LITTLE FLOWER ACADEMY

NAME	HR.	YR.
Shellby Sy	10-3	2007-2008
Anastasia Corbett	10-2	08-09

100074

HORIZONS
CANADA MOVES WEST

MICHAEL CRANNY
School District 91
Nechako, BC

GRAHAM JARVIS
Carson Graham Secondary School
North Vancouver, BC

GARVIN MOLES
Dover Bay Secondary School
Nanaimo, BC

BRUCE SENEY
Robert A. McMath Secondary School
Richmond, BC

Prentice
Hall

To Valerie, our families, and our students

Canadian Cataloguing in Publication Data

Main entry under title:
Horizons: Canada moves West

For use in grade 10 British Columbia.
Includes index.
ISBN 0-13-012367-6
1. Canada — History — 19th century. 2. Canada — History — 1867-1914.
2. Canada — Economic conditions — 20th century.* I. Cranny, Michael
3. William, 1947-

FC500.H67 1999   971   C99-931599-4
F1033.H75 1999

© 1999 Prentice Hall Ginn Canada, Scarborough, Ontario
Pearson Education Canada, a division of Pearson Canada Inc.

Prentice-Hall, Inc., Upper Saddle River, New Jersey
Prentice-Hall International (UK) Ltd., London
Prentice-Hall of Australia, Pty. Ltd., Sydney
Prentice-Hall of Hispanoamericana, S.A., Mexico City
Prentice-Hall of India Pvt., Ltd., New Delhi
Prentice-Hall of Japan, Inc., Tokyo
Prentice-Hall of Southeast Asia (PTE) Ltd., Singapore
Editora Prentice-Hall do Brasil, Ltda., Rio de Janeiro

ISBN 0-13-012367-6

Publisher: MaryLynne Meschino
Series Editor: Jessica Pegis
Developmental Editors: Jessica Pegis, Dayne Ogilvie
Copy Editor: Dayne Ogilvie
Permissions/Photo Researchers: Karen Taylor, Alene McNeill
Production Coordinator: Kathrine Pummell
Art Direction: Alex Li
Cover Design: Zena Denchik
Page Layout: Mary Beth MacLean
Illustrators: Alan Barnard, Nicolas Debon, John Fraser, John Mantha
Technical Art: Mary Beth MacLean, Deborah Crowle
Maps: Deborah Crowle, Steven Corrigan

Cover Image: *Through the Rocky Mountains: A Path on the Canadian Highway* (1887), Lucius O'Brien. Private Collection, Toronto. Photo courtesy the Art Gallery of Ontario.

Printed and bound in Canada.

10 TP 07

Note From the Publisher
The publisher of *Horizons: Canada Moves West* has made every reasonable effort to trace the ownership of data and visuals and to make full acknowledgement for their use. If any errors or omissions have occurred, they will be corrected in future editions, providing written notification has been received by the publisher.

CONTENTS

UNIT III:

BETWEEN TWO CENTURIES

PREFACE

Horizons continues the story of Canada begun in *Crossroads*. It chronicles the struggles and achievements of newcomers and Native Canadians as they adapt to the political, cultural, and economic changes in Canada from 1815 to 1914. The road to Confederation and the settlement of the West are examined through geography, history, and cultural developments. This book also introduces students to the economy of Canada and British Columbia, and to global economic trends.

Horizons builds on the skills and ideas introduced and developed in *Pathways* and *Crossroads*. Like these earlier books in the series, *Horizons* continues to integrate geography and history with other disciplines and to encourage skill development through the use of primary sources, map studies, statistical tables, and graphs.

A number of features are designed to engage the student in active learning and appear throughout the text. Windows on the Past, and in the later chapters, Windows on the Present, open all but the geography chapter. Most are fictional stories based on historical occurrences or contemporary issues. These Windows are designed to engage students creatively in exploring issues and ideas that are important to an understanding of Canada's past and present issues. The Cross Currents feature enhances students' understanding of a chapter's themes by examining present-day examples. Activities throughout each chapter develop and expand creative and critical thinking related to those themes and issues discussed in each chapter.

ACKNOWLEDGEMENTS

The authors would like to thank Bob Kirk, for his continuing commitment to this project, and Jessica Pegis and Dayne Ogilvie for their support and encouragement in the development of *Horizons*. Their thoughtful suggestions and editorial acumen were critical in melding the work of four authors.

The editorial team would like to thank the many reviewers of *Horizons* for offering their analyses and thoughtful advice, especially Cam Murray, who reviewed much of the book's geography, including Chapter 3; Richard Lonsdale, who reviewed different drafts of the manuscript; Dixon Taylor, former Coordinator for Aboriginal Education, BC Ministry of Education (now an educational consultant specializing in aboriginal affairs), who reviewed the entire manuscript for bias; Jennifer Hammond, of the Office of Communications, University of Northern British Columbia, who reviewed the Window on the Present for Chapter 9; and Patrick Kwok, of SUCCESS, who reviewed the Window on the Present for Chapter 10.

UNIT I
A DOMINION IS FORMED

In the decades following the War of 1812, immigrants from Europe and the United States flooded into British North America. Most came seeking land to farm, and a better life. There were few roads, and clearing the land was back-breaking work. In Lower Canada, immigration and colonial rule threatened French culture. Britain, however, maintained its rigid class system and undemocratic form of government.

In Upper and Lower Canada, reform movements sprang up demanding responsible government. Reformers wanted to strip power from the ruling-class groups in Upper and Lower Canada. Rebellions broke out in 1837, but were quickly put down. Captured leaders were hanged in public. In 1840, Britain passed the Act of Union. It formally joined Upper and Lower Canada as United Canada—but without the participation or support of Lower Canada.

Parliament burns. In 1849, riots led to the burning of the parliament buildings in Montreal. The city was then the capital of the Canadas. Clearly, the union of what is now Quebec and Ontario had left many tensions unresolved.

Native peoples and fur traders. Settlement was encouraged by the colonial government. Eventually, it would lead to many conflicts in territories of British North America where fur traders and the western Native peoples had a long-established relationship.

By the 1860s, as the American Civil War was fought, the threat of US invasion increased. Debates about the future government of the colonies intensified. In 1864, conferences were held in Charlottetown and Quebec. In the end, John A. Macdonald, Confederation's chief advocate, prevailed: He compromised enough to accommodate the many different demands. In 1866, the British Parliament passed the British North America Act. On July 1, 1867, Confederation was proclaimed. Nova Scotia, New Brunswick, and Canada (now Ontario and Quebec) became the Dominion of Canada.

In the years following the Rebellions of 1837, immigration continued to grow. As settlements grew, they encroached on Native land. Eventually, many of the treaty lands were absorbed. In the wake of the Rebellions, Lord Durham recommended that Britain unite its North American colonies. Later, Britain ended colonial trading privileges, and the economies of the colonies suffered. The move towards self-government and unification intensified.

During this period, Canadians adopted Victorian values and pursued Victorian pastimes. It was an age of breakthroughs in science, transportation, technology, and communications. Women began to question their limited social roles and rights. Steamships and steam-powered locomotives led to the beginnings of Canada's infrastructure.

Architect of Confederation. John A. Macdonald championed the cause of Confederation and negotiated it into a reality. For his work, he was knighted by the British government, and became Canada's first prime minister.

1 COLONIES IN THE WILDERNESS 1814–1840

CHAPTER OUTCOMES

This chapter examines the important social and political events in the history of Upper and Lower Canada in the early nineteenth century, leading up to the Rebellions of 1837. By the end of the chapter, you will

- assess the importance of geography in Canada's early development

- identify important political and social changes in the history of Upper Canada

- identify the reasons for political discontent in Lower Canada

- work in small groups to develop consensus

- synthesize information from a variety of sources

My Boy Life
Presented in a Succession of True Stories

John Carroll was born just before the beginning of the War of 1812. He was a respected and loved member of the community and wrote about his boyhood memories when he was in his seventies. As a Methodist minister who lived and worked in Upper Canada, Reverend Carroll witnessed many of the changes that occurred in Canadian society in the nineteenth century. His charming memoirs, which are easy to read and entertaining, tell us a great deal about everyday life during the pioneer period.

I never heard that any of my **forebears,** either on my paternal or maternal line, had been hanged, but the **waxed end** might be found if looked after in my genealogy.

My father was a **saddler** and **harness-maker** by trade and understood well his handicraft ... In his time in America, people travelled two or three, if not four, times as much on horseback as in carriages; hence the demand for saddles. Some of my earliest recollections are of amusing myself among the scraps and litter of his shop, and of some of the tools he employed—such as his tack-hammer, his wooden mallets (one faced with shark skin), and his long iron "collar rods" employed in stuffing the rims of draft collars with long straw, which are left as hard as wood and as polished as if made of marble ...

Of my father, physically, I have this to say: he was an old man when I first remember him. He was full twenty years older than my mother; I and my twin brother were the last of twelve children; he must, therefore, have been close on to sixty years of age when I was born. From what I saw and learned, he came of a strong, long-lived race of men. He was considerably above medium stature—about five feet, eleven—he may have been six feet before he began to settle down ... Sad to say, he was a poor manager; changeable in his plans—trying from time to time, hunting, fishing, and farming, as well as his own proper vocation. Then his convivial proclivities, induced by his song-singing and storytelling gifts, with the love of liquor acquired in his seven years' soldiering experiences, during which, he used to boast,

that he sometimes drank a dozen glasses of liquor in a morning and passed muster on the parade ground as a sober man. He was not, however, a lazy man, but quite disposed to labour, had not his work been often interrupted by the causes I have mentioned ...

My mother was in all respects the opposite of my father. The young and lovely daughter for she was a most comely woman—of a grave Quaker man, of a singularly amiable disposition, only eighteen when she was induced, ... to marry a man of forty (claiming of course to be much younger). Oh! What poverty, privations, shifts and turns, neglect and abuse, that poor woman suffered by being "lured" by the songs, blandishments, and persuasive tongue of a man, vastly her inferior, "from her native home," a home of full and plenty.

John Carroll's mother makes new clothes from the old.

Heroically she struggled with insufficient supplies of provisions and covering for day and night, living in dilapidated houses in that severe climate, to provide for and raise her large family of boys, preparing the materials from which their clothes were woven, and making it into garments herself when woven. The elder ones' garments were made of new cloth, and the little ones' clothes of the cast-off coats and trousers of the older ones. The first thoroughly new suit I ever wore, at the age of eight or nine, was of striped homespun **carded** and spun by my tireless mother's hands, while doing for a family of ten or twelve, without any domestic help—something she never had. Oh! My precious mother! My soul is agonized by the remembrance of thy sorrows! And glad I am that I had the chance of doing something to soothe thy mind in thy later years!

If I have not already told my readers, I will tell them now, that I spent three or four years (perhaps I ought to say five in all, including two or three several intervals) in a tannery, from the ages of twelve to seventeen, and that for two of those years I was considered a regular apprentice to the tanner's and **currier's** trade. Some will think I ought to be ashamed to make the confession. I would be ashamed if I thought there was anything sinful or mean in a business that is so important to civilized countries. My "boss," or master, raised himself by following this business from the low estate of a poor boy to be one of the very richest, most respected, and most useful men of the town during the course of a long life.

In every trade, "the youngest apprentice" has usually, for some time, to do many things not properly of the trade, but preparatory to it. In our establishment this bottom rung of the ladder was grinding the **bark.** In many large establishments at the present day, along with other advanced conveniences, the bark is ground by water or steam power; in earlier and ruder times it was ground by in an iron mill, by horse power. John Jones ... when I first knew the establishment, was the bark-grinder, but when John was promoted, others were employed to do his work. Two other boys **intervened** between him and me. At length I was called to mount the mill "brow," for the bark was pounded and put into a hopper above the stairs and fell into a place for its reception below, whence it was carried out as wanted to the tan vats. I ground the bark both before and after I became a regular "hand" in the tannery.

In several of my sketches I have made reference to a crisis in our humble family history by which our joint residence was broken up for a number of years, and several members of the household were scattered in various directions. Thomas, the patron of the rest, was married and had gone to live by himself, taking ... mother along. A temporary residence was found for poor James, though finally he followed me to the country. 'Thaniel was at a trade. An opening for business he understood opened itself to brother George ... And, as I had always showed a preference for country life, it was decided I should join my brother William on the bush farm ... This breaking up occurred in the month of March, or April 1822, when I was between twelve and thirteen years of age.

George's route and mine lay pretty much in the same direction, and it was decided we should travel together to the end of my journey at my brother William's. We were very disproportionate in size; he being a stout fellow of nineteen or twenty, and being of the tender age already given, and small even at that; but each had his wardrobe packed in a bundle on his back. We started, after an early lunch, on a raw short day, to trudge fourteen miles. Less or more, on foot. At Wilcox's Tavern ... we took a short rest; my brother regaled himself and me (such, alas! was the custom of the times, no one seeing the danger), each with his glass of whiskey. It was a mercy that converting **grace,** a little more than two years after, abruptly and completely put a stop to an indulgence which would have been very likely to have proved my total ruin.

About nightfall we reached our brother's log house and enjoyed his blazing fire of burning logs. His wife, for the season, was boiling all the sugar they made over the domestic fire, and the new sugar and molasses added to the social

Eventually, John became a regular hand in the tannery.

The sugar bush was far from the home of John's brother.

pleasure around the homely hearth …

It will devolve on me now to tell how I was employed, and some of the things which befell me during the year and a quarter or so, of my residence there. The sugar bush; learning to chop, reap, rake, bind and pitch grain; going to mill on horseback, hunting the cattle, getting lost, etc., etc., will probably be some of the subjects on which I will dwell for the entertainment of my readers.

First, the sugar seasons. I passed through two of those during the time I remained. At the period of my arrival it was

pretty well over for that year; and I have said the boiling was attended to in the house. The sugar bush was some distance, and the sap had to be gathered and poured into barrels on an ox-sled which was then slowly drawn to the house. The work of gathering the sap henceforth was mine; and, the next year, boiling it down over the campfire in the woods, to which was added the work of chopping and fetching the fuel to keep up the fire under the sugar kettles …

Sugar-making was the first thing I learned; the next thing I shall mention was driving oxen … As I became greatly attached

to them, I will describe their looks and other things about them. They were about four years old, more or less, when I began to drive them. Like many domestic animals, they had received the names of distinguished personages. Not wholly forgetful of old war memories, one was called The Duke of Wellington and the other, Prince Blucher, but for short … "Duke" and "Prince." Duke was a lively red colour, but his face was as white as the drifted snow and I think also his feet … He had a large, kindly eye, and a good temper … he was my favourite … Prince was not bad-tempered but … somewhat sullen. His colour was a dusky brown or dun. His horns were the thick, straight ones of a bullock, and would have been sharp-pointed, had not their tips been taken off with a saw. Only for their being blunted, no doubt one of them … would have put out my right eye …

I thought I had performed a great exploit when I first found I could yoke them up … the most of growing boys like any kind of teaming, and I was fond of driving the oxen; they were company for me, on which account I got very attached to them, and it was not hard work. The hardest work I had to do was **harrowing,** because the fields were full of stumps, around which I had to turn the harrow. This implement was made of strong, heavy wood, in the form of a letter A … penetrated with heavy iron spikes … a chain was attached and the oxen drew it over the ground, by which the soil was torn to pieces; but as it met with many obstructions, mostly undecayed roots in the ground, it twitched and jumped about, which tried my quick temper, I am ashamed to say, very much …

To keep as near the stump as possible, and to have the harrow directly behind them when they got around, I had to lift the harrow on its edge, so that the "teeth" would not fasten among the roots, and to hold it there till it had passed the stump, when, as quickly as possible, I had to throw it "teeth" downwards again … This required all my strength—for the harrow was very heavy, and all my patience, too; because the poor unknowing brutes would jerk it rudely out of my hands, defeating my purpose and giving my slender arms and back a great shock besides. I was then without grace, and often lost my temper and beat the poor oxen, much as I thought I liked them … using words the while that I have long since deeply repented of. I have heard of a wicked man who "did not believe that any but a real Christian could plough among stumps without swearing." … If he listened to me in those days, I'm afraid he could … have made such report.

I must [now] particularize two or three other kinds of boy's work on a bush farm. First, there is my learning to chop, and my efforts therein. I admired chopping very much, and aspired earnestly to possess the skill and do the work of an axeman. Chopping is indeed delightful work; it is clean; the smell of the newly cut timber is most agreeable; you are constantly seeing the result of your operations and the progress you are making; and there is a feeling of triumph when you have "knocked down" a tree two or three times the thickness of yourself and … a hundred feet high … But then an axe is seldom light enough for a growing boy … very often the handle is too long, with the danger of giving yourself a poke in the stomach.

William made his own axe-handles, and the shaping and smoothing of them was a nice little job for a long winter evening before the big open fire, which often furnished the only light for the operation … It was with something of the pride of manhood that, after my breakfast of a morning, I whetted my axe, tied my trowsers with a tow string around my legs to keep out the snow, and tramped the deep drifts to the "chopping" on the margin of the cleared land. The **underbrushing** being light and easier done by one of inferior strength, it usually fell to me …

Chopping was delightful—and sometimes dangerous—work.

The true way to escape a falling tree is to run to the right or left of them, not certainly opposite either **notch**, not even to the last made one; for if the tree should "lodge" against other trees, it will be liable to slide back over the stump and crush the chopper ... But most bushmen know how to plan the whole operation and to calculate their chances ... There was a tall Scotchman named Tom Bell in those new settlements, who had so good an eye and was so experienced, and so cool, that, on a bet of a quart of whiskey ... would walk (not run) out from under the falling tree and so calculate it that he would allow the branches of the tree top just to switch him on the heels as it reached the ground.

Planting potatoes was another part of my work ... the labour of planting was very hard, the ground being full of undecayed roots of trees and bushes which, after a slight harrowing, if it got that, had to be cut up and drawn to the potatoes with a hoe, purposely heavy for the purpose and made of a material with a sharp edge. I remember a hard day's work in planting a patch for myself ... at the foot of two large maple trees ... on a very hot day. It was a holiday ... cheered by the hope of raising a little crop, the sale of which was to procure me some pocket money, I worked away till I had completed the job, which left my hands, hardened as they were, blistered, and my slender arms so sore that they ached for days; but, alas! I never sold my crop, and therefore never realized the money.

Pulling and "topping" turnips was another of my attainments and occupations in the autumn. The turnips were a sweet and luscious kind, and I regaled myself while I worked. We had no apples and these were a fair substitute for them. The turnip harvest extended into the beginning of the cold weather, with rain and frost, and was sufficiently dreary, groping with the hands as we did, in the cold, wet earth.

The threshing was done with a **flail**, and took up a good part of the winter, as it was all done by my blind brother, who taught me the art, and myself. Standing on the barn floor was very cold for the feet, and the log barn was very open besides. All my toes were more or less frozen that winter of 1822-23.

I will leave the failure of some boyish hopes for another section—such as the fowling piece I failed in getting—my calf that died—my pet squirrel that was killed—and the pig I left and never claimed.

forebears: one's ancestors

waxed end: the end of the rope used to flog prisoners

saddler: one who makes and sells saddles and other equipment for horses

harness-maker: one who makes harnesses for animals who work on a farm

carded: fibres that have been cleaned and collected before spinning

currier: one who cures, or treats, leather

bark: the tannin from wet bark used to cure, or treat, leather

to intervene: to come between

grace: the love and awareness of God

to harrow: to break up and smooth the soil

to underbrush: to cut down the underwood and throw it into piles

notch: the mark made on a tree before cutting, which directs its fall

flail: an instrument made up of two pieces of wood used to break wheat kernels from stalks

parlance: way of speaking

ACTIVITIES

1. Reverend Carroll became a Methodist and, later, a minister of the church. What things did he do in his youth that he later regrets?

2. The life of a young person in Upper Canada was physically challenging. What makes your life easier? In what respects would your life be more difficult than Reverend Carroll's?

3. How does Reverend Carroll's way of expressing himself differ from modern **parlance?**

4. Based on Reverend Carroll's account, make up a seasonal calendar of activities for a fourteen-year-old boy or girl who lived during this period.

TIME LINE

1791 CONSTITUTIONAL ACT CREATES UPPER AND LOWER CANADA

1815 TREATY OF GHENT ENDS WAR OF 1812

1816 ROBER GOURLAY ARRESTED FOR CRITICIZING LAND POLICIES IN UPPER CANADA

1821 HUDSON'S BAY COMPANY AND NORTH WEST COMPANY AMALGAMATE

1824 WILLIAM LYON MACKENZIE BUYS THE COLONIAL ADVOCATE

1828 WILLIAM LYON MACKENZIE ELECTED TO THE LEGISLATIVE ASSEMBLY

1837 NOVEMBER BATTLE OF ST. CHARLES

1837 DECEMBER BATTLE OF MONTGOMERY'S TAVERN

1838 LORD DURHAM ARRIVES IN QUEBEC

1840 ACT OF UNION PASSED

A highly civilized and densely peopled state possesses extensive waste lands in the colonies. In a state possessing those waste lands (Canada), all citizens have equal rights—all have a share in the collective right to those waste lands; and if a few hundreds or even thousands by settlement acquire a further right in certain parts ... that right cannot extend to deprive the community at home of its interest in the whole ...

AN EDITORIAL IN THE BRITISH NEWSPAPER, *THE SPECTATOR*, SEPTEMBER 18, 1847

Most upper-class English settlers tried to recreate England in Canada, as well as they were able. They were in regular contact with "home" and imported the latest styles—or had them made up in the "waste lands." What kind of existence might these three young women have had in Canada?

INTRODUCTION

Upper Canada: "up" the St. Lawrence River; part of present-day Ontario

Lower Canada: "down" the St. Lawrence River; part of present-day Quebec

At the dawn of the nineteenth century, Canada was not the developed, prosperous country it would eventually become. Its vast spaces, often rocky and forbidding to farmers, and its cold winters made northern and western Canada far less attractive to settlers than the United States. For many years, these regions, including British Columbia, were inhabited by the Native peoples and a small group of daring fur traders, and no one else.

In the east, Canada was certainly growing. The population of **Upper Canada** (now southern and eastern Ontario) had risen rapidly after the end of the War of 1812, as immigrants from Europe and the United States arrived to take advantage of cheap land. **Lower Canada** (Quebec along the St. Lawrence), and the Maritime provinces (now Newfoundland, Prince Edward Island, Nova Scotia, and New Brunswick) prospered from close ties to Britain and New England. However, many Native peoples were dying of diseases introduced from Europe, and everywhere they were being forced out of good farmland. Although this was a great injustice, most settlers paid little attention to their plight.

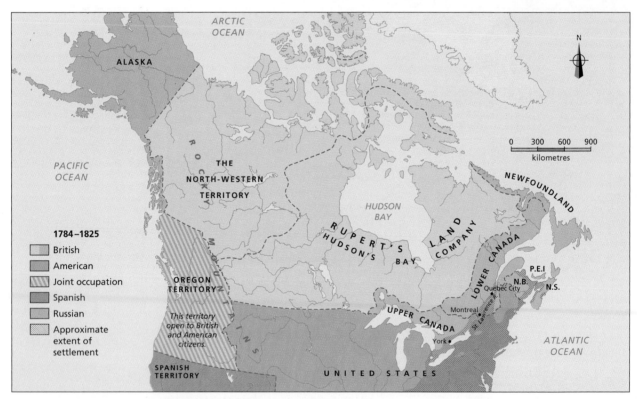

Figure 1–1 In 1825, the map of present-day Canada looked very different from what it does today. British North America consisted of six colonies—Upper Canada, Lower Canada, New Brunswick, Nova Scotia, Prince Edward Island, and Newfoundland. The Hudson's Bay Company controlled a huge amount of land in the Northwest, and Canada and the US claimed an area that is now part of British Columbia and California. Russia controlled present-day Alaska.

Around this time, many people viewed the United States as a possible enemy of Canada. Like today, Canadians had many interactions with Americans. In fact, many early settlers were Americans, and trade with the United States was important. But Canada had been invaded during the American Revolution and again during the War of 1812. These attacks, and the threat of others, reinforced ties to the British Empire. Community leaders were often members of **Loyalist** families, pensioned British army officers, or other members of the gentry. The lingering American threat had important consequences for Canada, as you will read in this chapter and in Chapter 2. Ironically, however, it helped Canadians to see themselves as different, which helped to foster a Canadian national identity.

The efforts of the ruling classes in Upper and Lower Canada to accumulate wealth and power, and to keep American-style government out of British North America, had other consequences for Canada. Britain had tried to copy its own society in its Canadian colonies, complete with gentlefolk with large estates. But immigrants from the United States believed in equal opportunity for all. British snobbery also angered immigrants from the British Isles, who had hoped to escape the rigid class system of their homeland. Unfair land policies, and bad government, set the stage for violent confrontations between the classes. In French Lower Canada, the French deeply resented the ruling class, which was English. Eventually, rebellions broke out in both Upper and Lower Canada. You will learn much about these rebellions in this chapter.

> **Loyalists:** Americans who did not support the American Revolution and who remained loyal to Britain

CANADA: THE LAND

Last year, you learned about Canada's early history, and how Canada's vast size affected its development as a nation. Prime Minister William Lyon Mackenzie King (1874-1950) once remarked that while other countries have too much history, Canada has "too much geography."

Although you will learn more about the geography of the regions of Canada in later chapters of *Horizons*, it may be helpful to remember what our country looks like before examining its history and cultures.

Figure 1–2 The Rocky Mountains viewed from the western side

Canada is a northern country. Most of it lies between 50 degrees and 70 degrees latitude and every part of it knows winter. Most Canadians live in towns and cities close to the southern border. Historically, this region was attractive because of its proximity to the United States. And, of course, the weather is warmer here. Windsor, Ontario lies just north of 42 degrees latitude—farther south than the French **Riviera!**

Canada is also a vast landscape, which is easier to say than to imagine. Leaving from Vancouver or Victoria, you could drive all day for four days and yet be only two-thirds of the way to the East Coast. It takes a full day to drive from Vancouver to Prince George—which is only half the distance to British Columbia's northern border. It is as far from Vancouver to Toronto as it is from Vancouver to Canada's northern boundary in the islands of the high Arctic. Canada is the second largest nation on Earth, with a total land area of 9 916 140 square kilometres.

If you were to set off on the Trans-Canada Highway from Vancouver for Halifax, what would you see? Early in your journey, you would notice that the highway runs through the fertile Fraser Valley and then into its great canyon. This is one of the few gates through the grey walls of the Coast Mountains. Like many mountain highways, the Trans-Canada in British Columbia often follows river valleys. The road crosses the Interior Plateau, then climbs into the Rockies. Other roads lead south into the deserts and dry lands of the Okanagan, or the steep-walled lake country of the Kootenays.

The Rockies form Alberta's western wall. The Trans-Canada passes through them, using the Kicking Horse Pass, and then crosses Banff, before descending into the foothills and on to Calgary. You've been driving for two days now. From Calgary, the highway crosses the southern prairie, moving quickly past oil wells and ponds filled with waterfowl. It's a long day. Once you pass Medicine Hat and Regina, you're ready to cross the old lake bed of Lake Agassiz (flat as a pool table and dark with rich, black soil) before arriving in Winnipeg.

Beyond Winnipeg, the prairie changes. Rocks start to appear—you haven't seen any for a thousand kilometres or more. The Trans-Canada probes the edges of the Canadian

Figure 1–3 Calgary, Alberta

Figure 1–4 Rock and forest—the Canadian Shield

Shield, a massive core of ancient granite that stretches from Manitoba to the distant edges of Quebec. Farms are much smaller at the edges of the Shield, and soon there are no farms at all. This is a country of deep forests and thousands of lakes—a landscape the **Group of Seven** made famous. You will travel through these forests for a whole day before you reach the shores of Lake Superior.

The highway follows the shore of Superior for many kilometres, curves around its corner, and strikes south for Sault Ste. Marie. East of the "Soo" you spot farmland again— a long, lakeside finger of it. The Shield appears again, then Sudbury. You can't miss the city's "Big Nickel," a sign of the mineral wealth of the region. After lunch, you drive southeastward to Ottawa, or south past Lake Simcoe, just north and east of the Industrial Heartland, which includes Canada's largest city, Toronto. The Trans-Canada skirts this region and travels on to Montreal, on the St. Lawrence. You have now been on the road for six days.

Canada's second largest city is full of history. Many people love Montreal because it feels like a

European city, and because it is so cosmopolitan. Now the highway leaves the city and heads east, passing along the southern shore of the expansive St. Lawrence River. Near Gaspé, it veers towards New Brunswick and the Saint John River Valley—renowned in fall for the glorious colours of the leaves of its maples. In the spring, the burnt, sweet smell of the sugar shack fills the woods. From New Brunswick, the Trans-Canada heads through Nova Scotia, the old city of Halifax, and up the peninsula to the ferry for Newfoundland. Here the journey will end, in St. John's. After nine days, you have reached your final destination. You have travelled Canada from coast to coast.

Figure 1–5 A bridge on the Hammond River in New Brunswick

THE LAND OF YESTERDAY

Métis: someone of French and Native ancestry

Canada's history has always been affected by its geography. Following the War of 1812, settlers poured into Upper Canada, attracted by rich and relatively inexpensive farmland. Quebec, then called Lower Canada, continued on its steady course, its economy based on farming practices that had endured for more than two hundred years. Its trading capital, Montreal, attracted Scottish and American entrepreneurs

The Maritimes, well-settled and stable, were a shipbuilding centre and traded with Britain and New England. Newfoundland prospered in its age-old economy based on fish and timber. By 1800, about 16 000 people lived along the coast of Newfoundland and fished for a living. In the north and west, from northern Labrador to the Rocky Mountains, the Hudson's Bay Company (HBC) claimed all lands drained by rivers flowing into Hudson Bay. In competition with the HBC, the North West Company fought for control of the southern fur trade and trade beyond the Rockies, and set up posts wherever it could. Russians and Americans, and even the Spanish for a time, claimed the coast of British Columbia.

Most immigrants to British North America wanted to farm. The fertile soils of Upper Canada, and the groves of timber-producing hardwoods, were very attractive. Of course, the lands closest to the United States and to the waterways were most desirable. These were all in the south. North of present-day Barrie, the rocky Canadian Shield was a barrier to agriculture. Even the woodlands south of Georgian Bay were often rock-strewn, and the climate was not ideal for agriculture. This was an era of few roads, and it often took days to travel 100 kilometres. Land just 50 kilometres away from York, Cornwall, or Niagara was considered to be remote.

Land for the Fur Trade

Most Europeans accepted that the lands west and north of the Great Lakes were reserved for the fur trade. In 1820, probably fewer than a dozen people lived west of the Great Lakes who were not **Métis** or Native, or who didn't work in the fur trade. Most aboriginal people and Métis were connected in one way or another to the "trade." Even if European or American immigrants wanted to farm the West, they usually did not, because the fur traders, the Native peoples, and the Métis

Figure 1–6 This painting shows the rustic living conditions of Canada's early settlers.

were determined to prevent settlement. Pioneers want boundaries, surveys, roads, canals, schools, and—most important—land of their own. These goals conflicted with the cultures, lifestyles, and economy of the westerners. The fur traders would become the natural allies of the Native peoples and the Métis against settlement. All three groups had everything to lose and nothing to gain from settlement, as you will read in Chapter 4.

Furs had been a precious commodity in Europe and Asia ever since the first furs had been brought back from Canada during the sixteenth century. By the beginning of the nineteenth century, fur-trading companies were locked in a struggle for survival that would not end until the two largest companies merged in 1821. Although independent traders dealt in furs, only the big companies with **monopolies** made a lot of money.

The largest company, as you have learned, was the Hudson's Bay Company. With a royal charter and a government monopoly, the Company held the exclusive right to trade furs in its vast territories. It could—and did—punish anyone found trading in its region. The Company's monopoly was seriously threatened by the French until the fall of New France in 1763. Afterwards, traders—most of them Scots—took up the old French trading networks. As the so-called "Montrealers," and then as the North West Company, these traders took on the Hudson's Bay Company and tried to break the monopoly.

monopoly: exclusive ownership because of legal privilege

Table 1–1	Recorded Fur Sales for One Year	
	Item	**Price in pounds**
124 000	Beaver skins	£ 69 922
14 000	Bears skins	£ 15 177
9 200	Otters	£ 22 892
4 600	Fishers	£ 1 365
52 000	Martins	£ 12 085
9 400	Wolves	£ 6 323
450	Wolverines	£ 392
9000	Cats (probably lynx)	£ 4 131
11 000	Minks	£ 1 294
7 000	Foxes	£ 2 836
113 000	Raccoons	£ 15 533
80 000	Musquash (Muskrats)	£ 2 223
14 000	Elks	£ 8 170
142 000	Deers	£ 34 416
2 000 lb. (900 kg)	Castoreum (beaver scent glands)	£ 1 518

Table 1–1 lists the Colonial Office's recorded fur sales in London for one year in the mid-1800s. Remember that the average wage in Britain at the time was less than £1 a week.

1. Refer to the text on pages 11 to 13 and use an atlas to do the following. Your teacher will provide you with an outline map of Canada.

   a) Plot the route of the trip described on pages 11 to 13 on the outline map of Canada. Include lakes, rivers, and other physical features, such as the Rocky Mountains, and cities.

   b) Measure the distances between the cities.

   c) How far is it from Victoria to Winnipeg? From Winnipeg to Sudbury? From Toronto to Halifax?

   d) Place all the cities in one column. In another column, write the distance of that city from Vancouver in kilometres.

2. Find a map of the physical regions and the vegetation zones of Canada in your atlas. Which physical regions do you pass through between Vancouver and Toronto? Which vegetation zones do you pass through between Victoria and Calgary?

3. Using the atlas and your own knowledge base, identify an interesting **landmark** between Victoria and Winnipeg. Why is it interesting? Design a postcard that shows this feature on one side. On the other side, write to a friend in Vancouver and describe the landmark.

UPPER CANADA

landmark: any prominent feature of the landscape, natural or human-made, that identifies the locality

physical map: a map that shows the major physical features of a region, including mountain chains, lakes, rivers, and so on. Physical maps use colour to show the varying height of the land

In the early nineteenth century, Upper Canada was the newest and most undeveloped of the colonies of British North America. During the War of 1812, it had almost fallen to the Americans, who made up its largest group of settlers.

There were few roads; even the military routes—Yonge and Dundas, for example—were just tracks through the bush. Places at a distance of 30 or 40 kilometres from the village of York (the capital) were considered to be remote. The forest cover was

Figure 1–8 Settlers were attracted to British North America by advertising campaigns and word of mouth. According to this map from 1825, where did most people choose to live? Now examine a **physical map** of southern Ontario and Quebec. What geographical features helped to determine settlement patterns? Compare the modern map with the 1825 map, and summarize your observations.

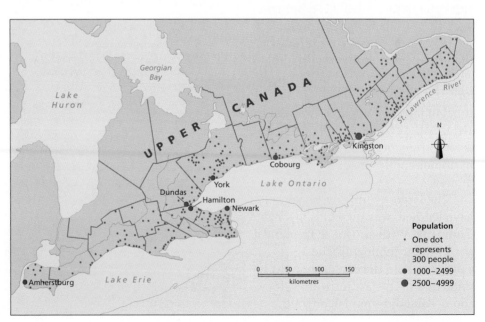

heavy, with great giant oak, walnut, ash, hickory, and maple trees. Native peoples had occupied this land for thousands of years, but to European settlers Upper Canada was a wilderness. Clearing the land was their first task, and it took time. No more than one hectare could be cleared in a year. Normally, it would take a family twenty or more years to clear a 25-hectare farm—a little larger than a city block.

What was it like to live in Upper Canada in the 1820s? If you could travel back in time, the first thing you would notice would be the quiet of the land. Those of us who live in today's cities are accustomed to non-stop noise; we live with a sort of background din. To pioneers, noises from animals, steam-powered saw mills, or perhaps a smithy would be considered loud. The sound of fiddles and musical instruments at occasional parties or important social events, such as weddings and christenings, was a treat.

It was much more common to help and visit one's neighbours than it is today. People looked forward to going to church, or to being visited by a travelling member of the clergy. Sometimes communities set up a small school and hired a teacher, often paying for the service with produce, lodging, and meals. Life was hard. It took years to raise a crop that would not be entirely consumed by the family or sold to pay off debt. Almost everyone was in debt at one time or another to merchants, and **mortgaged** their next crop to obtain supplies.

to mortgage: to use as security on a loan

Figure 1–9 Most settlers in Upper Canada had large families, but they lived in tiny cabins, like this one near Chatham, Ontario. It was common for a dozen or more people to live squeezed into only two small rooms. Occasionally, a loft would provide a third room. There were, of course, no indoor bathrooms, no closets—and no separate kitchen. Windows, often made of oiled parchment, were translucent but not transparent.

A Barter Economy

Figure 1–10 This Russian woman has some shoes to trade. What product or service might she accept as a fair exchange?

Modern people live in a **money economy.** This system differs greatly from the economy that operated in Canada during the early 1800s. At that time, most people living outside larger settlements participated in a **barter economy.** People barter when they exchange goods and services, rather than using money. For example, a farmer might pay a blacksmith, carpenter, or doctor for their work with wheat or maple sugar. First, the services and products were valued in dollars, and then the exchange was made. More than 70 percent of all transactions were made through bartering.

Bartering may seem like a difficult, inefficient way to do business, but prices for products and services were fairly fixed. Studies have shown that the price of a bushel of wheat, for example, varied little throughout Upper Canada during this period.

Barter economies persist today. During financial crises, such as the upheaval in Russia following the collapse of the former Soviet Union, bartering re-emerged as a way of distributing goods and services. Today, in Canada, struggling small companies often barter products or services with each other. For example, a small printing company might trade photocopying services for free advertising in a small newspaper.

However, Revenue Canada wants to know about these cashless transactions. Both parties must issue a tax slip stating the value of the product or service in cash, and both parties must report the amount received as taxable income.

money economy: an economy that uses cash

barter economy: an economy that works by trading of products and services

WHAT DO YOU THINK?

1. As a class, brainstorm some advantages and disadvantages of bartering from the standpoint of three entities:
   - Canadian teenagers
   - Canadian small-business owners
   - the Canadian economy

2. Students in younger grades often barter goods. Why might this be so?

3. Why does Revenue Canada want to keep track of bartering in the modern Canadian economy? What would happen if it didn't?

The Importance of Social Class

Social class and financial means would often determine how an immigrant reacted to the experience of moving to Upper Canada. But Upper Canada also had a way of levelling people, of making them change their priorities. Many younger children of English aristo-crats or pensioned-off army officers came with their families to settle in the colony. To their chagrin, they found they had to do most of the back-breaking labour of building and maintaining a farm themselves. Cheap labour and good, respectful servants were hard to come by. In Europe, overpopulation and a lack of labour laws made poorer people desperate for employment, so upper-

The Family Compact

Some settlers of Upper Canada saw themselves as superior to others. The Family Compact, for example, was a small group of officials who helped run Upper Canada. They were descendants of the Loyalist settlers and believed in the rightness of the aristocracy and the importance of ties to Britain. They made up most of the Executive Council, and had control over government budgets and appointments. On a social level, members of the Family Compact were snobbish in the extreme. Even aristocratic visitors from Britain had a hard time breaking into this group, which operated like a private club. All members knew one another, and were often related. They even dressed alike. Susanna Moodie, the pioneer author, described them in the excerpt that follows:

Figure 1–11 Members of the privileged upper class were known as the "Family Compact" in Upper Canada and the *Château Clique* in Lower Canada. In this painting, some members of the Château Clique watch the launch of the *Royal William*. Steamships were a new technology in the 1830s, and an important step forward in transportation for the colonies. Family Compact and Château Clique members invested in ships and canals. They used their influence to get government backing of these projects, and benefited financially from their success.

> **PRIMARY SOURCE** They dress well and expensively, and are very particular to have their clothes cut in the latest fashion. Men and women adopt the reigning mode so universally that they look all dressed alike … If green was the prevailing colour, every lady would adopt it, whether it suited her complexion or not; and, if she was ever so stout, that circumstance would not prevent her from wearing half-a-dozen more skirts than was necessary, because that absurd and unhealthy practice has for a long period prevailed.

Figure 1–12 Settlers often worked together to cut trees and burn slash, as this **romanticized** picture shows. In reality, this was back-breaking, dirty work. Slash—the dead branches, roots, and debris—was piled, left to dry, and burned a year or two after cutting. The ashes were sold to make potash and **lye**, which were then sold to make fertilizer and soap. Logs were sold to timber merchants. These, along with tobacco, barley, oats, and rye, were the first cash products of the new farm.

to romanticize: to make something look good, satisfying

lye: the liquid that is leached from wood ashes and is used to make soap

land speculators: those who buy property at a low price and sell it at a higher price without spending much of their own money

class people could live apart from the so-called lower classes. This was not the case in Upper Canada. Most settlers found they needed their neighbours, and socialized with them, no matter what their background. Some people, of course, continued to think of Britain as their real home. Educated people in particular were very interested in English culture. They did not see themselves as Canadians, but rather as English people settling a new land.

The Problem of Land

Almost everyone who came to Upper Canada had some interest in farming. Most people wanted land, and they wanted to be farmers on their own freehold farms. Other people were engaged in farm-support businesses or industries, such as blacksmithing and wagon-making. But many settlers arrived to find that much of the good land was already taken up by absentee landowners and speculators. This was not what they had been led to expect. Advertising campaigns in England— and later in other parts of Europe—

had led people to believe that they could get good, cheap farmland, with easy access to towns and markets. Problems associated with restrictions on land, and poor roads, caused great hardship for many, and much discontent. Even people from privileged classes in Britain found they had been duped. Land problems were at the root of the general dissatisfaction felt towards the colonial government, and a major cause of the Rebellion of 1837 in Upper Canada, as you will read later.

Many members of the Family Compact were **land speculators,** and profited immensely from this activity. Speculators took ownership of large areas of prime land in the southern part of Upper Canada, close to the Great Lakes and the United States. Like most commodities, the value of land is governed by the law of supply and demand. The less good land that is available, the higher its value. By keeping huge parcels of land off the market, speculators made money on land they sold, while keeping more land in reserve. The supply problem was further complicated by crown and clergy reserves.

Clergy and Crown Reserves

Crown and clergy reserves were blocks of land set aside to provide income (through sale or rent) for the government and for the Anglican Church—in total, two-sevenths of all the land in Upper Canada. For the most part, these lands lay idle. And because they were scattered through the townships and were not cleared, the reserves blocked road development, causing much grief to settlers. Farmers had to wind their way around reserves if they wanted to travel anywhere—a waste of time and a source of irritation. Moreover, the reserves often tied up prime, arable land. Because of the economics of supply and demand, this caused the value of land to rise even higher.

The Role of the British Government

Upper Canada's land problem was partly created by the attitudes of the British government and its desire to duplicate the English model of landowning. England was a land of large estates controlled by aristocrats. The government believed this group could best rule the country. Privileged owners of large blocks of land in Canada were also more likely, in the British government's view, to maintain strong ties with Britain and its institutions. This idea was completely contrary to the **republican** views of immigrant farmers, especially those from the United States. They felt that people should be able to succeed on their own efforts and that many of the principles of British policy towards the Canadas were discriminatory and anti-democratic. This was absolutely true. The last thing Britain wanted was to allow her British North American colonists to adopt American attitudes and values. Had not the Thirteen Colonies (the United States) successfully rebelled against Britain? One upper-class British immigrant remarked:

Possessing farms which render them independent of the better classes of society they can, within limits, be as bold, unconstrained, and obtrusive as they please, in their behaviour towards their superior …

Another wrote:

These emigrants, having generally been of the lowest class of society in their respective countries—and consequently mere cyphers [of no importance] in their own immediate spheres, as soon as they arrive in Canada, begin to assume an appearance of importance … They are (tireless) in acquiring a knowledge of The Rights of Man, The Just Principles of Equality, And The True Nature of Independence, and, in a word, of everything which characterizes an American; and they quickly become divested of common manners and common civility, and not uncommonly of common honesty too—indeed this latter virtuous quality is rather uncommon on this side of the Western Ocean.

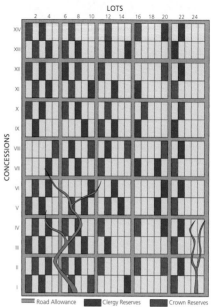

Figure 1–13 A typical township in Upper Canada. One clergy reserve could be as large as ten farms.

republican: democratic, without a monarch as head of state

A few communities, such as Sturgeon Lake in Upper Canada, were settled almost entirely by well-educated people. Two-thirds of the men at Sturgeon Lake had university degrees, indicating that they were Anglican—the official church—and members of the gentry. Women did not take degrees, but were usually educated by tutors.

Britain's plans for Upper Canada were first implemented by its first governor, John Graves Simcoe, but they continued even after the War of 1812. It proved difficult to attract true aristocrats to backwoods Canada, but many retired army officers and their families, who were members of the gentry, were interested.

English law favoured the first-born son in a family, who received the bulk of an estate when a landowner died. Younger sons joined the army or the Church, and they could not hope, under normal circumstances, to be major landowners in Britain. In Canada, the situation was different. Thousands of hectares were available to "take up" and develop. The government also allowed land companies, such as the Canada Company, to acquire vast tracts of prime land at a very low price. The Canada Company, with Family Compact connections, purchased lands that stretched from Lake Ontario to Lake Huron. In exchange for 1 million hectares, it agreed to pay the government £295 000 pounds over sixteen years! Although these terms were indeed generous, the Canada Company was responsible for attracting settlers. Even so, many speculators could double their money within ten years. In 1815, almost 50 percent of all farmland in western Upper Canada—the best available land because it was level, with deep soil and few rocks—was owned by speculators.

deferential: showing respect

Figure 1–14 Colonel Thomas Talbot acquired 2106 hectares around 1810. Within a few years, he controlled a wide swath of prime land where the cities of London, St. Thomas, and Chatham are now situated. The Talbot Settlement consisted of 30 000 people by 1830. Talbot personally interviewed each settler who wanted to take up residence on his land. If a settler did not meet his standards (Talbot preferred soft-spoken and **deferential** people), he would rub that person's name off his map and the land would go to someone else.

ACTIVITIES

1. Colonists often came to Upper Canada expecting to obtain land easily. Identify three barriers they actually faced. What role did the British government play in land disputes?

2. How did moving to Upper Canada level people? Which group maintained its ties to the British aristocracy? If you were a member of this group, in charge of admitting new members, what qualifications would you insist people have? Provide a reason for each one.

THE IMMIGRANT EXPERIENCE

No one who lived in British North America or in Lower Canada could have been prepared for the waves of immigrants who arrived at the close of the War of 1812. Most of these immigrants settled in Upper Canada. Some settled in Lower Canada's **Eastern Townships,** between Quebec and Montreal. The long-settled—and French—St. Lawrence corridor was unavailable. Here, life based on the seigneurial system continued as it had for generations. But Six Nations' leaders, such as the leaders of the Mohawks along the Grand River in Upper Canada, had to remain vigilant so that their lands would not be sold off by Britain. Other Native leaders signed treaties in attempts to

secure territory for their people. Surveyors always came before the settlers, dividing the land into townships, and laying out the routes for future roads.

Immigrants came primarily from Great Britain or the United States, but some came from European countries, attracted by widespread advertising campaigns. Potential buyers were wooed with promises of cheap, fertile land, close to towns and markets. Colourful posters, embellished with advertising **copy,** painted an optimistic picture of life in Canada.

The first rude awakening was the journey across the Atlantic. Moving to Canada was a costly and emotional venture. People spent all the money they had on the trip and

> **The Eastern Townships:** the region of south central Quebec between Montreal and Quebec City
>
> **copy:** the print part of a poster or advertisement
>
> **anglophone:** English-speaking

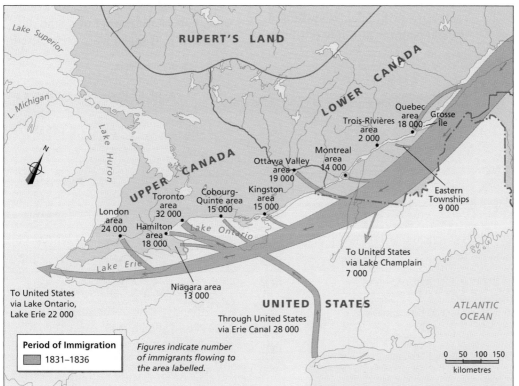

Figure 1–15 This map shows the number of immigrants who came to Upper and Lower Canada, and to the United States, between 1831–1836, and where they settled. Notice the number of people who moved to the Eastern Townships of Lower Canada, which included Montreal and Quebec City. By 1831, Quebec City was 45 percent **anglophone.** As you continue reading this chapter, think about the effect this might have on the rest of Lower Canada.

Map labels:

Lake Superior
L. Michigan
Lake Huron
RUPERT'S LAND
LOWER CANADA
UPPER CANADA
Quebec area 18 000
Grosse Île
Trois-Rivières area 2 000
Montreal area 14 000
Ottawa Valley area 19 000
Eastern Townships 9 000
Toronto area 32 000
Cobourg-Quinte area 15 000
Kingston area 15 000
London area 24 000
Hamilton area 18 000
Lake Ontario
To United States via Lake Champlain 7 000
Lake Erie
Niagara area 13 000
To United States via Lake Ontario, Lake Erie 22 000
UNITED STATES
Through United States via Erie Canal 28 000
ATLANTIC OCEAN

Period of Immigration
1831–1836

Figures indicate number of immigrants flowing to the area labelled.

0 50 100 150 kilometres

on supplies for a year or two of life in the colonies. New settlers also had to be prepared for long separation from family and friends. It took more than a month to travel by ship to Canada—a sea journey which many immigrants did not survive. Moreover, most settlers probably assumed they would never see their loved ones back in Britain or Europe again. Such separation is difficult for us to understand today. Those who embarked on the journey to Canada were brave and resolute—and sometimes desperate, especially the poorest people, who came in the infamous **coffin ships.**

Deadly Journeys

The overpopulated cities and countryside of Britain supplied Canada with many new immigrants. For poor and displaced **tenant farmers** from Ireland and Scotland, the chance to own a farm was very attractive, as was the chance to escape the stifling class system of the old country. But few of these

people could afford to travel, as could members of the upper class, in above-deck cabins on pleasant sailing ships. Instead, they travelled in **steerage** in filthy, overloaded cargo vessels. For many, it would be their last journey.

Cargo vessels regularly transported lumber and other products from North America to Europe. On the return voyage, however, they would sail empty. It quickly became apparent to ship owners that a profit could be made if below decks were converted to carry passengers. Tiers of bunks were built where cargo would otherwise be stowed. Other than pots and tubs, no bathroom facilities were constructed, and the poor hygiene posed a serious health risk. Steerage passengers were squeezed into extraordinarily close quarters, which encouraged the spread of contagious disease. Cholera and other deadly plagues killed many before they ever reached Canada's shores. In 1832, for example, half of all immigrants who did make it to Canada were seriously ill.

coffin ship: a death ship. Many people died while travelling in steerage. The bodies were dumped overboard.

tenant farmer: a farmer who works the land owned by another

steerage: below deck, where cargo is usually stored

Table 1–2	Immigration to Canada from Great Britain 1815–1850				
1815	680	1827	12 648	1839	12 658
1816	3370	1828	12 084	1840	32 293
1817	9797	1829	13 307	1841	38 164
1818	15 136	1830	30 574	1842	54 123
1819	23 534	1831	58 067	1843	23 518
1820	17 921	1832	66 339	1844	22 924
1821	12 955	1833	28 808	1845	31 803
1822	16 013	1834	40 060	1846	43 439
1823	11 355	1835	15 573	1847	109 680
1824	8774	1836	34 226	1848	31 065
1825	8741	1837	29 844	1849	41 367
1826	12 818	1838	4577	1850	32 961

Figure 1–16

Figure 1–17

The emotionally and physically challenging experience of emigrating to Canada is captured in these period illustrations, which show (clockwise) desperate crowds in the shipping agent's office (**Figure 1–16**); the grim conditions in steerage (**Figure 1–17**); and the docks teeming with people ready to board overcrowded ships to go to Canada (**Figure 1–18**). What advice would you give a family member embarking on such a journey?

Figure 1–18

The Multiculturalism of Pioneer Canada

Gaelic: the language of the Celtic highlanders of Scotland

Celtic: the early Indo-Europeans of the British Isles

Most of the better-known journals and accounts of life in British North America during pioneer days were written by relatively well-to-do English people. However, most settlers in Upper Canada were not English. Americans did not consider themselves to be English, nor did the Scottish and Irish, many of whom spoke **Gaelic**. They brought their own distinct cultures and values to Canada, including their own church traditions. Even the music of pioneer Canada was more **Celtic** than English.

In the past, the histories of Native peoples, and Irish and Black immigrants, have been mostly ignored in accounts of Canada's history. This tells us a great deal about how history is actually written. Historians create our official memories. If they ignore the contributions of some groups, while highlighting the contributions of others, how accurate can that history be? By detecting this kind of discrimination, we learn to pay more attention to the ignored groups—and we learn about the values of the time in which those histories were written. By our standards today, nineteenth-century Canadians were racist, the more so because they believed that Europeans had a duty to "civilize" the world. For example, a newspaper article that appeared in the *Owen Sound Comet* in June 1851 captures the idea of the English "destiny":

> In another half-century, therefore, the predominance of the Anglo-Saxon race, terming it in a general way, will be a thing to admire beyond all common admiration. There will be the British Isles with their family of fifty millions or so, and our Northern Continent, with eighty millions or thereabouts, and this South Pacific branch of the English-speaking household— say thirty millions at least; and these three branches of mankind working away in the illumination upwards of the nations—taking the lead in all things, by sea and by land, and lugging the civilization of the world with them!

Ideas like these were taught in schools and churches for many years—even well into the twentieth century, so it is hardly surprising that the contributions of many cultural groups were neglected. As a

Figure 1–19 Canadian fiddler Natalie MacMaster has drawn from Celtic traditions in music.

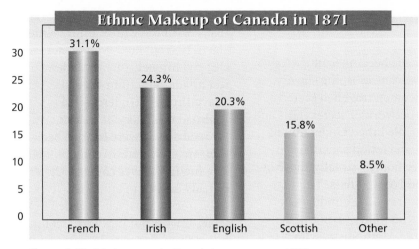

Figure 1–20 Ethnic groups in Canada by percentage, 1871

result, it is very hard to find accounts of Irish contributions to Canadian history, or those of the Native peoples. And it would be impossible in a book such as *Horizons* to tell everyone's story. That would take volumes. Still, it is tragic that the people not included in our official histories have become almost invisible. For example, many Canadians are unaware that Black men and women have been part of Canada's history almost since its beginnings because so few of their stories have been told.

Black Canadians

It may be hard to imagine, but slavery existed in New France during the late-seventeenth and eighteenth centuries. In addition, many Loyalists brought African slaves with them to Canada during the American Revolution. The deep wound that slavery has created in North American society will not be easily healed, as we now know. However, slavery stopped working in Canada long before it did anywhere else in North America. Slavery was abol-

ished everywhere in the British Empire in 1833, but courts in Lower and Upper Canada refused to support slavery long before that. One major factor was that most Black Canadians were free—in fact, many Black Americans had fled the slave states south of the border to find freedom in Canada. As well, during the Loyalist wave of immigration, many Black Americans came to Canada as free men and women, and as loyal subjects to the British throne. They were promised land in exchange for their loyalty.

In 1837, the Black Militia fought against the rebels in Upper Canada, led by William Lyon Mackenzie. You will read more about this important event in Chapter 2. Most Black pioneers believed that a victory for the rebels would result in American domination of Canada, and slavery. Following the rebellions, one member of the militia, Josiah Henson, became an educator and church minister, and a leading member of the growing Black community. He eventually established a technical school in Dresden, Ontario.

The Underground Railroad

Upper Canada became a refuge for Black Americans escaping slavery. Men and women travelled secretly through a network of secret trails and pathways called the "Underground Railroad," and found sanctuary in anti-slavery homes, usually those of Quakers and Methodists. The fugitives often travelled hundreds of kilometres on foot, staying with Quakers and Methodists, who thought slavery was a sin against God and humankind. Harriet Tubman, a Black activist, helped thousands to escape this way. Josiah Henson came up through the "railroad" with his whole family. One slave, Henry "Box" Brown, actually shipped himself—in a wooden box—to Philadelphia from Virginia. Travelling the Underground Railroad was risky. If caught, escaped slaves were handed back to their masters and severely punished. The fugitive slaves came to Upper Canada hoping to build new lives and to be free of fear. Many settled in the larger towns, but new Black communities were also founded by the fugitives. The excerpt that follows describes one such community near Lake Simcoe.

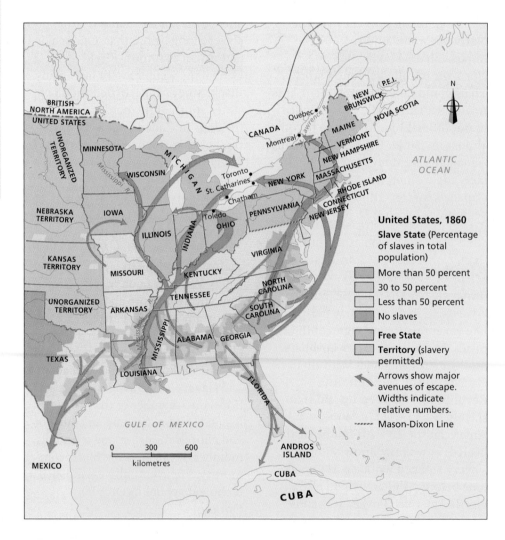

United States, 1860

Slave State (Percentage of slaves in total population)

- More than 50 percent
- 30 to 50 percent
- Less than 50 percent
- No slaves

Free State

Territory (slavery permitted)

Arrows show major avenues of escape. Widths indicate relative numbers.

------ Mason-Dixon Line

Figure 1–21 Safe houses which American slaves used to escape to Canada. How do you think slaves in the Deep South might have learned of the existence of the Underground Railroad?

In every town in the United States the free negroes, who were very numerous and possessed considerable property, were called upon to give security for their good behaviour or to leave the country. No cause is assigned for this requisition … They therefore deputed two of their number to seek a settlement for them in Canada. They have accordingly procured a large tract in the north of Lake Simcoe, and 1,100 have already come over to Canada and nine-hundred more are prepared to follow in the spring, and, as the matter is said to have been generally taken up, it is probable that it will not end there …

Unfortunately, few Black people found acceptance in Canada. Nor did they find a place in government for more than a hundred years. For years, they lived as communities within communities, sometimes just a half-dozen families in small towns here and there. Many took up land in the more remote parts of the country and were part of the pioneer experience of Upper Canada.

In fact, there were communities of Black men, women, and children in every colony in British North America. Those who came during the Loyalist wave of immigration settled in the Maritimes, where there are large communities today. The renowned preacher, David George, for example, arrived with 1232 others in the early 1780s. Many Black Maritimers are descended from these settlers. In British Columbia, there were several Black communities, including Saltspring Island. Some Black settlers remembered their lives before slavery, and wanted to see their African homelands again, as did Richard Pierpoint, a Black Loyalist, who wrote the poignant letter that appears at the right.

Figure 1–22
Maritimer Lucy Mitchell was known for her great sense of style. She lived in Nova Scotia in the nineteenth century.

The Petition of Richard Pierpoint, now of the Town of Niagara, a Man of Colour, a native of Africa, and an inhabitant of this Province since the year of 1780.

Most humbly showeth,
That Your Excellency's Petitioner is a native of Bondu in Africa: that at the age of Sixteen Years he was made a Prisoner and sold as a Slave: that he was conveyed to America about the year 1760, and sold to a British officer; that he served his Majesty during the American Revolutionary War in the Corps called Butler's Rangers, and again during the late American War in a Corps of Colour raised on the Niagara frontier. That Your Excellency's Petitioner is now old and without property; that he finds it difficult to obtain a livelihood by his labour; that he is above all things desirous to return to his native Country; that His Majesty's Government be graciously pleased to grant him any relief, he wishes it might be affording him the means to proceed to England and from thence to a Settlement near the Gambia or Senegal Rivers, from whence he could return to Bondu…"

York, Upper Canada
21st of July 1821

Mary Ann Shadd and the *Provincial Freeman*

To promote harmony—not based on complexional differences—among Her Majesty's subjects

By mid-century, the interests of Black Canadians were represented by the *Provincial Freeman*, a newspaper founded in Windsor, Ontario, by Samuel Ringgold Ward in 1853. Mary Ann Shadd was its first editor, and the first woman editor of a Canadian newspaper. Like other newspapers of the time, the *Freeman* was supported by advertisements and often had poetry on the front page and featured helpful hints and opinions, as well as local and international news.

Mary Ann Shadd was well-educated. She had escaped from the United States after a law was passed that might have returned her to slave status. An advocate for Black education, women's rights, and the abolition of slavery, she even founded a school before becoming the editor of the *Freeman*. This remarkable woman, widowed when her children were still small, also attended law school in the United States, at age forty-six. Denied graduation because she was a woman, Mary Shadd continued to write and speak on important issues. She finally was accepted to the bar and began to practise law when she was sixty.

mentor: a coach and advisor, often in business

Figure 1–23 Today in Ontario, more Black Canadians are being drawn to journalism. Suzanne Boyd, editor-in-chief of *Flare* (left), is **mentor** to Cassandra Leader (right), through the Canadian Association of Black Journalists program.

Women in Upper Canada

I had just finished the first stage of my cooking and was about to shift my character from cook to gentlewoman ...

—MARY O'BRIEN

Women in Upper Canada defined themselves in large part according to their social class. Like men, their expectations, lifestyle, prejudices, and beliefs depended on the class to which they belonged—a mark of their English heritage. But because women did not usually own property, or work outside of the home, they tended to think of their own success or failure in terms of the successes or failures of their fathers and husbands.

In pioneer society, almost all women of marriageable age were married. **Spinsters**, or unmarried women, were often pitied, in part because they had to rely on relatives for support and a place to live. A good marriage gave a woman status in ways it is difficult to understand today. Even intelligent, resourceful, pioneer women such as Susanna

spinster: out-of-date language for an unmarried woman

Moodie, Catherine Parr Traill, Anna Jamieson, and Mary O'Brien wrote often about the activities of their husbands. It was assumed, at least among the gentry, that women would idolize their husbands. Finding a good marriage prospect for a young woman was of great interest to all the family members. Less importance was attached to romantic love than today, and more emphasis was placed on the duty to make the right match.

Of course, no upper-class woman was idle in Upper Canada. Cutting new farms out of the wilderness was hard work, and it often depended upon the help of women from the lower classes, with whom they worked cooperatively. This tended to break down social barriers, which many found quite refreshing. Mary O'Brien, for example, was a pioneer woman who knew the governor and most high government officials in Upper Canada personally, and visited them in their homes.

Nevertheless, she took part in the running of the farm, along with some hired staff, as she records in a diary entry for November 13:

> It was very busy again until twelve o'clock, first in directing my old Yorkshire man how to cut up a fat pig which was slaughtered last night, and then in assisting the old Irishwoman to salt and pack away the same. I value myself on being able to put more into a barrel than anybody else except Southby, though this part of the business is usually the province of the man.

Mary also had a keen sense of justice. She felt it was her duty, and the duty of the men of her social class, to maintain community standards. Spousal and child abuse were not uncommon in the colony, although many people were shocked when it came to light. Mary O'Brien mentions one such incident in her diary:

Figure 1–24 Anne Langton (shown near the fire) was able to maintain a genteel life in Upper Canada. She settled in Sturgeon Lake in 1837 and later penned *A Gentlewoman in Upper Canada*, published by her nephew in 1950. What upper-class English traditions are evident in this painting?

Her husband had used her so ill so as to drive her away from him about two years since, and he has just taken another wife. Not content with that, on her return to the neighbourhood he seeks out to abuse her by threatening her life. Edward has for some time had his eye on the culprit and urges her to prosecute him ... as the crime is fearfully common ... Edward has been out to consult and stimulate the magistrate on account of the deserted wife ...

For poor immigrant women, hard work and long hours were the norm. Although there was a division of labour, it was one-sided. Men never looked after the household jobs, but women did the housework, planting, and harvesting. All pioneer women worked to preserve the harvest, and they made candles and soap. They were expected to have large families because this was a rural society where children were required to do chores as soon as they were able.

Childbirth was hazardous for all women because of a shortage of medical care and little knowledge of proper hygiene during birthing. The overcrowding and poor sanitation in small cabins probably made the process even more dangerous for poor women, who, of course, could not afford the midwives or servants hired by the upper classes.

ACTIVITIES

1. Create an organizer to show who came to Upper Canada in the early nineteenth century and why. Some possible headings are Country of Origin and Means of Transport.

2. Table 1–2 on page 24 shows British immigration to Canada from 1815 to 1850. Can you find any pattern in the figures? In several years, the number of immigrants changes dramatically. Select one year, 1837, for example, and explain what event or events in Canada, Britain, or the United States might account for the change. Consult this chapter and an encyclopedia for background information.

3. Imagine it is 1830 and you have immigrated to Upper Canada. Write a short letter to a family member you have left behind in Ireland. Your letter should report what life is like in the colony and convey your feelings, hopes, and disappointments.

4. a) Create an organizer to show the starting point of African-Americans fleeing slavery in the US, and their final destination. Which seems to be the most popular destination? Explain why.

   b) Name the non-Canadian and non-US destinations of some slaves.

c) Why did people fleeing Missouri take a detour through Kansas and Nebraska to get to Iowa?

5. What do you think were the three greatest risks a fugitive slave might face on the Underground Railroad? Keeping these in mind, imagine that you are a father or mother explaining the need to escape to your children. Write a short dialogue about your plans and the family's reaction to them.

6. Why might Black Americans look towards Canada for a better life? Give three reasons, after you have thought about economic, legal, and social factors.

7. Using the slogan of the *Provincial Freeman* as your model, develop a five-point editorial policy for a newspaper. Your policy should describe the paper's mission, the type of articles it will publish, and the kind of advertising you hope to attract.

8. The painting of Anne Langton (Figure 1–24) and the painting of the Robinson sisters that introduces this chapter (page 9) differ in many ways from the other images of pioneer life presented in Chapter 1. Select one image that seems to contrast with these two paintings (see, for example, page 4 or page 14) and write a paragraph about the differences that strike you the most.

COLONIAL GOVERNMENT AND THE NEED FOR REFORM

Government in the colonies of British North America was neither representative nor responsible. These are important terms. A representative government is one in which representatives are elected by people to make laws on their behalf. Responsible governments can be voted out if elected representatives fail to please a majority of the people who elected them. Democratic governments are usually both representative and responsible. Colonial government, on the other hand, placed power in the hands of a small group of rich and influential men. This type of government is known as an "oligarchy." Although Britain appointed a governor who was supposed to control the oligarchy, in reality, he ruled according to the wishes of its members. As an aristocrat, the governor had much more in common with the colonial upper crust than with the ordinary farmers who made up the bulk of the population.

The government of Upper Canada had been established in 1791 by the Constitutional Act. This divided Upper Canada from Lower Canada, and gave the colony an elected law-making assembly, known as the Legislative Assembly, an appointed governor, and two appointed councils. Since all male citizens who owned property could vote for members of the Assembly, the government gave the appearance of being democratic—and it was. The problems arose because the actual power was held by the governor and his appointed councils, who could **veto** any laws or regulations proposed by the Assembly. The Assembly wanted the government to spend money on projects that would benefit ordinary people, such as schools and roads, and it wanted land reform. The councils, whose members came from the Family Compact, wanted the government to build canals and improve business, and to ignore the problems of land speculation and Crown and clergy reserves. Naturally, conflict was bound to occur. We can only imagine how frustrating life was in a limited democracy. Elected members of the Legislative Assembly were constantly frustrated, which led to calls for reform.

to veto: to stop with authority

Figure 1–25 This diagram illustrates the structure of Upper Canada's colonial government.

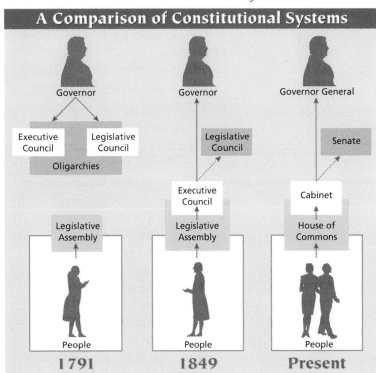

A Comparison of Constitutional Systems

Governor
Executive Council — Legislative Council
Oligarchies
Legislative Assembly
People
1791

Governor
Legislative Council
Executive Council
Legislative Assembly
People
1849

Governor General
Senate
Cabinet
House of Commons
People
Present

Figure 1–26
William Lyon Mackenzie, leader of the reform movement

A List of Grievances

The most extraordinary collection of sturdy beggars, parsons, priests, pensioners, army people, navy people, place-men, bank directors, and stock and land jobbers ever established to operate as a paltry screen to a rotten government ...

–WILLIAM LYON MACKENZIE, WRITING ABOUT THE FAMILY COMPACT

Settlers complained most loudly about land. As you read on pages 20 to 21, speculators (often members of the Family Compact) and absentee landowners either overpriced or tied up prime land, while Crown and clergy reserves hindered development of roadways.

Many settlers knew the Family Compact was to blame and did not disguise their anger. When Robert

Gourlay, a Scottish land agent, surveyed farmers about life in Upper Canada, he was shocked to discover the extent of their discontent. People were fed up with the government and its land policies. Gourlay drew up a list of grievances and, with the settlers, a petition. He was arrested and sent out of the country. The government was in no mood to listen to complaints, and it was not about to change its policies—no matter what the average farmer thought. Gourlay's arrest had the effect, however, of hardening opposition to the Family Compact. His place as a leading radical reformer was taken by another Scot, William Lyon Mackenzie.

Mackenzie did not do things by half measures. As with Gourlay before him, he had strong political convictions and a sincere interest in the well-being of others. Red-haired and argumentative, he often disagreed with other, more moderate reformers, such as Egerton Ryerson and Robert Baldwin, among others. Ryerson and Baldwin were also often frustrated by the government and the Compact, but they hoped to bring about change through negotiation and debate. Mackenzie took a more direct approach: He bought a newspaper. In *The Colonial Advocate*, he published articles that strongly criticized the government and the Family Compact. When angry young members of the Family Compact ransacked his offices, Mackenzie did not back down—he sued. Soon he was at the centre of a group of people who wanted radical change—a more American style of government, but one which would remain loyal to Britain. As a member of the Legislative Assembly, to which he was elected in 1828, Mackenzie became a leader of the reform movement.

Political Action and Protest

Canadian elections have changed considerably since the 1830s. In some ways, modern political rallies do resemble the gathering shown in Figure 1–27. However, you might be shocked to discover some of the goings-on at the polls in the early days. There was, for example, no secret ballot. Voters—men only—had to openly declare their candidate of choice. Votes could be bought, and voters might be intimidated by thugs hired by the supporters of one candidate or another. Many men came to the polls drunk, or would sell their vote for liquor.

Election reform later in the century eliminated most of these problems and made elections fairer and more honest. Today, Canadian elections are well-run. We even send representatives to other countries to set up and monitor their elections. This does not mean that political action in Canada is a thing of the past. Citizens are legally free to criticize the government and to protest its actions, as guaranteed by the Charter of Rights and Freedoms. However, even today Canadian citizens can be thwarted in their attempts to voice their criticisms of government.

Figure 1–27 When voters still had to declare the candidate of their choice from a special platform, such as the one shown here in 1828, election day often turned into a brawl.

Figure 1–28 In the 1830s, the government of Upper Canada could and did arrest and imprison political protesters. Canadians today have a legal right to protest, but how absolute is that right? Protesters at the 1997 Asia-Pacific Economies (APEC) Conference, held in Vancouver, were pepper-sprayed and arrested as part of a security operation by the RCMP. The protesters were publicizing human-rights abuses, in particular those of Indonesia's then-President Suharto. The RCMP and the Prime Minister's Office were criticized in the media for their handling of Suharto's demands. Cries for a public inquiry into the "APEC affair" were only partially satisfied. Is a government ever justified in using violence to suppress protest?

Using Opinion as a Primary Source

William Lyon Mackenzie was a controversial figure, and his actions were much discussed in Upper Canada. Because the reform movement demanded significant changes in the colonial government, he was quickly branded as being an American agent. This was no minor accusation. Memories of the American invasions were still vivid, and many people knew that American immigrants often radically opposed the Canadian government, saying that it curtailed their rights.

Was Mackenzie a patriotic reformer who wanted improvements in British government, or was he an American sympathizer? Even in his day, opinions about him varied. Now, you be the judge. Read the excerpts from the documents quoted and test them, as you would any primary source. Are these documents useful to a person wishing to describe Mackenzie's character and goals? If you were on a committee to determine whether Mackenzie should be named a founder of Canadian democracy, would you support his nomination?

1. ...The people of this Province (Upper Canada) neither desire to break up their ancient connection with Great Britain, nor are they anxious to become members of the (U.S.A.). All they want is cheap, frugal, domestic government, to be exercised for their own benefit and controlled by their own fixed landmarks: they seek a system by which to insure justice, protect property, establish domestic tranquility, and afford a reasonable prospect that civil and religious liberty will be perpetuated, and the safety and happiness of society affected.

    –William Lyon Mackenzie, 1830

2. ... with the eccentricity, the volubility, and indeed the appearance of a madman, the tiny creature (Mackenzie) raved in all directions about grievances.

    –Bishop John Strachan, friend of the Family Compact, 1836

3. ... a wiry and peppery little Scotchman, hearty in his love of public right, still kore in his hatred of public wrongdoers, clever, brave, and energetic but, as tribunes of the people are apt to be, far from cool-headed, sure-footed in his conduct, temperate in his language, or steadfast in his personal connections ...

    –G. Smith, author of Canada and the Canadian Question, 1891

4. So far as any of us, at any time, may have supposed that the cause of freedom would be advanced by adding the Canadas to [the United States], we were under the merest delusion.

    –William Lyon Mackenzie, 1838

5. ... Mackenzie is doing all he can to make a riot but I believe he will not succeed, and the business of the House (Mackenzie was elected to the legislature) proceeds so much more effectively since his absence from it that I think his credit must suffer. Besides that, his unwarranted attack on the Governor will disgust many of his advocates.

    –Mary O'Brien, 1830

WHAT DO YOU THINK?

1. How does knowing something about the source of the opinion affect your evaluation of it?

2. Which opinion did you find the least helpful in evaluating Mackenzie's contributions to the democratic foundations of Canada? Which opinion did you find the most helpful? It would be interesting for you to return to this question once you have finished reading this chapter.

3. Categorize these five opinions as Conservative, Moderate, or Reform, or as being a combination of any two categories. Which category represents the Family Compact?

Stirrings in Lower Canada

The time has come to melt our plates and spoons to make bullets.

–WOLFRED NELSON SPEAKING TO THE PATRIOTES, 1837

As with Upper Canada, Lower Canada had serious political problems. In some respects, these problems were more serious than those of its English-speaking neighbour. With language and cultural roots going back to Champlain, the French population of Lower Canada had not completely adjusted to the British conquest. Exposed to the ideas of the French and American Revolutions, and to the democracy of the United States, educated French-Canadians found British rule without democracy difficult to accept. Control of the colony was in the hands of an oligarchy of merchants and ex-army officers—all English-speaking. Profit was the only reason they maintained ties with the Church and with some wealthy French-Canadian landowners.

The old power structure based on the **seigneurial system** was changing slowly.

Seigneurial families, and the Church, had considerable influence in Lower Canada. Even those who were destined to become leaders of the Rebellion of 1837, such as Louis-Joseph Papineau, came from seigneurial families. Since the St. Lawrence River Valley had been settled for centuries, Lower Canada never experienced the problems associated with land that plagued Upper Canada, except in the northwest region and in the Eastern Townships.

However, French-Canadians had many other grievances. The English seemed to have most of the advantages, even though there were only 80 000 English-speaking people in a population of 420 000. Many French people believed that the seigneurs and the Church had "sold out" to English interests. An attempt to join the two colonies in 1822, and to make English the official language of the union, as you will read, seemed like an attack on French society. Most certainly, it seemed to make the French a minority in a larger English colony.

seigneurial system: the old system of New France whereby seigneurs, or lords, were granted parcels of land by France

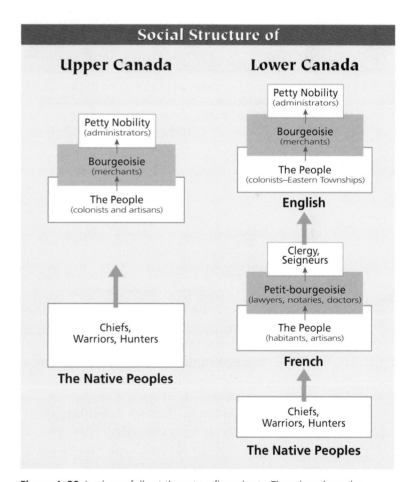

Figure 1–29 Look carefully at these two flow charts. They show how the conquered population of Quebec saw the power structure of their society. The British left the Church and the seigneurs as part of the power structure in Lower Canada. Why would they do that? What was the result?

Figure 1–30 Louis-Joseph Papineau is a hero in Quebec to this day. He was a seigneur and a lawyer, and he became a French-Canadian nationalist. As the Speaker of the Assembly in Lower Canada, he earned the respect of both French and English members. Under his direction, the Assembly changed the way the governor could use tax money, thereby gaining more power for elected representatives. In the 1830s, he became a principal leader of the Patriotes and of the rebellion which broke out in Lower Canada. He escaped to the United States when the revolt failed.

Feelings of Nationalism

French-Canadians also feared that Great Britain might be trying to solve its "French problem" by bringing more English-speaking immigrants into the colony. The government worked to change the old seigneurial system into a British freehold land system by offering land in the Eastern Townships to people from the British Isles. The short-lived British American Land Company, chartered in 1834, bought 343 995 hectares of land in the Eastern Townships for £120 000. Its members were all land speculators. Some time later, when ships loaded with cholera-stricken Irish immi-grants began landing in Quebec, many thought that Britain had plans to kill off the French-Canadian pop-ulation with disease.

Reformers in Lower Canada were frustrated in their attempts to bring about change in the govern-ment and to reduce the power of the Château Clique, whose members included British brewers and bankers. They felt discriminated against, both economically and politically, because of their lan-guage, culture, and ideas. They also objected to the government's "per-manent civil list," which guaranteed salaries for the members of the two councils. French farmers, for their part, resented the British govern-ment's attempts to raise their land tax, while leaving business revenues untouched. And no one believed that Britain had an interest in solv-ing these problems.

These three issues—discrimina-tion against the French, unequal tax-ation, and lack of power within the government—became the focus of reform in Lower Canada. Louis-Joseph Papineau, the leader of the radical reformers in Lower Canada, was a powerful public speaker. At one time, he had been a supporter of British rule. Other leaders, however, were not French. Wolfred Nelson, for example, was an English physician, and Edmund O'Callaghan was an Irishman who started a pro-Patriote newspaper, the *Vindicator*. They all believed that the Assembly should have complete control of the govern-ment's budget, and they wanted a more American-style republic.

In rival newspapers, and in gov-ernment, the Château Clique and reformers squared off against each other. Britain did little to ease ten-sions. In 1810, the colonial office appointed the anti-French James

Craig as governor. Craig arrested those who criticized the government and brought in soldiers to intimidate the French population. He also closed the *Canadien*, a reformist newspaper. A proposal to unite Upper and Lower Canada in 1822, which would have made the French a minority in a huge English colony, only fanned the flames of discontent.

Although French protest quashed the so-called "Union Proposal," the feelings of Lower Canadians were turning bitter towards the government. After British soldiers shot protesters in Montreal in 1832, Papineau and other reformers in the Assembly submitted their "Ninety-two Resolutions" to the governor. It demanded a complete change in the way the colony was governed. When Lord John Russell, in charge of the Colonial Office in Britain, replied with Ten Resolutions denying the rights of the Assembly, the Patriotes, led by Papineau, openly rebelled against the government.

The Rebellions of 1837

Reformers in the colonies of British North America stayed in contact with each other. They shared their views on government and the economy, and exchanged possible solutions to problems. Leaders of the reform movements of Upper and Lower Canada were particularly close, although their goals were not

Figure 1–31 Sir John Colborne, the former governor of Upper Canada, was placed in charge of the British forces. During the Battle of Eustache, he had about 2000 troops under his command. The British forces crushed the 250 Patriotes by setting fire to the church in which they were hiding, then shooting them as they escaped.

always in harmony. Mackenzie and his followers wanted to copy the United States, for example. All realized, however, that change in any one colony would set a pattern for change in the others. When it became clear that government could not be reformed from within—and that it was nearly impossible to weaken the powers of the Château Clique and of the Family Compact—Mackenzie and Papineau prepared for armed attacks on the government.

Radical leaders planned revolts in both Upper and Lower Canada, since Britain did not have enough troops to fight back everywhere. Although there was a reform movement in the Maritimes, led by Joseph Howe, Maritimers did not become involved. In spite of the best-laid plans, the revolts in Upper and Lower Canada were not well-coordinated. Rebellion first broke out in Lower Canada, led by the *Fils de la Liberté* (Sons of Liberty), who were named after radicals of the American Revolution.

A Patriote Song

Political ideas and stories are often communicated through song. Songs can also record important events. After the Rebellion of 1837 in Lower Canada, many rebels, including Papineau, went into exile. This sad song, "Un Canadien Errant," written by Antoine Gérin-Lajoie (translated by Edith Fowkes), describes the feelings of a French-Canadian exile who cannot return home.

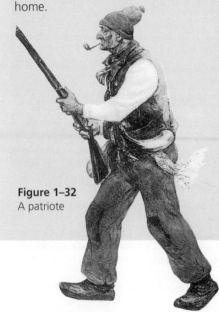

Figure 1–32
A patriote

Un canadien errant
Banni de ses foyers,
Un canadien errant
Banni de ses foyers,
Parcourait en pleurant
Des pays étrangers,
Parcourait en pleurant
Des pays étrangers.
Un jour, triste et pensif,
Assis au bord des flots,
Au courant fugitif
Ill adressa ces mots:
Si tu vois mon pays,
Mon pays malheureux,
Va, dis à mes amis
Que je me souviens d'eux.
Ô jours si plein d'appas
Vous êtes disparus…
Et ma patrie, hélas!
Je ne la verais plus!
Non, mais en expirant,
ô mon cher Canada!
Mon regard languissant
Vers toi se portera.

Translation
Once a Canadian lad,
exiled from hearth and home,
Wandered, alone and sad,
through alien lands unknown.
Down by a rushing stream,
thoughtful and sad one day,
He watched the water pass
and to it he did say:
If you should reach my land,
my most unhappy land,
Please speak to all my friends
so they will understand.
Tell them how much I wish
that I could be once more
In my beloved land that I
will see no more.
My own beloved land I'll
not forget till death,
And I will speak of her with
my last dying breath.
My own beloved land I'll not
forget till death,
And I will speak of her with
my last dying breath.

Had the Catholic Church supported the rebels, the Patriotes might have been more successful. As it was, Church leaders strongly advised their parishioners to stay loyal to Britain. The Rebellion began with the attempted arrest of Papineau, who immediately fled Montreal. In a series of skirmishes and brief battles—at St. Denis, St. Charles, and St. Eustache—British troops defeated the Patriote forces. At St. Eustache, many Patriotes were killed or wounded. By December of 1837, most rebel leaders and supporters had been arrested. Papineau escaped to the United States. The Rebellion in Lower Canada ended quickly, but resentment against the British has lingered to this day and remains a factor in Quebec politics.

Rebellion in Upper Canada

Nationalist feelings among the French in Lower Canada helped convince the colony's reformers that they were part of a larger cause. This was not the situation in Upper Canada. Mackenzie and other radical leaders wanted an American-style democracy. This approach distanced them from many English immigrants, who thought of the United States as an enemy power. Nevertheless, many people—even members of Mary O'Brien's social class—wanted better government.

Moderate reformers found their hopes for more responsible government dashed by John Russell's Ten Resolutions, and by the appointment of Sir Francis Bond Head as

Figure 1–33 The Capital of Upper Canada, York (now Toronto), grew rapidly during the 1830s. English architects relied on English design for the important buildings. Why would Canadians copy English buildings rather than create their own architectural style? What do you think the term "colonial architecture" means?

governor in 1836. Head's sympathies were firmly with the Family Compact, and his heavy-handed administration was bound to provoke a violent response. After the Assembly reprimanded him, he dissolved the House and went on to win an election by advocating loyalty to Britain. Mackenzie took the defeat of the reform movement as a call to arms, and to rebellion.

Whatever their motives, Mackenzie and the radical leaders made plans that bordered on treason. Mackenzie spent a great deal of time and energy organizing resistance to the government and actually training rebels to fight. Some soldiers had gone to war during the War of 1812, but military experience on both sides was minimal. Mackenzie himself lacked military experience. This factor, and poor planning, would ensure his defeat.

Mackenzie decided to strike after hearing that Governor Head had sent soldiers to help fight rebels in Lower Canada—which left Toronto (renamed York) virtually unguarded. A quick march, Mackenzie reasoned, would allow his rebel force to take over the arms and ammunition stored in the arsenal. In addition, they could take Governor Bond Head prisoner. Mackenzie's plan was to set up a new and independent government if rebel demands were not met. Although he tried to convince other radicals to join him, they would not. Unable to count on widespread support, Mackenzie ordered an attack to begin at Montgomery's Tavern on Yonge Street. He led the attack in person, mounted on a white horse.

Marching down Yonge Street, the rebel force met a small group of militia led by Sheriff Jarvis, a local

insurrection: revolution against the established government

official. During the first skirmish, the rebels' lack of military experience became painfully obvious. Jarvis's men fired and ran away. Returning fire, rebel troops shot and then fell to reload, but this confused the rear ranks, who thought they had all been killed. In the confusion, rebels abandoned the little battlefield and retreated back up Yonge Street. At the Battle of Montgomery's Tavern, the rebels were attacked and defeated by militia led by Colonel Alan MacNab. William Lyon Mackenzie escaped, disguised as a woman, to the United States. Although Mackenzie worked to keep the rebellion alive from the other side of the border—and although rebel incidents continued until 1838—the Rebellions of 1837 were a failure.

Punishing the Rebels

Those who rebelled against the government, and failed, probably expected little mercy. The British legal code prevailed in the colonies, and it prescribed the death penalty for more than a hundred crimes, including **insurrection** against the government. British justice concentrated on punishment, rather than rehabilitation. Judges hoped that quick and severe punishment would deter others from committing similar acts. Flogging was common, for example.

After the Rebellions of 1837, the major leaders of the revolt were publicly hanged. Others were "transported" to Bermuda for seven years. In fact, transportation was a very severe punishment. During the long sea voyage from Britain or Canada to Bermuda or Australia, prisoners were kept in a low-ceilinged, cramped lock-up between decks.

They were chained to the walls or to the deck, with no bathroom facilities or ventilation, beyond a small grate or window. In the suffocating heat of the tropics, many became sick and died. Upon arriving at their destination, prisoners were used as slave labour for Britain, working in plantations and on government projects, on starvation rations. Many of Australia's early settlers were convicts.

Figure 1–35 These British convicts have just arrived in Tasmania, off the coast of Australia.

Lord Durham's Report

I found two nations warring within the bosom of a single state.

–LORD DURHAM, 1838

In the wake of the 1837 Rebellions, Britain realized that the old ways of administering the colonies would have to change. The British cabinet established a commission to investigate the situation and to recommend solutions. It was led by John

Lambton, the Earl of Durham, an aristocrat and reformer politician who was appointed Governor-in-Chief of the Canadas. Politically, however, his appointment was not straightforward, and Durham soon found himself in a no-win situation.

Durham, supported by his wife, Lady Durham, arrived in the spring of 1838. Prejudiced and irritable, Durham did possess certain strengths. Where other governors

Figure 1–36 Lord Durham was a young aristocrat who made a fortune from the coal mines he owned. The leaders of the reform movement in Britain, in fact, usually were aristocrats. How would this affect the movement and its leaders' proposals?

had blended quickly into the local power structure of Clique and Compact, Durham was seen as an independent representative of a powerful empire. He even travelled to the United States and patched up relations there. This was strategically important because it froze support for the rebels who had been operating from the northern states.

Though a wealthy man, Durham had progressive ideas. He appointed colonial experts—Charles Buller, Thomas Turton, and Gibbon Wakefield—to his staff. He treated captured rebels as leniently as possible, and pardoned most of them. Papineau was advised to remain in exile. Unfortunately, without the councils and the Assembly, Durham was really a dictator. In addition, British law was being flouted. Even though the results of Durham's actions were beneficial, those who

had fought the rebels, or had had property destroyed in the rebellions, were angry. And they had a legitimate complaint that could be used against him in Britain.

When Durham saw that he had little support in the Canadas (even his pardons were overturned), he resigned and went home. There he completed his report, which recommended that the colonies be joined together and that they be given responsible government. He also recommended that all of British North America be united in time, a forerunner of later proposals for a Canadian confederation. The Durham Report was not well-received by the French in Lower Canada. His prejudices against them were well-known. His goal, through unity, was to force the French to assimilate into English culture.

Union and Beyond

Durham resigned and died soon after his return to Britain. He had correctly reasoned that peace would never be achieved in Canada without some form of democracy—the United States was just too close for comfort. His recommendation for responsible government came as a result of his own liberal ideas and those of Gibbon Wakefield and reform leaders such as Robert Baldwin and Louis Lafontaine. Responsible government, as Durham proposed, was not, however, full democracy or independence. The elected assembly would have power over internal affairs (taxation, for example) that only affected the colonies. Britain would keep control of foreign affairs and the military.

However, Durham proposed that the Executive and Legislative

Councils change substantially. The Executive Council, which would become the Cabinet, would be chosen from elected members of the House of Assembly, and the Legislative Council would no longer have the power to make laws. In fact, the Legislative Council would evolve in time into what we now call the Senate. Although Durham's proposal became the basis of our present system of government, his successors were either unwilling or unable to institute this particular recommendation. It would not become a fact of government for several years. To complicate matters even further, the constitution of Lower Canada had been suspended in the wake of the rebellions. As a consequence, French-Canadian representatives were denied a voice in government until 1843. Nevertheless, reform leaders in both colonies continued to press for the implementation of responsible government.

Durham's proposal for union was accepted by the British government, and by his successor, Lord Sydenham. A wealthy merchant, and a newly appointed peer, Sydenham had a great interest in transportation and development, particularly in building roads and canals. These kinds of projects were dear to the hearts of members of the Clique and the Compact, but not necessarily to French-Canadians. Sydenham was instructed by the British government to press for unity, and this he did, in spite of protests from Lower Canada's reformers. In 1840, the Act of Union united Upper Canada and Lower Canada: they became United Canada in 1841, with the capital in Montreal. However, this was accomplished without the support or participation of the French, which created many problems that linger to the present day.

ACTIVITIES

1. Re-examine Table 1–2, on page 24, which shows immigration to Canada from 1815 to 1850. Explain why immigration declined dramatically in 1837.

2. Develop a "position paper" for the colonial government. In it, you will represent the wishes of either the Family Compact or Upper Canada reformers; or the Château Clique or the Patriotes. Your paper should be a point-form list of grievances and recommendations

3. Create an announcement or poster that will attract volunteers to serve in either the government militia or the rebel forces in 1837. Be sure to use information in such a way that it stirs emotions. Consider how much distortion you can get away with in getting your message across.

4. Give three reasons why you think the Rebellions of 1837 were quickly put down by the colonial government.

5. Imagine that you are a member of the British government and are displeased with the results of Lord Durham's efforts in Upper and Lower Canada. Draft a letter, giving him at least three reasons why he must resign.

6. Explain why few Black people, Native people, or other minorities became involved in the Rebellions of 1837.

CONCLUSION

The years following the War of 1812, and leading to the Act of Union in 1840, were important to the development of our nation. It was a time of turbulence, consolidation, and growth. At the end of the period, one very important political change had occurred: in passing the Union Act, the British government united Upper and Lower Canada into a single colony. Unfortunately, this came about undemocratically. Recommended by Lord Durham, the conditions of the union were extremely unpopular in French Canada. Not only was the process undemocratic, but the act itself was a product of Durham's undisguised racism. Political changes also occurred in the Maritime colonies, but in a more gradual, moderate way. Responsible government, one of Durham's major recommendations and a demand of many colonists, was not immediately granted. Resistance to this was strong both in England and in Canada, especially among the supporters and members of the Family Compact and the Château Clique. The power of these conservative elements had yet to be shaken.

SUMMARY ACTIVITIES

1. Create a newspaper broadsheet for the years 1837–1838. Your broadsheet should be composed to highlight events and feelings of the Rebellion period. It should have an original name, a price, three local stories, two international stories from the period, and any other newspaper features, such as cartoons and advertisements that you think will make your broadsheet interesting and readable.

2. Debate the following resolution: "Upper Canada Needs an American-style of Government, beginning in this year 1837." The debate should be properly organized with speakers for and against the proposal, rebuttals, and all the other elements of formal debate.

3. Examine maps of Upper and Lower Canada in 1830. Prepare a detailed itinerary for Lord Durham that will enable him to restore relations with the United States and to find solutions for the problems of the Canadas within the five months he will spend in the colonies. Include Wakefield, Turton, and Buller in your plans, and meetings with Baldwin, Archbishop Strachan, and other colonial leaders.

ON YOUR OWN

1. Imagine you are part of a committee planning a class trip to cross Canada in a chartered bus. Your role is to plan one-day side trips from three provincial capitals. The challenge is to make these trips both interesting and educational. Students should learn about the history, geography, culture, and economy of each area. Research one province and its capital and prepare an itinerary. Then write a one- or two-page "pitch" for your choice to represent to the whole committee.

2 BUILDING A NATION 1840–1867

CHAPTER OUTCOMES

In this chapter, you will continue to examine the social and political life of the Canadas and how the colonies came to be united in Confederation. By the end of the chapter, you will

- use pictures as a source of information about other periods in history

- use period newspapers as sources of information on social history

- describe the process which led to Confederation

- empathize with people from other eras

- read and interpret primary sources

- identify individuals and events important in Canada's pre-Confederation history

- explain arguments for and against political union

A Trip Across Canada
Selections from the Journal of Walter Cheadle

Walter Cheadle and his friend, Lord Milton, left England in 1862 with the intention of crossing Canada to the Pacific. Unlike other Europeans of the period, however, they had no purpose for their trip other than to see the country. As a result, they have been called the first "Trans–Canadian tourists."

After arriving in Quebec in July, they travelled to Toronto and Niagara Falls, crossed the northern United States by train and steamboat, and then canoed up the Red River to Fort Garry. From Fort Garry, an Assiniboin family guided the two tourists across the prairies to Fort Edmonton. At Fort Edmonton, they were joined by Mr. O. B., an "egotistical, arrogant, and ungrateful" Irish teacher, according to Cheadle. Here and elsewhere, Cheadle's descriptions of events and activities on the trip—and his frequent complaints—are hilarious. The party then travelled across the Rockies to Victoria, on to the goldfields of British Columbia, and then back to Victoria. They sailed for home in December 1863, and Cheadle's account of the journey became a bestseller in Britain.

Later, Cheadle devoted his life to children's medicine and, incidentally, supported the cause of women's right to practise medicine. This selection begins in Fort Edmonton, where Cheadle and Lord Milton meet up with Mr. O. B.

Friday, May 22

Mr. O. B. returned from the Lake to worry us about taking him across with us. As I have omitted to mention him, I will give his history and our acquaintance with him here. He introduced himself to Milton on Sunday evening and talked at him furiously, and shortly after, at me. From his own account it appeared he was a graduate of **Cambridge** ... he crammed birth and aristocracy down my throat in nauseating doses ... He is a great talker and I fancy a great **humbug** and

ne'er do well who has been a dead weight on his friends throughout. Seems a well-informed fellow, however, and nearly knocked my head off with Latin quotations. Horribly afraid of bears and even wolves, [so the other] men amuse themselves by **exciting** false alarms of bears being seen in the neighbourhood ... [H]e is a man of 60, clothed in long coat and walking with a stick. He wishes to go with us, and intimates it will be in our interest to take him, which we don't see, as he is the most helpless fellow in the world ...

Tuesday, June 2

Yesterday we made Mr. O. B. very happy by consenting to take him with us; he made a most pathetic appeal to me as a Cambridge man, and although we knew it was foolish to burden ourselves with an extra mouth, yet we could not find the heart to refuse him. Resolve to set out tomorrow.

Wednesday, June 3

[T]he men of the fort ... commenced a subscription [to buy] Mr. O. B. a horse ... O. B. did not seem very grateful. Wanted

O.B. was a great talker, though horribly afraid of bears.

hardly help laughing at his continual questions at the chance of meeting grisly bears. The Assiniboin today stopped in the bush to light his pipe. O. B. … passed him without seeing him and when he had just got by, the Assiniboin set up a most fearful growling. O. B. took to his heels and ran for it immediately.

Friday, June 12

All through the day, bad swampy ground, often covered with heavy timber, and very heavy work for the horses; in the morning heard a rustling in the bushes, probably a wolf, which horrified O. B., who was sure it was a grisly bear. Weather sunny and breezy.

Thursday, June 18

Nothing of consequence; made short journeys to rest the horses, and stopping early; in pretty good feeding grounds to make up for yesterday. Along the banks of river all day in the thick pines. At noon Milton found very good "colours" of gold in this river … we fix to move on to the river, and fish and hunt for one day.

Friday, June 19

[Our Assiniboin guide] and I off at sunrise after moose; the others move camp to fishing place. After a hard day's work we cannot find fresh moose tracks …we saw nothing; very hot. O. B. set fire to the country … Baptiste and Milton quarrel over the site of the lodge …

me to send a man over to the guard and take another Company's horse on my own responsibility which I, of course, refused and felt rather disgusted at his suggesting it.

Friday, June 5

O. B.'s horse is very satisfactory now. A trouble arranging all the **packs** … but fortunately all the horses prove quiet except O. B.'s, which is the fastest runner we have. Weather continues fine and hot. No incident occurred

after departure; reached fine and **copsed** country, pines and aspens, and camped near a pretty wooded river. O. B.'s assistance is nil; he is the most helpless fellow I ever saw; frightened of a horse and shows very little disposition to help in anything without I ask it. Asks the men, or rather tells them, to do little things for him, as if they were his servants and he an emperor. Does not even attempt to pack his own horse … He is the greatest coward I ever saw, and I can

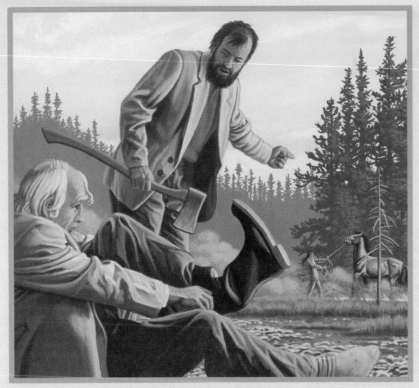

"Mr. O'Byrne, what on earth are you doing?"

Monday, June 22

Can't get up as early as I wish … and Milton's laziness is a great drawback. About noon we begin to suspect that we have taken the wrong track … The path we were following is merely a hunting road. It led us through a bog and to the top of a high bank … The matter was now getting serious, and we therefore unpacked horses, although there was nothing for them to eat … In the meantime we had dinner, and very nearly set the forest on fire … and I thought we could not save it. I seized an axe and cut down the nearest trees. [T]he black horse got frightened and rolled in the fire and I had to seize a great pole and beat him around the head before he would get out again. I thought

he was done for, but he turned out little injured. Whilst this was going on, the fire had again got [out of control], and I set to work with the axe … Milton's presence of mind in helping me at once saved us … Whilst I was energetically cutting trees and crying for water, I observed O. B. sitting down, tugging away at a boot. I shouted at him very angrily:

"Mr. O'Byrne, what on earth are you doing! Why the devil don't you bring water?"

"I can't. I've only got one boot," he said.

"Are you such a fool staying to put on a boot, when the forest will be on fire in a minute and you burnt to a cinder?"

This frightened him, and he jumped up, and limped up with

a pan of water … we packed off … going at a great pace, keeping O. B. at a run, for he dared not be left behind for fear of bears and losing the road. Quite exhausted when he came in. Camped for the night in pretty open space where the road forks.

Next the party crossed the Rockies, following the Athabaska River to Jasper House, then on to Tête Jaune Cache, a trying and difficult journey of more than 1000 kilometres. Mr. O. B. described the trip from Jasper past Moose Lake toward Tête Jaune as the worst journey of his life. Cheadle records that much of the pemmican was bad and that they "starved utterly" for five days. They reached the Fraser River, and the route to Kamloops.

Tuesday, July 14

We started early, and in an hour arrived at the Grand Fork of the Fraser; here we unpacked the horses to feed a little, whilst the guide went to explore the passage of many streams … In about half an hour, we again started and crossed five or six streams, very rapid and swollen, but not more than up to the horses' bellies. O. B. in a great funk. One of the horses took it into his head to swim down the main Fraser and soak our **pemmican** again. I thought he might be drowned, but he came safely under the bank; we hauled him out with a rope. Another [horse] carrying flour walked into a deep place out of the road and soaked that also. We had an awful bother with them and were very glad to be past all the water. The Grand Fork is the original *Tête Jaune Cache* and is certainly the finest scene I have ever viewed. To the right, Robson's Peak, a magnificent mountain, high and rugged, covered with deep snow, the top now clearly seen, although generally covered with clouds. Ranges of other mountains along the Fraser on each side, and in the blue haze were quite fairy-like …

Monday, July 27

Milton's birthday, but a day of work, putting the raft together and crossing. Mosquitoes and sand flies fearful at night. No rest today as provisions are running short … I assist our guide to cut logs for raft, very hot

work … O. B. gave vent to usual groans and sighs whilst staggering under a small tree …

Wednesday, August 5

Late start owing to necessary repair of moccasins … Killed two partridges … Papillon [the dog] killed a skunk for supper … Vast woods still before us … Mosquitoes murderous.

Thursday, August 6

Dull morning. Early start for us …obstructions became greater and greater, and the underwood thick. It was terribly hard work forcing one's way thro' all this, and about 2 o'clock I felt rather weak and doubled up … some hope of better country. We should be glad to see someone; pemmican the size of a fist; flour very

little in bottom of sack! Discussion about killing horses …

Thursday, August 13

Everybody anxious to see what is at the end of the rapid … All keep spirits up, though it is disheartening work … we see nothing before us but the continuation of this rapid thro' its narrow gorge … We have only provision for three days more, and seven or eight charges of powder … Dried, clean horse meat goes fast.

Monday, August 17

Rainy morning; refitting in every way and drying meat [they killed another horse for food]; trousers all torn and in rags … a sorry turn-out. We shall go into the Fort nearly

The party arrives at the Grand Fork.

O.B., of course, did more justice to the grub than anyone else.

consisted of a greasy soup of bacon, cabbages, and peas in a tin dish, beautiful white gallette [probably **bannock],** and tea and sugar. Milton and I did wonders … O. B. appeared shortly and joined us heartily and coolly, altho' I informed him it was a dollar a head! … All anxious to know who we were, where from, whether we intended to mine or seek employment, and seemed rather incredulous when informed that we were a mere party of pleasure, our ragged appearance and gaunt looks greatly against us: Milton's trousers literally rags, mine little better; shirts the same, moccasins in holes; our persons dirty, unwashed and unshaven. The Assiniboin and wife in same condition. Horses and dog skeletons.

naked … This horse-killing is most unprofitable work, delays us two days, and after we have dry meat for only five or six more [days] … Only Milton advocates the raft. He is very irritable and provoking and tries my temper continually. I am terribly bored by being compelled to be at a standstill for two days. I think of home with its comforts, and the eatables and drinkables till we were quite wild with appetite for them … But I cannot stand this, I must change my thoughts, and resort to gnawing the shoulder blade of a horse …

On August 24, the travellers met a family group of Shuswap people. Having finished the last of their dried horse meat, the tourists were desperate.

Cheadle was troubled by a boil the size of "two fists" on his knee. Milton and O. B. could barely walk. Without the Assiniboin guide, and his wife and son, the three Europeans would have been lost and starved. The Shuswaps fed the party and guided them to Fort Kamloops.

Friday, August 28

[A]t last at twilight we discern a long rambling shanty, and … to the front found several people seated round a tarpaulin stretched upon the ground eating … An old man jumped up and in a curious mixture of French, English, and Indian invited us to eat … [We] sat down to the remains of a repast

Saturday, August 29

[G]oing forward across the South Branch in a canoe … [saw] two notices fixed up to trees, "Indian Reserve Lands," "Not to be Trespassed Upon."—Cox Chief Magistrate. We were landed close to the Fort which consisted of two or three detached wooden buildings, not yet completed … quarters for us in the house. We then purchased trousers and shirts in the store, towels and soap, and Burgess [the clerk] showed us a good bathing place, we went down to the river and had a regular scrub-down, and swim afterwards; put on our new apparel and felt really comfortable ... Then, Ah! Then, dinner! ... Mutton chops, potatoes, fresh butter, delicious *gallette*, rice pudding! Never shall forget that delightful meal. Strong tea and plenty of sugar. Talk of intellectual enjoyment! Pooh! Pooh! Your stomach is the door of true delight ... O. B. of course coolly entered and sat down without explaining his case to anyone and did more justice to the grub than any of us. We heard a good deal of what was news to us. Taking of Vicksburg by the North; Mexico by the French; marriage of the Prince of Wales and ... 300 Indians carried off by smallpox last winter. Order famously kept in the Cariboo; Governor Douglas very efficient—only two murders this year.

Monday, August 31

[A]sked O. B. what he intended to do. He said that he thought of waiting here until we went forward ... In the evening he called me aside and asked me if I could supply him with a pair of socks, a silk necktie, some tea and sugar, a little bread, and money enough for the steamer from Yale to Victoria ...

Tuesday, September 1

Milton kindly wrote O. B.'s letter [of introduction] and supplied him with tea, tobacco and matches for his journey ... He then called me aside and said, "Look here, I've got no money for the road," in the coolest manner, as if it were my duty to supply anything he liked to order ... [They had an argument.] He then bid us good-bye coolly and set out, pack on back, saying we would probably never meet again, and that he bore us no ill will! ...

Thursday, September 3

... we are now rested and anxious to get to Victoria for letters ...

After arranging with the chief trader of the Hudson's Bay Company for horses, Milton, Cheadle, and the Assiniboin guides set off for the coast by way of Lillooet and the precipitous Fraser Canyon. They saw the famous, but unfinished, Cariboo Wagon Road,

American and Chinese gold miners, and found the decayed body of a murderer. Passing Hell's Gate, they came to Yale, a wild town filled with gold miners and saloons. Yale was a short steamer trip from New Westminster (present-day Burnaby), their next destination. They sailed for Victoria, where 30 000 **gold rushers** *lived in tents. Milton and Cheadle went to the theatre, dined with the governor, and generally enjoyed themselves before returning to the mainland to continue their tour of the goldfields.*

Cambridge: Cambridge University in Cambridge, England, one of the two prestigious British universities of the day. The other one was Oxford.

humbug: a boaster, a liar

exciting: stirring up

packs: the bags containing all the supplies and gear for a cross-country trek

copsed: an old-fashioned word used to describe countryside that features mostly small trees

pemmican: ground-up meat, lard, and berries

bannock: a type of flatbread

gold rushers: people who travelled to sites where gold had been discovered. There were a number of gold rushes in North America in the nineteenth century.

ACTIVITIES

1. Cheadle published a book loosely based on his journal when he returned to England. Later, the journal itself was published. Which would be of the most value to historians? Why?

2. What does Cheadle's expedition reveal about travel and communications in western Canada at the time of Confederation?

3. Read some of the more humorous passages of Cheadle's journal as a radio drama. Imagine the tone of voice and inflection of the real Cheadle, who was educated at Cambridge University. Another person could provide O. B.'s voice or some appropriate background noises, for example, mosquitoes, rushing water, or even the fake bear roars that frightened O. B. Present your radio drama to the class.

[Those who support Confederation] are ... a few ambitious individuals, who feel our legislature too small for their capacity ... who feel anxious to strut in embroidered court suits ... and enjoy fat salaries far away from the provinces whose best interests are to be shamefully voted away in return for a fortnight's feasting ...

–EDITORIAL, *THE HALIFAX CITIZEN*, 1864

Have you ever felt as though you were being swayed from your better judgement in "return for a fortnight's feasting"? A fortnight is two weeks, but hastily made decisions often haunt people for years. What does this statement say about anti-Confederation sentiment?

INTRODUCTION

The Rebellions of 1837 temporarily slowed the rush to settle Upper Canada. Soon, however, emigrants began to arrive by the thousands, and the population of English-speaking Canada surpassed that of French Canada. Concerned that their language and culture were under attack by the British government, politicians in French Canada formed political parties to defend their interests. After all, in his report, Lord Durham had recommended that English culture and values should prevail, and that the colonies should be joined in a union. If such a union were extended to include the Maritime colonies of Nova Scotia, Prince Edward Island, New Brunswick and Newfoundland—or even, after 1852, British Columbia—French Canada would be forever under siege.

Canada West (formerly Upper Canada) grew rapidly after the rebellions. Toronto became a city with substantial buildings, businesses, banks, and busy thoroughfares. New roads linked bigger towns to the hinterland. Many new towns were incorporated, each with a row of brick or **clapboard** houses for the doctor, the dentist, and the leading merchants. As business grew, so did the challenges of getting goods to market and to the consumer. Canada West was an exciting place to be—a place of growth and opportunity.

As the British government became less interested in its colonies, it amended or cancelled

clapboard: horizontal boards, the outer "skin" of a house

Figure 2–1 Toronto's Crystal Palace was fashioned after a similar building in London, England.

laws which had given them special benefits. Britain refused to finance new projects. Now colonial governments and private developers were responsible for raising cash to build new ships, canals, and railways. Some projects, such as an intercolonial railway, seemed to make more economic sense if the colonies were joined together. Many people believed that the union of all the colonies would make each stronger and richer. Not everyone agreed. The emergence of political leaders who powerfully articulated the advantages of union marked a turning point in the debate—as did the American Civil War, which posed a serious external threat.

This chapter is about the building of Confederation. In other words, it is about the building of Canada. You will learn much about the politics and government of the era, but these are only one part of the story. You will also learn about the people of the time. Who were the men and women in those early photographs and paintings? They are long dead, but once they talked and ate and laughed and schemed and took holidays. They loved, grumbled, gossiped, listened to music, played games, cried, and feared disease and death. Try to see these people as they were—in many ways just like you, but also different. That is really what history is all about. When you come to understand that you too are living in history, not simply studying it, you will have built a bridge between the past and your present.

THE REIGN OF QUEEN VICTORIA

Immigrants, Rich and Poor

In the mid-nineteenth century, life in Canada could be luxurious or burdensome, depending on your social class. With money, education, and social standing, life was very good indeed. It was possible to make a vast amount of money and to keep most of it, since there was no income tax. The very rich, who lived lavishly in splendid houses with many servants, grew even richer after Confederation. On the other hand, many people had to struggle to make a living. Thousands and thousands of people lived below the poverty line in tiny one- or two-room cottages. Workers, in general, were not paid well and worked long hours for little reward. There was no employment insurance, no universal health care, no government assistance as we know it today. If a person could not find work or became ill, he or she depended solely on relatives or the church.

Many of the new immigrants to Canada came from Ireland and Scotland. Most of these people were desperately poor and had little education. Some went to Toronto or to growing towns, where they could find work as manual labourers. Others rented land in return for part of the harvest. Rocky land with thin

Figure 2–2 This picture was taken at the end of the Victorian era in Toronto. It shows housing in one of the poorest sections of town.

soil was the cheapest, and poor immigrants bought land whenever they could. Near present-day Owen Sound, near Meaford and Orangeville, for example, areas today are still known as the "Irish Block" and the "Scottish Settlement." While it was true that new immigrants had opportunities in Canada that simply did not exist for them in the United Kingdom or Europe, in reality they often faced disappointment and hardship.

Many Irish immigrants were Catholics, while many Scots were Presbyterians. People in the establishment, however, belonged to the Anglican Church, which was the official church of the colonies. Most towns had at least one Anglican, Presbyterian, Methodist, and Catholic church. Indeed, religion was very important to the **Victorians.** Almost everybody attended services. Churches were, in effect, communi-

ties within communities. Their leaders made decisions about education, schools, and community matters, and church congregations served as one of the few agencies that helped the destitute. People gave to the churches and helped to build or improve them, often as a way to display their own wealth.

The Native Peoples

The original people of the Eastern Woodlands—the Native peoples— were often pushed aside in pioneer Canada, especially in southern regions of the colonies. Not only were aboriginal reserves located on the edges of the main settled areas, but the Native peoples tended to be forgotten and ignored, unless, of course, Europeans wanted to buy "Indian" lands or to employ "Indian" labourers.

One way or another, the Native peoples were forced to adjust to

Victorian: someone who lived during the era of Queen Victoria, from 1837–1901

Figure 2–3 An Ojibwa chief in the 1850s

European ways of doing things. The Algonkians, for example, had traditionally relied on hunting and fishing for food. With the growth of immigrant settlements throughout the Eastern Woodlands, they turned to small-scale fruit and vegetable gardening and even started to shop at the local food stores. The Ojibwa had never grown a single crop, and they resisted any attempts to force them into farming. Other groups, such as the Mohawks along the Grand River, were long-time agriculturalists, and had their own local governments. They were well-equipped to deal with the colonial officials, merchants, and speculators who had recently appeared on the scene.

Around this time, land claims and territorial disputes were common. Land claims may be in today's news, but they are hardly new. Many claims have histories that go back more than a century. (You will read about one such British Columbia claim, and its resolution, in Chapter 7.) By mid-century, the Ojibwa who lived in the Lake Superior region were embroiled in a

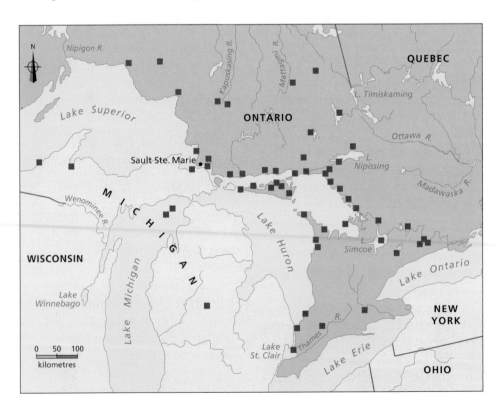

Figure 2–4 A map of Ojibwa reserves in the mid-1800s

land dispute with the new government over miners trespassing on their property. In 1845, the government had given several mining companies the go-ahead to explore the mineral wealth of the Shield. A few years later, it agreed to fund the mining operations. The new governor of the Canadas examined the Native claims and found they were "favourable to the Indians," but this could not stop the development of the Shield—or the encroachment on Ojibwa territory.

The Ojibwa also had reserves on on Lake Huron and Georgian Bay on the edges of European settlements. As settlers moved closer to their lands, they often pressured the Ojibwa to sell their best land. Sometimes, settlers and local governments challenged the terms of previous treaties. One late-century dispute over boundaries forced the Ojibwa to meet with the colonial government at Allenford, Ontario. In the end, the government backed down and accepted the Ojibwa interpretation of their treaty.

The government also tried to persuade bands to rent out good reserve lands, and would pay an annual fee in return for land it could sell to settlers. Since many Native

Figure 2–5 In 1995, the Ojibwa challenged the municipal government to return lands used as a golf course, one frequented by members of the Canadian military, at Ipperwash, Ontario. The confrontation escalated, and actions taken by both sides in the dispute resulted in a violent confrontation.

people were desperately poor, the struggle to hold onto their lands was difficult. Much of the territory that had been recognized in early treaties was eventually lost. But in spite of the tremendous pressure to change and **assimilate** into White society, Native culture remained essentially intact. Elders kept alive many traditions and oral histories, which persist to the present day.

to assimilate: to join the majority group and give up the traditions of one's own group

ACTIVITIES

1. Create an organizer or a web diagram to display information about new immigrants to Canada in the mid-nineteenth century. Show their country of origin, where they settled, and their church affiliation. As part of your web, include information on the lives of the rich and the poor.

2. **a)** Do you think it was possible for a Native person to adapt to Victorian society? Was such adaptation necessary? Was it right? Why or why not?

   b) Why did the settlers not adapt to Native customs and traditions?

3. What economic, environmental, and social difficulties would Native communities face as they tried to preserve their own culture?

VICTORIAN ATTITUDES AND VALUES

Queen Victoria came to the throne in 1837, while she was still in her teens. During the years that she reigned, 1837 to 1901, her tastes, values, and behaviour set the standard. In fact, people who lived in Britain and the British Empire at this time are often called "Victorians." Most Canadians, and those who lived in other colonies of British North America, were British citizens and followed Victorian values. Even Americans adopted the tone and values of the period: Victorian ideals complemented their own beliefs about morals, hard work, success in business, and power. The Victorians had what we call "attitude." They were very sure of themselves and had few doubts about their values and beliefs.

Victorian society was distinctly Christian. The people of this era placed a high value on personal modesty and on "gravity," a kind of seriousness, particularly as the century wore on. The queen was a model for the age. After Victoria's husband, Albert, died, she wore mourning clothes for the rest of her life. But the Victorian era was not grim—in fact, it was very optimistic. The British Empire grew larger and stronger, and its armed forces, particularly its navy, were almost beyond challenge. New discoveries in medicine, science, and technology were reported almost daily. In the

Figure 2–6 Queen Victoria appears at one of her Jubilees (in either 1887 or 1897). Notice that even during a celebration she is wearing black under her robe. Several poor Irish families are shown to the left. The Catholic Irish experienced many hardships under British rule.

latter half of the century, Victorian adventurers embarked on daring journeys. These romantic quests typically involved searching for the sources of the great rivers or other mysteries of the world. The journey of Walter Cheadle and Lord Milton, excerpted in the opening "Window on the Past," typifies this yearning for romantic adventure. Understandably, newspapers were filled with accounts of British triumphs. Many Canadians enjoyed reading these stories because they thought of themselves as British. Most English Victorians had no doubt that they were superior to all other peoples, and that to be born British was "to win the lottery of life."

Victorian values included a strict moral code and an obsession with social status. The class system of Britain and Europe still operated in the US and Canada, but to a lesser extent. This meant that your occupation and social standing was still largely determined by family background and social connections. Although many Europeans had emigrated to North America to escape the class system, they found no shortage of snobbery when they arrived.

Middle-class Victorians were very prudish, and they believed that people could be easily tempted to stray from proper behaviour. They were also extremely materialistic—they liked nice things, and spent freely on clothes, homes, and furnishings. The Victorian obsession with status extended to church buildings, which were often the largest and most important buildings in town. Many social activities took place on church property. Weddings and funerals were important community events, and helped people to build strong relationships with one another.

Fashion and Decor

Although Canadians were less formal than Europeans, keeping up appearances was important. Clothing indicated social status and Victorian values, so even labourers tended to dress formally. Women wore long dresses and aprons; men wore hats and ties, even to sporting events. The

Figure 2–7 Architecture tells us much about the people of an era. After 1840, house styles in Canada West changed almost every decade, often copying English or US fashions. How do you think people earned the money to build large, lavish homes, such as this one, on Jarvis Street in Toronto? Now a restaurant, The Keg, this mansion was once the home of the Massey family.

Figure 2–8 A typical Victorian drawing room. Notice the heavy drapery and tassels.

Figure 2–9 A Victorian hairbrush

parasol: a fancy umbrella to keep out the sun

wealthy dressed extremely well. Men wore long jackets and high, stiff collars; women wore long dresses made of the finest cloth, with high collars to protect their skin from the sun. **Parasols** and broad-brimmed hats were used for the same purpose. Unlike today, a tan was a sign that a person worked outdoors and was, therefore, lower class. No one ever tried to sport a tan.

Victorians were most demonstrative about wealth. Houses of the rich professionals and merchants were large and substantial, indicating the owners' importance in the community. Large houses were also necessary because large families were

common. Often grandparents and other relatives lived in the house, as did servants. Because houses were usually heated with coal or wood fireplaces, rooms were small, with doors to keep in the heat. Victorians loved heavy, decorated furniture, heavy curtains, and knick-knacks. To modern eyes, Victorian rooms would look cluttered and overdone. Of course, the poor could not afford large houses and rich furnishings. They lived in small houses in the poorer sections of town, or in the country; and they decorated with what they could afford. Grown children often lived with their parents, sometimes even after marriage.

ACTIVITIES

1. It is important, and fair, to judge people by the standards of their own time. Make a PMI chart for Victorian values and sensibilities. (Your teacher will review the PMI with you.) Assess your own bias after you have done so, and summarize your assessment in two or three sentences.

2. Is there anything in Victorian society that strikes you as a contradiction? If so, what is it?

3. Examine Figure 2–8. Imagine you are a magazine editor compiling a list of fashion and decor "do's" for trendy Victorians. Using this scene as a model, make a list of at least six "do's".

A NEW AGE OF SCIENCE AND MEDICINE

These three things, will, work and success, between them fill human existence.

–LOUIS PASTEUR

Science and technology dominated and shaped the Western world after 1860. In the nineteenth century, people were astonished as scientists and inventors made discovery after discovery, many of which seemed almost magical. Discoveries came so fast, and many ideas were so new, that understanding was often incomplete. Scientists debated the origin of disease, the causes of which were not well understood. When germs were first seen under a microscope in the 1870s, some scientists theorized that germs ("animalcules," as they were originally called) grew spontaneously out of liquids. Other scientists thought that they were laid as eggs by insects. Educated people took a keen interest in science and its future. As empires and trade networks grew, people came into contact with new, and sometimes unexpected, forms of life. Newspapers and journals carried accounts of discoveries in Africa, northern Canada, and Asia—and to stir public curiosity, journalists often mixed fiction and fact.

Exciting medical discoveries were regularly featured in the news of the nineteenth century. Aspirin, antibiotics, antiseptics, x-rays, vitamins, and hormones were discovered in the latter half of the century. Although the pioneering work on vaccinations had been done at the end of the eighteenth century, it wasn't until the Victorian era that vaccinations became available to ordinary people. Science excited people, but it also frightened them—unlike today, few people had access to reliable information and news reports. People living in Canada's cities, however, were more likely to be aware of what was happening than those who lived in isolated communities.

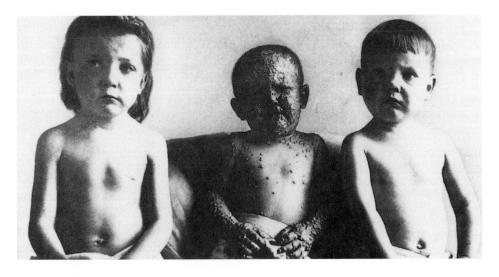

Figure 2–10 The child in the middle has smallpox, a terrible disease that left many scarred for life in the nineteenth century.

The Europeans Meet the Gorilla

Victorians were interested in learning more about the natural world, but they liked their news on the sensational side. This account, published in *The Gentleman's Magazine* in the mid-nineteenth century, describes the gorilla, an animal first encountered and described by a European, a French naturalist, in 1847. How does this account compare with what is known about the gorilla today?

Figure 2–11 A Victorian-era poster of the gorilla. This one seems to have toned down the ferocity!

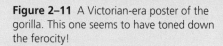

The gorilla is a fruit-eater, but as fierce as the most **carnivorous** animals. He is said to show an enraged **enmity** against men ... he shows a similar hatred to the elephant ... We are told that when the gorilla "sees an elephant busy with his trunk among the twigs, he instantly regards this as an infraction of the laws of property, and ... he suddenly brings his club down on the elephant's (trunk), and drives off the alarmed animal trumpeting shrilly with rage and pain." His enmity to man is more terrible ...

The hideous aspect of his face (his green eyes flashing with rage) is heightened by the thick and prominent brows being drawn **spasmodically** up and down, with hair erect, causing a horrible and fiendish scowl. Weapons are torn from their possessor's grasp, gun-barrels bent and crushed in by the powerful hands and vice-like teeth of the enraged brute. More horrid still, however, is the sudden and unexpected fate which is often inflicted by him. Two people will be walking through one of the woodland paths, unsuspicious of evil, when in an instant one misses his companion, or turns to see him drawn up into the air with a convulsed choking cry ...

carnivorous: flesh-eating

enmity: hatred

spasmodically: in spasms

carbolic acid: an acid compound present in coal tar that can be used as a disinfectant when diluted with water

suffrage: right to vote

People hoped science would find cures for the many serious and deadly diseases that afflicted society. Cholera, smallpox, typhoid fever, influenza, and tuberculosis were very common and killed millions of people in the nineteenth century. Children were particularly susceptible to rheumatic and scarlet fevers. Childbirth was very hazardous, and many women died as a result. Yet very little was known about disease or hygiene. Until germs and antiseptics were discovered, doctors often infected patients during operations. Surgeons performed major operations without washing their instruments or, sometimes, even their hands. Operating rooms were never sterile, and smoking in an operating room was fairly common. So many new germs were introduced into a patient's body during surgery that it is astonishing that people survived surgery and recovered at all.

In 1857, a French scientist, Louis Pasteur, discovered the tiny organisms—the *bacilli*—that cause many diseases. Pasteur also discovered the cause of anthrax (a deadly disease that wiped out cattle and sheep and could infect humans), cholera, and rabies. He used **carbolic acid** as an antiseptic, and vaccinated people and animals against disease. Incidentally, Louis Pasteur did not become wealthy because of his discoveries, as medical researchers often do today. He chose instead to live a simple and generous life, and found satisfaction in his work.

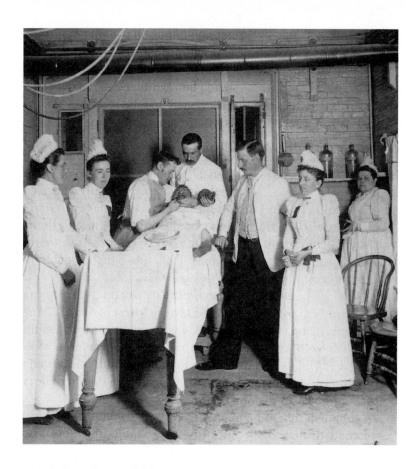

Figure 2–12 This early Canadian photo shows conditions in hospital operating rooms in the mid-1800s. Because germs had not been discovered, the doctors have made no attempt to keep the room—or the patient, the instruments, guests, and themselves—sterile.

Breaking the Barriers: Emily Stowe

Emily Stowe, a Canadian woman, was one of the first female doctors in the British Empire. Born in 1831, she was provided with a good education by her Quaker parents. At sixteen, she became a school teacher, and at twenty-three, she became Canada's first woman school principal. Emily married John Stowe, and they had three children. When her husband became ill with tuberculosis, Emily Stowe realized she wanted to become a doctor. However, she couldn't pursue her studies in Canada—no Canadian medical school would accept a woman applicant in the mid-nineteenth century.

Stowe looked to the United States, and was accepted at the New York Medical College for Women. Upon graduating in 1867, she faced another barrier: She would have to practise illegally in Canada because Canadian law required physicians to do some training in Canada. Stowe bravely set up an illegal practice in Toronto. Finally, in 1880, the rules were changed and Emily Stowe was able to practise legally. In her spare time, she campaigned for women's **suffrage** (see Chapter 7) and other feminist issues, founded the Toronto Women's Literary Club, and helped establish the Toronto Women's Medical College. She died in 1903.

Figure 2–13 Emily Stowe was a feminist and one of the first female doctors in the British colonies. She became a physician in 1867, after studying in the United States. Many Victorians believed that women should never enter medical school because they might be corrupted as they studied the human body.

Using an Editorial as a Primary Source

Whether women should pursue higher education, including medical school, was a question frequently debated at mid-century. One newspaper published in Canada West reprinted this editorial from the *Edinburgh Review*. In it, the author argues for the admission of women to medical school.

Editorials in major publications are useful primary sources for the historian because they usually express an opinion that has attained some popularity. The fact that this editorial had been published in the United Kingdom and was reprinted by a local Canadian newspaper indicates how seriously people took the fight of women to educate themselves.

The question of the right or no right of women to avail themselves of a university education has been raised in a somewhat unexpected form at St. Andrews. A young English lady, Miss Elizabeth Garrett, visited St. Andrews during the summer, and intimated her desire to become a student of medicine.

This lady arrived in St. Andrews a few days ago and on Wednesday last applied to the Rev. Mr. Mcbean, secretary of the university, for a **matriculation ticket**, paid the usual fee, received the ticket, and signed her name in the matriculation book .... All this was very well, and just what might have been expected, from the distinguished and accomplished professors of this ancient and celebrated university. But, unluckily, they seem somehow to have become alarmed at the idea of being first to take the lead ... in the so-called "innovation" of educating women in college, and in those branches of learning that have been generally confined to men, or at least not sought after by women. Accordingly, on Saturday the Senate [of the university] met and passed a resolution to the effect that the issuing of a matriculation ticket ... to Miss Garrett was not sufficiently authorized; that this novel question raised ought to be deliberately considered and decided; that the opinion of other universities and of lawyers should be taken.

It may be doubted that any Senate can exclude ladies from those universities that are established by law and funded by public money. Where do they find the right to do it? Girls are not yet prohibited from attending parish schools—they are rather encouraged to attend. What difference is there, unless arising from custom, between parish schools and universities? We are not aware of any difference in law. Males are admitted and in Acts of Parliament the "male includes the female." It may have been decided by the Court of Session at some time or another that a woman was not entitled to a university education, but we have never heard of such odd decisions. Most likely the question was never raised and we presume that but for custom it is still open. A custom that regulates the measure of rights may be very important but when there has been no exercise of the right at all, there can be no custom, and it is not in every circumstance that non use of a right is followed by the loss of it ...

WHAT DO YOU THINK?

1. In point form, list all the arguments the writer makes in favour of admitting women to medical school.

2. What phrases are most effective in communicating the writer's viewpoint?

3. Knowing what you do about Victorian values, why do you think some people thought that women would be corrupted by studying the human body?

1. In your opinion, what was the most important medical/scientific discovery of the Victorian era? Design a plaque to honour the scientist responsible. The plaque should include three or four sentences about the specific value of this discovery.

2. Who was Emily Stowe? What difficulties did she face and surmount?

3. Louis Pasteur did not become wealthy from his scientific discoveries. Should he be a model for today's scientists? Explain.

LEISURE AND TRAVEL

matriculation ticket: a piece of paper indicating that a student is enrolled in a course and will matriculate, or graduate

serial format: in weekly or monthly installments

droll: humorous

Victorian Canadians liked to be entertained. Those who lived in cities had many opportunities to go to parties, concerts, fairs, circuses, and shows. In the country, barn raisings, quilting bees, weddings, *ceilidhs* (parties with Scottish or Irish music, dancing and stories), barn dances, and other diversions were freely available. Books and magazines were very popular because many people could read. Stories were published in **serial format** so that people had to read the next week's issue to follow the story. Charles Dickens's stories were serialized, for example.

The Victorians had a taste for many amusements that are still enjoyed by modern Canadians—but some of their amusements would today be considered brutal or bizarre. Sports achieved a new popularity. Swimming for pleasure, a fashion started in Europe, quickly caught on in Canada. But so did "blood sports," such as bear-baiting and dog-and-bull fighting. Bare-knuckle boxing matches always drew plenty of spectators—the boxers would hammer away at each other, with bouts often lasting more than a hundred rounds. Boxing remained a brutal sport until

Britain's Marquis of Queensbury issued his famous rules for boxing in the 1860s. These rules, which recommend boxing gloves and limit the duration of rounds, form the basis of today's boxing etiquette. They are also unintentionally **droll** because they capture the Victorian spirit—proper, but fascinated with impropriety. Rule Five, for example, notes: "A man hanging on the ropes in a helpless state, with his toes off the ground, shall be considered down."

The Victorians loved medicine shows. The patent medicines sold at these affairs promised to cure anything and everything, but many of the medicines were actually made from alcohol, pepper, or turpentine. They would often intoxicate or nauseate people, but with no medicinal effect whatsoever. This was also a new era of travelling circuses. Many disabled people, including children, found jobs in the sideshows,

Figure 2–14 Bare-knuckle boxing was strongly discouraged with the publication of the Marquis of Queensbury's rules for boxing.

whist: a card game for four players divided into two teams

where people paid money to gawk at their handicaps. A travelling circus came to Charlottetown, Prince Edward Island, during the conference on Confederation held in 1864. You will read more about this important conference later in this chapter.

Parlour Games

With no television or radio, no movies, videos, or recorded music, people relied on more personal ways to entertain themselves, particularly on winter evenings. They made music, held dances, talked, and played parlour games. Card games, such as **whist**, were very popular, as were checkers and chess. Since large gatherings provided a venue where young people could meet each other in a socially acceptable way, games served as a natural icebreaker and entertainment. Some games were hundreds of years old and had been passed down through the generations. Those of Native, Black, French, and English ancestry had distinct cultural traditions and developed their own games. In time, many parlour games crossed cultural boundaries and were played in homes and halls everywhere.

These parlour games, for example, originated on L' Ile Vert, a farming community on the St. Lawrence

Figure 2–15 Children formed a larger proportion of the population in Victorian times than today. Society was more youthful, since life expectancy was much lower than it is today and people tended to have large families. Victorian children amused themselves with games and outdoor activities, but most were expected to behave properly and to help out with family chores. What clues in this painting would help you identify the social class of these children?

River. Primarily tests of strength and coordination, these games would mainly have been played by men, but would have served the social purpose of allowing the sexes to mingle. What other social purposes might they have served?

Pulling Up The Stump

The first player gets down on his hands and knees; the second sits on the shoulders of the first and, facing toward his feet; he crosses his feet under the first. By giving some jerks, the second player tries to make the first player raise his hands from the floor and to tip him backwards.

Pulling the Leg

The two players lie side by side on their backs with the head of one by the feet of the other; they hold each other by the forearms and raise the left leg three times; the fourth time, they catch the other's leg and each tries to overturn the other.

Kissing His Thumb

The player, hanging by his right arm from a pipe or beam, must raise his body so as to kiss his thumb.

Getting Around

Leisure travel became immensely popular in the Victorian era. People with money to spare travelled to Europe or America whenever they could. There they experienced the nightlife, parties, and entertainments of great cities such as Paris, where they could see the most famous people in the world. Transatlantic travel became much easier after the invention of the steamboat, which reduced the time for an ocean crossing to a few weeks. The *Royal William*, built in Quebec in 1833 (see page 19), crossed the Atlantic in just seventeen days. A few years later, steamships made the

Figure 2–16 Victorian railway travel. Passenger cars were not comfortable by today's standards, but people still enjoyed themselves. How do these sleeping arrangements strike you?

crossing in less than two weeks. In our era, this seems like a very long time, but for people accustomed to crowded sailing ships that took five weeks to travel from Britain to Canada, the steamship was wonderful. And for those who could afford it, steamships had luxurious cabins and recreation facilities.

Changing Technology

The new steam locomotives made land travel more attractive for everyone, not just the wealthy. Imagine how thrilling it must have been to discover you could travel by train to some distant place in a fraction of the time it had taken just a few years earlier.

Railways and steamships also helped to build the **infrastructure** of Canada after 1830. Canada's first railway was the Champlain Saint Lawrence Railroad, which ran from La Prairie, a suburb of Montreal, to

infrastructure: the community systems that make travel, communications, and business easier: for example, roads, canals, transportation, and postal service

DID YOU KNOW?

The idea of a vacation was radically new in the nineteenth century, and it quickly became a status symbol. People often planned their trips years in advance.

Sarah Bernhardt, Superstar

The life of Madame Sarah Bernhardt may prove the greatest marvel of the nineteenth century.

—EDMOND DE GONCOURT, NOVELIST

Sarah Bernhardt, perhaps the most famous person in Europe, was one of the first "superstars." Americans and Canadians who travelled to Paris to see her perform in a Victor Hugo play or in the Théâtre Français could tell their friends that they had witnessed one of the most magnetic performers of all time.

At the time of Confederation, most people in Canada would have recognized her name. She was also known as the "Divine Sarah," "The Greatest French Woman since Joan of Arc," or even "The Eighth Wonder of the World." Marvelously talented, Bernhardt was an actor, sculptor, painter, art critic, singer—and extremely temperamental. She was fired from her first job for slapping the face of another performer and breaking an umbrella over the head of the doorman. Like some performers today, Bernhardt loved publicity and spread shocking stories about herself to attract attention. She let it be known, for example, that she slept in a coffin.

Sarah Bernhardt had an unusual and beautiful face, and a magnetic, forceful personality. People said she had the "eyes of a cat and the smile of a llama." As a young woman, she was so thin that people joked that "an empty carriage pulled up at the stage door and Sarah Bernhardt got out." As one of the most important people in Paris, Sarah Bernhardt was someone to know. In 1870, when the Prussian army was attacking Paris, Sarah set up a hospital and worked day and night as an administrator, fundraiser, and volunteer nurse.

Figure 2–17 The "Divine Sarah" shocked and fascinated the public, which gave her great power. As a public figure, her actions and accomplishments challenged the traditional Victorian view of women as being passive and dutiful. She was for some not only a "superstar," but a role model.

WHAT DO YOU THINK?

1. What are your criteria for a performer to be called "superstar"?

2. How would easier transatlantic travel and the rise of newspapers (see pages 71 to 72) help to create a superstar such as Sarah Bernhardt?

3. What entertainers today could be compared with Sarah Bernhardt? Why? Refer to your criteria in question 1.

4. How do bizarre, sometimes unflattering, details of a superstar's life enhance the public's interest in that person?

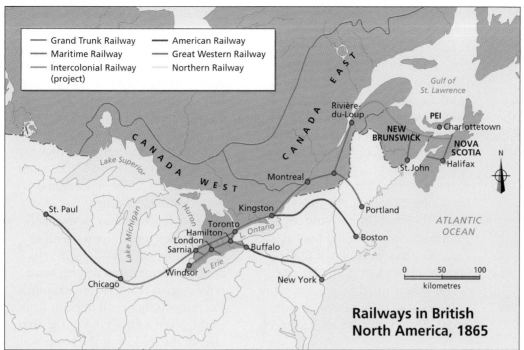

Figure 2–18
Canada entered the railway age after 1837. By the end of the nineteenth century, rail lines linked all the cities in Canada with each other, and with the United States. Today, many of those lines have been abandoned. In fact, many railway beds are now used for bike trails. What transportation system took the place of the trains? Why would another system be more efficient and profitable now, but not in earlier times?

Legend:
— Grand Trunk Railway
— Maritime Railway
— Intercolonial Railway (project)
— American Railway
— Great Western Railway
— Northern Railway

Railways in British North America, 1865

Saint-Jean-sur-Richelieu, 40 kilometres southeast of Montreal. It was completed in 1836. The railway's steam locomotive, which had been built in England and shipped to Canada, transported people and freight at speeds of up to 48 kilometres an hour.

By 1850, regularly scheduled trains moved goods and people at speeds of 80 kilometres an hour or more, and rail lines linked towns from Canada West to the Maritimes. The Champlain and Saint Lawrence Railroad, for example, was extended in 1852 to Saint Lambert, Quebec, and also travelled further into New York state. The St. Lawrence and Atlantic Railroad, completed in 1853, gave Montreal and other Quebec towns access to an ice-free port by connecting them to Portland, Maine. The railways had strict timetables, as much to avoid collisions on the same length of track as to accommodate passengers. For this reason, a train could arrive late, but never early. Train engineers and brakemen were on the job throughout their shifts, even cooking their meals on a shovel in the steam engine's **firebox**.

The Rise of Newspapers

In the mid-nineteenth century, every city and most small towns in Canada had one or more newspapers. In fact, newspapers had existed in Canada since the eighteenth century—*The Halifax Gazette* was the country's first paper, founded in 1752. The Victorian era saw the rise of the dailies—newspapers that are published every day of the week. The dailies began in Montreal in the 1840s. By 1873, Canada had forty-seven dailies. Because more and more people could read, and because so many people lived in cities, where access to information was considered important, dailies caught on rapidly.

Victorian newspapers had many features that we recognize in today's

firebox: the steam boiler

DID YOU KNOW?

Professional sports would have been an unusual concept for Victorians. They recognized only a few professions, all of which required a university degree.

bushel: an old measure of dry goods equivalent to roughly 35 litres

peck: one-quarter of a bushel

newspapers, but there were major differences. Professional sports, other than boxing and horse racing, were not a feature of Victorian life, so there was no sports section. Aside from the odd political cartoon, Victorian newspapers had no comics section. They had no professional advice columns, or horoscopes, and few non-news or special-interest features—"helpful hints" were an exception. Moreover, by today's standards, they had limited sources of information. So how did they attract readers? They were one of the few sources of news from the outside world—the United States, the other colonies, and from places far from home. They were also far less interested in respecting people's privacy. Local news was very important because people loved to know what their neighbours were up to. Court reports and the names, sentences and fines of offenders were usually published, and made for interesting reading. For example, William Wilson sold "spirituous liquor without a license" and was fined $5.00. Mary Morrison used "abusive language" and was fined 25 cents.

People would buy newspapers only if they found them useful or interesting—as a result, self-help articles, recipes, and helpful hints were regular features. For example, "to remove the smell of paint from a room, place a vessel of lighted charcoal in the middle of the room and throw on one or two handfuls of juniper berries." There were recipes for curing ham ("a **bushel**-and-a-half and a **peck** of salt is required for every 1000 pounds of pork"). There was late-breaking news on fad science, for example, phrenology (the science of personality study based on the bumps on a person's head) and the water cure (the theory that water could cure all ailments).

Today, Victorian newspapers may seem hopelessly old-fashioned—as do steamships and steam locomotives. At the time, however, they were revolutionary, and they reshaped society.

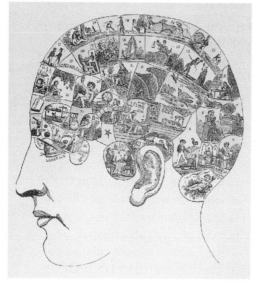

Figure 2–19 Can the bumps on the human skull hold the secrets to the personality within? This drawing from the Victorian era demonstrates that the fad science of the day—phrenology—inspired much enthusiasm. How does this drawing reflect Victorian values and attitudes?

ACTIVITIES

1. Describe all the ways in which Canada's infrastructure developed after 1830. In your judgement, which contribution to infrastructure was most important?

2. Reread the section, Changing Technology, on page 69. What was the first railway in British North America? When was it extended, and to where? What does this say about trade links between Canada East and the US?

3. Urbanization is about the growth of cities and the change, for many people, from a farm-based to a city-based life. Describe the beginnings of urbanization in Canada, and list some of the changes you would expect to see.

BUILDING A NATION

… the scheme as a whole has met with almost universal approval.

–JOHN A. MACDONALD, 1864

Some politicians had been dreaming of Confederation—the union of the colonies of British North America into a **federation**—since the days of Lord Durham. It is safe to say, however, that their dream was far less popular in Canada East, with its French culture, than it was in Canada West. The idea was also unpopular in the Maritime colonies. Macdonald's speech to the Canadian Legislature, excerpted above, was a magnificent piece of rhetoric, but it virtually ignored the fact that almost as many people opposed union as favoured it.

Union would mean a central government, one that would most likely control defence, **external relations**, currency, postage, taxation, and other concerns. Britain already administered most of these functions, however, and many people preferred this arrangement to one that would shift that kind of power to central Canada. In general, those living in the Maritime colonies felt they had little in common with the growing province of Canada, and French-Canadians were wary of any attempt that would make them a minority in an English-speaking nation. Yet the idea was intoxicating—people could create, in their own lifetime, a new country stretching from sea to sea. And that new nation would be immense, one of the largest on Earth.

Like many big ideas, the concept of Confederation started at the top. Those who shared this dream had to sell their vision. They had to win over politicians and business people who regarded union as a bad idea. Through political manoeuvring, persuasion, and debate, they had to quash the notion that big ideas for governments are usually expensive. In the mid-nineteenth century, many people were as skeptical about the motives of politicians as the public is today. The builders of Confederation had started a long process. The first hurdle they had to overcome was to convince skeptics of the merits of these proposals.

Towards Confederation

In Chapter 1, you learned that the Rebellions of 1837 resulted in the Durham Report, and that the **Canadas** were joined by the Act of Union in 1840. Many people in French Canada opposed Durham's recommendation to unite the Canadas, but the British government favoured the plan and acted upon it immediately.

Durham had also recommended **responsible government** for the colonies. This created trouble for Britain and her Canadian governors. The idea that colonies could govern themselves was entirely new. Nobody knew if, or how, self-government would work. Many thought it would seriously weaken the British Empire, and perhaps even strengthen Britain's potential enemies (such as the United States and France). On both sides of the Atlantic, many feared that self-government could create economic problems both in Canada and in Britain. Many people still clung to

federation: a federal union in which the members keep certain powers themselves, and give certain powers to a central government

external relations: dealings with other countries

Canadas: Upper and Lower Canada, whose names were changed to Canada West and Canada East—modern Ontario and Quebec

responsible government: a government in which the executive council is responsible to the legislative assembly, whose members are representatives of the people

Figure 2–20 Lord Elgin came from a wealthy, well-connected family. In spite of Elgin's privilege, he was well-suited to be governor. Like his father-in-law, Lord Durham, he believed in responsible government, and he had considerable experience in colonial matters. Why do you think Britain would appoint Elgin governor rather than a Canadian?

mercantilism: an economic system based on colonialism. The home country takes raw materials in from its colonies and manufactures goods, which it sells for profit.

Corn Laws: laws which protected British agriculture

depression: a period of low economic activity marked by high unemployment

the old idea of **mercantilism**, which defined the colony's economic relationship to the home country.

Britain's economic relationship with the colonies, however, was already changing. In 1846, the British government repealed the **Corn Laws**, which had given trading privileges to the British colonies. Up to this point, Canadian grain had entered Britain with low duties, which had helped wheat and flour production to expand in Upper Canada. Now Britain wanted to move towards free trade—it wanted to buy wheat, flour, and other products at the lowest price, and from any country. After the Corn Laws were repealed, Canada's economy went into a **depression**. Canadians had built ships for the British trade, and they had exported raw materials and agricultural products, but they manufactured very little. With the old economic relationship in tatters, and with few existing industries to revive the economy, Canadians began considering the possibility of creating a country. Then a Canadian government could create its own economic policy—one that would best serve its people.

Support for the idea of self-government was limited. For the most part, the governors who succeeded Durham had not liked the idea, but some, such as Governor Charles Bagot, had brought reformers into the councils. As you learned in Chapter 1, Bagot chose Robert Baldwin and Louis Hippolyte Lafontaine as unofficial joint premiers. Bagot did not believe, however, that he had to do what these men demanded on behalf of the people—the key principle of responsible government. When Britain decided that free trade was in its own best interests, its attitude towards government for Canada changed completely.

In 1847, Britain named James Bruce, the eighth Earl of Elgin, governor of the Canadas. Lord Elgin, who was Lord Durham's son-in-law, was charged with the task of putting responsible government into operation. The colony was to become Britain's economic partner, and it

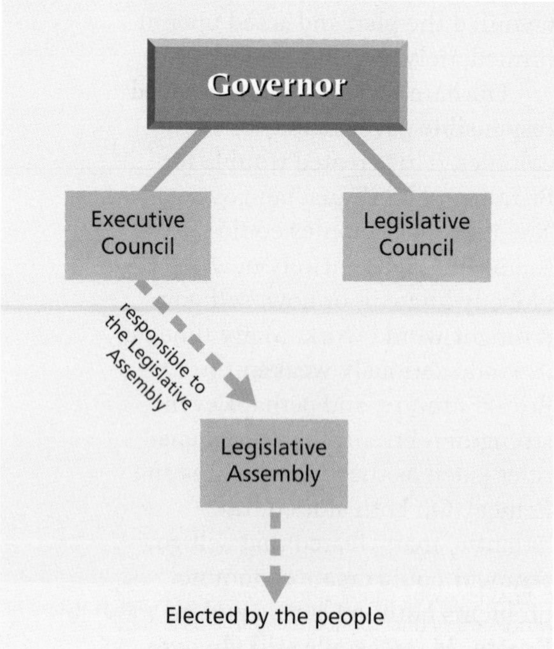

Figure 2–21 The relationships of responsible government

```
                    Governor

        Executive                Legislative
        Council                  Council

            responsible to
            the Legislative
            Assembly

                    Legislative
                    Assembly

                Elected by the people
```

would cease to be Britain's responsibility. From Britain's standpoint, this was an advantage. It was expensive to govern, defend, and financially support the colonies. Responsible government would be a new and exciting chapter in the colony's history, to be sure. Yet no one expected the explosive incident that was to occur.

In Chapter 1, you learned how the Rebellions of 1837 pitted the British establishment against a faltering people's crusade. While many people supported an end to privilege and corruption, others believed the reformers had betrayed the government. When, in 1849, the elected—and reformist—government of Canada passed a bill giving financial compensation to anyone, including the rebels who had lost property during the rebellions, anti-rebel forces

were outraged. In their eyes, **treason** was being rewarded. Even the governor, Lord Elgin, was against the Rebellion Losses Bill. But under responsible government the governor had no right to veto a bill: he had to sign it into law. Never had a governor been in such a predicament. Many people were so opposed to the bill that they attacked Elgin's carriage. The violence escalated into a full-scale riot, which **culminated** with the burning of the parliament buildings. Following the riot, angry merchants and citizens who had condemned the rebels published an Annexation Manifesto—a plan for the United States to take over Canada. Nevertheless, Elgin's signature had laid the foundation for a new form of government for the Canadas—democracy.

treason: betrayal of one's country

to culminate: to climax

Figure 2–22 This painting depicts the burning of the parliament buildings in Montreal on April 25, 1849, after the passing of the Rebellion Losses Bill. The riots involved thousands of people and lasted for two days. Why were the parliament buildings located in Montreal at this time?

1. Create an organizer. In one column, list factors that supported Confederation. In the other, list factors that went against Confederation. Based on your observations, which side do you support? Explain.

2. **a)** How did Britain's economic attitude towards its colonies change in the 1840s?

   b) What economic impact did the repeal of the Corn Laws have on the colonies? In your opinion, would this help or hinder promoters of Confederation? Explain, with reasons.

3. Imagine that you are a witness to the burning of the parliament buildings, shown in Figure 2–22. Write a 1-minute news item for radio, vividly describing the scene and outlining the reasons for the riots.

THE ADVANTAGES OF CONFEDERATION

to annex: to incorporate a territory or country into another country

American Civil War: a war between the southern and northern American states over states' rights. The divisive issue was slavery.

There were many reasons why uniting the British North American colonies into one country would benefit everyone. As a nation, Canada would enjoy economic stability—economic union could even bring back prosperity. Tariffs and trade barriers which then existed between the colonies could be abolished, and the colonies could begin trading with each other.

A strong central government could also build an intercontinental railway to link the colonies for the purposes of trade and defence. A railway on this scale was something separate colonies could never finance on their own. Linking the central colonies to the Maritimes would mean that goods travelling to Europe in winter could go to a Canadian ice-free port—Halifax—instead of Portland, Maine. Eventually, a railway could extend to the Northwest as far as the Pacific. Although the smaller railways of the Victorian era had been greeted with much enthusiasm, they had never made much money,

and often teetered on the verge of bankruptcy.

In the West, Confederation would help to ensure that the western region of British North America—British Columbia and Rupert's Land—was not **annexed** by the United States. Canadians were very suspicious of US intentions. Some American politicians made speeches about Manifest Destiny, the idea that the destiny of the United States was to include all of British North America. Americans had invaded Canada during the War of Independence and the War of 1812. The scattered British colonies had weak defences against the Americans, but as a united and independent nation, that could change—and the United States would be far less likely to invade an independent nation. The **American Civil War**, which began in 1861, heightened the US threat. When the war ended in 1865, the army of the victorious North had more soldiers than the combined population of the British colonies. It could easily strike across

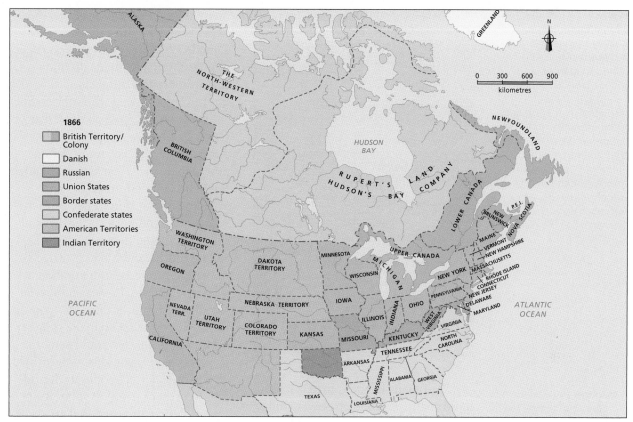

Figure 2–23 Canada and the US immediately following the Civil War

1866
- British Territory/Colony
- Danish
- Russian
- Union States
- Border states
- Confederate states
- American Territories
- Indian Territory

the borders. Moreover, Britain had angered the northern states by supporting the South during the war. Many wondered if the North would retaliate by invading Canada.

Confederation could also improve the way the colonies were governed. The government of the province of Canada was markedly inefficient. The Act of Union had given Canada East and Canada West an ineffective system saddled with numerous elections and plenty of idle time. In addition, there was little structure. Modern political parties maintain internal organization and discipline so that everyone acts together and speaks with one voice. A modern party also has a **whip** to ensure that members vote together on bills. While this reduces the independence of members, it makes the party stronger and more effi-

cient. By contrast, the government of the Canadas was filled with "loose fish," or independent members of the Legislative Assembly. These members could topple a government by voting against one of its bills. Since the colony was governed by alliances of political groups, rather than by single parties, the defection of independent members often created a political crisis.

In a way, the government of early Canada operated like the modern governments of Italy and Israel. In these countries, governments are formed by coalitions of political parties because the party that wins an election seldom has enough seats to rule on its own. Its leader must ask other parties to help form the government, and to compromise. If even a minor party leaves such a coalition, the government can fall.

whip: the person responsible for ensuring discipline and solidarity within a political party

Figure 2–24 George-Étienne Cartier was a wealthy businessman who had invested in and promoted railways. As a young man, Cartier had fought with the rebels in the Rebellion of 1837, and had spent time in exile. He became leader of the *parti bleu*, and was a joint premier of Canada with John A. Macdonald. Cartier was one of the driving forces behind Confederation. He died in 1873.

Clear Grits: so-called because a brave person has "grit"

Politicians in the Canadas had to build coalitions to keep power, and they were often frustrated by the problems this created. For example, members from French and English provinces rarely agreed on an issue, since what was good for French Canada invariably hurt English Canada, and vice versa. In Canada East, the small, radical *parti rouge*, led by Louis-Joseph Papineau, attracted French-speaking farmers and business people opposed to English commercial interests. They also favoured an American-style government, and hated the Act of Union.

George-Étienne Cartier led the most powerful political group in Canada East. The *parti bleu* focused on the economic development of Canada East, and on the protection of French-Canadian rights. Because the *parti bleu* defended traditional French cultural values, and had a working relationship with the Catholic Church, it had wide support in the province, and in govern-

ment. The *parti bleu* was also prepared to work with politicians in Canada West to achieve its goals, as long as English Canada did not threaten French interests.

In Canada West, the more radical party was known as the **Clear Grits**. Led by George Brown, the publisher of the Toronto *Globe* newspaper, the Clear Grits defended English-Canadian interests and attacked corruption in government. Brown disliked both Catholics and the French, and he made enemies easily, but he and his party tried to make the province more democratic. For example, Brown supported the idea of representation by population, which meant that the number of members an area could send to the legislature would be determined by the number of people in the riding. Representation by population was violently opposed in Canada East, where there were now fewer French-speaking people than in Canada West. The middle ground in Canada West belonged to the Tories, led by John A. Macdonald. Macdonald's views were less democratic than those of Brown, but he was a more astute politician. Macdonald made a deal with the *parti bleu* that enabled the combined party—the Liberal-Conservatives—to form a government. In a backhanded compliment to Macdonald, a reporter once said of Brown:

Now that he is a member of parliament, we venture to remark … What is he going to do? That is the question. Will he become finance minister in the present government? Will he give members of this administration a violent personal opposition? Will he join John Hillyard Cameron to secure Rep-by-pop? Will he coalesce with John A. Macdonald? These are things everybody wants to know and which, in due time, will be known, but to gratify natural curiosity, we give the prophetic answer: No!

Another barrier to good government was the so-called "double majority." In order for a bill to pass in the Legislative Assembly, there had to be a majority vote in both the Canada East and Canada West sections of the assembly, rather than just a simple majority. Imagine how hard this would be—rather like passing identical laws in Quebec and British Columbia. Usually one section or the other was not really affected by the laws which were being passed. French or English voted against, or worked against, important bills that the other side wanted passed, particularly when the bills concerned schools, religion, or language.

The problems arising from French-English and Catholic-Protestant divisions were insurmountable for the Union government. Moreover, without having their own provincial governments to legislate matters of provincial interest, both groups were forced to conduct themselves as a single government.

Figure 2–25 George Brown was an imposing figure. He had popular support all over Canada West and owned a newspaper with which to spread his views. It was well known that Brown hated John A. Macdonald, and that the two were political and personal enemies. Like many people, Brown was contradictory. He was prejudiced against Catholics and French-Canadians, but he was also an abolitionist and fought against slavery. After Confederation, Brown and Macdonald reportedly never spoke to each other again.

ACTIVITIES

1. Explain the "double majority" principle of government. How did it affect good government?

2. Chart the major political parties in Canada East and Canada West, with two or three characteristics for each.

3. In what ways did politicians expect Confederation to solve economic problems in the colonies?

4. Explain the concept of Manifest Destiny. Why was the United States such a threat to British North America?

5. Discuss the American Civil War as a factor in Confederation.

CONFEDERATION ACHIEVED

homogeneous: similar to everyone else

franchise: a special privilege granted to a group

sovereignty: the right to self-determination

It may have been portrayed as a lofty political goal, but Canadian Confederation was actually more "deal" than "ideal," and the colonies would join only if they received favourable terms. With the exception of Canada East and Canada West, the colonies were completely separate before 1867. This meant that the citizens of each colony were British subjects, and that the British colonial office was responsible for their well-being and defence. The colonies were often on friendly terms, economically and socially, but they had separate legislatures.

When Confederation was proposed, the various colonies wanted to know how the deal would benefit them. Although MacDonald favoured a strong national government and limited powers for provincial governments, very few colonial politicians agreed with this idea. People who lived outside of central Canada were not eager to be ruled by a government in central Canada—a sentiment that enjoys some popularity today.

The Maritime provinces—Nova Scotia, New Brunswick, Prince Edward Island, and Newfoundland—regarded themselves as mature, independent colonies. Though they

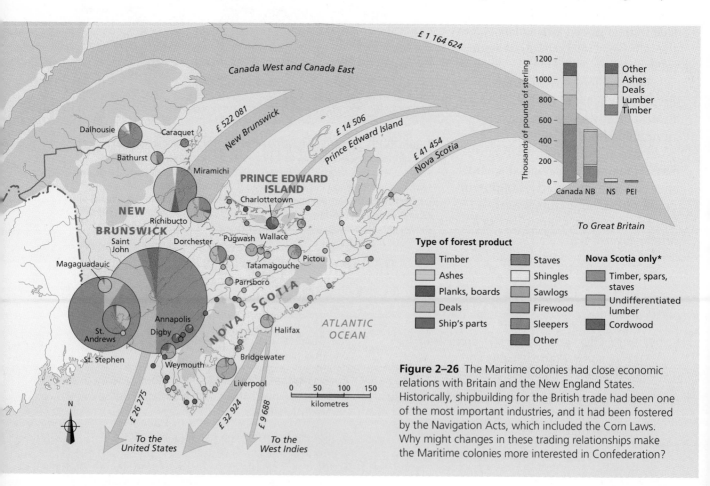

Figure 2–26 The Maritime colonies had close economic relations with Britain and the New England States. Historically, shipbuilding for the British trade had been one of the most important industries, and it had been fostered by the Navigation Acts, which included the Corn Laws. Why might changes in these trading relationships make the Maritime colonies more interested in Confederation?

Confederation: For and Against

Confederation stirred emotions for many reasons, perhaps because it raised questions about identity—in particular, the question of a Canadian identity. In the following excerpts from speeches by John A. Macdonald and Joseph Howe, notice how identity is cleverly linked to other issues. What are some of these issues? Joseph Howe, a long-time Nova Scotia politician who had guided the colony to responsible government, strongly opposed Confederation.

Let us see what the Canadians desire to do. They are not, as we have shown, a very harmonious or **homogeneous** community. Two-fifths of the population are French and three-fifths English. They are therefore per-plexed with an internal antagonism which ... must ever be a source of weak-ness. They are shut in by frost from the outer world for five months of the year. They are at the mercy of a powerful neighbour whose population already outnumbers them by more than eight to one ... on the opposite side of a natural defenceless frontier. Surely such condi-tions as these ought to repress inordi-nate ambition or lust of territory on the part of the public men of Canada.

[I]t is evident that a more uncompromising nucleus of a new nation can hardly be found on the face of the Earth, and that any organized com-munities, having a reasonable chance to do any-thing better, would be politically insane to give up their distinct formations and subject themselves to the domination of Canada.

... When **franchises** were conferred upon the people of the Maritime Provinces, and legislatures given to them, these could only be yielded up by voluntary consent, or be forfeited by misconduct. When self-government was conceded, it could never afterwards by withdrawn.

–Joseph Howe

For twenty long years I have been dragging myself through the dreary waste of Colonial politics. I thought there was no end, nothing worthy of ambition; but now I see something which is well worthy of all I have suffered in the cause of my little country ...

The dangers that have risen from this system we will avoid if we can agree upon forming a strong central government—a great central legislature—a constitution for a union which will have all the rights of **sovereignty** except those that are given to the local governments. Then we shall have taken a great step in advance of the American Republic. If we can only obtain that object—a vigorous general government—we shall not be New Brunswickers, nor Nova Scotians, nor Canadians, but British Americans ...

In the case of a union, this railway must be a national work, and Canada will cheerfully contribute to the utmost extent in order to make that important link, without which no political connection can be complete. What will be the consequence to the city [Halifax], pros-perous as it is, from that communication? Montreal is at this moment competing with New York for the trade of the great West. Build the road and Halifax will soon become one of the great emporiums of the world. All the great resources of the West will come over the immense railways of Canada to the bosom of your harbour.

–John A. Macdonald

WHAT DO YOU THINK?

1. In an organizer, list Joseph Howe's points against Confederation in one column and Macdonald's points in favour of Confederation in another.

2. How do Macdonald and Howe represent the presence of the United States? In a paragraph, describe who, in your opinion, used the American factor most effectively.

3. What does Macdonald say citizens of his proposed Confederation would call themselves? Would this be a selling point for French-Canadians? Explain your answer.

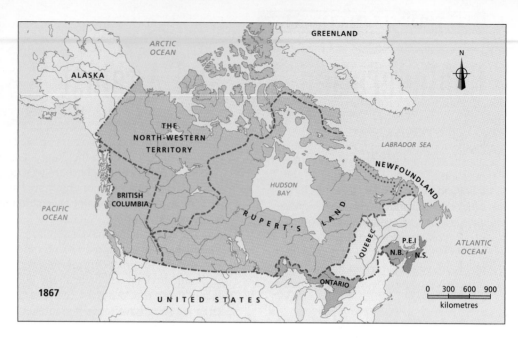

Figure 2–27 Canada at Confederation

THE NORTH-WESTERN TERRITORY

ARCTIC OCEAN

ALASKA

GREENLAND

BRITISH COLUMBIA

PACIFIC OCEAN

HUDSON BAY

RUPERT'S LAND

LABRADOR SEA

NEWFOUNDLAND

QUEBEC

P.E.I

N.B.

N.S.

ATLANTIC OCEAN

ONTARIO

1867

UNITED STATES

0   300   600   900
kilometres

had problems, a distinctive Atlantic outlook gave these colonies a sense of shared identity. They also had responsible government and independent trading relationships with Britain and the United States. Newfoundland, for example, had almost no trade with Canada, so there was little or no economic benefit to be had from union. Building a railway to link the colonies, a major argument for union, held no promise for Newfoundland or Prince Edward Island. But there were threats on the horizon. The United States planned to end its Reciprocity Treaty, which had allowed goods to pass into the US duty-free, in 1866. Britain had already repealed the Corn Laws, which had put a damper on trans-Atlantic trade. Moreover, the development of steam and steel technology seriously threatened the Maritime shipbuilding industry. Macdonald and his supporters had to show how Confederation would resolve some of these concerns. Even then, Prince Edward Island and Newfoundland could not be convinced.

The Conferences

Most of the colonies of British North America were facing difficult times by the mid-1860s. The northern US states, who were winning the American Civil War, were not on good terms with Britain. In the Maritimes, the loss of favourable terms in British markets for Canadian products (see pages 73 and 74) had damaged the economy. Canada East and Canada West were nearly bankrupt as a result of their depressed economies, and their union government barely worked at all. Between 1849 and 1864, twelve different governments had been in power. Many leaders saw Confederation as the only solution to these crises. Even George Brown, to the astonishment of friends and allies, agreed to work with Macdonald and Cartier in what has been called the "Great Coalition"—first to save the government of Canada, then to try to unite the colonies.

The next step on the road to

Confederation was a series of meetings known as the "conferences." At these meetings, representatives from all the colonies hammered out details of a new union. The meetings began in 1864 in Charlottetown, Prince Edward Island, where the Maritime colonies had planned to discuss a Maritime union. Accompanied by the land speculator and railway builder, Alexander Tilloch Galt, the three members of the Great Coalition asked to join the discussion to present their plans for Confederation. They were so convincing that Samuel Tilley and Charles Tupper, from New Brunswick and Nova Scotia, respectively, and Edward Whelan, from Prince Edward Island, agreed to work out the details with the Canadian delegates at another conference at Quebec. Newfoundland also came to the Quebec Conference, but its voters were not enthusiastic about Confederation.

The delegates to the Quebec Conference, held in the fall of 1864, planned the birth of a new nation, a difficult, time-consuming task. After much discussion, and much disagreement, they decided that provincial governments should retain

> **Potato Famine:** the failure of the potato crop in Ireland in 1840s, which caused widespread starvation and caused many people to emigrate

The Fenian Raids

Figure 2–28 This modern wall mural depicts the Irish Potato Famine of the nineteenth century.

When the American Civil War ended in 1865, an Irish society known as the "Fenians" planned to harm Britain by striking at Canada. Britain had occupied Ireland for centuries, but most Irish deeply resented their British rulers. Many of the Irish who emigrated to the United States carried their anger with them, particularly since it seemed that the **Potato Famine** had been caused by Britain.

Many Fenians had been soldiers in the army of the northern states—and they were eager to invade the British colonies. In May 1866, the Fenians captured Fort Erie but turned back to Buffalo when back-up troops failed to arrive. That same year, they crossed into Quebec, remaining there for two days, and also launched an unsuccessful raid against the New Brunswick border.

The Fenian attacks convinced many people, including Maritimers, that the US threat to Canada was real. John A. Macdonald, acutely aware of the significance of this turn of events, was able to turn the raids to his political advantage in developing support for his dream of Confederation.

Figure 2–29 John A. Macdonald, our first prime minister, was born in Scotland, like many other early Canadians. His politics were conservative, and he was part of the militia unit that fought against the rebels at Montgomery's Tavern. As a lawyer, however, he defended the rebels in court. He also had ties to the Family Compact. As a leader of the Conservative, or Tory, party, he built an alliance with George-Étienne Cartier of Canada East. MacDonald's strengths included his energy, vision, and public-speaking skills.

many powers. This made the nation a federation. The country would not have the strong national government that Macdonald had envisioned, but he had to compromise, just like the other delegates. In the end, the Quebec Conference produced seventy-two resolutions—statements on government—and a blueprint for Confederation.

It was not enough for the delegates to meet and decide the fate of Canada amongst themselves. Each of the colonies had responsible government, and the proposal had to be debated and approved by each legislature. Opposition greeted almost every point—whether the issue was railway-building or the powers of Ottawa, the proposed new capital. Powerful speakers such as A. A. Dorion, of Quebec, and Joseph Howe, of Nova Scotia, spoke against Confederation. One of the most inspiring speakers for union, Thomas D'Arcy McGee was eventually assassinated, probably by a Fenian (see The Fenian Raids, on page 83).

Although all the delegates to the Charlottetown and Quebec conferences were men, they were accompanied by their families. Unofficial activities included banquets and parties (a painting of a Charlottetown Conference ball is shown on page 54). Only recently have historians begun to write about the influence of the women present at these events who were, in a typically Victorian arrangement, relegated to the background. Certainly they played a role. As one historian has put it, they were a force that helped to build a "sense of communal solidarity" among participants who were divided by language, region, and political beliefs. Native peoples were absent from both conferences—an omission that can never happen again.

In the end, New Brunswick, Nova Scotia, and Canada decided to join together as one nation, and to ask Britain for permission to do so. This event took place in London, England, in 1866, after which the British Parliament passed the British North America Act, creating the Dominion of Canada.

1. Build three-point arguments both for and against Confederation. For example, use the point-of-view of a citizen of the colonies and of a Native person. Consider political, economic, and social costs and benefits.

2. In a brief report, describe how technological changes and trade developments with the US and Britain affected the colonies' economic prospects. Describe how these set the stage for the Confederation Conferences.

3. Did Macdonald succeed in getting the kind of Confederation he had hoped for? Explain your answer.

4. In what ways did the Conferences reflect Victorian social values and beliefs? In your answer, consider the roles that women and Native people were allowed to play in the negotiations.

THE BRITISH NORTH AMERICA ACT: CANADA'S CONSTITUTION

Canada became a country because the parliament of Britain passed an act, the British North America Act, making it a country. This was in sharp contrast to the United States, which had declared itself a nation, fought a revolution, defeated the British, and formulated its own rules. Because the BNA Act was based on the Quebec Resolutions, most of it was written by Canadians, in Canada, and it became the **constitution** of the new Dominion. However, the BNA Act recognized the supreme authority of the monarch in these sections:

3. It shall be lawful for the Queen, by and with the Advice of Her Majesty's Most Honourable Privy Council, to declare by Proclamation that, on a Day herein appointed—the Provinces of Canada, Nova Scotia, and New Brunswick shall form and be One Dominion under the Name of Canada

4. Canada shall be divided into Four Provinces named Ontario, Quebec, Nova Scotia, and New Brunswick.

Because Canada emerged as the result of negotiations between equal partners, the BNA Act is full of compromise. By reading it carefully, you can almost imagine delegates sitting around the table until dawn, thrashing out details of issues large and small—ferry services, for example. Try to see beyond the legal language as you read the following sections of the BNA Act. Remember that Canada has a federal, or national, government—the Parliament of Canada—and a government in each of the provinces—the provincial legislatures.

constitution: the laws that set forth the powers and responsibilities of the government and guarantee the rights of the people

The Powers of the National Government

Authority of the Parliament of Canada extends to all Matters coming within the Classes of Subjects next hereinafter enumerated: that is to say,

1 a. The Public Debt and Property.

2. The Regulation of Trade and Commerce.

2a. Unemployment insurance.

3. The raising of Money by any Mode or System of Taxation.

4. The borrowing of Money on the Public Credit.

5. Postal Service.

6. The Census and Statistics.

7. Militia, Military and Naval Service, and Defence.

8. The fixing of and providing for the Salaries and Allowances of Civil and other Officers of the Government of Canada.

9. Beacons, Buoys, Lighthouses, and Sable Island.

10. Navigation and Shipping.

11. Quarantine and the Establishment and Maintenance of Marine Hospitals.

12. Sea Coast and Inland Fisheries.

13. Ferries between a Province and any British or Foreign Country or between Two Provinces.

14. Currency and Coinage.

15. Banking, Incorporation of Banks, and the Issue of Paper Money.

16. Savings Banks.

17. Weights and Measures.

18. Bills of Exchange and Promissory Notes.

19. Interest.

20. Legal Tender.

21. Bankruptcy and Insolvency.

22. Patents of Invention and Discovery.

23. Copyrights.

24. Indians, and Lands reserved for the Indians.

25. Naturalization and Aliens.

26. Marriage and Divorce.

27. The Criminal Law, except the Constitution of Courts of Criminal Jurisdiction, but including the Procedure in Criminal Matters.

28. The Establishment, Maintenance, and Management of Penitentiaries.

29. Such Classes of Subjects as are expressly excepted in the Enumeration of the Classes of Subjects by this Act assigned exclusively to the Legislatures of the Provinces.

And any Matter coming within any of the Classes of Subjects enumerated in this Section shall not be deemed to come within the Class of Matters of a local or private Nature comprised in the Enumeration of the Classes of Subjects by this Act assigned exclusively to the Legislatures of the Provinces.

The Powers of the Provincial Legislature

92. In each Province the Legislature may exclusively make Laws in relation to Matters coming within the Classes of Subject next hereinafter enumerated; that is to say,

1. The Amendment from Time to Time, notwithstanding anything in this Act of the Constitution of the Province, except as regards the Office of Lieutenant Governor.

2. Direct Taxation within the Province in order to the raising of a Revenue for Provincial Purposes.

3. The borrowing of Money on the sole Credit of the Province.

4. The Establishment and Tenure of Provincial Offices and the Appointment and Payment of Provincial Officers.

5. The Management and Sale of the Public Lands belonging to the Province and of the Timber and Wood thereon.

6. The Establishment, Maintenance, and Management of Public and Reformatory Prisons in and for the Province.

7. The Establishment, Maintenance, and Management of Hospitals, Asylums, Charities, and Eleemosynary Institutions in and for the Province, other than Marine Hospitals.

8. Municipal Institutions in the Province.

9. Shop, Saloon, Tavern, Auctioneer, and other Licenses in order to the raising of a Revenue for Provincial, Local, or Municipal Purposes.

10. Local Works and Undertakings other than such as are of the following

Classes: —
(a) Lines of Steam or other Ships, Railways, Canals, Telegraphs, and other Works and Undertakings connecting the Province with any other or others of the Provinces, or extending beyond the Limits of the Province;
(b) Lines of Steam Ships between the Province and any British or Foreign Country;
(c) Such Works as, although wholly situate within the Province, are before or after their Execution declared by the Parliament of Canada to be for the general Advantage of Canada or for the Advantage of Two or more of the Provinces.

11. The Incorporation of Companies with Provincial Objects.

12. The Solemnization of Marriage in the Province.

13. Property and Civil Rights in the Province.

14. The Administration of Justice in the Province, including the Constitution, Maintenance, and Organization of Provincial Courts, both of Civil and of Criminal Jurisdiction, and including Procedure in Civil Matters in those Courts.

15. The Imposition of Punishment by Fine, Penalty, or Imprisonment for enforcing any Law of the Province made in relation to any Matter coming within any of the Classes of Subjects enumerated in this Section.

16. Generally all Matters of a merely local or private Nature in the Province.

---

2. Education is given exclusively to the provincial legislatures in section 93.

While British Columbia was not officially present at the Charlottetown and Quebec conferences, people in the colony were not indifferent to Confederation. Western supporters of Confederation, such as Amor de Cosmos (then a member of Vancouver's Legislative Assembly) did attend the events. Moreover, most Westerners believed that a railway link to central Canada would foster growth and development of their region. The great Northwest, which was controlled by the Hudson's Bay Company, was bought by Canada in 1867—but no one bothered to consult the Native peoples, including the Métis, who lived there. This aspect of Canadian history will be more closely examined in later chapters of *Horizons*.

ACTIVITIES

1. a) In what key way did Canada's approach to achieving nationhood differ from that of the United States?

    b) Would you say that the new Dominion of Canada was truly independent? Explain your answer.

2. Look at the image on page 54. According to it, what was the class and social status of the people present at the Charlottetown Conference? How are women portrayed? Based on what you have studied, would you paint a different picture? Explain your answer.

3. Create a Confederation time line that includes important events leading up to the proclamation of the Dominion of Canada on July 1, 1867.

4. Do a PMI chart on the sections of the BNA Act featured in this chapter.

CONCLUSION

On July 1, 1867, Canadians celebrated their new Dominion in style. Communities all across the new provinces organized parties and concerts. Fireworks shot into the sky, bands played, and crowds cheered speakers who promised a glorious future for a nation that would one day take its place among the great nations of the world. Plans were already in the works to bring the Northwest and British Columbia into Canada. Many hoped that the objections of the two hold-out Maritime colonies could be overcome. As Canada's first prime minister, John A. MacDonald had initiated a national policy that would establish Canada's infrastructure and industrial base, forever changing the old colonial relationship with Britain.

Yet the new nation had some old problems. Soon the Métis made it known that they violently opposed plans that deprived them of land and rights. Trans-provincial and transcontinental railways were extremely expensive, and as they were built, corruption crept into the very highest levels of government. Long-standing disputes between French and English Canada did not vanish, and remain unresolved to the present day. Still, Canadians, who had forged a country through compromise, had embarked on a new, exciting enterprise. Today, Canada ranks as one of the world's most prosperous and democratic nations, with a good record for tolerance, social responsibility, and peace. Truly, Victorian Canadians, enthusiastic and naive as they were, had left a great legacy to future generations.

SUMMARY ACTIVITIES

1. Historians tend to specialize. Some study economic history; others study political history; some are interested in military history; others study social history. What kind of history makes up the first section of this chapter? Make a list of things that a social historian would focus on. Make another list for one of the other areas of specialization in history.

2. Make up a constitution—real or imaginary—for the governing of a small community, club, or organization.

3. Create a dialogue between an American president who is in favour of Manifest Destiny, and a Canadian, such as John A. Macdonald, who is opposed to the idea.

4. In a small group, develop an advertising campaign, with posters, a slogan, a song, and other materials, which you feel might have influenced the delegates to the Charlottetown Conference.

5. Research Canadian history from 1837 to 1867. Based on what you discover, build a portrait gallery of important people from the period, with captions explaining their importance.

ON YOUR OWN

1. Canada has a strong party system, and almost every adult can vote. Does this make Canada's democracy function as well as it could, or would many smaller parties be preferable? In an oral report, describe how you think government should operate to best serve the people it represents.

2. Create a "Victorian Evening" program for either upper- or lower-class people. List the events, including entertainments, for the evening. Create a "guest list" with the names and occupations of the people you want to invite. Remember that women will usually have no occupation outside the home.

UNIT II
THE LAND AND THE PEOPLE

The geography of western Canada has played a great role in the history of its people. By the beginning of the nineteenth century, the prairie had been home to the Assiniboin, Cree, Sarcee, and Blackfoot for more than a thousand years. The North American bison numbered 60 million, and the prairie was covered with a variety of grasses—many now extinct. In the Western Mountains and on the Pacific Coast, the Native peoples made the forest their home, using its wood to build their homes, boats, and totems—even to make clothes and utensils. A mild climate lessened the struggle for survival and encouraged the development of a complex social life.

Métis protest. When the Scottish Selkirk settlers came to the Red River Valley area in 1811, many Métis were alarmed. They balked when the settlement leader tried to stop them from selling pemmican to the North West Company. As a result, the NWC and the Métis started to harass the settlers, hoping they would leave. Here, two members of a Métis family discuss their plan of action.

Mighty bison. Both the Plains peoples and the Métis hunted bison, which numbered more than 60 million until the mid-nineteenth century. The systematic slaughter of the bison by the Canadian and American governments, and the building of the Canadian Pacific Railway, forever disrupted the herds. Bison now remain as a protected species in parks such as Elk Island National Park, Alberta.

Into this milieu came the Europeans—as fur traders and, later, as permanent settlers. In present-day Manitoba, the French fur traders married into Native families, forming a unique culture—the Métis. Métis culture dominated the Red River Valley area until the the arrival of hundreds of Scottish settlers in 1811.

In 1860, a new wave of Upper Canada immigrants came to Red River, contributing to rising tensions. The climax of these conflicts was the Red River Rebellion, led by Louis Riel, and the creation of the province of Manitoba and the North-West Territories.

Meanwhile, British Columbia was undergoing its own changes. Two gold rushes—one along the Fraser River, and one in the Cariboo region—caused wild population fluctuations as immigrants from the US, Britain, Europe, and China poured into the area. As fast as some people came, they left, or so it

seemed. Economic woes forced the union of the colony of Vancouver Island and British Columbia into the new colony of British Columbia, which joined Confederation in 1871. Then, things began to look up. Vancouver became the terminus for the Canadian Pacific Railway, and the province started to diversify its economic base.

As the century progressed, the Canadian government worked hard to open up the West for settlement. Between

1870 and 1877, under the leadership of John A. Macdonald, it concluded seven treaties with the western Native peoples so that "immigrants could come and fill up the country," as one government official put it.

Western settlement and protective tariffs for farmers were just two of Macdonald's ideas for Canada. The third was perhaps the most ambitious—the building of a transcontinental railway to link east and west. This was the future Canadian Pacific Railway. The CPR required the labour of tens of thousands of workers, including 17 000 Chinese immigrants, who laboured in the difficult terrain of British Columbia. Completed in 1885, the railway became a political tool for the Canadian government to finally quash Louis Riel during the Northwest Rebellion of 1885.

Bitter disappointment. Tens of thousands of Chinese immigrants came to British Columbia to help build the railway. They often toiled without knowing that the cost of their supplies and room and board was being deducted from their wages.

3 THE GEOGRAPHY OF WESTERN CANADA

CHAPTER OUTCOMES

In this chapter you will examine the geography of western Canada. By the end of the chapter, you will

- identify and understand the major themes of geography

- identify and understand the different physical and natural regions of western Canada

- read and interpret maps, climographs, and technical illustrations

- describe the interactions of physical and cultural factors in the environment

- evaluate the impact of human actions on the environment

INTRODUCTION

Although you may not be aware of it, you experience geography every day. Geography is about location—where people live on the Earth. But geography also embraces many other aspects of your life. The weather, the economy, and even the sports you play are all shaped by geography.

Consider the following Canadian newspaper headlines:

Death of local pulp mill town in BC

Local tree war spreads to Europe

Migration to BC slows

Warm seas ruining BC fishery

Recyclables one-third of landfill

Toxins found in bodies of harbour seals

You probably noticed that these headlines are extremely timely. But did you know that they also relate to the broad area of study known as "geography"? Geography explores much about human behaviour—how humans react with their environment, and how they occupy and exploit the physical environment.

When the Royal Geographic Society was founded in 1830 in London, England, its goal was to promote an "important and entertaining branch of knowledge—geography." Like the founders of the Royal Geographic Society, modern geographers want to unlock the mysteries of the Earth. However, they are less interested in exploring unknown places than they are in understanding the "why" and "how" of the physical world. Geography brings together many fields of study: it draws on a wide range of subjects, such as climate, geology, hydrology, economics, and biology. It looks for spatial patterns on Earth in order to understand how humans live.

In this chapter, you will explore the geography of western Canada and how human activity changed the ecology of the prairies. For thousands of years, the prairies were home to many aboriginal nations. European settlement, which began by the 1860s, was the driving force of change. The aboriginal peoples saw that European settlement would change their world forever and fought against it. You will read more about the political resistance to settlement in the next chapter. By examining the geography of the region in this chapter, you will be able to link these two factors in your appreciation of western Canada's history.

Figure 3–1 European settlement changed the face of the prairies. In this painting of the Plains Indians hunting bison, the prairie grasses are shown in their natural state. What is your image of the prairie today?

THE IMPORTANCE OF PLACE

latitude: the distance of any point north or south of the equator, measured up to 90 degrees

longitude: the distance of any point east or west of the Prime Meridian, measured up to 180 degrees

Geography begins with the posing of questions and the gathering of information. What is a place like? How is it similar to, or different from, another place? Geographers use five organizing principles to help them gather, organize, and analyze their information:

- Places have a location.
- Places have physical and cultural characteristics.
- Places change.
- Places interact with other places.
- Places are in regions.

Places have a location. Many people think that geography is simply about finding places on a globe or map. While modern geographers would scoff at this as a definition, location nonetheless is the first step in the process of geography.

All places can be located in precise terms, in other words, a place has a position on the globe and a specific relationship to other places. For example, Winnipeg is located at 49 degrees north **latitude** and 97 degrees west **longitude,** and it is 650 kilometres away from Moose Jaw, and 550 kilometres away from Regina.

However, location also has significance, and this is even more important for geographic study. It is more important for geographers to know that Winnipeg is located in western Canada, is the geographic centre of North America and the historic gateway to the prairies from eastern Canada, and that it functions as Manitoba's economic, administrative, and transportation centre. You can reach Winnipeg by travelling from the east or the west along the Trans-Canada Highway. And if you lived in Minnesota, in the United States, you could drive to Winnipeg in the space of an afternoon.

Figure 3–2 Winnipeg, Manitoba

Where (Exactly) Are You?

It's 5:30 p.m.
You're at the mall.
You've spotted the perfect shoes.
You've just realized that your bank card's sitting on your dresser at home. Phone home with the news, and the response is pretty much guaranteed: "Where ARE you?"

Now, thanks to the **Global Positioning System** (GPS) you can state your latitudinal and longitudinal coordinates with amazing accuracy, give or take a few metres. The GPS is a new technology that it is being used by researchers and map-makers to pinpoint exact locations.

All you need is a GPS receiver, which looks like a cell phone. The GPS receiver picks up radio signals from twenty-four US Department of Defense satellites orbiting 17 600 kilometers above the Earth. Equipped with four highly accurate atomic clocks, the satellites continuously transmit their positions, time signals, and other data. The GPS receiver compares the positions of three satellites and the length of time it took the signals to reach it. In this way, it calculates your exact position on Earth. GPS calculations are based on the same system of triangulation that was used by Canada's early map-makers, but the new technology eliminates the back-breaking work.

The US military introduced GPS technology in 1974 to aid in naval navigation and to locate foreign military targets. It was used extensively in the Gulf War to help American troops move around the desert in Saudi Arabia. Today, GPS technology is used much more widely. It is used to survey land, monitor geologic fault lines, explore resources, track wildlife, and fight fires. As receivers become smaller and cheaper, they are being used by hikers, boat owners, and even by golfers who want to figure out how far they are from the hole.

DID YOU KNOW?

Canada is in the process of modifying GPS technology to implant in children's knapsacks, to foil child predators.

Figure 3–3 Right: With GPS technology, you could offer your exact location. Left: GPS technology is useful in remote areas such as the Canadian Arctic. Here an Inuit fisher is using a GPS receiver to track a whale.

Some California companies are now using GPS to market a "personal satellite tracking device" that will allow parents to locate their children, or even the family pet.

Global Positioning System: a system that uses satellite tracking devices to establish the latitude and longitude of a person or object

WHAT DO YOU THINK?

1. If your were given a GPS receiver, in what ways could you use it?

2. Imagine that you represent a company selling GPS locators. What kind of customer would be interested in your product? Why?

3. Prepare a five-point company brochure that describes the advantages of GPS locators.

Places have physical and cultural characteristics. Physical characteristics include the landforms and bodies of water found in a place, as well as its soil and mineral deposits. These characteristics have a great impact on how people live, and they usually present distinct advantages or disadvantages, or a combination of both. For example, Prince Rupert has rugged terrain and heavy rainfall, but it also has rich vegetation and abundant water sources.

Virtually every human activity leaves its mark on the physical environment. The visible results of human activity are known as the "cultural landscape." Peoples of different cultures usually affect the landscape in distinct ways. For example, in the Prince Rupert area of northwestern British Columbia, the Northwest Coast peoples removed bark from standing trees to make blankets, clothing, and fishing nets. Because the trees renewed their bark,

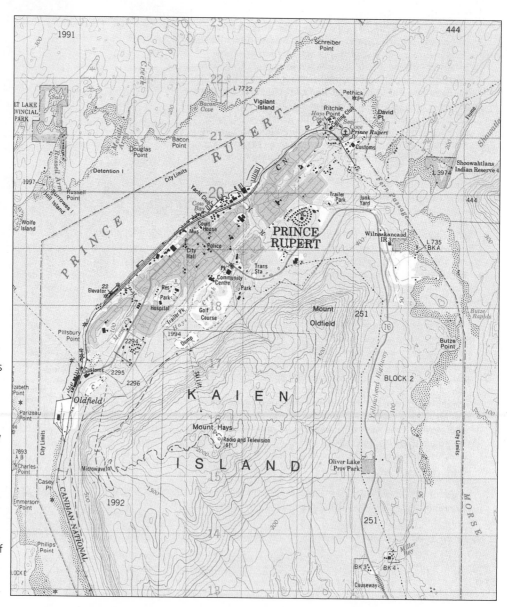

Figure 3–4 Prince Rupert's rugged landscape and shoreline is evident in this topographic map. The changes in the physical environment caused by settlement are particularly evident along the shoreline. In what way has the pattern of development been adapted to the landscape? What cultural features and patterns of land use would you spot if you were on a boat approaching the yacht club at Cow Bay?

and because the bark itself was recyclable, the long-term impact on the environment was minimal. This was not the case with the activities of later settlers. From its founding as a terminus of the second transcontinental railway (see Chapter 7), Prince Rupert experienced a dramatic alteration of its physical environment: as European immigrants settled in the area, they cleared land and built houses, roads, and port facilities. Eventually they exploited the area's fish and forest resources on a massive scale.

Places change. Nothing in nature stays the same. Landforms and **vegetation** are changing all the time, as are political boundaries and patterns of human settlement. How a place looks today is the result of changes that occurred over time. Geographers are especially interested in knowing how the natural environment changes through human actions. For example, how do river dams upstream affect people living downstream? How does a new highway affect the development of nearby real estate or industry? Knowledge of past changes helps us to make informed decisions about future changes.

Places interact with other places. In the past, the size and location of a place determined its level of contact with the rest of the world. Today, however, new transportation and communication technologies have made all but the most remote loca-

vegetation: the natural and undisturbed plants of a region

Figure 3–5 Before Richmond's population rapidly increased in the 1980s and 1990s, the area was mainly devoted to agriculture. Farmland was displaced by housing developments and new commercial and light industrial activities.

tions accessible. We live in a world of rapid movement and instant communication. People travel, communicate, and use products, information, and ideas from around the globe. In this way, the places we inhabit have an impact on one another.

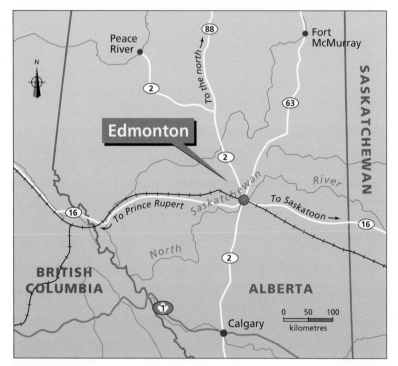

Figure 3–6 Edmonton's position in northern Alberta makes it a crossroads for travel east, west, north, and south. In particular, it is the gateway city for road and air travel to Canada's northern territories. As the capital of the province, Edmonton also regulates and controls the province's resources and industry.

Places are in regions. A region is an area where certain characteristics prevail. The concept of a geographic region allows the geographer to organize information about the great diversity of the Earth's surface. You already use the idea of region in your everyday speech. For instance, you travel to "the coast," "the interior," "the prairies"—or to the "Caribbean" for holidays. You have a clear image of these regions. You also know that no two places in any of these regions are the same, but that they are similar enough to allow you to make general statements about the area.

There are as many regions as there are ways to examine and classify the similar physical or cultural characteristics of an area. Natural regions are identified by characteristics such as the prevailing climate, landforms, vegetation, and soils. Economic regions have prevailing industries. Government regions can be as large as a province or as small as a school board. There are also political-economic regions, such as all the countries who participate in NAFTA (the North American Free Trade Agreement). In this and later chapters, you will be introduced to the regions of western Canada as a means of analyzing regional issues.

ACTIVITIES

1. **a)** Record the latitude and longitude of your community by using an atlas and copying the information in your notebook.

   b) Describe the location of your community in such a way that a person on another continent could find it easily on a map—without reference to latitude and longitude.

2. As a class, create a time line to display the effects of human activity on the cultural landscape of your local area. You could choose four or five main periods, beginning with the culture of the aboriginal peoples and ending with the twentieth century. Groups of students could be responsible for gathering information from the school library on one time period and filling in the information on the time line.

3. List as many regions as you can in your community. Beside each region, briefly describe what type of region it is. Remember that there are many categories of regions.

THE PHYSICAL REGIONS OF WESTERN CANADA

Our country has a difficult landscape. Its mountains and plains, its massive Shield, and its harsh lands in the North have made the development of Canada a challenge. The physical geography of western Canada is dominated by the presence of the Canadian Shield, the Interior Plains, and the Western Mountains. Each of these regions has distinct **geological** features, landforms, and climatic conditions. The Canadian Shield is the oldest region; the Interior Plains have the most uniform physical characteristics; and the Western Mountains have the most complex physical structure.

The Canadian Shield

Canada is a young country in political years but one of the oldest in geologic years. Large masses of rock, known as shields, are the oldest parts of the Earth. They are hard, rigid blocks around which the younger areas of the continents have formed.

geological: having to do with geology, the study of the history of the Earth as found in rocks

topography: the shape of the land

Figure 3–7 The physical regions of western Canada are based primarily on the age and type of rock and on **topography.**

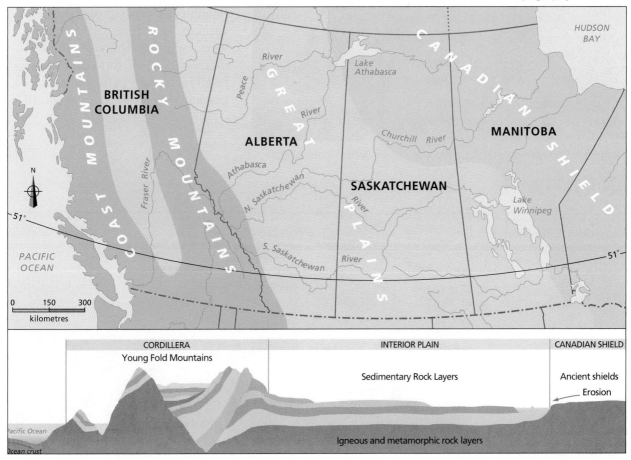

The Canadian Shield stretches from the Arctic islands around Hudson Bay to the Adirondack Mountains in the United States, and east across Labrador. The Shield was once a volcanic mountain range as high as the Himalayas. Over millions of years, weathering and erosion wore it down into a landscape of exposed rock and lakes. The Shield was originally made up of **igneous rock** from its volcanic state.

Much of this rock has been changed by heat and/or pressure into **metamorphic rock.** This process also created the Shield's vast storehouse of minerals, such as copper, gold, lead, and nickel. The exposed rock, however, makes the land unsuitable for agriculture and large-scale settlement.

The Interior Plains

In Canada, the Interior Plains region stretches from the Canadian Shield to the Rocky Mountains. It covers almost all of Alberta. The Interior Plains were formed as eroded material from the Canadian Shield was deposited in layers at its edges. These generally horizontal layers of **sedimentary rock** make up the plains. Millions of years ago, when the area had a tropical climate and was covered by water, occasional flooding left deposits of plants and animals. Over time, these deposits were compressed between the sedimentary layers to form deposits of **fossil fuels,** such as oil and natural gas, and **evaporites,** such as potash.

Figure 3–8 The worn-down landscape of the Shield is evident in this photo.

Figure 3–9 The farms of the Interior Plains

Figure 3–10 The Rocky Mountains near Banff

fossil fuel: a natural fuel formed by geological forces from the residue of living organisms

evaporite: a type of sedimentary rock that originates by the evaporation of sea water

plate: a slab of the Earth's crust. Plates are underneath all the continents and oceans. They regularly move away from, and collide with, each other.

tectonics: the study of forces within the Earth that form its surface features, such as mountain ranges and ocean basins

> **DID YOU KNOW?**
>
> *The mountain-building process continues today in the St. Elias Range, where British Columbia, the Yukon, and Alaska meet. The force of plate collision is pushing up these mountains, including Canada's highest, Mount Logan, at a rate of 4 centimetres a year.*

The Western Mountains

The Western Mountains are made up of parallel mountain ranges that are separated by a series of plateaus and valleys. Mountain ranges of this type are known as a "cordillera." The Rocky and Coast mountain ranges and the Interior Plateau were formed when **plate** collision caused the Earth's crust to buckle, which lifted sections of it into the air. The pressure of plate **tectonics** also caused the terrain to form valleys, plateaus, and trenches. Erosion from rivers and glaciers sculpted the rugged, mountainous landscape that we know today. Sediments carried off by rivers, called "alluvium," formed fertile river valleys, such as the Fraser River Valley. The area is also rich in minerals, such as copper, gold, molybdenum, and coal.

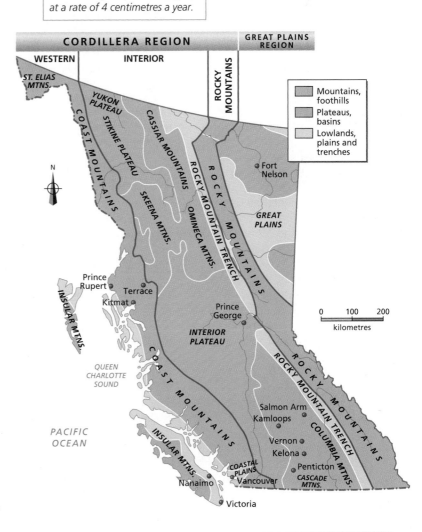

Figure 3–11 The diverse landscapes of British Columbia form six parallel regions. This has made east-west travel in BC particularly difficult.

Apply Your Knowledge

Waiting for the Big One

You may think you're standing on rock-solid, immovable earth on Canada's West Coast. Think again. The area is located where two plates are on a collision course. As the Juan de Fuca plate collides with the North American plate (see Figure 3–12), grinding occurs. When the Juan de Fuca plate becomes stuck under the North American plate, pressure and tension build up. When The Juan de Fuca plate breaks free, it generates seismic waves and **tsunamis,** which can have catastrophic results.

In fact, the west coast of British Columbia is the most active **seismic** area in Canada. Approximately 300 small quakes occur along the 1500-kilometre Juan de Fuca **subduction zone** every year. Most of these quakes are too small to be felt. The strongest tremors recently recorded originated in Courtenay in 1946, and under the Gulf Islands in 1976. The Courtenay tremor registered 7.2 on the **Richter scale**; the Gulf Islands tremor registered 5.4.

In recent years, there has been little significant tectonic activity off the coast of British Columbia. For this reason, some **seismologists** think the "big one" is overdue. They have found evidence of earlier, more serious, ground movements in altered landscapes and in coastal sediment layers that are significantly disturbed. Their research indicates that one serious earthquake, registering as high as 9 on the Richter scale, may have occurred around 1700. Oral

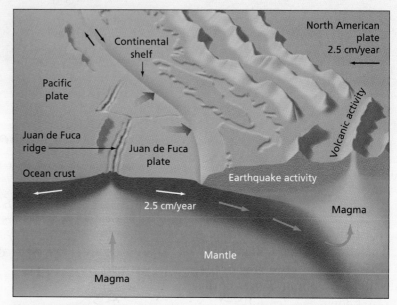

Figure 3–12 The Juan de Fuca ridge is a crack that allows **magma** from the Earth's **mantle** to reach the ocean floor. As magma cools, it builds up on either side of the ridge. The altered sea floor pushes the Pacific plate to the west and the Juan de Fuca plate to the east. The Juan de Fuca plate collides with the North American plate, which is moving west. As the oceanic plate is pushed under the continental plate, at a rate of 45 millimetres a year, it is destroyed and returns to magma.

histories of the Northwest Coast peoples seem to confirm the theory. Their accounts describe a great shaking and refer to huge waves hitting Vancouver Island. Japanese reports of a tidal wave that engulfed their shores in that year lend further support to this theory.

Some scientists fear that as each plate strains against the other, the pressure of 300 years may be released in a mega-quake. Using GPS tracker stations (see page 95) across south-western BC to determine distances between locations, seismologists have discovered that portions of Vancouver Island's west coast are rising 5 millimetres each year. The east coast of Vancouver Island is being pushed toward the mainland in a big squeeze. When the tension is released, the earth will shift and bend, sending waves through the ground and water. Damage will be extensive and severe.

Old brick buildings and bridges are the most vulnerable and could be heavily damaged in even a moderate earthquake. Many older buildings are not built to withstand the powerful shaking and swaying that could last for several minutes. Few buildings will be as secure as Vancouver's West Coast Energy Building, which is suspended on cables to absorb the swaying motion caused by an earthquake. The low-lying Fraser Delta, and other areas not built on **bedrock**, will be highly unstable. Their surface will turn to the consistency of porridge, a process known as "liquefication."

Scientists studying the faults and plate movements off the British Columbia coast are convinced that the earthquake will happen. The question they can't answer is: Where and when?

magma: molten rock material within the Earth from which igneous rock is formed through cooling

mantle: the interior part of the Earth that lies directly above the core

epicentre: the Earth's surface directly above the quake—the middle of the quake

tsunami: a great sea wave produced by an earthquake or by a volcanic eruption

seismic: to do with earthquakes

subduction zone: a long region with a trench through which a descending tectonic plate is assimilated into the earth's mantle

Richter scale: a measure of the power of earthquakes. Each step on the scale is ten times the previous one, so an earthquake that registers 7 is ten times greater than a 6 and one hundred times greater than a 5.

seismologist: someone who studies earthquakes

bedrock: solid rock underneath looser materials such as soil

Figure 3–13 When the Big Earthquake happens, the plates beneath BC will come unstuck, sending waves outward from its **epicentre.** The land will shake uncontrollably and create enormous damage to the built environment. This illustration depicts the possible damage to a typical neighbourhood. Examine Figure 3–13 for a few minutes. How has the infrastructure of this community been damaged? For more information about infrastructure, see Chapter 2, page 69.

ACTIVITIES

1. In groups of four or five students, create a Disaster Education Program to help community members prepare themselves for a major earthquake. With members of your group, create a ten-point brochure that outlines the provisions and equipment people will need in the event of an earthquake. In an opening paragraph, describe the damage to the community infrastructure that may make these emergency items necessary. Add pictures, diagrams, and captions to explain the impact of an earthquake.

1. Use the following headings to create an organizer comparing the Western Mountains, the Interior Plains, and the Canadian Shield:
   - original state
   - significant changes
   - result of changes
   - appearance today

2. Using a medium of your choice, create a small visual display to illustrate the principles of mountain building. Review pages 101 to 103 for information. You may have to experiment with a number of media in order to represent the results of tectonic plate collision.

THE CLIMATES OF WESTERN CANADA

continental climate: the climate of a continent's interior

maritime climate: a coastal climate, usually referring to the West Coast

Western Canada lies above 49 degrees latitude. Most areas experience a **continental climate** of temperature extremes and low precipitation. Coastal areas of British Columbia are moderated by a **maritime climate** of mild temperatures and high precipitation. Temperature and precipitation differences among communities in western Canada reflect their location and local conditions. These are described in the next section.

Factors Affecting Temperature

Latitude. The distance of an area from the equator determines the amount and intensity of sunlight it receives. In northern latitudes, the sun's rays strike the Earth at a lower angle than they do closer to the equator. As a result, there is greater seasonal variation in the length of day and night. Another effect is that temperatures are generally higher in southern Canada, because the higher angle of the sun in the sky results in more intense heating of the land.

Altitude. The higher the altitude, the colder the temperature. In general, for every 150-metre rise in altitude the temperature drops by 1 degree Celsius.

Distance from the Sea. The surface of land heats and cools more quickly than the surface of water. A large land mass such as western Canada can swing between temperature extremes—high temperatures in the summer and low temperatures in the winter. By contrast, the summer and winter temperatures of areas such as the West Coast of Canada are moderated by the water.

Wind Direction. Winds blowing from the ocean increase the moderating effect of water. The reverse is true for winds blowing off the land. West Coast communities are the only communities in Canada with winter temperatures above freezing. Prevailing winds are those that blow most often in an area. In western Canada, these winds are generally westerlies, that is, from the west, or northerlies, from the north.

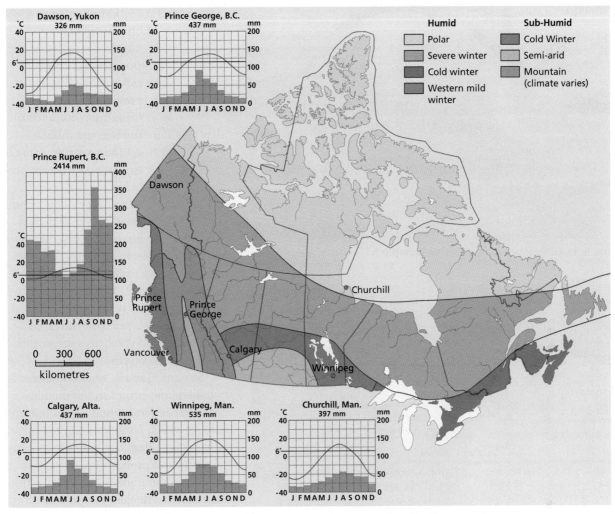

Figure 3–14 Climographs show the average monthly temperature of a community with a line graph and the average monthly precipitation with a bar graph.

Ocean Currents. Ocean currents are either warm or cold, depending on their origin. Ocean currents affect the temperature of the land by warming or heating the air blowing over them. Warm air can absorb more water than cold air. This is why the West Coast enjoys a mild, wet climate. The prevailing westerlies blow over the warm Alaska current, which comes from warm southern waters.

Precipitation. The amount of precipitation received by a location is determined by its distance from the sea and by the prevailing winds.

Heavy precipitation is often confined to a season, or seasons. In turn, the form of precipitation—for example, drizzle, heavy rain, snow, or hail—will have an impact on the location. Western Canada experiences three basic types of precipitation: orographic, convectional, and frontal.

Prevailing westerly winds push warm, moist Pacific air up against the mountains of Vancouver Island and the Coast Range and create orographic precipitation. As the winds force the air up the mountainside, the air cools and shrinks, losing its moisture as rain or snow. As the air

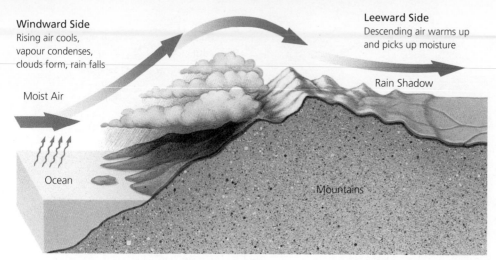

Windward Side
Rising air cools, vapour condenses, clouds form, rain falls

Leeward Side
Descending air warms up and picks up moisture

Rain Shadow

Moist Air

Ocean

Mountains

Figure 3–15 Orographic, or mountain, precipitation

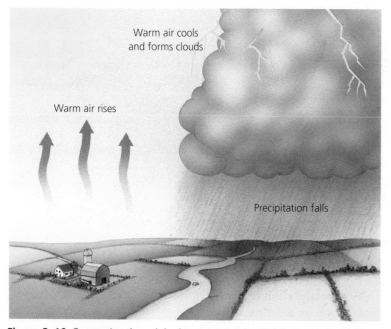

Warm air cools and forms clouds

Warm air rises

Precipitation falls

Figure 3–16 Convectional precipitation

> **DID YOU KNOW?**
>
> *Convectional precipitation is commonly known as a thunderstorm.*

convection: transference of heat by upward movement

Convectional precipitation is caused by **convection** currents in the atmosphere. It falls primarily on the prairies and on the Canadian Shield during the hot months. As the ground heats throughout the day, it heats the air. This warm air expands and rises, and meets cool air, which also warms, rises, and cools, eventually forming a cloud of rain or hail, which falls back to the Earth. While this type of precipitation provides much-needed moisture to the arid prairies, it is unreliable, and the heavy rain or hail often damages crops.

Most of Canada lies in a zone between cold polar air, which originates in the North, and warm tropical air, which originates in the Gulf of Mexico. These two air masses cannot mix, and their line of contact is called a "front." Because warm, tropical air is less dense than cold air, it rises over the cold air. As the warm air rises, it condenses and forms clouds, usually resulting in prolonged precipitation. There is more frontal activity during the Canadian winter because the polar air extends further south and the two air masses—warm and cold—vary most dramatically in temperature. Fierce frontal activity, known as "cyclonic storms," result, and are pushed from west to east by the prevailing westerlies.

Water Resources Of Western Canada

Most of the rivers of western Canada begin in the cordillera. The high levels of precipitation and melting

descends on the eastern slopes, it becomes warm and dry; this area is called the rain-shadow. Orographic precipitation also occurs on the Rockies, although less rain falls on the western slopes. In winter, the winds that descend the eastern slopes of the Rockies—called "chinooks"—warm so quickly that they can raise the temperature 20 degrees in a matter of hours.

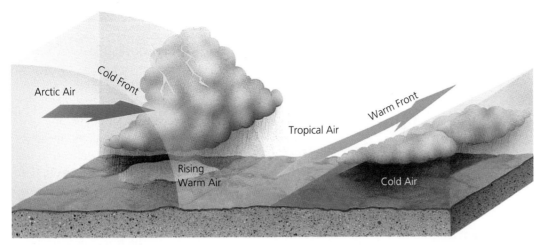

Figure 3–17 Frontal precipitation

snowpacks provide a constant flow of water. Rivers flow east or west from the highlands of the Rockies and Coast range until they meet a major body of water, such as Hudson Bay or the Pacific Ocean. Along the way, they join other rivers, flow through lakes, and form river systems that drain the land. A drainage basin is an area of land drained by one river system. Basins are formed as the rivers carry away eroded material from the land.

The abundance of water in most parts of western Canada has made many Canadians complacent. However, as population and development have increased, so too have threats to water quality. Today, seri-ous efforts are underway to find solutions to these problems. For example, the Lower Fraser River Basin, which includes the greater Vancouver area, has been a dumping ground for industrial and municipal **sewage** and agricultural **run-off** for decades. In the early 1990s, communities in the lower mainland of British Columbia, along with the provincial government, set aside $50 million to clean up the Fraser. At that time, most experts estimated it would take more than ten times that amount to treat the sewage dumped into the Fraser each year. For Canadians, water quality, not water supply, will be the issue for the future.

sewage: municipal and industrial waste

run-off: pesticides, herbicides, and other materials that drain from fields into rivers and lakes

ACTIVITIES

1. Examine the climographs in Figure 3–14 to identify and explain which locations have the following: highest rainfall, lowest precipitation, lowest monthly temperature, highest monthly temperature, and the greatest range in temperature between summer and winter.

2. Explain why most rainfall in Winnipeg occurs in the summer months.

3. Explain which climograph location would have the most precipitation in the form of snow.

4. Use the map of physiographic regions on page 101 to list the three major drainage basins in western Canada. Which of the drainage basins is the biggest? Which of the drainage basins are likely to suffer from pollution from: a) urban sources, b) agricultural sources, c) industrial sources.

DID YOU KNOW?

The word "ecology" comes from the Greek oikos, which means "home." Ecosystems are homes to living things.

DID YOU KNOW?

More than 500 species of plants now found in British Columbia—approximately one in five of the total flora—have been introduced by humans either by accident or intention.

biome: an ecological community of plants and animals extending over a large area

interdependent: being dependent on each other

system: a group of things that interact with each other and together form a whole

THE NATURAL REGIONS OF WESTERN CANADA

Ecosystems and Biomes

A natural environment is defined as the conditions under which plants and animals live in relation to each other and with the non-living parts of the environment. The natural environment of western Canada is made up of a number of large ecosystems, or **biomes,** each with its own characteristic type of vegetation and animal species.

A biome contains a number of smaller ecosystems—natural areas where the life cycles of plants, animals, and other organisms are linked to each other and to their physical surroundings. Smaller ecosystems are in turn made up of habitats, places where plants and animals

have adapted to a set of specific conditions, for example, a bog. Because all the elements of an ecosystem are **interdependent**, altering one part of the system, or introducing a new organism into the system, usually sets off a chain reaction. For example, removing the forest cover has a dramatic impact on the animals that use the forest as a habitat. Here is another example: During this century, rats were introduced to Haida Gwaii—the Queen Charlotte Islands—by coastal trading ships passing by. The rats dramatically reduced the number of nesting bird colonies. In 1995, a rat control program was established to rid the islands of this unwanted species.

Systems

Geographers use the model of a **system** to explain natural events. A system can show how parts of something, such as an ecosystem, are linked together.

When the parts of an ecosystem are in balance, the system functions smoothly. If one part of the system is altered, however, the balance of the entire system is upset. For example, deforestation reduces the ability of the soil to hold water. Prolonged rainfall causes flooding of rivers and increases soil erosion. This leads to larger sedimentary deposits downstream, which in turn upset habitats.

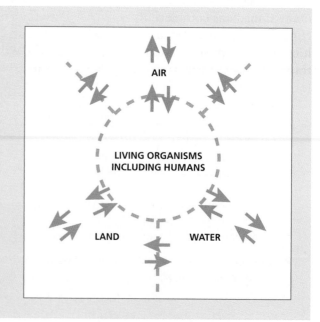

Figure 3–18 This simplified example of an ecosystem shows how the physical and natural environments are balanced and interdependent. Interruptions and reorganizations in the system lead to imbalance and often undesirable side effects.

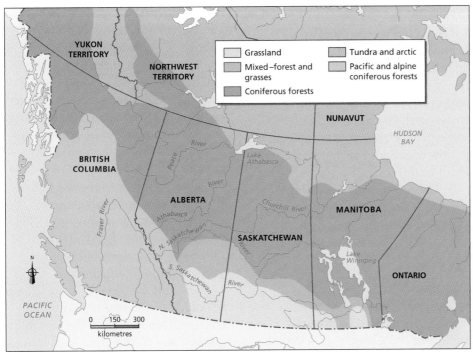

Figure 3–19 Most of western Canada is covered by forest and grasslands. Natural vegetation is the result of many factors that work together—temperature and precipitation combined with other factors such as rock type, soil composition, slope of the land, and drainage. The grasslands, in particular, show the effect of human activity—agriculture has replaced the natural vegetation.

Map legend:
- Grassland
- Mixed–forest and grasses
- Coniferous forests
- Tundra and arctic
- Pacific and alpine coniferous forests

coniferous tree: an evergreen tree

humus: the remains of decomposing plants in the soil

The Western Biomes

Biomes are usually named for the dominant vegetation type of a region.

Boreal Forest

Most of this region is made up of **coniferous trees.** Needle-leaf evergreen trees, such as spruce, fir, and pine, are able to survive the very cold winter temperatures and erratic precipitation. Very little moisture is lost through the needles, and they do not freeze, even in frigid weather. Evergreens begin growing in early spring to make use of the short growing season.

The soil type of this region is known as "podzol." It is acidic, due to leaching from the surface layers and needles, and is not very fertile because it contains only small amounts of **humus.** Deer, moose, black bears, wolves, and many fur-bearing animals such as beaver, otter, and muskrat, inhabit this biome. Many species of owls and blue jays, and many other types of birds, frequent these forests.

Figure 3–20 This white-tailed deer has made a home in the boreal forest of Prince Albert National Park, Saskatchewan.

erosion: the wearing away by action of wind, water, or ice

slough: depression filled with fresh water from rain or melting snow

Parkland

Parkland is a transitional area between the dry prairie grasslands and the coniferous forest regions of the North. The natural vegetation is long grass, with isolated stands of trees—mainly aspen, willow, and some pine. The long grass, after it decays over many years, provides a lot of humus, resulting in rich, black soil. This is an ideal region for growing wheat because the soil is rich and precipitation is sufficient.

The Prairie

The prairie, sometimes called the "grasslands," is a vast area of western Canada located between Winnipeg and Calgary. It is very dry in the southeast, around the Alberta-Saskatchewan boundary. The driest area is known as the "Palliser Triangle," after the 1857–1860 expedition of Captain Palliser, who mapped British territory from Lake Superior to the Okanagan Valley. The prairie is sufficiently moist in the northwest to support ranching and agriculture, but never moist enough to support trees.

The natural vegetation of the grasslands includes several types of short grasses—sagebrush and cactus in the south, and some areas of long grasses. Agriculture has completely destroyed some of the indigenous grasses. In addition, human activity has led to wind **erosion**, although there is less wind erosion on the prairie today than during the 1930s. At that time, much of the topsoil of the region was blown away after years of prolonged drought.

The soils of the region are brown in colour and have a high mineral content. Depending on the length of grasses, and so the amount of humus they would provide over many years, the soils will vary from light to dark brown. The dark brown soil type, known as "chernozem," is ideal for growing wheat and other grain crops. Ground squirrels, gophers, and prairie dogs abound in this region. Hawks, owls, and badgers are the predators of the gophers. Deer and antelope have replaced the exterminated bison as the largest animals in this biome. Wild fowl are found in the region's many **sloughs**.

Figure 3–21 In the 1920s, poor farming practices and a prolonged drought had catastrophic consequences on the prairies. Much of the topsoil of the short-grass prairie turned to dust and blew away. The so-called Dust Bowl ruined the wheat economy of the prairies and forced many farmers to abandon their farms.

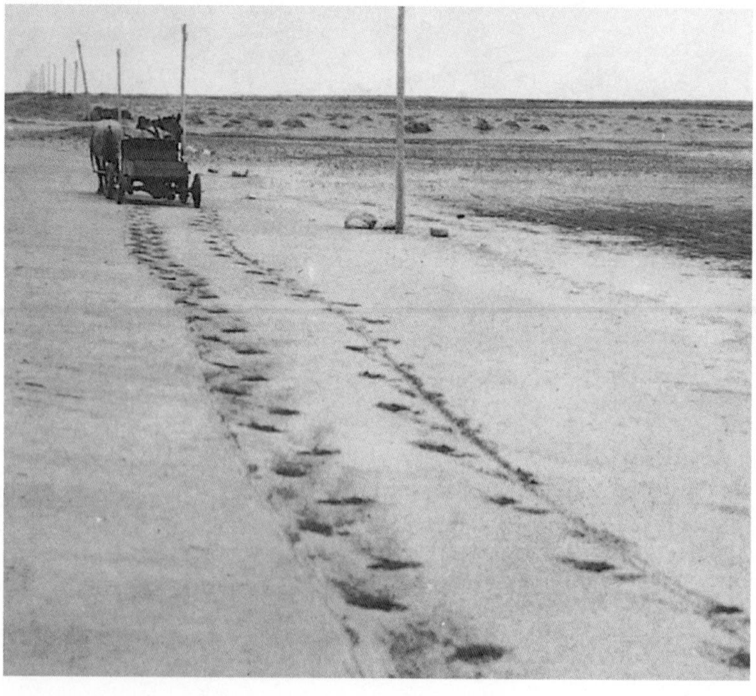

The Interior Mountain Region

The Interior Mountain Region consists of a variety of landforms—meadows, plateaus, and mountains. Vegetation is also highly varied, and includes pine forests, sub-alpine forests, and, in the high meadows, areas of tundra that resemble vegetation found in the Arctic, such as dwarf shrubs, lichens, and grasses. The region has as many soil types as varieties of vegetation. Soils of coniferous regions are found on the mountains, whereas the grasslands have prairie soils. Tundra soils—typically thin, with little humus, and a permanently frozen subsoil—are found on the meadows. Wildlife is abundant in this region. Bears, deer, mountain goats, and sheep are easy to sight, as are varieties of owls, woodpeckers, and bluebirds. Canada's only preying mantis—the ground mantis—is found in this region, as is the rattlesnake.

Coastal Forest

The forests of the Pacific Northwest are rain forests, but they are coniferous, which distinguishes them from the world's other temperate rain forests. They receive most of their rain from November to March—and conifers can grow during mild winters. Owing to the mild temperatures and abundant precipitation, the trees of the coastal forest are huge, although many of the tallest trees have been cut down. Today, many Douglas firs, red cedars, and hemlock trees remain. The largest trees are close to 90 metres high,

with diameters ranging from 1 to 2 metres. Soils and wildlife of the region are the same as those found in the boreal forests. Not surprisingly, the forests of the Pacific Northwest are much sought after by the lumber industry.

treeline: the upper limit of tree growth on a mountain

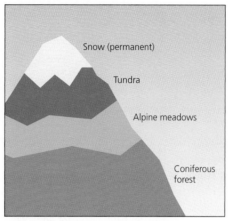

Figure 3–22 Coniferous forests grow on the lower slopes of the mountains. As altitude increases, temperature decreases and the growing season shortens. As you ascend the mountain, an area known as the **treeline** is reached. Above the treeline, alpine flowers and grasses grow. Further up, only mosses and lichens can grow. Finally, at the permanent snow line, no forms of vegetation can grow.

Figure 3–23 A thick blanket of giant conifers covers the windward slopes of the Coast Mountains. The trees tend to have shallow roots, which spread like mats beneath the surface of the soil. As in any rain forest, almost 97 percent of the seedlings germinate on decaying logs and stumps, often called "nurse trees." These provide humus, which is otherwise unavailable in the moss-covered forest floor and nutrient-poor, acidic soil.

THE PRAIRIE GRASSLANDS:
A Changing Ecosystem

As a resident of British Columbia, you have probably taken many strolls through the forest. Vast tracts of old-growth forest still remain in the western provinces, and it is possible to see what the original landscape looked like in areas such as Clayoquot Sound. The same cannot be said of the prairie grasslands. Only in isolated locations, such as Elk Island National Park, can you see the original landscape.

What happened to the prairie? In a word: settlement.

Figure 3–24 Bison are now being protected in Elk Island National Park, Alberta.

First Impressions of the Prairie

Newcomers to the prairie usually had strong first impressions of the landscape. This letter from Edgar Dewdney, Indian Commissioner of the North-West Territories (1879–1888), to Sir John A. Macdonald reflects the awe with which many viewed the region:

The next excerpt comes from the diary of Henri Julien, a reporter from *Canadian Illustrated News*. Julien accompanied the North West Mounted Police on their initial—and disastrous—trek west. He had a less positive view of the landscape:

I felt on the plains even more than when I was hacking out the trail across British Columbia years ago that here for me was indeed God's great, good plenty. There are terrors on the plains, of course, and emptiness will forever keep it as Butler [the explorer] has it, the great lone land, but at almost any point one can gain some elevation and see and see. It is all so vast, so laid out in unending curving lines that you can begin to lose the sense of yourself in relation to it. Believe me, Sir John, it can drive a small man to madness, this incomprehensible unending at any point seemly unresisting and unchecked space.

Here we first encountered the hostility of the mosquitoes. We had men from all parts of the world ... but they all agreed that nowhere had they seen anything equal to the mosquitoes of the prairie.

As soon as twilight deepens, they make their appearance on the horizon, in the shape of a cloud ... At first, a faint hum is heard in the distance, then it swells into a roar as it comes nearer. The attack is simply dreadful. Your eyes, your nose, your ears are invaded. If you open your mouth to curse at them, they troop into it. They insinuate themselves under your clothes, down your shirt collar, up your shirt sleeves ...

They send dogs off howling in pain. They tease horses to desperation. They goad even the shaggy buffalo ...

For thousands of years, the vegetation of the prairies supported an abundance of animal life. In the seventeenth century, an estimated 60 to 70 million **bison** roamed the grasslands, together with 50 million antelope, grizzly bears, wolves, prairie dogs, and many species of birds, reptiles, and insects. Today, few of these larger mammals survive, and the habitats of many smaller species are threatened.

Human activity has dramatically altered the prairie ecosystem. Other than the temporary effects of drought, fire, and overgrazing by animal herds, the prairie grasslands had remained in a state of natural balance until the mid-nineteenth century.

Both in Canada and the United States, the Native peoples who lived in the region did little to alter the ecosystem. They maintained the natural grasses and subsisted almost entirely on the bison. The opening of the West to settlement eventually led to the virtual extinction of the bison. In fact, US government policies in

Figure 3–26 These maps show the location of the bison at the beginning and the end of the nineteenth century.

the late nineteenth century actively contributed to the vanishing herds. The slaughter of the bison became part of the campaign to force Native peoples onto reservations so that the West could be made available to European settlers. In 1870, American General Philip Sheridan advised the Texas legislature to stop a bill that would have protected the bison. Instead, he suggested, hunters should be offered a bronze medal featuring a dead buffalo on one side and a discouraged-looking Native person on the other.

When the migrating herds of bison failed to reappear in Canada, the way of life of the Canadian Plains Indians and the Métis was also seriously threatened. As one observer noted in a letter to John A. Macdonald:

It seems Laird's Indian Affairs office was almost totally unprepared for the starvation [of the Plains Indians] of the past year. Once fires began to burn along the border, set, of course, by American soldiers, the depleted buffalo herds would not move north even if General Miles' troops had not patrolled the border continuously all winter.

By contrast, General William Sherman, Commander of the US Army in Sioux territory in the 1800s, had little good to say about the bison. In a letter to General Philip Sheridan, Commander of the US Army in the Southwest, he noted:

Invite all the sportsmen in England and America this fall for a Great Buffalo Hunt and make a grand sweep of them all.

Fur traders moving West had already helped to reduce the population of bison. Then in the

Figure 3–25 Cattail, an original prairie long grass

1880s, the building of the transcontinental railways in both Canada and the United States divided the great herds and accelerated the arrival of hunters and settlers. In less than a century, what was possibly the world's largest population of wild, herding animals was on its way to becoming a memory.

A prairie free of bison, and with Native peoples confined to reserves, was a prairie wide open to settlement. Cattle ranching on the western prairies replaced the bison herds and, in some areas, led to problems of overgrazing. Today, overgrazing is not a problem in the huge **feedlots**, where intensive cattle production is practised. However, the high concentration of animals results in pollution of both soil and water if disposal of the wastes is not handled adequately and sanitarily.

Settlers also introduced cereal farming, particularly wheat, to the prairies. Large waves of immigration to Canada after 1900 (see Chapter 7) coincided with the development of hardier strains of wheat. These settlers, mainly from Eastern Europe, ploughed under the prairie grasses and planted Marquis and Red Fife, new strains of wheat that matured early and had superior baking qualities. They made Canada famous for its high-quality wheat and made wheat the most important cultivated crop in Canada.

Over-cultivation and drought in the 1930s, however, led to soil erosion on the prairies. Soil conservation methods, such as **contour ploughing** and **wind breaks**, have helped to reduce this problem. Monoculture—the cultivation and reliance on a single crop—has also created problems. Both insecticides and pesticides must be used in order to protect a single crop from insect damage and disease. Critics of monoculture say that the reliance on chemicals adversely affects many prairie ecosystems and habitats. They claim it reduces the area's biodiversity— the variety of insects, birds, and predators that make up a living system, an ecosystem. Monocultures are incapable of protecting themselves because they are single systems and must be supported with chemicals. Farmers counter that single-crop farming produces higher yields and helps feed the world's growing population.

Settlement and development led to extreme alterations of the prairie ecosystem, and to both negative and positive consequences. The balance between the two is very much open to debate. The natural prairie biome has been mostly replaced by extensive farms and cattle operations. Its large mammals have been hunted to near extinction and many of its smaller species have been greatly reduced in numbers. The extinction of the bison contributed to the loss of territory for the Native peoples in both Canada and the United States. In return, cereal farming and grazing herds have made Canada one of the world's leading exporters of food and have contributed to a high standard of living.

bison: North American buffalo

feedlot: an enclosed area where large herds of cows eat high-quality feed

contour ploughing: ploughing along the shape of the land to prevent erosion

wind break: a line of trees planted to prevent wind erosion by shielding the soil

Figure 3–27 Saskatchewan grows approximately 60 percent of Canada's wheat. The prairies produce an average of three times as much grain as Canadians consume, which makes Canada one of fewer than half-dozen countries that have a large grain surplus for export.

1. Sketch a flow chart of the possible impact of one of the following on an ecosystem or habitat: a road is built through an area of untouched wilderness; the number of tourists to a scenic location increases dramatically.

2. Find or make a sketch or flow chart of an ecosystem in your vicinity. Annotate the sketch with information on the interrelationships of its various parts. Determine to what degree the ecosystem is threatened and by what. Develop a plan of action to protect it.

3. Make a flow chart of your school as an open system. Buildings and grounds can be the habitat, and students, teachers, and support staff can be the organisms. Books and other materials are included. You could add variables—such as new courses, or new technology—and note the impact on the system.

4. Search out some of the many excellent accounts of the prairies before settlement, such as William Butler's *The Great Lone Land*. Share descriptions from these books with your class and combine your findings with pictures to form a collage of the Canadian prairies before settlement.

5. Compare the fate of large herding animals in Africa with that of the North American bison. What effect is the fate of the animals having on the people?

6. Write an e-mail to a farmer or environmental group, stating your opinion of monoculture on the Canadian prairies.

7. Investigate the issue of genetically altered seeds and the control of these seeds by multinational chemical companies.

◆ ◆

THE CULTURAL LANDSCAPE

Environments that have been used and altered by humans are called "cultural environments" or "cultural landscapes." Culture—and cultural attitudes—determine how people view and use the land. For example, the Cree of the Interior Plains did not view the land and its resources in the same way as did the fur traders, and the fur traders did not view the land with the eyes of European settlers. Opposing attitudes can often result in a crisis, for example, the extinction of the North American bison, or the conflict that has arisen between environmentalists and the logging industry in BC. You will read more about that particular conflict in Chapter 9.

Settlement and Population

At the beginning of the twentieth century, western Canada was only beginning to experience the effects of large-scale settlement. The Native peoples had used the environment for millennia without significantly changing the landscape. Wherever they lived—on the Canadian Shield, the Interior Plains, or the Western Mountains—they used land and water resources in a way that respected the natural environment. The prosperity of the Laurier era, which will be described in Chapter 7, brought large-scale settlement to the Canadian West and upset this balance.

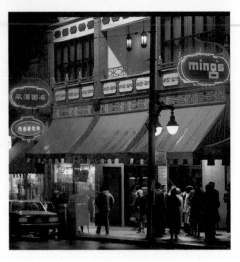

Figure 3–28 Human culture is often reflected in architecture. The diversity of Canada's population and the origin of its settlers can be seen in these buildings: a Haida village, with its distinctive elevation and totem poles; a Ukrainian settlement on the prairie; and one of British Columbia's many Chinatowns.

boom and bust: words used to describe a healthy (booming) economy or one that is slow (bust)

Waves of immigrants have also changed the way the land looks. Métis farmers in Manitoba followed the French practice of dividing their farms into narrow strips along rivers. The Canadian government followed the English grid system when it surveyed the West, while Mennonite farmers in Manitoba used a combination of both systems. During the twentieth century, extensive farming and cattle ranching, mining, manufacturing, and urban development have all contributed to the alteration of the natural environment in western Canada.

Where people decide to settle depends on several factors, but the principal factors are the physical environment and its economic possibilities. Landforms and climate play a key role in determining how many people will permanently settle an area. Flat land, mild winters, adequate precipitation, and good soil are some of the factors that often entice people to settle permanently in an area. The agricultural areas of the prairies and British Columbia follow this pattern.

Areas that lack these features can also experience population growth in brief spurts. This is because people almost always live where they can find work. Resource towns on Canada's frontier go through cycles of **boom and bust** as the resource is developed and then exhausted. Barkerville, British Columbia, was created in the 1860s after gold was discovered in the Cariboo region of the British Columbia interior. Its population climbed to 5000 people, but eventually it became a ghost town. Ocean Falls, British Columbia, a former pulp-and-paper town, and Uranium City, Saskatchewan, are other examples of towns that fell into decline when their resources were exhausted. This story has been repeated all across western Canada's resource frontier, and is still being repeated today.

The Function of a Settlement

All settlements have a function, which is defined as the activities responsible for the economic and social development of the place. A place can be considered a successful settlement when it has an economic base to support the people living there. This economic base—along with the kind of place it is—will usually determine the community that results. For example, a suburban residential community with most of its population working elsewhere will look different from a single-industry town. Smaller communities usually have fewer functions, acting as service centres or single-resource-based communities. Today, most cities have a number of dominant functions and many minor ones. Some of the common functions of settlements in western Canada are found in Figure 3–29.

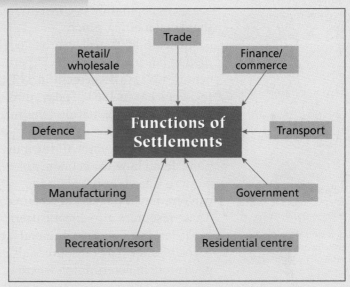

Figure 3–29 Would a small village of 100 people have all these functions? Explain.

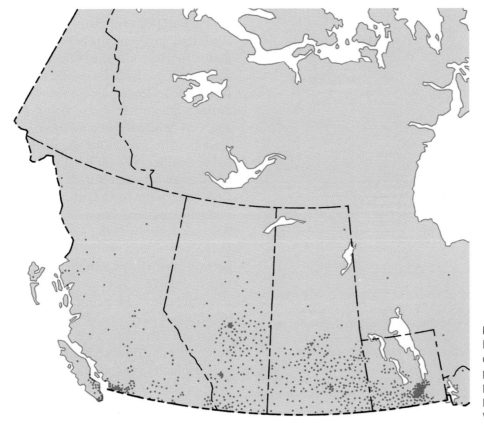

Figure 3–30 How land is used helps to determine the distribution and density of the population (see definitions, page 118). This map shows the population distribution of western Canada in 1911.

Canada's resource towns do not employ as many people as do the manufacturing and service industries of cities. That is why western Canada's population is concentrated in its major cities. Since Confederation, Canada's urban population has increased from 17 percent in 1871, to 45 percent in 1921, to 54 percent in 1951. Today, three quarters of the population lives in an urban area.

In Chapter 9, you will learn in more detail how the economy of western Canada is based on the exploitation of its natural resources. These resources also affect patterns of settlement. Soil type, mineral deposits, and energy resources all play a role in determining where

population distribution: where people live within a given area

population density: the average number of people in a given area

people will come to live, known as **population distribution,** and how many people will eventually settle in the area, or its **population density.**

Boundaries: The Lines on a Map

The provincial and territorial boundaries of western Canada are so familiar that it is easy to forget how abstract they are. These political boundaries are what geographers call "artificial" boundaries. Before European settlement, the Native peoples, Métis, early explorers, and fur trappers divided western Canada according to its natural boundaries—the recognized physical features of Shield, plains, mountains, rivers, and forests. Such boundaries are ill-suited for the purposes of the modern state: political leaders like to have clear lines indicating the extent of their authority.

As European and, later, North American governments began to dominate the continent, frontier zones were replaced by political boundaries. Geographic knowledge of the more remote areas, however, was very limited. Dividing these regions with boundaries inevitably led to conflict. The establishment of a boundary between British Columbia and Alaska is an example you will study in Chapter 7. Another example is the 49th parallel of latitude, which set the boundary between British and American territory in the West. Because it cut through plains and mountains, people who had been accustomed to crossing a natural area were now hemmed in by lines on a map.

The Native peoples living in the frontier regions did not have the power to draw these lines on the

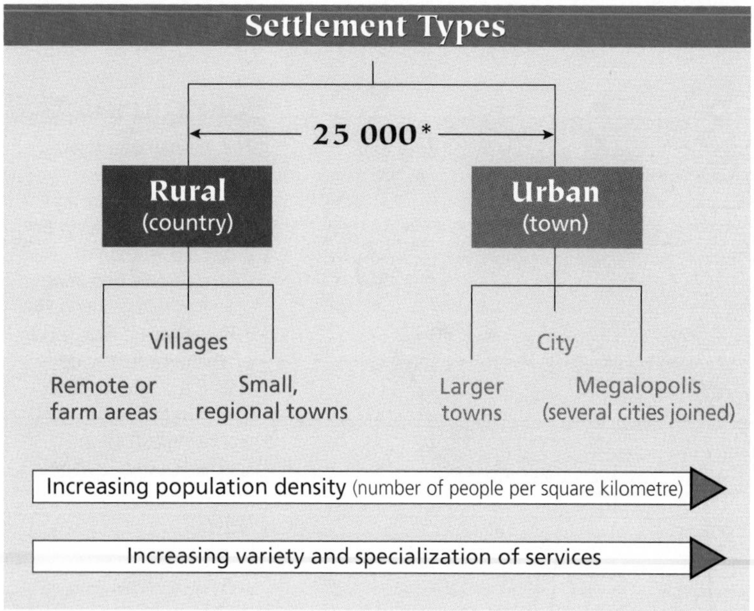

Settlement Types

25 000*

Rural (country)   **Urban** (town)

Villages   City

Remote or farm areas   Small, regional towns   Larger towns   Megalopolis (several cities joined)

Increasing population density (number of people per square kilometre) ▶

Increasing variety and specialization of services ▶

* Statistics Canada dividing point

Figure 3–31 The definition of a rural area versus an urban area varies throughout the world. Statistics Canada defines an urban area as one with a minimum population concentration of 1000 and a population density of at least 400 per square kilometre. Below that figure, an area is considered rural. As a settlement grows, the number of services it provides usually increases in variety and specialization. This is known as the "hierarchy of services." For example, within the health-care field, the number of specialized services and treatments usually increases with the size of the community. Only large cities have the resources and population to supply specialists in organ transplants or even heart surgery.

map themselves. In the last decades of the twentieth century, however, the power to do so shifted. The Inuit and other aboriginal Canadians became more successful in reclaiming control of their traditional territories. In British Columbia, the wheel came full circle. Because the right of aboriginal title had been recognized in the Constitution Act of 1982, and was later confirmed in court decisions, new lines marking First Nations land claims appeared on BC maps. Negotiations continue to determine where those lines will finally be drawn. In 1998, the Nisga'a signed the first treaty in British Columbia since Confederation, and gained title to some of their ancestral lands. You will learn more about this in Chapter 7.

Figure 3–32 Physical features such as mountains and bodies of water are natural borders. Political borders are actually artificial.

Canada's Newest Regions

Something happened to Canada on April 1, 1999. The Northwest Territories were split in two. Nunavut and the Western Territory (Denendeh) form Canada's newest political regions. Canada has witnessed a number of provincial and territorial boundary changes since Confederation.

Cartographers last redrew the map of Canada in 1949, when Newfoundland joined Confederation. And the Northwest Territories were actually divided once before—in 1905, when the provinces of Alberta and Saskatchewan were created.

While the new territories share an Arctic climate, they also differ in many ways. In every region of the Arctic, physical characteristics have a dramatic impact on the cultural and economic life. With its vast stretches of permanently frozen ground and polar islands, Nunavut supports little vegetation. Trapping has been the mainstay of the Inuit economy for thousands of years. By contrast, most of the Western Territory lies below the treeline, making its resources of diamonds, gold, oil, and gas easily accessible. Nunavut also has large stores of gold, lead, zinc, and oil and gas, but the climate and physical characteristics of the region will make it a challenge to retrieve these resources—both from the viewpoint of economics and environmental safety.

cartographer: someone who draws maps

Time Line 3–1

Creation of Nunavut and the Western Territory

1960+	Federal government considers dividing the NWT
1967	Yellowknife becomes capital of the NWT
1976	Inuit propose land claim and creation of Nunavut
1982	Most voters in the NWT want to divide the territories
1991	Boundary between the Eastern and Western Arctic approved
1993	Nunavut Land Claims Agreement and Nunavut Act approved by Parliament
1999	Nunavut and Western Territory become Canada's newest political regions

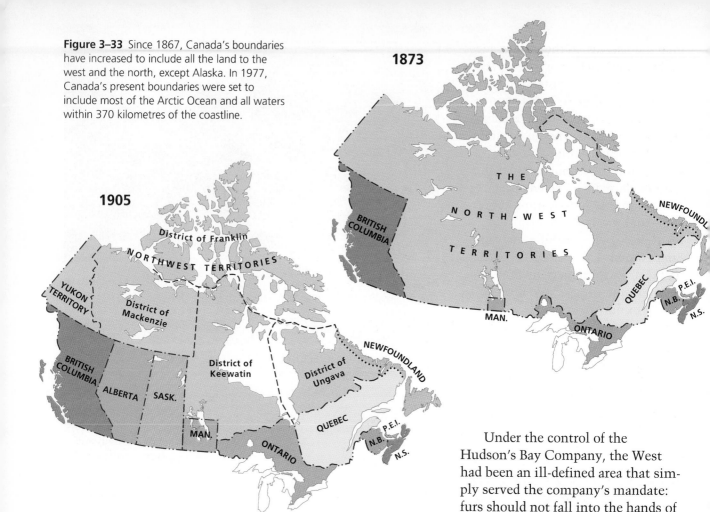

Figure 3–33 Since 1867, Canada's boundaries have increased to include all the land to the west and the north, except Alaska. In 1977, Canada's present boundaries were set to include most of the Arctic Ocean and all waters within 370 kilometres of the coastline.

1873

1905

Under the control of the Hudson's Bay Company, the West had been an ill-defined area that simply served the company's mandate: furs should not fall into the hands of rival companies. With Confederation and the purchase of Rupert's Land by the Canadian government (see Chapter 4), more specific boundaries were needed to establish whether areas were controlled by the federal government or the provinces. As more areas of the West were settled, people asserted their right to local control in such areas as transportation, resources, and civil law. By 1949, provincial status had been granted to all areas south of 60 degrees north latitude. In 1999, the division of the Northwest Territories into the eastern territory of Nunavut and the Western Territory completed the expansion of self-government

Figure 3–34 This family is using a new, light-weight kayak.

from the shores of the St. Lawrence River to the Pacific and to the Arctic oceans.

Boundaries are not visible on the landscape, but they have profound effects on people's lives. They determine the amount of taxes you will pay, what form of education you will receive, what form of government you will have, how—or whether— your environment will be protected, and a host of other regulations. As Canada enters the twenty-first century, however, the very concept of "boundary" is being challenged. By determining boundaries, groups establish power and control over their own fate and region, often by taking away power and control from other groups. Today, in response to a global revolution in technology and communications, areas of international control are being established through agreements such as the North American Free Trade Agreement. This is challenging older concepts of boundaries. Will there ever come a time when people and goods can move freely anywhere in the world? What power and control will be exerted by national governments within their boundaries? These are questions for economists, politicians, concerned citizens, as well as for geographers. You will learn more about these issues—and their effect on Canada—in later chapters of *Horizons.*

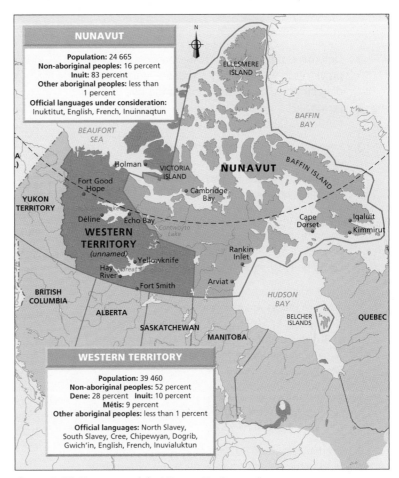

NUNAVUT

Population: 24 665
Non-aboriginal peoples: 16 percent
Inuit: 83 percent
Other aboriginal peoples: less than 1 percent
Official languages under consideration: Inuktitut, English, French, Inuinnaqtun

WESTERN TERRITORY

Population: 39 460
Non-aboriginal peoples: 52 percent
Dene: 28 percent   Inuit: 10 percent
Métis: 9 percent
Other aboriginal peoples: less than 1 percent

Official languages: North Slavey, South Slavey, Cree, Chipewyan, Dogrib, Gwich'in, English, French, Inuvialuktun

Figure 3–35 Nunavut and the Western Territory

Figure 3–36 Paul Okalik (left), the Premier of Nunavut, shakes hands with Nunavut Commissioner Helen Mamayoak Maksagak as she is sworn in as a member of the legislature in Iqaluit on April 1, 1999.

1. Determine the most and least urbanized provinces in western Canada. Use a venn diagram to compare and contrast the two provinces as a way of discovering the reasons for their differences.

2. Research the history of a resource town in western Canada. Find out what resource was extracted, the town's peak population and lifespan, and its status today.

3. Research the origin and growth of your community. Plot its development on a time line, dividing it into sections according to your community's functions and stages of growth.

4. Refer to an atlas to classify the following western places according to size and function(s): Whistler, Trail, and Prince Rupert, in British Columbia; Calgary, in Alberta; Regina, in Saskatchewan; and Churchill, in Manitoba.

5. Draw a flow chart showing the hierarchy of services for a retail item such as an automobile or a specialized service.

6. Examine Figure 3–30, and refer to information in this chapter and Chapters 6 and 7 (you may also need an atlas). Explain:
   - the absence of significant population above 55 degrees north latitude
   - the relatively even distribution of population in the southern prairie region

   - the concentration of population in the southwest corner of Manitoba
   - the concentration of British Columbia's population in the southwest corner and the narrow threads of population in the rest of the province.

7. Look up and study maps of the region where you live. Examine how your region's "artificial" boundaries—such as your school district, regional district, sports leagues, and electoral ridings—correspond to its "natural" boundaries.

8. With a partner, examine an up-to-date map of Canada in an atlas. Suggest further divisions or changes in boundaries that might be made in the provinces or territories. Defend your choices in a presentation to the class.

9. Use a webbing technique to brainstorm the characteristics of the Nunavut region using the headings Physical, Natural, Cultural, Economic, and Influence, as described above.

10. "Those with power draw the lines on the map." Evaluate this statement in light of the establishment of Nunavut and the Western Territory.

11. Compare and contrast your lifestyle with that of a young person in one of the new northern territories. Consider the influence of the natural and cultural environments and any unique attributes that may result.

CONCLUSION

Geography is a diverse field of study. It incorporates many other disciplines in studying how humans interact with their physical environment. In particular, geography examines the spatial relationships and connections between people, resources, settlements, ideas, and their physical environment.

Western Canada is a region of diverse landforms, vegetation, and climate. Historically, people have responded to the natural environment in different ways. The lifestyles of the Native peoples had little impact on the landscape over a period of thousands of years. European contact and settlement, however, had an enormous impact on the landscape, and within a brief period of time. The cultural landscape we see today in western Canada has evolved over a century of resource development and settlement. Canadians are increasingly aware of the beneficial impact these activities have had on their living standards. They are also becoming increasingly aware of effects—both damaging and beneficial—that these activities have had on the natural environment of the Canadian West.

SUMMARY ACTIVITIES

1. In groups of three, present the major regions of western Canada as a colourful, illustrated poster-map. Use illustrations to show the most outstanding features, challenges, and attractions of each region. For example, a picture of a skier could be used to show the recreational potential of the Rocky Mountains.

ON YOUR OWN

1. With a partner, create an earthquake-awareness brochure for distribution in threatened communities.

2. Research a current conservation issue in western Canada, using the library or the Internet as a reference resource. Write a letter to the appropriate agency expressing your views on the issue.

3. Imagine that you have to move to one of the regions of western Canada other than the Western Mountains. Make a list of the changes you would have to make to adapt to living in that region. Think of such factors as climate, vegetation, economy, and size of population.

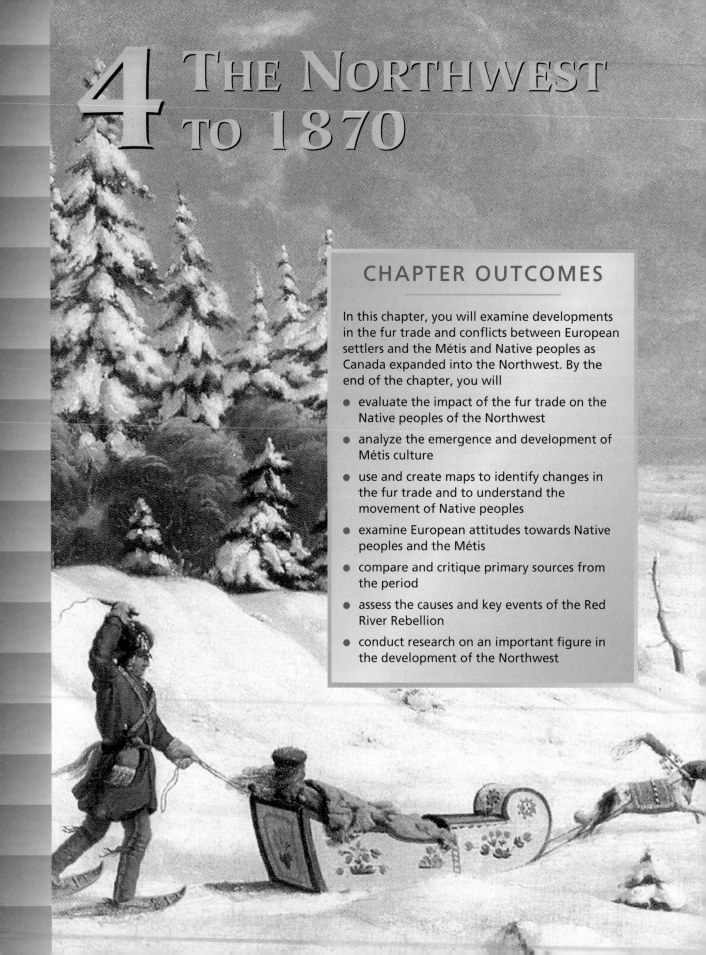

4 THE NORTHWEST TO 1870

CHAPTER OUTCOMES

In this chapter, you will examine developments in the fur trade and conflicts between European settlers and the Métis and Native peoples as Canada expanded into the Northwest. By the end of the chapter, you will

- evaluate the impact of the fur trade on the Native peoples of the Northwest

- analyze the emergence and development of Métis culture

- use and create maps to identify changes in the fur trade and to understand the movement of Native peoples

- examine European attitudes towards Native peoples and the Métis

- compare and critique primary sources from the period

- assess the causes and key events of the Red River Rebellion

- conduct research on an important figure in the development of the Northwest

I Am Anne-Marie Lepine

The Métis are a unique people, descended from two cultures—Native and French. Their communities began to form hundreds of years ago along the banks of the Red River in what is now southern Manitoba.

In this Window on the Past, you will get to know Anne-Marie Lepine, a Métis teenager who lived in one of these communities in the early nineteenth century. It was around this time that the Métis began to view themselves as a distinct society. While Anne-Marie is a fictional character, many of the events described really took place.

I am Anne-Marie Lepine and I am seventeen years old. I live on a farm with my father and mother, who are both Métis. Our farm is long and narrow, but larger than it looks, because it stretches far back from the river.

Who are the Métis? We are a new people, the children of Native mothers and European fathers. Both my grandfathers were French fur traders for the North West Company. They lived with us until they died two years ago in a canoeing accident. My father's mother is still alive; she is **Saulteaux.** My mother's mother was Cree. I can still remember stories my two grandfathers used to tell me about the fur trade. I know they got very bored with life on the farm, but I still miss them a lot.

We have everything here, I guess. The nice thing is, we are really only part-time farmers. We grow all the vegetables we need to live throughout the year, and we keep chickens and two cows—they give us milk, butter, and cheese. Everyone pitches in. I have to milk the cows, which I do not enjoy, especially in the winter, when my fingers are frozen with the cold. The men of our village also work for the North West Company, working as packers and voyageurs. Those are European jobs. We are also great hunters of the bison—a skill we learned from our mothers' peoples. The bison hunt is the great event of the year and not, as you might expect, just for the men!

In the spring and in the early autumn, we all set out for the hunt. Men, women, children and the old people—we all go. We load up the wagons with everything we will need for several weeks, and set off in great anticipation. Our wagons are made entirely of wood, and they squeak horribly. My father calls them the "devil's fiddle," but it's more like the devil's marching band when we all squeal together across the plains. After we set up camp, the men ride out on their trail horses to find the bison. Some of the unmarried women, like me, who have shown strength, ride with them, although I know my mother would like me to stay behind.

We are under strict orders from the Captain of the Hunt, Mr. Grant. Cuthbert Grant is the leader of all our people. He is a tall man, very strong, and a wonderful speaker. He can persuade almost anyone to see things his way. Mr. Grant runs the bison hunt as though it were a military expedition. He has absolute control, and everyone must obey him.

In the spring of this year, I was riding at the front of the men seeking the bison. The prairie was green in its new growth, the sun was warm, and a gentle breeze was blowing over the prairie grass. All was still and quiet, except for bird song. Slowly I became aware of a noise ahead of me, like the distant rumbling of thunder, yet

125

I watch the hunt from my horse on the ridge.

there were no clouds in the sky. Bison! I urged my horse on, and as I came to the crest of a low ridge, I saw them. Thousands and thousands of bison—they covered the ground as far as the eye can see, all moving slowly northward. I immediately swung my horse around, and galloped towards the men behind me. I did not cry out, but rode straight to Mr. Grant. He knew what I had found before I arrived, for as I approached, the men got off their trail horses and mounted their bison runners. These are superb horses, swift and bold, trained to obey their riders instantly. Because the hunters have both hands occupied with powder horn and rifle, they have to direct the horses with their knees.

I am not allowed to hunt the bison because my parents think I could be killed. I disagree, but I obey them. So, like last year, I watched the hunt from my horse on the ridge. The men rode right into the herd and started following individual bison very closely. It's dangerous work, because the bison is huge. If a hunter falls, he will die instantly, trampled under thousands of hoofs. My own cousin died so last year— his horse tripped on a gopher hole, and he fell. This is the way of things sometimes.

When we have taken enough bison, the rest of the community arrives to prepare the animals. We use all parts of the bison, as do the people of the Plains. Our moccasins, clothes and winter robes come

from the hides; we use the horns to make powder horns, which hold our gunpowder; we use sinew to sew clothes together; and we use the meat. Some of the meat is eaten right away, but most of it is dried and made into pemmican, which we sell to the North West Company in exchange for trade goods. Pemmican is not my favourite food; it is dull and rather smelly, but a small portion makes for a meal, and it is an ideal food on the trail.

Well … those were happy days I like to think about when I drift off to sleep. These days, things are not so happy. There are strangers in our midst. They came four years ago, from Scotland, my father tells me. Last winter, in our house on the banks of the river, he tried to explain things to me. I confess I do not fully understand the explanation.

"Many, many years ago," my father told me, "an English king gave all the land drained by rivers flowing into Hudson Bay to some men. Those men started the Hudson's Bay Company. Five years ago the Hudson's Bay Company gave part of those lands, where we live now, to a Lord Selkirk, so he could settle his countrymen."

"Why did they do that?" I asked. "Doesn't the land belong to the people who already live there?

My father was silent for a few seconds. "It is true that those who live in a land have the right to it, but not all people recognize that right. The Hudson's Bay Company says that the law of England is greater than the claim of having lived here so long, and so they've sent these newcomers to be among us. Now, to be fair, they were thrown out of their farms in Scotland because of some bad laws."

"I suppose," I said, "that the land is large, and there is enough room for all."

"That's also true," my father said, "but the new leader of these people—Semple is his name—is a haughty man, and he has made a rule that hurts us. These settlers have no experience with life on the plains, and they nearly starved the first two years they were here. If it were not for us, they would have died. Now, in return for our kindness and generosity, Semple has said that we can no longer trade our pemmican—it must all be given

to him, and his people. This is terrible, because it means that if we cannot sell our pemmican to the Nor'westers, then we too will feel hardship in the coming winter."

"Don't we have enough pemmican for everyone?" I asked. "Couldn't the colonists trade things for the pemmican?"

"That is also true," my father said, "but the leader of the colonists hates us for who we are. I'll tell you, he wants us to move away so he can have all the land for himself."

"Why would he hate us?" I asked.

"I don't know, but if the colonists decide to make war on us, we will have to fight for what is ours rightfully."

"I don't like this either," I said. "Fighting is wrong when the reason makes no sense."

Later that winter, Mr. Grant came to our house. He does not want a war, but he wants the colonists to leave if they will not share the land and its resources. He told my father that we are all supposed to start harassing the colonists—if we bother them enough, they might go away. So, this spring we started our campaign of harassment. At night, when all are asleep, we go near their homes, and fire off guns and shout at irregular intervals, so that the dogs bark wildly and everyone in the family wakes up. Our young men like this, but I do not, because I think of the terror it causes the little children. We also set fire to the colonists' barns and burn their crops. This also disturbs me because destroying food will mean starvation for these people in the winter. It is terrible to see the smoke rising from

"It is true," my father said, "that those who live in a land have the right to it."

Why can't we live together in peace?

the colonists' fields. At these times, it saddens me that we can't live together in peace.

The last part of my story is even harsher. Last month, the killing started. The colonists' leader, Robert Semple, heard that Mr. Grant and some Métis were on their way to Fort Gibraltar. Mr. Semple thought they were after pemmican, so he took twenty men, and confronted Mr. Grant. Angry words were exchanged, and then a colonist shot at one of our people. The colonists are farmers, not soldiers, and they stood no chance against our skilled hunters. My father says that the colonists were all killed within a quarter of an hour, and their bodies still lie out on the prairie. As soon as word of the battle reached the colonists, they packed up their belongings and left with great speed. Mr. Grant and some of our men burnt the colonists' homes the next day. The colonists are gone, but I do not think the trouble is over yet.

While I am sad that killing took place, I have been giving this situation a lot of thought. I guess you could say that while I disagree with some of the actions, I have a new respect for my people. We stood up for what is rightfully ours, and declared that this is our land, for all time.

Saulteaux: the western Ojibwa

ACTIVITIES

1. In what ways are the Métis European? In what ways are they Native?

2. Describe how the Métis of the Red River were self-sufficient.

3. What is Anne-Marie's opinion about the conflict between the Selkirk settlers and the Métis? How would you feel in a similar circumstance? Could a peaceful solution have been found? Why or why not?

4. How have Anne-Marie's views developed by the end of the story?

TIME LINE

1670	FOUNDING OF THE HBC
1783	FOUNDING OF THE NWC
1810	MÉTIS COMMUNITY THRIVES IN THE RED RIVER VALLEY
1812	FOUNDING OF THE SELKIRK SETTLEMENT IN THE RED RIVER VALLEY
1814	PEMMICAN PROCLAMATION
1816	CUTHBERT GRANT RAIDS AN HBC PEMMICAN SUPPLY
1817	SELKIRK'S TREATY WITH CREE AND OJIBWA NATIONS
1821	HBC AND NWC MERGE
1869	CONTROL OF RUPERT'S LAND TRANSFERRED TO CANADIAN GOVERNMENT
	RED RIVER REBELLION
	MÉTIS LIST OF RIGHTS AND FREEDOMS
1870	EXECUTION OF THOMAS SCOTT MANITOBA ENTERS CONFEDERATION

Neither French nor Indian, but intermediate, [the Métis] claimed to unite the civilization of their fathers with the rights of their mothers' people in a new nationality of the Northwest. The "new nation" was a unique ethnic and political reality, sprung from the continental fur trade, and it was not unaware both of its uniqueness and of its dependence on the old way of life ...

–MODERN HISTORIAN W. L. NORTON

What does "nationality" mean to you? Do you think this concept will be important in the twenty-first century? What would a world without nationality be like?

INTRODUCTION

In the early years of the nineteenth century, the Northwest was known only to the Native peoples, the Métis, and people who worked in the fur trade. If you look back to the map shown on page 10, you will see how vast this area was, and how tiny the colonies of Upper and Lower Canada, and the Maritime colonies, were by comparison.

In this chapter, you will focus on the heartland area of the fur trade and follow its development up to 1870. By this time, the region had become a thriving community made up of the earliest settlers, the Métis, along with many newcomers from Europe and Upper and Lower Canada. As you read in this chapter's Window on the Past, this settlement was not entirely free of tensions, but there were many peaceful decades. In many ways, The Red River Settlement, as it came to be known, was a microcosm of modern-day Canada—a small cultural mosaic, long before multiculturalism became official.

This chapter will introduce you to one of the most controversial figures in Canadian history—Louis Riel, the leader of the Métis. If you ever have the opportunity to scan an early twentieth-century history textbook for Riel's name, you may be surprised, especially after reading about Riel in *Horizons.* Riel is a prime example of what historians call "revisionism," which means that the passing of time can sometimes revise the meaning of events, or change someone's reputation for better or worse. In Riel's case, the passing of time has only benefited his reputation. Executed by the Canadian government for his role in the Northwest Rebellion—an event you will read about in Chapter 5—he is considered a Canadian hero by many people today.

THE NORTHWEST IN 1800

The Hudson's Bay Company

Last year, you learned that the Hudson's Bay Company (HBC) was founded in 1670 following Pierre Radisson and Médart de Groseilliers's successful journey to the wilderness region beyond New France. Returning to London, England, loaded down with precious furs, the pair made a pitch to King Charles II. If he would back their business, they could help him wrest a portion of the fur trade from the French, who had controlled the trade since 1616. The king not only agreed, but claimed the area around Hudson Bay and named it after his cousin, Prince Rupert. That year, the HBC received its royal charter from the king, which gave it exclusive trading rights in a vast area—approximately one-third the size of modern Canada. Rupert's Land included all lands drained by rivers flowing into Hudson Bay.

Rather than risk sending traders inland, the HBC built trading posts at the mouths of rivers emptying into Hudson Bay. It encouraged the Assiniboin, Cree, and Ojibwa trappers and traders to bring their furs to the trading posts where they would be exchanged for trade goods. The HBC followed this "stay by the Bay" policy for the next century. Because beaver was the most prized fur, the HBC used it as a form of currency. All furs brought to the post were assessed in terms of their value relative to a beaver pelt, called "made beaver" by the HBC. Once the pelt's value had been established, traders could purchase other goods at the post's company store. The HBC's standard of trade was very strict, and there was little room for bargaining.

The HBC had a rigid **hierarchy**. The company directors ran the business from London, England. The local bosses, known as "Factors" were also British, as were the clerks and labourers at the post. Everyone who worked for the HBC was a salaried employee—only the London partners actually shared in the profits from the fur trade. The HBC shipped furs directly to England every summer, and received its trade goods at the same time, also directly from England. This exchange of goods had to be carried out swiftly and precisely because Hudson Bay is ice-free only from July to mid-September. The rest of the year, it is frozen over.

hierarchy: people in authority ranked from top to bottom

Figure 4–1 Major posts of the Hudson's Bay Company around 1820

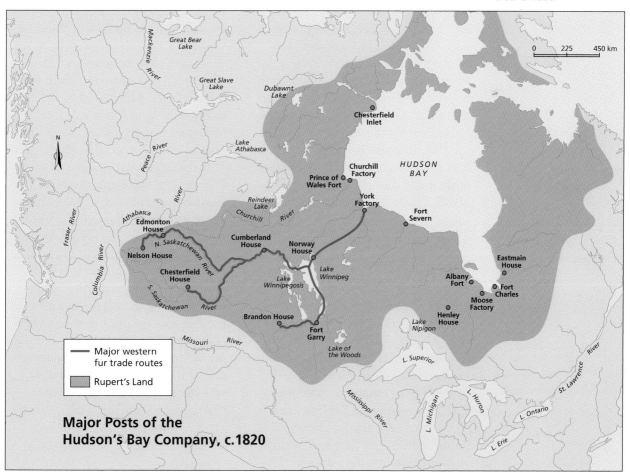

Major Posts of the Hudson's Bay Company, c.1820

Legend:
— Major western fur trade routes
�mineGrey Rupert's Land

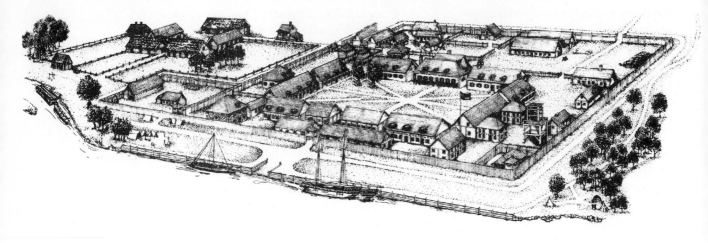

Figure 4–2 Fort William, headquarters for the North West Company

In 1783, the North West Company (NWC) was established. Now the HBC had a rival, and its stay-by-the-Bay policy was put to the test. Soon NWC posts dotted the western and northern interior. Native trappers found it much easier to get to these posts and were much less willing to make the long journey to the Bay. By the end of the 1780s, the HBC had also established a number of inland posts to win back some of the trade that had gone to the NWC. The race for furs was on.

The North West Company

By the 1750s, the French-Canadian fur trade had moved deeper inland. French traders knew that the HBC's policy of staying close to Hudson Bay occasionally made HBC posts inaccessible. When New France fell in 1763, the French fur trade was seized by a group of English merchants from Montreal. The "Montrealers," as they were called, expanded trading networks in the interior and continued to employ French-Canadians as traders. In 1783, several of these companies merged to form the North West Company.

There were geographic reasons why the NWC started to build posts inland. NWC furs had to be shipped to England from Montreal, and Montreal was too far for Native trappers to travel, especially when many of them lived west of Lake Winnipeg. As a result, the NWC company established a major trade depot at Fort William, at the head of Lake Superior. In the spring, trade goods were shipped from England to Fort William. From there, NWC employees transported the goods to the inland posts. In late summer the process was reversed, and furs were transported to Fort William and then on to Montreal to be shipped to England. Timing was critical. As was the case with the HBC, the NWC had to contend with a short ice-free season on the rivers and lakes.

The NWC was a vigorous, aggressive operation. Its structure was based on partnerships and so was much less rigid and **top-down** than that of the HBC. The NWC's Montreal partners stayed in Montreal, bought trade goods from England, and arranged for the sale and shipment of fur pelts to England. The *hivernants* (wintering partners) remained in the Northwest and did the actual fur trading. Because the hivernants were partners in the company, not simply salaried employees, they shared in profits. They had a strong motive to make sure the company prospered. The NWC also employed *voyageurs*, who provided the muscle power to paddle canoes and carry cargo in both the Northwest and on the long lake journey from Fort William to Montreal. It actively sought out new trading areas, employing explorers who travelled extensively throughout the Northwest mapping new territories and establishing new trading posts. The NWC was also much more relaxed in its trading standards than the HBC; it was willing to dicker over the price of furs, and it also traded alcohol for furs, something the HBC refused to do. All this **bullishness** eventually paid off for the NWC. By 1800, it had a network of trading posts that stretched as far west as the interior of what is now BC and as far north as Great Slave Lake.

top-down: dictatorial, bossy

bullishness: optimism in money matters

Figure 4–3 Major posts of the North West Company around 1820

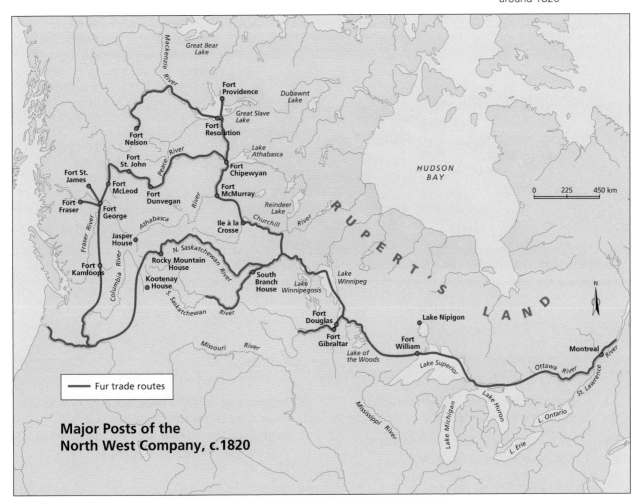

Major Posts of the North West Company, c.1820

— Fur trade routes

Boats, Canoes, and the Portage

Last year, you learned that the voyageurs relied on small and large canoes to transport goods. By 1750, the HBC had developed something better than the canoe. The York boat was a double-ended wooden boat. It was about 13-metres long and could either be rowed or sailed, depending on the winds. The first York boats could carry a cargo of up to 3000 kilograms—much more weight than a small canoe. Later models could carry up to 6000 kilograms. There was one drawback. A fully loaded York boat was extremely heavy, weighing about 1 tonne, and so was difficult to **portage**.

With an experienced crew, a York boat could make the round trip journey from Fort Edmonton to York Factory in about 30 days. But the work was physically draining. York Boat crews travelled from dawn to dusk, pulling heavy oars at a rate of 30 strokes a minute; and crews often worked in cold, wet conditions.

The NWC continued to rely on the canoe throughout the nineteenth century. In the Northwest, the NWC used *canots du nord*. These canoes were about 7-metres long and a metre wide. They carried about 1500 kilos of cargo, and were paddled by a crew of six. For the journey from Fort William to Montreal, the NWC used *canots de maitre*. These were about 11-metres long and about 1.5-metres wide. Crewed by twelve people, they could carry cargoes of up to 4000 kilograms. Both types of canoes were constructed of birch bark stretched over a light wood frame.

Travelling the lakes and rivers of Canada is not like travelling the modern Trans-Canada Highway. The fur traders had no ramps or exits to get from one river system to another, and sometimes the waters were not navigable. If rapids or waterfalls made a river impassable, or if travellers had to switch from one river system to another in order to complete their journey, they would have to portage. This meant that the cargo would be unloaded and carried to a place where the water journey could continue. Cargo—furs or trade goods—was packed in 40-kilogram bales called *pieces* that the voyageurs carried on their backs. There were thirty-six portages between Fort William and Lachine, near Montreal.

to portage: to carry from one body of water to another

head hunter: someone who looks for skilled employees on behalf of a company

Figure 4–4 The canot du nord

ACTIVITIES

1. Suggest reasons why the HBC initially adopted its stay-at-the-Bay trade policy.

2. List the advantages and disadvantages of the York boat versus the canot du nord.

3. Imagine that you are a **head hunter** who has been asked by the NWC to recruit new employees. Describe the company to a potential employee and compare and contrast it to the rival HBC.

THE NATIVE PEOPLES OF THE NORTHWEST

The Northwest is dominated by the Canadian Shield, which is covered mostly by boreal forest. Closer to Hudson Bay, the trees become small and the ground is covered by lichen. Southwest of the Shield lies a small portion of the Interior Plain. Before European contact, the Northwest was home to four aboriginal nations—the Ojibwa, the Assiniboin, the Cree, and the Chipewyan. A fifth group, the Inuit, lived along the northern edges of Hudson Bay, outside the main corridors of the fur trade.

By 1800, the aboriginal peoples of the Northwest had a long history of involvement in the fur trade as trappers, traders, or **middlemen.** Chipewyan guides had helped Samuel Hearne explore the northern part of Rupert's Land in the 1770s. For the next few decades, the Chipewyans supplied most of the furs to the posts being built around Lake Athabasca. By the seventeenth century, the Cree, who lived in the territory south and west of James Bay and south of Hudson Bay, were firmly established in the fur trade

middleman: someone who acts as a dealer between two parties who want to exchange goods

Figure 4–5 The Ojibwa originally lived in the region north of Georgian Bay and east of Lake Superior. They acted as some of the first middlemen for European fur traders.

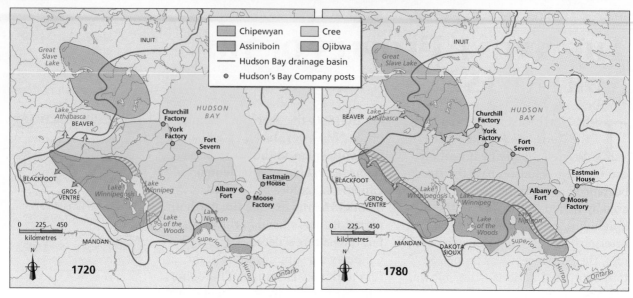

Figure 4–6 The fur trade drew Northwest aboriginal groups from their original territories. As fur-bearing animals became scarce in one region, trappers would move into another area.

and had close dealings with the HBC. As the fur trade moved west, so too did the Cree. Simultaneously, the Ojibwa began moving north into the former territory of the Cree. By 1740, the Ojibwa were also becoming established in the fur trade, and commonly traded at the posts north of Lake Superior, as did the Assiniboin.

Many Native peoples became so involved with the fur trade that it disrupted their way of life. As competition between the HBC and NWC intensified, Native trappers tried to keep up with the demand for furs. This forced full-time trappers to abandon their yearly cycle of fishing, hunting, and preserving food. In addition, the fur trade caused a real clash of cultural values. For example, the Native peoples did not subscribe to the Protestant work ethic of "work for work's sake." They worked to sustain themselves and their families. When Native guides decided they had escorted a European trader far enough inland, they would often abandon them without any sense of guilt—an act that Europeans viewed as irresponsible. On the other hand, the Native peoples did not always retaliate when traders from the HBC or the NWC stole their canoes, fish, or furs. There is even one account of a Cree trapper rescuing a NWC trader who had previously stolen his canoe and winter supplies.

Contact with Europeans also exposed the Native peoples to diseases. The two most deadly were smallpox and measles. While smallpox and measles could kill Europeans, many had developed an immunity to smallpox, and most survived the measles. This was not the case for Native peoples. An outbreak of smallpox in 1780–82 in the region around Hudson Bay killed off much of the Chipewyan and Cree populations. One eyewitness account noted that a village had twenty-nine people in the autumn, but only three by the following spring, entirely as the result of smallpox.

Apply Your Knowledge

The Importance of a Mind Map

It was once assumed that European explorers were moving into uncharted territory as they began to travel deeper into the Northwest. The assumption is largely false. All explorers relied on people from the aboriginal nations, both as translators and guides. The knowledge of the Native peoples about the Northwest was extensive and valuable. Not only did they know the region's topography better than anyone, they also knew how to locate valuable resources, such as food and water.

The map shown below was drawn by an HBC employee in 1802, but it was based on a sketch by Ki oo cus, a Blackfoot chief. It shows the topographic features of the central region of the prairies in what is now Saskatchewan and Alberta. This map is what geographers call a "mind map." Topographical

Legend highlights

2. hill, no pines, but plenty of other [kinds of trees]
9. a little hill, plenty of berries
16. stinking lake—10-miles long
19. rock high; pines
25. a little hill
26. a little poplar
33. Red Deer Lake
oo day's marches

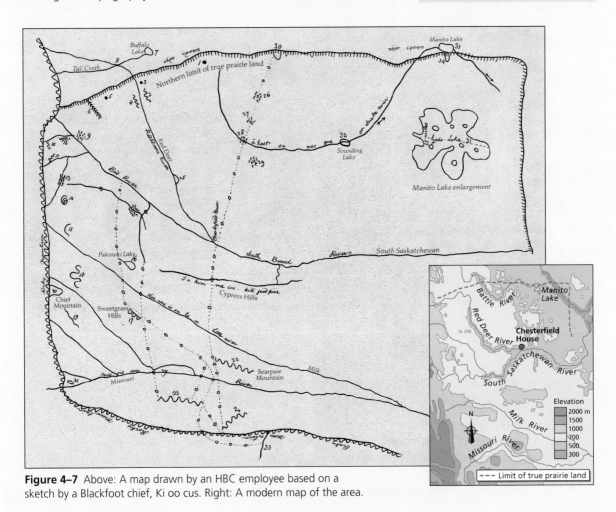

Figure 4–7 Above: A map drawn by an HBC employee based on a sketch by a Blackfoot chief, Ki oo cus. Right: A modern map of the area.

accuracy is not the primary purpose of such maps, but practical usefulness is. Mind maps usually indicate why a certain location is important, the distance between important locations, and the degree of difficulty of the terrain. For example, Ki oo cus noted a number of berry bushes in the region, but he was specific about the "little hill, plenty of berries" because this would probably be most useful to a tired, hungry traveller.

Ki oo cus's map was one of several adapted by Peter Fidler of the HBC. It has been said that Fidler made frequent use of Native sketches, and always acknowledged his source of information. The region shown in Figure 4–7 would not be formally mapped until 1865, when the explorers from the Palliser Expedition published their map of Canada from Lake Superior to the Okanagan Valley. This map would confirm that most of Ki oo cus's information—though collected without any mapping devices— was accurate.

ACTIVITIES

1. According to in Figure 4–7, how many days would it take to travel overland from the Missouri River to the northern edge of the prairies?

2. What physical features does Ki oo cus include on the map? Why would he consider these to be important? What is the modern name for "Chief Mountain"? Why would berry patches be indicated on the map?

3. Why would fur traders consider this map to be useful? Offer three reasons.

4. Create your own mind map of the area near your home and school. Include these key locations:
   - your house
   - your school
   - main roads
   - bus stop, if you take public transportation
   - shops that you frequent along the way (to buy a drink, for example)

   Display the distance between these key locations in a user-friendly way, for example, how long it takes to walk from your home to the bus stop at a brisk pace.

   Now branch out and add some landmarks that have meaning to you, for example:
   - homes of friends that you pass along the way
   - a mailbox you use
   - a park you love to visit
   - a bird's nest you look for
   - a garden you think is lovely
   - a wall mural you hate or admire

   Use your imagination to add more items.

   Do not worry too much about accuracy, for example, the precise distance between locations. Your map should show what is important in your home base.

5. Exchange your map with the map of a classmate and take his or her route home. Once you get back (to your real home), evaluate your partner's map on the basis of:
   - whether or not it was easy to use
   - the number of interesting landmarks included (or omitted)
   - whether it displayed distance in a useful way

   Exchange comments with your partner the following day.

ACTIVITIES

1. The fur trade brought many changes to the lives of the Native peoples of the Northwest. Name three changes, and evaluate whether they were positive or negative—or a mixture of both— from the standpoint of the Native peoples.

2. List all the roles played by the Native peoples in the development of the fur trade. Evaluate whether or not it can be said that the trade could not have existed without the Native peoples.

THE NORTHWEST FROM 1800 TO 1860

The Battle for the Fur Trade, 1800 to 1810

As the nineteenth century began, competition between the NWC and the HBC grew fierce. Fur resources in established trading were becoming depleted, so both companies moved deeper inland in a race to gain control of untapped resources. The NWC was especially aggressive. It established new posts in what is now British Columbia and north of the sixtieth parallel. Both companies sharpened their competitive edge by promising more valuable trade goods in exchange for furs and by opening new posts next door to the competition.

The Métis

As NWC traders began pushing deeper into the Northwest in the last decades of the eighteenth century, they began wintering in their trading areas and staying with local groups of Native peoples. As had occurred during the earliest years of the fur trade, a number of fur traders married the daughters of Native families. This was encouraged by both the NWC and the Native peoples. The NWC thought such marriages would help ensure trading loyalty, and Native elders thought it advantageous to have one or more of the family's daughters marry fur traders. Wives of fur traders enjoyed an improved standard of living and their lives were generally easier than those of most women.

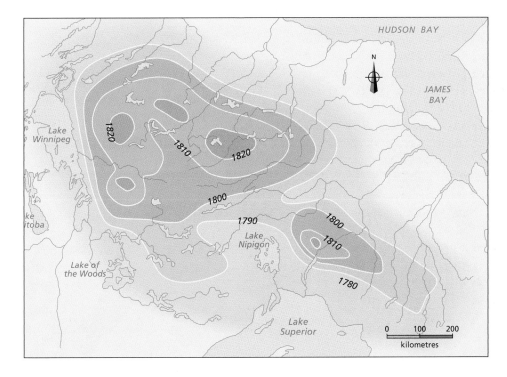

Figure 4–8 This map shows the depletion of beaver in the Northwest from 1780 to 1820.

celibacy: abstinence from sexual relationships

The marriages were important social events. Traders would ask the father of the intended bride for permission to marry and would pay the young woman's father a sum of money. At the ceremony itself, the bride would be ritually dressed by her family members and the groom would receive a set of traditional garments. By 1800, some 4000 voyageurs and hivernants were living in the Northwest, and many of them had married Native women. In contrast to the NWC, the HBC forbade its employees to marry—the Company was concerned about supporting too many dependents. In fact, it actually tried to enforce a policy of **celibacy** among its employees. Isolation in the remote northern environment, however, led to several marriages, including a number of cross-cultural marriages.

By the early nineteenth century, a sizeable number of the people living in the Northwest were of European-Native ancestry. As they began to marry among themselves, a new culture gradually evolved. Later generations began to think of themselves as a distinct people. Initially, persons of French-Native ancestry called themselves *bois brule* (literally, "burnt wood"). By about 1810, they began using the term "Métis" (from the French word for "mixed"). Because most Europeans in the Northwest were French-Canadian, the Métis formed the largest group of people with mixed ancestry. People with Native and Scottish or Native and British ancestry preferred the term "country-born." The Métis usually spoke French and Algonkian, or a dialect that combined the two languages, and they were usually Roman Catholic. By 1810, a large number of Métis were living near the junction of the Red and Assiniboin rivers in the Red River Valley. Here they developed communities and a lifestyle that combined both Native and European customs.

The Métis lived on some of the best prairie soils, and they built farms along the banks of both rivers.

Figure 4–9 The marriages of Native women to French fur traders were especially supported by the North West Company.

Their farms were laid out in the **seigneurial pattern**, which had been the long-standing French custom. Like the Plains Indians, the Métis hunted bison, but they were not exclusively dependent on it for survival. The bison hunt developed slowly. By the 1820s, it had become a seasonal event for all Métis. The hunt took place in the early summer and in the autumn, and had several purposes. It not only provided fresh meat and bison hides, but also all the meat and fat that was required to make pemmican. At first the Métis sold pemmican only to their ally, the NWC. After the merger of the NWC and the HBC in 1821, they also sold pemmican to the new HBC.

The bison hunt was a spectacular event that involved the whole community. Métis women, men, and children would set out across the prairie in **Red River carts**, travelling many days in search of the right herd. The Métis used two types of horses: saddle horses and buffalo

Figure 4–10 This sketch shows the Métis returning from the hunt.

runners. The saddle horses pulled the carts until the herd was spotted. Then the riders would mount the buffalo runners, which were fast, responsive horses that had been trained exclusively to hunt bison. The riders guided the horses by knee pressure, since both hands would be busy loading **muzzle loaders** with

seigneurial pattern: the long-lot pattern of the seigneuries of New France

Red River cart: a two-wheeled cart used on the prairie

muzzle loader: any firearm loaded through the muzzle

Rules of the Bison Hunt

The Métis developed a number of rules for the bison hunt. These were so strictly enforced that the hunt was something like a military expedition. Every aspect was approached with discipline. The captain of the hunt, who was elected by the hunters before the party left the Red River, was in command. In turn, the captain would often organize different troops of hunters, each having its own captain.

The Rules of the Hunt
1. No buffalo to be run on the Sabbath day [Sunday].
2. No party to fork off, lag behind or go before, without permission [of the Captain of the Hunt].
3. No person or party to run buffalo before the general order.
4. Every captain with his men, in turn, to patrol the camp and keep order.
5. For the first trespass of these laws, the offender to have his saddle and bridle cut up.
6. For the second offence, the coat to be taken off the offender's back and cut up.
7. For the third offence, the offender to be flogged.
8. Any person convicted of theft, even to the value of a sinew, to be brought to the middle of the camp, and the crier to call out his or her name three times, adding the word "thief" each time.

shot: the pellet discharged from the firearm

gunpowder and **shot** (all guns until the middle of the nineteenth century were muzzle loaders). The hunt was extremely dangerous. Guns could explode, horses could trip and fall because of gopher holes, and the pointed horns of the bison could swing unexpectedly. Death and serious injury were not uncommon. Once enough bison had been killed, community members, including children and the elderly, would help butcher the animals and prepare pemmican. Then the whole hunting party would return to the Red River.

During the hunt, the Métis sometimes came into conflict with the Plains Indians, who also hunted bison.

However, the strict discipline of the Métis made them formidable opponents. In 1851, a small Métis hunting party was attacked by 1000 to 2000 Sioux warriors. For three days, sixty-four Métis fighters held off charge after charge. In the end, the Sioux retreated, vowing never to attack "The Wagonmen"—in reference to the Metis' Red River carts—again. The bison hunt did more for the Métis than simply supply a large amount of meat and clothing. It fostered in them a strong sense of community, pride, and discipline. This would have profound implications for the Métis in the later-nineteenth century.

Figure 4–11 Above, a muzzle cover and a fine example of Métis needlecraft. How is the image at right a romanticized image of the bison hunt?

ACTIVITIES

1. Compare Figure 4–8 with Figure 4–1 and Figure 4–3. What is the relationship between the location of trading posts and the depletion of the beaver?

2. How did the HBC and NWC differ in their policies concerning marriage? What was the reason for this difference?

3. With a partner, determine which aspects of Métis life seemed to draw on Native traditions, and which seemed more European.

4. Why were the rules of the bison hunt so strict? Why might some punishments involve the destruction of property?

The Colony on the Red River

In 1812 an event took place that would have profound implications for the Métis community—and for the Hudson's Bay Company and the North West Company. In fact, it would bring the rivalry between the HBC and the NWC to the point of warfare. Eventually, the two companies would merge and a unique settlement in the Northwest would be created.

Thomas Douglas, the Fifth Earl of Selkirk, was a man with a vision. He was also a man with the means to carry out his plans. As a **liberal democrat,** Selkirk had been deeply troubled by the plight of poor tenant farmers in his native Scotland. During the later part of the eighteenth century, many large landowners in Scotland had "enclosed" their farmland. Enclosure meant that tenant farmers were evicted from the land so that it could be converted for sheep-grazing. Wool was more profitable for the landowners than the rent being paid by tenant farmers, or "crofters," as they were known in Scotland. The displaced crofters had two choices, if they were to survive. They could move to newly industrialized cities, especially Glasgow, and become factory workers, or they could emigrate to British North America and become farmers. Most crofters were too poor to take advantage of the second option. So Selkirk used his fortune to create agricultural colonies for the displaced crofters in the colonies. By 1810, he had established settlements in the Maritimes and in Upper Canada. Since Selkirk was also a director of the HBC, he decided to use his influence to launch a much more ambitious project.

Figure 4–12 Lord Selkirk

Selkirk learned that the soil in the Red River Valley was especially fertile. He also knew that it was costly for the HBC to ship foodstuffs from England to feed employees in the Northwest. Selkirk calculated that he could solve the problems of both the crofters and the HBC by establishing a farming colony in the Red River Valley. The farmers would be able to maintain their way of life in a new land, and the HBC could use their produce to supply employees at much less expense.

In 1811, Selkirk convinced the HBC to give him some 300 000 square kilometres in what is now southern Manitoba and North Dakota. It was called "Selkirk's Grant." Selkirk and the HBC felt they had a legal right to this territory because it was part of Rupert's Land—and the king had granted the HBC a monopoly in the Northwest. Neither Selkirk nor the HBC gave much thought to the people already living in the region, or how they

liberal democrat: in the nineteenth century, someone who fought for the rights of the underprivileged

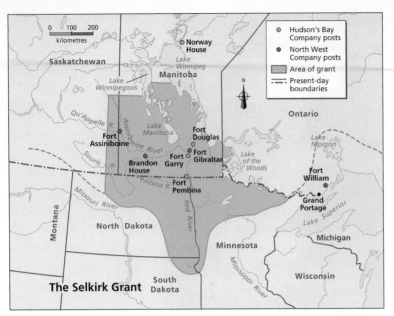

Figure 4–13 The Selkirk Grant. Why would someone call Selkirk's plans "futile"?

might react to an influx of farming colonists. Moreover, Selkirk overlooked the difficult climate of the region, which was much harsher than the climate of Scotland. Upon learning of Selkirk's plan for a farming colony, one of his London friends was cynical:

> By God, Sir, if you are bent on something futile ... why not plough the deserts of the Sahara, which is so much nearer?

And when the first contingent of Scottish colonists arrived, an NWC employee remarked on their future prospects:

> [T]he emigrants ... will be subject to constant alarm and terror. Their habitations, their crops, their cattle will be destroyed, and they will find it impossible to exist in the country.

An advance party of thirty-six Scottish and Irish labourers left Britain in 1811 under the command of Miles Macdonell, an ex-militia officer who had a reputation for belligerence. The group was supposed to reach the Red River and prepare for the main party of colonists, who were due to leave England in 1812. Macdonell's party, however, reached York Factory very late in the year. They did not reach the Red River until August 30, 1812. A few months later, they were joined by the main party of 120 colonists—men, women and children who had arrived at York Factory that summer. Winter begins early on the Red River, and both groups had to winter at the NWC post of Fort Pembina, some 110 kilometres south of the site intended for the colony.

In the spring of 1813, Macdonell led the group back to Red River, to begin clearing land for the colony. Already overwhelmed by the work and climate, the colonists were devastated when they discovered that all the crops they had sown in the spring had failed. Faced with starvation, they had no choice but to return to Fort Pembina for the winter. In the meantime, a second group of eighty-three colonists landed at Fort Churchill by mistake. They marched—in winter—to York Factory, a journey that brought them to the brink of death. In the spring of 1814, they arrived at the Red River Colony.

While the crops survived the second year, Macdonell feared the colonists would run out of food during the winter. He issued his Pemmican Proclamation to make sure they had a food supply. It effectively banned the sale and export of pemmican from the Red River. The Métis, who relied on the proceeds of selling pemmican to the NWC, were infuriated. The proclamation also ran contrary to Lord Selkirk's instructions to Macdonell: "keep clear of … the NWC." Undaunted, Macdonell followed up by ordering NWC employees to vacate all their posts in the Red River Valley within six months. By the spring of 1814, the NWC and the Métis, under the direction of the NWC Chief Trader Duncan Cameron, were retaliating. They harassed the colonists by burning buildings, trampling crops, and firing rifles at night. Cameron personally convinced 133 colonists to leave in early 1815. They were taken by canoe to Fort William. Cameron then arrested Macdonell and took him to Fort William for trial. The remaining colonists left in June and made their way to Jack River House at the north end of Lake Winnipeg.

Under the command of Colin Robertson, an HBC trader who had once worked for the NWC, the colonists returned to Red River by summer's end. Robertson was far less belligerent than Macdonell and soon made peace with the Métis and the NWC. In the fall, a new governor of the colony, Robert Semple, arrived with eighty-four new colonists. Before leaving the colony, Robertson warned Semple to remain on guard from possible attacks. Semple did not follow his advice. In a show of force, Semple attacked and burned the then-empty NWC Fort Gibraltar. This action convinced the Métis that the Selkirk colonists intended to declare war on them.

In May 1816, a group of Métis, led by the young leader Cuthbert Grant, raided a brigade of HBC boats on the Assiniboine River, to the west of the Red River. They seized a supply of pemmican, which they viewed as reasonable compensation for Macdonell's Pemmican

Figure 4–14 This romanticized view of the Battle of Seven Oaks (see page 146) shows Semple and his army of twenty-eight colonists taking a brave stand against the Métis. How does the event shown here compare with the description of the battle on page 146?

Proclamation two years earlier. A month later, Grant and a party of Métis arrived at the Red River Colony. They were better armed and trained in military discipline this time, and they firmly believed they had more claim to the area than recently arrived colonists. Grant, an intelligent, well-educated leader, was also an employee of the NWC. Semple and his underlings, however, regarded all Métis as inferior, because of their mixed ancestry. He decided that such people would only understand brute force.

Late in the day, Semple and twenty-eight men rode out to confront the Métis, who were approaching the colonists' settlement. The Métis split into two groups, one in front of the colonists, one behind—a strategic move that escaped Semple's attention. Within fifteen minutes, Semple and twenty of his men, but only one Métis, were killed. This skirmish, which was later called the "Battle of Seven Oaks," turned the simmering dispute between the HBC and its colonists, and the NWC and the Métis, into a full-scale conflict.

Once again, the colonists retreated to Jack River House. Once again, the colony was destroyed. While the situation at Red River deteriorated, Selkirk travelled west from Montreal to visit his colony for the first time. He had hired a group of ninety-five Swiss mercenaries to accompany him, planning to offer them land to settle. On the way, he met the recently released Macdonell, who told him of the Battle of Seven Oaks. Angered, Selkirk moved west with his troops, seized the NWC depot of Fort William, and descended on the Red River. He took military control of the area. Protected by the Swiss soldiers, the colonists started over again for a third time.

In the spring of 1817, Selkirk made a treaty with the local Ojibwa and Cree nations, gaining possession of the Red River Valley along both the Red River and the Assiniboine River. Selkirk's payment, for what amounted to a lease, was 100 pounds of tobacco a year. By the time Selkirk left the area in the fall of 1817, he believed he had settled the many disputes between the colonists and the Métis and the NWC.

When Selkirk returned to London in late 1817, he was confronted by a deluge of lawsuits arising from the actions of his employees in the Red River. For the next three years, he battled the NWC in the courts. Worn out by this litigation, he died in the spring of 1820, just short of his forty-ninth birthday.

Figure 4–15 Robert Semple

THE MERGER OF THE HBC AND THE NWC

The conflict between the North West Company and the Hudson's Bay Company over Lord Selkirk's Red River Colony was part of a larger struggle for commercial control of the Northwest. By 1820, however, both companies were suffering financially. The lawsuits over the Red River Colony dragged on for three years in the British courts, and at great expense. Moreover, the 200-year-old fur trade was rapidly depleting its resource base—there were not enough furs in the Northwest to justify full-scale operations by both companies. Profits were shrinking.

In 1821, the HBC and the NWC decided that the only way to survive was to merge their companies into one. A new company was formed— The Hudson's Bay Company—with 100 shares. The NWC partners controlled fifty-five shares, and the HBC controlled forty-five shares. The British parliament passed legislation that gave the new company control over Rupert's Land and extended the trading monopoly enjoyed by the old HBC. In fact, the legislation extended both the landholdings and the monopoly to west of the Rocky Mountains. This gave the new HBC control of more than half of the territory of modern Canada.

While the share distribution seemed to favour NWC partners, the HBC had no intention of giving up control of the new company. It was still cheaper and more efficient to ship furs out of the Northwest by the Hudson Bay route. The old NWC company route—via Fort William to Montreal—was rarely

Figure 4–16 This sketch of a Cree family was done in the 1820s, just after the merger of the HBC and NWC. The HBC relied on the skill of the Cree extensively after the 1821 merger. The iron pot is probably a new household item, and the tobacco would have been traded for furs.

used after the merger. By 1825, the Montreal fur partners from the old NWC had sold their shares in the new company back to the HBC.

As is often the case when companies merge, the HBC decided to reduce its workforce after 1821. As a result, the Native peoples became even more important to the success of the operation. In many regions of the Northwest, the HBC continued to rely on the knowledge and cooperation of the Native peoples—not just as trappers, but as translators, guides, and map-makers. They also built, repaired, and paddled the canoes, which continued to be used for lighter hauls. If the HBC's delivery system of pemmican failed, it turned to the Cree to supply meat. At the posts, Native women and young people—family members of Native traders—pitched in to help a downsized staff. During the summer months, a post could employ as few as two HBC clerks, but there were still plenty of chores, including gardening, tending the livestock, and chopping wood. Unfortunately, very little has been written about such contributions, but they were nonetheless important.

At the same time as it was reorganizing its operations, the HBC also appointed a new head. His name was George Simpson, and he was a Scottish sugar broker. Simpson knew very little about furs when he arrived in Montreal in 1820, but he did know how to run a trading company. In 1821, he was named Governor of the HBC's Northern Department—

Figure 4–17 Simpson was a blend of the new and the old. A "hands-on" businessman long before it became a trend, he was also an old-fashioned boss.

Cuthbert Grant and George Simpson

Although he has been overshadowed by Louis Riel, the first acknowledged leader of the Métis was actually Cuthbert Grant. He provided strong direction for his people during the first half of the nineteenth century.

Grant was born in 1793. His mother, a Métis, and his father, a Nor'wester, sent him to Montreal and Scotland to be educated. Upon returning to the Northwest, Grant started working for the NWC as a trader and clerk at about the time the first Selkirk colonists arrived. Fluent in both English and French, he quickly became a leader of the Métis and a rising star in the NWC. Grant quickly saw that European settlers could come to dominate the Red River, and he was instrumental in formulating the NWC-Métis policy to harass the Selkirk settlers. After the Battle of Seven Oaks, he was arrested and sent to Montreal to face several murder charges, but he was acquitted.

Returning to the Red River, he resumed his place as leader of his people.

Grant was soft-spoken, but large and powerful—he was able to persuade almost anyone to see things his way. It did not hurt that he was also handsome and courteous. This combination of characteristics made him the most prominent person in the Red River when George Simpson arrived in 1821. Simpson knew that he needed to get along with the Métis, but he also knew he could not employ Grant in the HBC. The Selkirk colonists still resented Grant for his role at the Battle of Seven Oaks.

With typical ingenuity, Simpson made Grant "Warden of the Plains." The position provided Grand with an annual salary of £200 and a grant of land on White Horse Plains, near the Red River Settlement. In return, he was expected to enforce the HBC's trading monopoly among the Métis. In fact, Grant played a number of roles. He was the Captain of the Hunt for decades; he used his medical knowledge to treat the sick; he allowed his home to be used as a school; and he policed the area, acting as both magistrate and sheriff. Simpson also relied on Grant to keep American traders out of the Red River area—a job he carried out with tact and force. In addition, Grant made sure that the bison hunt was protected against encroachment by other Plains nations, and he fought a number of battles with the Sioux.

By the 1840s, Grant's time as leader of his people was passing. Many young Métis resented his close association with the HBC, whose trade monopoly was despised. By 1849 Grant had lost all control over the younger Métis, and the HBC had abolished the post of Warden of the Plains. Grant retired to his farm, where he died in 1851 after falling off his horse.

he was actually in charge of all HBC operations in North America. Simpson was a dynamic man who took a hands-on approach to management. He refused to run the HBC from behind a desk. Instead, he spent much of his forty-year tenure as Governor travelling throughout the territory he controlled. Between 1821 and 1829, Simpson criss-crossed Rupert's Land, from Hudson Bay to the Pacific Coast, and everywhere in between. Typically, he would set off in the spring and spend the summer and autumn travelling to as many trading posts as he could. Simpson preferred to arrive without warning. Traders and Factors would be grilled unmercifully for hours if the post did not measure up to his exacting standards. Simpson was called the "Little Emperor" by his workers, because of his small stature and **autocratic** manner. In 1829, he left for England on an extended leave of absence, tired out from his exertions of the preceding decade.

Simpson returned to the Red River Colony in 1830. Although now a man in his forties, he brought with

autocratic: in a manner suggesting absolute power

Figure 4–18 Frances Simpson

ter of 1831–32. With few people to talk to, Simpson began to note the faults in virtually every HBC employee at the settlement. He recorded his views in a document known as the "Character Book." Two examples of his observations follow. One colleague was described as

> exceedingly vain, a great Egoist, swallows the grossest flattery, is easily cajoled, rarely speaks the truth, indeed, I would not put him upon Oath …

Another was

> a frothy, trifling, conceited man who would starve in any other country and is perfectly useless here: fancies, or rather attempts to pass himself off as a clever fellow, a man of taste, talents and refinement; to none of which I need scarcely say he has the smallest pretension.

In a letter to a friend, Simpson was no kinder:

> I could fill volumes with the details of the most Vindictive and Malicious intrigue that ever entered the mind of man which I have witnessed since I came here. In short, I am sick and tired of Red River and would be off tomorrow if I currently could …

him his new, 18-year-old bride, Frances. Simpson, who had married at Red River, and had several children of Métis heritage, did not want his new bride to meet his family members. They were packed off before the Simpsons arrived at Fort Garry. Once installed, the new Mrs. Simpson announced that she would not socialize with the Métis relatives of HBC employees. Racism aside, in a small community like the Red River Colony, this was a foolhardy move, and the Simpsons soon found themselves socially isolated. One person Frances did entertain was the wife of the Reverend Cockran, who, as Frances noted, "shines … when talking of elbow grease and the scouring of pots and pans."

This isolation took its toll on George Simpson during the hard win-

In the spring of 1832, Simpson's infant son died, and he and his wife left the Red River the next year for England. When Simpson returned to British North America, he settled in Montreal, where he and Frances found society more to their liking. Knighted in 1841 for his services to the HBC, Simpson continued to travel far and wide throughout his empire. He died in 1860.

THE RED RIVER SETTLEMENT, 1821–1860

After 1821, peace came to the Red River Settlement. For the next forty years, it was a remarkably stable, close-knit community. The settlement included the Métis, the country-born, Scottish and Swiss colonists, and HBC employees. This was an isolated community, with very little contact with the outside world. The inhabitants were, of necessity, self-sufficient. In this respect, the colony resembled Upper Canada in the earlier nineteenth century.

In 1821, the population was evenly divided between the Métis and country-born, and the European settlers. As time went on, more and more of the population was of mixed descent. By the end of the period,

more than 80 percent of the population was of mixed descent. Because it was primarily a farming community, the birth rate was high, and families often had more than ten children. As people matured and started families of their own, the population began to grow rapidly from the 1840s onwards.

The economy of the Red River Settlement was built around the needs of the HBC. The Scottish settlers grew many of the crops and sold their produce to the HBC. This supplied the HBC with food for its network of fur-trading posts throughout the Northwest. The Métis also farmed, but they contributed to the economy primarily through the bison hunt: they supplied pemmican to the HBC, as well as buffalo robes

Figure 4–19 Upper Fort Garry in the later nineteenth century

The Red River Cart

The Red River cart was unique to the Canadian prairies. It was built entirely of wood, using simple hand tools and not a single nail. It had one axle, two large wheels, and a wooden box that could hold people or goods. In short, it was not a luxurious vehicle.

The Red River cart was capable of carrying loads of up to 550 kilograms, and it was usually pulled by a team of two oxen, which drivers preferred to horses—oxen were slower than horses, but they could pull more

Figure 4–20 Below, Winnipeg's Main Street, to the right, the Red River cart

weight. Because of prairie dust in the summer, the axle was never greased. As a result, the Red River cart made an incredible amount of noise as the wheels turned, earning it the nickname the "Northwest fiddle." One eyewitness noted the effect:

It is like no sound ever heard in all your life, and makes your blood run cold. To hear a thousand of those wheels groaning and creaking at one time is a sound never to be forgotten—it is simply hellish.

Because of the dust, carts did not travel in single file, but side by side. A large number of carts travelling together could stretch 10-kilometres across as they traversed the prairie. Because the cart was so simply built, it was also easily repaired, making it the dominant vehicle on the prairies until the arrival of the train in the 1880s.

and other goods to the other settlers. The country-born tended to see themselves as superior to the Métis because they held typically **white-collar** jobs—as clerks, teachers, magistrates, and store owners. The law was upheld by the HBC, who

appointed the Recorder of Rupert's Land, in other words, the chief justice for the area. Despite their different backgrounds, the inhabitants of the settlement got along fairly well.

However, a disagreement eventually arose over the free trade of furs. It was a crime in the Red River Settlement for anyone to trade in furs or other goods because it violated the HBC monopoly, which had been upheld in the 1821 merger with the NWC. The Métis started fighting for the right to trade furs in the 1840s and, in 1849, four Métis fur traders were charged with illegal trading. When the trial began, the courtroom was packed and 300 Métis surrounded the building. The presiding judge, Adam Thom, was known to be hostile to the French-speaking Métis. When the time came to charge the jury, Thom said the jury had no choice but to return a verdict of guilty, which it did—to the dismay of the angry crowd. The foreman, however, recommended mercy for the four offenders. Thom quickly agreed, and ordered no sentence. While the HBC felt it had made its case, the Métis proclaimed: *Le commerce est libre! Vive la liberté!* ("Business is open! Long live freedom!")" The HBC monopoly had been broken.

A Self-Sufficient Community

Because of its isolation from the rest of the continent, the Red River Settlement fostered a sense of self-reliance among its inhabitants. Crop failures meant real hardship, and ordinary foods, such as fruits and vegetables, were rare. One settler later recalled seeing a ripe tomato for the first time in fifteen years in 1834. There was little variation in diet, especially in winter, when pemmican was the staple. Windmills provided power for grinding grain and pumping water. There were eighteen windmills and several water mills in Red River by the late 1840s.

Women and men worked side by side, though a woman's life was probably harder. Women helped in the grain harvest, using sickles to cut the wheat by hand. They also processed all the wool used in the community, including the cleaning, carding, and spinning, tasks that took a great deal of time. Once the

white-collar: referring to clerical or professional workers (as opposed to farmers or other labourers)

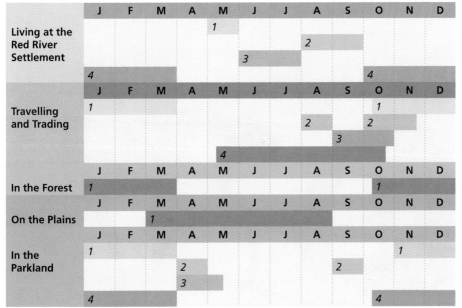

Living at the Red River Settlement
1. Planting vegetable and grain crops
2. Harvesting and haying
3. Cultivating crops and looking after animals
4. Making items for household, including carts

Travelling and Trading
1. Fur trading
2. Trading pemmican to HBC and Red River settlers
3. Trading farm produce to HBC
4. Travelling to York Factory and other destinations

In the Forest
1. Hunting and trapping

On the Plains
1. Organizing and conducting the annual buffalo hunt

In the Parkland
1. Fishing at the lake
2. Hunting geese
3. Sugaring
4. Trapping; occasionally buffalo hunting

Figure 4–21 The seasonal activities of the Métis in Red River

bannock: a kind of flatbread

day's labour was over, the men rested, but the women could not—they had to bake the **bannock** for the next day's meals. In addition, families were large. Many women had as many as fifteen children, despite the shortage of health care.

The Red River Colony was also socially isolated, and residents had a small-town mentality. Like other small communities, it was a place where secrets were hard to keep because everyone knew everyone else. If someone behaved improperly, the news spread quickly. Moreover, gossip must have been a constant temptation. In one instance, the consequences were quite serious. In 1850, Anne Pelly, the wife of the community's physician, accused

Sarah Ballenden and Captain Christopher Foss of having an affair. Prejudice may have been a motive, because Ballenden was a Métis, and already married to Chief Factor John Ballenden. However, no one was more aghast at the accusation than Captain Foss, who sued Pelly for defamatory conspiracy. When the case came to trial, Ballenden and Foss testified they were just good friends. Judge Adam Thom, the Recorder of Rupert's Land, agreed, fining Pelly and three others 400 in damages. However, the damage done to Ballenden's reputation was so great that she could no longer live in the settlement without people whispering behind her back. She decided to move to Scotland.

Figure 4–22 The Red River Settlement had a typically small-town atmosphere. How would you like to be a newcomer in this community?

1. Why was the bison hunt so important to Métis culture? How did the Rules of the Hunt help to shape Métis society?

2. Lord Selkirk can be said to have been an "unrealistic idealist." Find evidence to support or refute this claim.

3. Was conflict over the Red River Settlement inevitable? Provide reasons for your answer.

4. How did the old HBC retain control over the new HBC after the merger with the NWC?

5. Describe the attitude of George and Frances Simpson towards the Native peoples and Métis. How were their views racist? What impact did these views have on the Simpsons? On the Red River Settlement?

6. How was the free-trade trial of 1849 a victory for the Métis?

7. What roles did women play in the daily life of the Red River Settlement? How does this compare to life for women colonists in the "wilderness" of Upper Canada?

CHANGES: THE RED RIVER SETTLEMENT BETWEEN 1860 AND 1870

The decade of the 1860s brought many profound changes to the Northwest. More people immigrated to the area; Canada became a dominion; and the HBC started to decline. Perhaps the most noticeable change was the arrival of Canadians moving west into the Red River Valley. The rapidly rising population in **Canada West** during the 1850s meant that most of the land suitable for agriculture had been settled and cleared. By 1860, many Canadians were looking for new areas to settle and farm. The Red River Valley, with its rich soils and small population, was an appealing prospect.

Most of the new Canadian settlers to the Red River were Protestant and members of the Orange Order, a violently anti-French, anti-Catholic movement. Not surprisingly, they were prejudiced against the Métis. Not only were the Métis French-speaking and Catholic, they were also viewed as inferior because of their bicultural heritage. Although they were small in number, the presence of the Protestants increased tensions in the Red River Settlement.

One of the first immigrants to arrive in 1860 was Dr. John Christian Schultz. Schultz had never completed his medical degree and had no interest in practising medicine. Instead he wanted to start several businesses. He opened a general store, took over the only newspaper in the settlement, the *NorWester*, and championed Canadian interests

Canada West: Upper Canada, after the Act of Union in 1841

Figure 4–23 John Schultz

dominion: a country that rules itself

diversify: to branch out

by agitating against the Métis. By the late 1860s, he had organized a small group of supporters into the Canadian Party, which he hoped would eventually gain control of the settlement. Schultz used the *NorWester* as a platform for his anti-Métis views. In numerous editorials, he made statements that under current Canadian human rights legislation would be regarded as promoting hatred. Statements such as the following led to increasing tensions and uncertainty for the Métis:

[The Métis should] either be driven from the country, or kept as cart drivers.

[The Métis], the indolent and the careless, like the native tribes of the country, will fall back before the march of superior intelligence.

Economic problems during the 1860s also contributed to rising tensions at Red River. Crop failures were frequent, the bison were disappearing from the prairies (see

Chapter 3), and the cash-strapped HBC was losing interest in the area. An additional complication was that the Métis, although long-time farmers, had never made a legal claim to their territory. In the tradition of the Red River Settlement, all employees of the HBC were entitled to take up farmland and live on it after three years. On the surface, this posed no problem for the Métis, who believed that if a person cleared land and farmed it, he or she had a right to it. This attitude would lead to problems in the late 1860s.

Canada Purchases Rupert's Land

When the Fathers of Confederation drew up the British North America Act in London in 1866 and 1867, they included provisions for the eventual admission of all colonies in British North America and for the acquisition of Rupert's Land from the HBC. John A. Macdonald and D'Arcy McGee, in particular, were extremely interested in creating a **dominion** of Canada which would stretch from sea to sea. The HBC was also interested in relinquishing control of Rupert's Land. As the 1860s had progressed, the HBC had found it difficult to maintain control over such a vast territory. More and more settlers were moving into the Northwest, and the fur trade was declining. The HBC realized that if it were going to survive as a business, it would have to focus on and **diversify** its commercial operations and drop its administrative duties to the territory.

Between 1867 and 1868, the Canadian government and the HBC began negotiations to transfer control of Rupert's Land. The HBC did not consult the people who lived in the Red River Settlement, and it

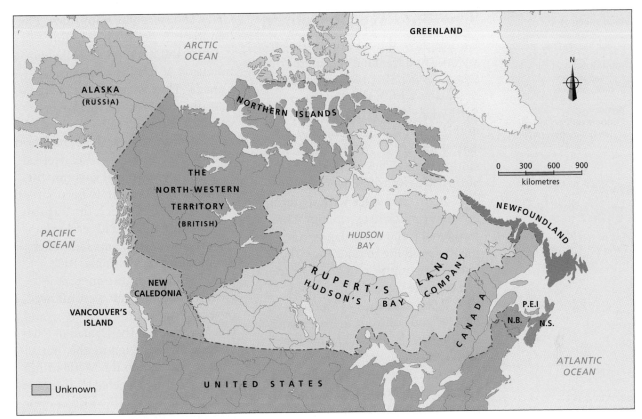

Figure 4–24 Rupert's Land and the North-Western Territory were joined together in 1869.

paid no heed to their special interests. Rumours of the impending deal circulated in the Red River Settlement and everyone felt ill at ease and angry, especially the Métis. The HBC and the Canadian government reached an agreement in November 1869. The Canadian government received title to Rupert's Land, which it joined with the North-Western Territory, and renamed them as the North-West Territories. Canada doubled in size. The HBC received a cash payment of 300 000 ($1.5 million), 2.8 million hectares of prairie farmland, and the right to continue the fur trade, although without the monopoly it had previously enjoyed.

Both the Canadian government and the HBC knew they would make this deal long before negotiations concluded. In 1868, Dominion of Canada surveyors had arrived in the Red River area to begin laying out the grids of townships. The surveyors operated on the assumption that the current occupants of the Northwest did not own their property, and the surveyors did not recognize the seigneurial pattern of farms that had existed along the Red and Assiniboine rivers since the 1820s. That same year, Louis Riel returned to the Red River. Born in 1844, he was the son of Louis Riel, Sr., who had been leader of the Métis people until his death in 1864. The younger Riel was a literate and well-educated lawyer, and he was fluent in both French and English. Like his father, and Cuthbert Grant before him, Riel was an excellent orator. Although only twenty-four when he returned to the settlement, he soon assumed the role of leader of his people.

The Red River Rebellion

During 1869, the actions of the surveyors—and the **land speculators** who followed them—raised the level of tension within the Red River Settlement. The settlers were angry at the HBC for proceeding with the sale of Rupert's Land without consulting them. They were also angry at the surveyors, who were laying out square townships with no regard for their traditional strip lots. They wondered if the Canadian government was trying to take away their land. That summer, in an effort to preserve the rights of his people, Riel organized bands of Métis to observe and confront the surveyors.

One week later, he formed the Métis National Committee to fight for Métis concerns about their land. One of its first tasks was to greet the new governor of the North-West Territories, William McDougall. The welcome was not warm. Members of the committee told McDougall to go back to Ottawa because they intended to govern themselves. Next, several Métis under Riel's command occupied Fort

Garry and seized its **munitions.** The Red River Rebellion had begun.

Riel and his supporters had no intention of rebelling against Canada. They wanted only to ensure that the people of the Red River would retain their rights and traditions after the region was transferred to Canadian authority. Riel decided to set up a **provisional government** to maintain order and to negotiate an agreement by which the territory surrounding the Red River Settlement could enter Confederation as the province of Manitoba. Riel feared, with justification, that if Governor McDougall were allowed to take charge of the area, he would give members of the Canadian Party all the power and ignore the Métis. This would lead to the Métis losing all their rights. Angered by recent events, the Métis of Red River drew up a List of Rights (see page 159).

Riel was determined to work to protect the rights of not only the Métis, but of all groups in the settlement. However, he feared civil war because the Canadian Party was already armed and prepared to attack the Métis. In early December, Riel

Figure 4–25 Louis Riel and the provisional government

The Métis List of Rights and the Charter of Rights and Freedoms

The Métis List of Rights is an important Canadian document. Here are those rights, as agreed to by the convention of the Red River Settlement. These resolutions were adopted at a meeting held in Fort Garry on Wednesday, December 1, 1869.

1. That the people have the right to elect their own Legislature

2. That the Legislature have the power to pass all laws local to the Territory over the veto of the Executive by a two-thirds vote.

3. That no act of the Dominion Parliament (local to the territory) be binding on the people until sanctioned [approved] by the Legislature of the Territory.

4. That all Sheriffs, Magistrates, Constables, School Commissioners, and so on, be elected by the people.

5. A free Homestead and preemption Land Law.

6. That a portion of the public lands be appropriated for the benefit of Schools, the building of Bridges, Roads and Public Buildings.

7. That it be guaranteed to connect Winnipeg by Rail with the nearest line of Railroad, within a term of five years; the land grant to be subject to the Local Legislature.

8. That for the term of four years all Military, Civil and Municipal expenses be paid out of Dominion funds.

9. That the Military be composed of the inhabitants now existing in the Territory.

10. That the English and French languages be common in the Legislature and Courts, and that all Public Documents and Acts of the Legislature be published in both languages.

11. That the Judge of the Supreme Court speak the English and French languages.

12. That Treaties be concluded and ratified between the Dominion Government and the several tribes of Indians in the Territory to ensure peace on the frontier.

13. That we have a fair and full representation in the Canadian Parliament.

14. That all privileges, customs and usages existing at the time of transfer be respected.

Excerpts from the Charter of Rights and Freedoms

The Charter of Rights and Freedoms was entrenched as part of the Constitution of Canada under the terms of the Constitutional Act, 1982. Here are some excerpts.

....

WHAT DO YOU THINK?

1. How are these two documents similar? Dissimilar? Discuss in a group or with a partner.

2. Why do you suppose the provisions of the List of Rights are so precisely stated?

habeas corpus: requiring that the lawfulness of a person's arrest or detention be investigated by a judge or court

Fundamental Freedoms

2. Everyone has the following fundamental freedoms: (a) freedom of conscience and religion; (b) freedom of thought, belief, opinion and expression, including freedom of the press and other media of communication; (c) freedom of peaceful assembly; and (d) freedom of association.

Democratic Rights

3. Every citizen of Canada has the right to vote in an election of members of the House of Commons or of a legislative assembly and to be qualified for membership therein.

Legal Rights

7. Everyone has the right to life, liberty and security of the person and the right not to be deprived thereof except in accordance with the principles of fundamental justice.

8. Everyone has the right to be secure against unreasonable search or seizure.

9. Everyone has the right not to be arbitrarily detained or imprisoned.

10. Everyone has the right on arrest or detention (a) to be informed promptly of the reasons therefore; (b) to retain and instruct counsel without delay and to be informed of that right; and (c) to have the validity of the detention determined by way of **habeas corpus** and to be released if the detention is not lawful.

12. Everyone has the right not to be subjected to any cruel and unusual treatment or punishment.

Equality Rights

15. (1) Every individual is equal before and under the law and has the right to the equal protection and equal benefit of the law without discrimination and, in particular, without discrimination based on race, national or ethnic origin, colour, religion, sex, age or mental or physical disability.

Official Languages of Canada

16. (1) English and French are the official languages of Canada and have equality of status and equal rights and privileges as to their use in all institutions of the Parliament and government of Canada.

led a party of armed Métis to Schultz's home, which was used as headquarters for the Canadian Party. Schultz's house was surrounded, and he and forty-eight of his followers were taken to Fort Garry. Riel now declared that he was prepared to negotiate with the Canadian government. Prime Minister John A. Macdonald, however, refused to recognize Riel, let alone negotiate with him. Macdonald said:

> Smith goes to carry an olive branch. We must not think of military force until peaceable means have been exhausted. Should these miserable half-breeds not disband, they must be put down.

Undaunted, the provisional government met to draft a proposal for the creation of the province of Manitoba, which Métis representatives could take to Ottawa.

In the meantime, Schultz had escaped from Fort Garry and plotted to free the other prisoners. But before Schultz could attack, his raiders clashed with the Métis, and several of his followers were arrested yet again. One of these prisoners was Thomas Scott, the most belligerent member of the Canadian Party. In prison, Scott loudly publicized his anti-Métis views, verbally and physically abused his guards, and threatened the life of Louis Riel. On March 4, he was executed by firing squad by Riel's provisional government.

Many people in the Settlement regretted the execution of Thomas Scott, but many also believed the crisis had passed. On March 9, Riel formally proclaimed that the trouble had subsided. A few weeks later, the Ottawa delegation departed in an optimistic mood—they were on their way to negotiate the creation of the province of Manitoba. Unfortunately for Riel and the Métis, Schultz had also left the Northwest for Ontario. Arriving in early April, he began to publicize his views on the Métis and the execution of Thomas Scott. Gradually the Orange Order created a mythology around Thomas Scott— he was transformed into a Protestant martyr who had been cruelly murdered by the Métis. The circumstances of Scott's execution fuelled this interpretation. Although the six members of the firing squad had taken careful aim together, they did

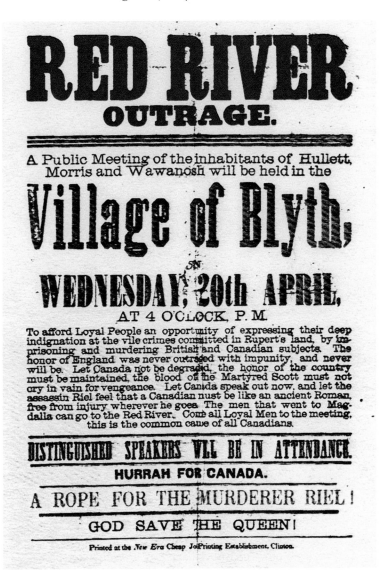

Figure 4–26 An anti-Riel poster announcing a meeting in 1870

not kill Scott instantaneously. The squad director, Francois Guillemette, had to step forward and deliver one more bullet to Scott's head. Cries for justice and retribution soon reached government ears in Ottawa.

The delegates from Red River had a hard time getting recognition from Macdonald's government. Their case was finally heard in late April, and the government agreed to the terms for Manitoba's admission to Confederation. Macdonald refused to allow provincial control of public lands, but he did offer a compromise: a grant of 200 000 hectares of land for the Métis, in recognition of their aboriginal title. On May 2, legislation confirming Manitoba's admission was passed by the House of Commons.

Macdonald was also determined to show his support for the calls demanding justice from Ontario. He dispatched a force of 1200 to Winnipeg under the command of Colonel Wolseley, with the instructions that they keep the peace until the transfer of power to a new provincial government could be made. He also made it clear that they were not to treat Riel or his followers as being a legitimate government. When Wolseley's force arrived in late August, Riel had wisely fled the area—fearing, with justification, that his life was in danger. Eventually, all members of the provisional government were granted amnesty, with the exception of Riel. The Canadian government decreed that he be banished from Canada for a period of five years. The architect of Manitoba departed quietly, and spent the next fifteen years in exile in the United States.

Figure 4–27 These troops have arrived too late to "restore order" to the Red River area. Although the troops are clambering up the hill in great anticipation, Riel has already fled.

ACTIVITIES

1. Did immigrants from Canada drastically change the composition of the population of the Red River Settlement between 1860 and 1870? Why?

2. How was the Orange Order racist? Why would politicians like Macdonald be influenced by such an organization?

3. What did Canada need in order to acquire Rupert's Land? How did this action precipitate a rebellion?

4. Was Riel's provisional government legal? With a partner, discuss this question and share your findings with the class.

5. Evaluate key incidents of the Red River Rebellion. Consider the execution of Thomas Scott, the Métis List of Rights, and the actions of John Shultz and Macdonald's government. Refer to Figure 4–26 and then create a poster that you think presents a fair view of Riel.

6. Did Sir John A. Macdonald demonstrate a lack of understanding about the Northwest? Explain your answer, with reasons.

CONCLUSION

The Northwest experienced many changes during the nineteenth century. The ancestral home of many Native peoples, it was also rival territory for the Hudson's Bay Company and the North West Company. By 1800, contact between the European fur traders and the Native peoples had led to the emergence of a new people—the Métis.

In 1812, Irish and Scottish settlers came to the Red River area, the region where the Métis had settled. They had been brought there through an arrangement of the HBC. Conflict quickly erupted over entitlement to land, and the Métis became angry when the HBC tried to stop them from selling pemmi-can to the NWC. However, by the 1820s, fur resources had been depleted in the Northwest, and the two companies were forced to merge.

As the century progressed, the Métis and the later settlers lived together peacefully. By the 1860s, however, an influx of settlers increased tensions. After Confederation, the Canadian government negotiated to acquire Rupert's Land from the HBC. The Métis, never consulted, adopted a List of Rights to protect the rights of all citizens in the Red River Settlement. In 1869, Louis Riel led the Red River Rebellion, but John A. Macdonald's government ignored their demands. However, the region became the province of Manitoba in 1870.

SUMMARY ACTIVITIES

1. With a partner or in a group, do a PMI on the effect of the HBC on the history of the Northwest. You should consider social, political and economic factors. Share your findings with the rest of the class.

2. In what ways did the development of Métis culture affect the development of the Northwest? Think about the origin of various aspects of Métis culture and why most people in the Northwest were Métis by the 1860s.

3. You are a resident of the Red River Settlement. It is March 5, 1870, and Thomas Scott was executed yesterday. In a letter, poem, essay or drawing, relate your feelings about this event. You could take the viewpoint of a Métis supporter of Louis Riel, or a Selkirk settler, or a Canadian who was a member of the Orange Order.

ON YOUR OWN

1. Pick one of the people identified as important in this chapter. Do some library research and prepare a biographical report or essay on this person's contributions to the development of the Northwest. Why is this person important? Present your report to the class.

2. Do some more research into Métis needlecraft. What influences shaped this art form? Is it still alive today? Prepare a report on this topic and include some photos of present-day examples.

5 THE PRAIRIES 1870–1896

LEARNING OUTCOMES

In this chapter, you will focus on Canada's western expansion and its impact on the Métis and the Native peoples. By the end of the chapter, you will

- identify the impact of Canadian policy on Métis settlement and self-government

- critique the Canadian government's treaties with the Native peoples and suggest alternatives

- analyze the impact of the National Policy on different parts of the country

- describe the development of the CPR under the Macdonald and Mackenzie governments

- describe and analyze the causes and outcome of the Northwest Rebellion

- explain symbolism in paintings and monuments

Life in New Iceland

Between 1873 and 1876, many people from Iceland emigrated to Canada, driven from their homeland by a series of volcanic eruptions. They docked at Quebec, and then eventually moved west, some to Winnipeg, but the majority to the western shore of Lake Winnipeg. This area became known as "New Iceland" and was then part of the North-West Territories.

The story of the Icelanders has much in common with the stories of other immigrant groups, yet it is also unique. This Window offers of glimpse at the challenges faced by these settlers. The true accounts that follow have been excerpted from newspaper articles and journal entries, or from the personal reminiscences of the people of New Iceland.

This account describes the situation in Iceland around the time of the volcanic eruptions:

The accounts just received by the last mail from Iceland assume a far more serious impact than the first news have led one to anticipate. A resident of Bardardal ... writes: "What fearful times we have had of it north here this winter! First we were visited by earthquakes, which in some places, terminated all but fatally, and then came the eruption, with its concomitant dust-gloom and fall of ashes..." On March 29 the fall of ashes was at its thickest; and all that day, although it was bright and sunny, the people spent in absolute pitch darkness ... The farmers have fled out of the ash-covered countrysides with their cattle in quest of pastures not yet destroyed ..."
–*The London Times*, May 20, 1876

This editorial describes the arrival of the Icelanders. Note how the editorial calls them a "valuable addition" to the province.

The first installment of these people arrived on the International last evening. There are in all 285 souls in which number is included 216 adults, 60 families and 80 men. They are a smart looking, intelligent, and excellent people, and are a most valuable addition to the population of our Province. Their Icelandic experience, supplemented with some experience with our mode of life, is quite sufficient to give them that peculiar off-hand manner of overcoming obstacles, and an energy of character, which will ensure their success here, and make their settlement, in a very few years, one of the best in their province ... It is understood that the Dominion Government are to make an advance to the Icelanders, to assist them in settling themselves.
–*Manitoba Free Press*, October 12, 1875

The following are the reminiscences of Simon Simonson, one of the first settlers. Simonson mentions Sygtryggur Jonasson, who was the first Icelander to emigrate to Canada (in 1872), and the founder of New Iceland.

The first group of Icelanders prepare to make their home in Canada.

About midnight the people were dumped out of the wagons, under the trees, in darkness such as I have scarcely seen the like. We knew not where to go, and had the sick children on our hands. At last, after a long and distressing wait, with the people milling about in the mud, two of our countrymen came, bringing a faint light, and directed us to a hovel which was under construction, and at the building where a few Icelanders had worked. Tired and hungry, we arrived at these miserable quarters. There was some food on the table, but only the strongest secured this, while the weak and the sick received nothing. Each thought of self, and no one else. I could not bring myself to act like a wild beast.

Sygtryggur's plan was to have a communal table, with all alike sharing expenses. His system, however, did not do so well, and there were those who pilfered supplies ... [W]e had to wait for our bed-comforters several days. All this was hard on the children, who were continuously taking ill. As for the men, they were unused to the work, and all were ignorant of the language. Most bitter of all, for me, it was to see my little Gudrun suffering intensely and to be unable to ease her suffering. She kept nothing down. There was little milk, and what little there was, was not good. About nine days from the time she became ill, God took her to himself ... Gudrun was a lovely and pleasant child, well developed for her years, and appeared to be endowed with good intelligence. I shall mourn the loss of my loved one as long as I live.

–Icelandic Canadian, Winter 1946 issue

This letter was found in the Manitoba Archives. It refers to the smallpox epidemic of December 1876, which killed many Icelanders as well as many Native people.

Sir: I have the honour to inform you that in consequence of the disease of smallpox being greatly and virulently present in the Icelandic and Indian settlements on the west side of Lake Winnipeg it has been found expedient in order to as much as possible to isolate and repress the spread of the pestilence to prohibit traffic southward eastward and westward of the line of demarcation ... as well as communication with the area from northern points ... Frank G. Beecham, Justice of the Peace for the District of Keewatin."

The Icelandic settlement, known as "Gimli," was described in this article in the Manitoba Free Press *on September 17, 1876. Note the contrast between the harsh landscape and the interior of people's homes mentioned at the end of the excerpt.*

Gimli is about one-and-one-half-miles [2.4 kilometres] long by half-a-mile [.8 kilometres] broad. There is but one street in it, which, running between two rows of fences, half-cleared grass and with stumps of felled trees cropping up, is more like a cattle-track than a street, but is not as muddy as the main street of Winnipeg after a heavy fall of rain. On each side of the road are the houses of the inhabitants, removed from the street some little distance. Most of them are logs and floored with logs, the doors low, the windows small, and, as far as could be seen, without any chimney, so the air and light are excluded to a great extent. But in many of these

close atmospheres and squalid cottages were to be found little libraries of from 30 to 40 books. A few of the houses are quite roomy and more comfortable.

–*Manitoba Free Press*, September 17, 1876

These oral histories of Gimli have been handed down to us by Ted Kristjanson and David Arnason, former community members.

Ted Kristjanson
Sailing to beat old hell. That's George's Island with all the sailboats. They were brought down without the masts. The masts were always left out on the lake. These are no bigger than the skiffs that we used for fishing. Not a lot of room, but

you know what we had on those things? Up to 4000 pounds [1810 kilograms] of fish. There was nothing sticking out. No, you never thought nothing about it ... No, there was no more than this sticking out and you were out in the middle of the lake. Today I'd be scared unless I'm on a great big boat. No, we didn't have sense enough to be scared.

David Arnason
The Indians taught them how to fish, those Icelanders who thought they were the world's greatest fishermen. My great-grandfather, Captain Baldi Anderson (he was twelve when he came, gave himself the title captain and insisted on it until he died), soon after the arrival walked to the mouth of the Red River where an old Indian

Children pose outside their home in the 1880s.

woman taught him how to cut a hole in the ice, how to bait a hook to catch jackfish. She helped him catch fourteen big jacks, and he lugged them home to a family desperate for food. On the way back he followed a trail where bags of flour had leaked enough that he could scoop flour into his hat and his mother could make pancakes.

David Arnason

After the bleak and treeless sweep of Iceland's coast, those forests you could get lost in with a second's inattention must have been the most foreign thing. They came in October when the trees were stark and so much firewood. But what a flowering in the spring that followed that first awful winter: elm, oak, ash, spruce, cottonwood, poplar, willow, maple, birch, blackberry, pinchberry, chokecherry, thornberry, sandberry, hawthorn, elderberry, wild plum, sumac, cedar, balsam, fir. A catalogue of names their language had no need for, more greens than any language has words for.

A Cree woman teaches an Icelander how to fish in the Canadian North.

Ted Kristjanson

There's 220 hundred-pound [45.4 kilogram] boxes on the sleigh. I've figured it out. It took sometimes three teams to start it in the morning, but once the iron got warm— they've got iron runners, so it was a plowed trail—they just went by themselves. But to start them was the job. There was, say, 125 pounds [57 kilograms] in each box at least. That would make 15 or 16 tons. But once they got goin', it just ran by itself. But what an awful time to start it. See the loads? It's unbelievable, eh?

ACTIVITIES

1. Why did many people leave Iceland in the 1870s? Why do you suppose they chose Canada as a destination?

2. Contrast the report in the *Manitoba Free Press* (page 165) with the actual situation of the Icelanders when they arrived. Why are the reports so different?

3. How did the Icelanders adapt to their new home? What factors contributed to their success?

4. What did David Arnason mean when he said "more greens than any language has words for"?

GIVE ME A HOME MARKET FOR MY PRODUCE, AMONGST THE WELL PAID MECHANICS, EVERY TIME!

EGGS
BUTTER
WHEAT
CORN

UNDER THE NATIONAL POLICY.

WHERE ARE ALL MY OLD FRIENDS THE MECHANICS? TO WHOM CAN I SELL MY PRODUCE NOW?

FOR SALE

UNDER A FREE TRADE OR REVENUE TARIFF.

TIME LINE

1870	MANITOBA BECOMES A PROVINCE
	TREATY PROCESS WITH THE NATIVE PEOPLES OF THE NORTHWEST BEGINS
1871	CANADIAN PACIFIC RAILWAY IS FORMED
1872	SANDFORD FLEMING COMMISSIONS CANADIAN PACIFIC SURVEY
	"PACIFIC SCANDAL" ROCKS MACDONALD'S GOVERNMENT
1873	THE LAWS OF ST. LAURENT
	LIBERALS COME TO POWER UNDER ALEXANDER MACKENZIE
	NORTH WEST MOUNTED POLICE FORMED
1874	CYPRESS HILLS MASSACRE
1877	OTTAWA CONCLUDES TREATY PROCESS WITH THE NATIVE PEOPLES
1881	BUILDING OF THE CPR BEGINS
1885	CPR IS COMPLETED
	NORTHWEST REBELLION
	EXECUTION OF LOUIS RIEL

So far as we could see, they [the Native peoples] wished to have about two-thirds of the province. We ... told them that it was of no use for them to entertain any such ideas ... Whether they wished it or not, immigrants would come in and fill up this country.

—REPRESENTATIVE OF THE CANADIAN GOVERNMENT, JULY 1871

Settlement of the West was part of Macdonald's National Policy, and the reason behind the treaty process between the Native peoples and the Canadian government. What seems to be the government's view of the treaty process?

INTRODUCTION

In the wake of the Manitoba Act, the future looked bright for the Métis, but the promise soon dimmed. Many decided to leave their original territory near Red River and scattered across the prairies. Throughout the 1870s, the Métis would continue to feel threatened by many forces, such as the future Canadian Pacific Railway (CPR) and the steady stream of settlers from eastern Canada who came to build farms in the West. In 1885, the Métis and the Canadian government reached an impasse, which resulted in the Northwest Rebellion.

In this chapter, you will follow the story of the CPR, and the treaty process pursued by the Canadian government with the Native peoples of the prairies—two stories that are intertwined. Between 1871 and 1877, the government concluded seven treaties with the Native peoples, which gave Canada access to much of the land included in present-day Manitoba, Saskatchewan, and Alberta. As you are reading about this process, think about the consequences of these historical events.

THE MÉTIS FLEE WESTWARD

homesteader: a settler who had a place to live granted by the government

land speculator: someone who makes money by buying and selling land

The passing of the Manitoba Act in 1870 had been welcomed by the Métis. They made up the majority of people in the new province, and their rights seemed to be protected under the new legislation. The Manitoba Act made French and English the official languages of the province, and it provided for two education systems—Protestant and Roman Catholic. In addition, 1.4 million acres [566 580 hectares] of land were reserved for the Métis to use as farmland.

But the transition from settlement to province was not smooth. In the wake of the Red River Rebellion, Macdonald ordered troops into the area to keep the peace, but they did not act as peace agents. The Métis were brutalized almost as a matter of course. Many died as a result of the beatings they received. Although these actions were not officially condoned, the soldiers who engaged in violence were not punished for their actions.

Macdonald noted that:

> These impulsive Métis have got spoilt by the emeute [uprising] and must be kept down by a strong hand until they are swamped by the influx of settlers.

Moreover, the issue of land ownership was not straightforward. In order to gain title to the land that had been reserved for them, all settlers in Manitoba were required to have scrip, a piece of paper that was similar to money. Two kinds of scrip were issued to the Métis. Money scrip had a value of $160. This amount was based on the value of a quarter section of land, which was then worth $1 an acre [.405 hectares]. Money scrip was also convertible to

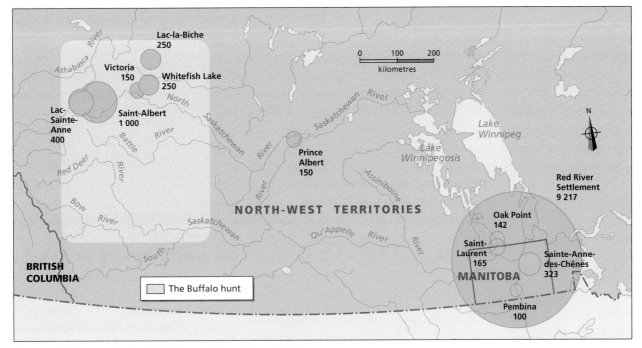

Figure 5–1 The population distribution of the Métis in 1870

cash to $160. Land scrip entitled a person to exchange the scrip for a **homesteader's** quarter-section land grant (160 acres, or 64.8 hectares).

Problems occurred, however, when **land speculators** arrived in the Red River Valley. They were successful in buying up almost all the scrip from the people who held it—usually for an amount far below the actual value of the land. Most Métis did not understand the value of the scrip because their traditional economy did not include money or deeds. The speculators could then use the scrip as **collateral** for much larger bank loans, which provided them with even more **investment capital**. For example, scrip to the value of $160 could be used to obtain a loan of as much as ten times that amount. The government of Manitoba often threatened the Métis with imprisonment if they did not turn over their scrip to the speculators.

As a result, many Métis left Manitoba in the early 1870s. They

gravitated to the Northwest, where they tried to recreate the culture they had enjoyed in the Red River settlement before 1869. Some Métis settled near Fort Edmonton on the North Saskatchewan River. Others took up land near the junction of the North and South Saskatchewan Rivers, near Prince Albert. Some Métis also left for the Dakota and Montana territories in the United States.

collateral: something offered as security when asking for a loan

investment capital: the start-up money used to invest in a project

Figure 5–2 Scrip issued to the Métis

1. Why do you suppose the government issued scrip to the Métis in Manitoba?

2. Imagine you are a Métis in Manitoba in 1871. You receive land scrip for 160 acres. You have no job and food is scarce. A speculator offers you $80 for your scrip. What do you do?

3. Why did the Métis leave Manitoba in the early 1870s?

THE MÉTIS IN THE NORTHWEST

In the Northwest, the Métis recreated the pattern of settlement established at Red River at the beginning of the nineteenth century. They laid out their farms in the traditional manner—long lots "10 chains across and two miles deep" with frontage on the river; and the Catholic church was always at the centre of the community. Their income was drawn from three sources: subsistence farming on small garden plots on their land, hunting buffalo, and hauling freight for the HBC. In the beginning, life was good. Buffalo and other game were still plentiful, the soil was rich in nutrients, and doing business with the HBC provided cash, which could be used to buy manufactured goods.

Figure 5–3 These women lived in one of the new Métis communities of the Northwest. What are they doing?

The Laws of St. Laurent

The Laws of St. Laurent were an extension of the Métis List of Rights, and they formed the **constitution** of the community. These laws were both enforceable and fair to the community members. Here are some of the main features of the Laws of St. Laurent.

Excerpt from the Preamble of the Laws of St. Laurent

It is well understood that in making these laws and regulations the inhabitants of St. Laurent in no wise pretend to constitute themselves an independent state, but the actual situation of the country in which they live, obliges them to make some measures to maintain peace and union amongst them, knowing that so large a society as theirs can only exist under some organization to preserve mutually their rights, but in forming these laws, they acknowledge themselves as loyal and faithful subjects of Canada, and are ready to abandon their own organization and to submit to the laws of the Dominion as soon as Canada shall have established amongst them regular magistrates with a force sufficient to uphold in the country the authority of the law.

Laws of St. Laurent: Highlights

- ◆ The community elected a president and a council. They were required to meet on the first Monday of the month. Members of the council who did not have a legitimate excuse for being absent were censured and fined.
- ◆ The council had the final authority to rule on any disputes in the community.
- ◆ The captain of the bison hunt regulated the hunt and all the provisions.
- ◆ The Laws of St. Laurent did not usurp the authority of the Canadian government. The Métis believed that the Canadian government would respect their community laws.

constitution: the body of principles used to govern a nation or community

However, by the early 1870s, the bison were beginning to disappear. Settlement in the United States and the Canadian Northwest was possible only if the bison were removed—these great animals could not coexist with farming homesteads. The decline of the bison greatly alarmed the Métis, because the hunt was a large part of their livelihood. In December 1873, the Métis adopted the "Laws of St. Laurent." These laws governed all aspects of life in the settlement, including the bison hunt. The new hunting rules were very strict, because Métis leaders knew it was necessary to conserve the bison for as long as possible.

The Chief Factor at Fort Carlton—the main HBC post in the area—was Lawrence Clarke, who had been with the HBC since the age of nineteen. Clarke was ambitious, and he made a show of getting along with both the Métis and European settlers. However, Clarke strongly believed that the Métis were inferior, and he used his position to lower the Métis standard of living. He hired Métis carriers on temporary **contracts** instead of offering them full-time work with the HBC, and he paid them as little as he could. By 1875, Clarke was paying

contract: an agreement for a fixed amount of time

Figure 5–4 These buffalo bones were awaiting shipment to the NWT. What impact would this slaughter have on the bison and on the Métis?

DID YOU KNOW?

Gabriel Dumont spoke six First Nations languages, but he could not speak English, and he could neither read nor write.

magistrate: a judge

the Métis in trade goods rather than cash, which reduced the expenses of the HBC. Clarke also asked the Canadian government to provide a **magistrate** to enforce Canadian law in the Fort Carlton area. The government responded by making Clarke magistrate, and it gave him sweeping powers to maintain order. Clarke used these powers for the benefit of the HBC. Any Métis who objected to the low pay, or who attempted to strike for better wages, could be imprisoned.

In 1873, the Liberals came to power under Alexander Mackenzie. During this administration, which lasted from 1873 to 1878, the Canadian government left the Métis alone. There were other issues developing on the prairies which required the attention of Ottawa—

you will learn about these in the next section of this chapter.

The winter of 1874–1875 was very difficult for the Métis, as it was for the other aboriginal nations living on the prairie. By now, the bison had all but been eliminated, and there was very little to eat. It was impossible to make pemmican, which meant loss of food and income for the Métis (pemmican was the principal winter food). In the spring of 1875, a group of Métis who were not members of the St. Laurent community began hunting bison before the official St. Laurent hunt had begun. Gabriel Dumont, the Métis president of St. Laurent, arrested and fined the participants, according to the new laws of the hunt. However, those who were charged in the incident appealed to

The Hunt of 1875

Were the Métis being unreasonable in setting out strict rules for the hunt and punishing people who disobeyed them? The accounts that follow take very different sides. The account at right, written by Chief Factor Clarke to the Lieutenant-Governor of the North-West Territories, seems to dispute the right of the Métis to enact laws at all. Why would Clarke take this view?

Below, an account of the same incident, written by a priest at St. Laurent, takes a very different view.

The hunters left as usual under the leadership of brave Gabriel Dumont... After twelve days' march ... they began to sight buffalo which gave them courage and hope. [Then they learned] that many Métis [of another parish] without respect for the laws and rules and without concern for their brothers went on ahead. Immediately it was decided in a general meeting that it was necessary at any cost, and in the interest of everyone, to observe the laws.

The leader [Gabriel Dumont], with his captains and soldiers, faithfully carried out the decision of the meeting, brought to the camp willy-nilly all the delinquents with the exceptions of two who preferred to pay an **indemnity** which was granted to them on condition that they would go immediately to Carlton. Hardly had they arrived at Fort Carlton when they complained of having been maltreated, robbed, almost assassinated. They knew whom to make these complaints to; it was to people who had looked askance at the creation of the laws of the Colonies. If one were to believe the celebrated knave and his agents, the Métis of Carlton, joined with the Indians, were in full revolution against the Dominion of Canada.

Two-thirds of this population (150 families constituting the settlement of St. Laurent) are connected by intermarriage and other degrees of kinship, and have assumed to themselves the right to enact laws ... which the minority of the settlers are perforce bound to obey or be treated with criminal severity. From this body, a court has been constituted numbering fourteen persons presided over by a man named Gabriel Dumond [sic] who is designated president before whom all delinquents are made to appear, or suffer violence in person or property.

... The past spring a party of "freemen" numbering four families made their way to Carlton ... and having disposed of the products of their hunts, purchased fresh supplies of necessaries and started prairie wards to hunt ... joining a party of other hunters and Indians who were leaving for the same purpose. Dumond dispatched a courier with a letter ordering the party ... to retrace their steps and join the St. Laurent camp. To this the Indians and Métis demurred; when Dumond with 40 of his bodyguards fully armed ... followed in pursuit, and having come up with the party seized all the horses and carts together with provisions and effects they had secured leaving the plundered people on the plains naked of transport. Dumond ... then returned the stolen property and, after using violent personal threats to individuals, levied by force a heavy fine upon the party and returned to their camp.

indemnity: compensation for loss

WHAT DO YOU THINK?

1. How is each account biased? Provide examples to illustrate your answer.

2. How do these accounts corroborate, or support, each other?

3. How do these accounts contradict each other?

4. Who are the "knave and his agents"?

Figure 5–5 Gabriel Dumont

insatiable: impossible to be satisfied

avarice: extreme greed

anarchy: chaos, lawlessness

acted properly, it did not censure Clarke, who went ahead and arrested Dumont and his men. He tried them at Fort Carlton, acting as magistrate. Although Clarke imposed only minor fines, this incident invalidated the Métis's Laws of St. Laurent. Ottawa had extended its power to control the Métis—who would now have no authority to regulate the buffalo hunt.

Following the incident, a priest living in St. Laurent wrote:

> It was after the humble legislation of the Colony of St. Laurent, having no longer the right to punish the delinquents naturally lost all sanction … Everyone took their freedom and ran on the buffalo without any other guide than their **insatiable** keenness, passion for killing, greed and **avarice**. **Anarchy** and self-interest reigned on the prairie. They exterminated the poor buffalo with more frenzy than ever.

Chief Factor Clarke, who issued warrants for the arrest of Dumont and others.

While the Canadian government admitted that Clarke had engineered the crisis and that Dumont had

In the end, the Métis found themselves in a terrible situation. Already struggling to survive, they were now deprived of the right to make their own laws and conserve their livelihood. As the 1870s drew to a close, the Métis saw themselves as being powerless to deal with the changes that were sweeping the Northwest.

ACTIVITIES

1. List the ways in which Lawrence Clarke lowered the standard of living of the Métis and chipped away at their right to govern themselves.

2. Why would the responsibilities of the captain of the bison hunt be noted in the Laws of St. Laurent?

THE FIRST NATIONS PEOPLES IN THE NORTHWEST

The Whisky Traders and the NWMP

During the 1870s, control of the Northwest gradually passed from the HBC to the Canadian government. Even so, one of the first problems facing Ottawa was a fur-trade issue. By the early 1870s, American fur traders in the southwest part of the North-West Territories—in what is today southern Alberta—were causing trouble. While the Canadian fur trade had been controlled by the HBC since 1821, the American fur trade was dominated by several smaller, independent companies. These companies traded strong, cheap liquor to the Native peoples of the region in return for buffalo robes and other furs. The principal trading post was Fort Whoop-Up, and it was soon the centre of a trade that devastated the local Native groups. The liquor trade led to widespread alcoholism among the Native peoples, resulting in malnutrition, disease, and death.

By 1872, the Canadian government decided that the Northwest required some form of policing. It feared that the presence of the whisky traders could lead to the loss of some or all of the territory to the Americans. The government established the North West Mounted Police in 1873. The NWMP was both a police force and a **paramilitary**

paramilitary: an unofficial military organization

Figure 5–6 A present-day photo of Fort Whoop-Up

organization. Its first task was to drive out the whisky traders and regain control over the entire North-West Territories. This process was hastened in 1874 by an incident involving the whisky traders and the Assiniboin people.

In the spring of 1874, a group of Assiniboin was attacked by a party of whisky traders in Cypress Hills, in what is now southern Saskatchewan. The Cypress Hills Massacre took the lives of about thirty Assiniboin, and caused outrage in Eastern Canada. In the wake of the incident, the NWMP sent 300 officers into the prairies to establish Canadian control over the area. By the time the NWMP reached Ft. Whoop-Up later that summer, the whisky traders had fled across the border back into the United States. Initially, the NWMP was welcomed by the Native peoples, who believed that the police might put an end to the lawlessness that had plagued the region for more than a decade.

Figure 5–7 This modern-day photo shows how some of the first NWMP officers would have looked. These actors are dressed in authentic period costumes.

Firewater

The whisky traders did not trade whisky as it is known today, which is usually about 40 percent alcohol. They traded an extremely powerful liquor, which the Native peoples called "firewater." It was almost pure alcohol, and **distilled** from grain in stills. Pure, distilled liquor is colourless, so the whisky traders usually added other ingredients to give it colour and taste—molasses and Tabasco sauce were used often. Alcohol of this strength is extremely dangerous, and can cause death in even small quantities.

to distill: to heat liquid until it vaporizes and then condense it

Figure 5–8 This painting is called *The Treaty Line*. What does it express about the treaty process? What is the symbolism of the painting?

Treaties with the Native Peoples

Once the Canadian government had established the North-West Territories and Manitoba, it turned its attention to the prairies. The goal was to open the area to Canadian and European settlement. However, this would not be possible until the question of aboriginal title had been settled. By 1870, all the land in the Northwest—with the exception of the Selkirk settlement—was still held by the aboriginal nations. These groups wondered about their fate under a Canadian government, and they wanted to make the best possible deal for their future.

In 1870, the Canadian government began negotiating treaties with the Native peoples through the Department of Indian Affairs. It sent Indian Commissioner W. Simpson to Manitoba to begin talks with the Cree and Saulteaux peoples. By the end of August 1871, Simpson had concluded Treaties 1 and 2, and the Native peoples of Manitoba had signed away their claim to their traditional homeland. Over the next six years, this pattern would be repeated across the prairies. The Canadian government wanted this outcome, and there was little room for negotiation. Simpson was ordered to conclude treaties that would terminate Native title to the land—only then could settlers take up homesteads in the area. At the beginning of talks for Treaty Number 1, Simpson said:

> God intends this land to raise great crops for all his children, and the time is come when it is to be used for that purpose. White people will come here to cultivate it under any circumstances. No power on earth can prevent it.

Figure 5–9 A Cree chief talks to the Red River community about the treaty process.

Ay-ee-ta-pe-pe-tung, a Cree elder, replied to Simpson:

> I have turned this matter of a treaty in my mind and cannot see anything in it to benefit my children. This is what frightens me. After I showed you what I meant to keep for a reserve, you continued to make it smaller and smaller ... Let the Queen's subjects go on my land if they choose. I give them liberty. Let them rob me. I will go home ...

Henry Prince, chief of the Saulteaux, whose father had concluded the Selkirk Treaty in 1817, had this to say:

> How are we to be treated? It is said the Queen wishes Indians to cultivate the ground. They cannot scratch it— work it with their fingers. What assistance will they get if they settle down?

The Cree and the Saulteaux did not want to give up all their land— they wanted to control about 60 percent of the land that made up Manitoba. However, Simpson had been instructed to offer 160 acres [64.7 hectares] for every family of five.

Figure 5–10 Farming was not the traditional occupation of the Native peoples of the prairie, but they had to adapt.

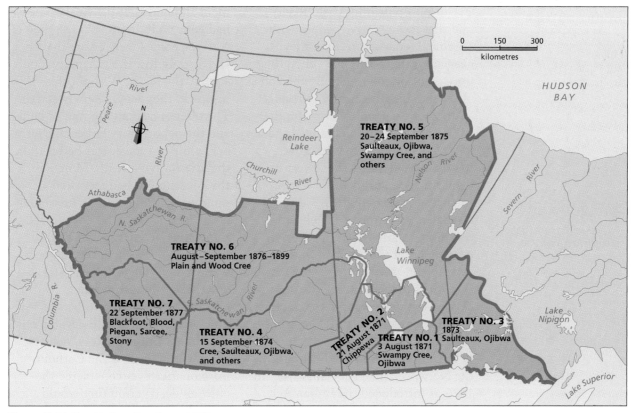

Figure 5–11 First Nations Treaties to 1877

While this offer was not really acceptable to the Cree or to the Saulteaux, they knew that no other offer would be made. However, they were successful in imposing some conditions. In return for land, the government agreed to give both nations farm equipment, supplies, and instruction in farming techniques.

Treaty Number 1 was finally signed on August 3, 1871. Treaty Number 2, which gave the government title to the forest lands between Lake Winnipeg and Lake Manitoba, was signed on August 21, 1871. Compared to the lands originally held by the Native peoples, the reserves set aside for them were tiny. As they would later discover, the Canadian government had no intention of living up to its part of the bargain.

The aboriginal peoples of the prairie welcomed the prospect of becoming farmers. After all, their traditional lifestyle had been endangered by the extermination of the bison herds. But as they began to farm, they realized that the promised tools, supplies, and animals would never materialize, and their standard of living declined rapidly. The Canadian government justified this betrayal by blaming the people they had promised to help.

Years later, Indian Commissioner Hayter Reed would say that it was "unnatural" for the Native peoples to use farm machinery, even though it is impossible to grow and harvest wheat without it. In fact, the government did not want the Native peoples to prosper as farmers, and they certainly did not want them selling

missionaries: people
concerned with
spreading religious
beliefs

DID YOU KNOW?

*The Indian Act banned the
potlatch (see page 280),
but Northwest Coast
peoples continued to hold
potlatches in hiding.*

any surplus wheat for cash. Reed said that if the Native peoples grew too much food—more than they needed for their own use—then they were planting too much. By the end of the nineteenth century, virtually all the Native peoples living on the prairie reserves had abandoned the idea of farming. They were now totally dependent on the government for their survival.

Between 1874 and 1877, the Canadian government concluded five more treaties with the aboriginal peoples of the prairies. In this way, it gained access to all the land that was suitable for agriculture. The government wanted to conclude the treaty process as quickly as possible, because European settlement of the prairies could not begin until the Northwest had been surveyed. In 1876, it introduced the Indian Act, which confirmed that the Native peoples would be required to live on reserves, and stipulated that Native children would have to attend residential schools.

In general, the Canadian govern-ment thought that the treaty process had gone well. In most cases, the Native peoples were aware that they had already lost their primary food source, the bison. Without this resource, they would slowly starve. The offer of a small amount of land, and the opportunity to become farmers, while not ideal, was better than the alternative—death. Moreover, the government had recruited a number of local Catholic **missionaries** as translators, who encouraged the Native peoples to sign the treaties. The missionaries did not want the Native peoples to starve— and they truly wanted them to become productive members of the new society that would develop on the plains. Unfortunately, neither the government nor the Catholic missionaries ever considered the cultural destruction that would accompany this plan. As soon as each treaty was signed, the NWMP was summoned to escort the Native peoples to their reservations. The course of Canadian history had been altered forever.

ACTIVITIES

1. What was the effect of the whisky traders on some of the aboriginal peoples?

2. Why did the Canadian government wish to see the whisky traders removed from the Northwest?

3. With a partner or in a group, discuss possible alternatives to the treaty process as conducted by the Canadian government. Was there a better way of ensuring settlement without as much disruption to the Native peoples? Discuss your findings with the class.

4. Provide two reasons for the creation of the North West Mounted Police.

5. Why do you suppose the Canadian government did not provide an effective program of financial and technical support for the Native peoples relocated on reserves?

6. Were Canada's treaties with the Native peoples freely negotiated? Was there coercion? If so, by whom was it applied? Provide reasons for your answer.

THE NATIONAL DREAM

As you will learn in Chapter 6, British Columbia entered Confederation in 1871, with the promise of a transcontinental railroad link to the rest of Canada within ten years. At the time, this promise seemed extravagant, if not rash. No politician had a clear idea of the route the railroad would follow, nor did they know how much a railroad would cost. It is conceivable that if Macdonald had known the final cost of building the railroad, or the problems it would entail, he might never have made such a promise to British Columbia.

Macdonald had a dream of creating a British North American nation that would rival the United States. He understood correctly that the only way to realize the dream was to build a transportation and communication link that would join all the parts of British North America. Macdonald also knew that the railroad had to be built quickly, Otherwise, Canada ran the risk of being assimilated by the United States.

Macdonald's first task was to find **backers** for the project. He and his government had no intention of building the railway themselves; they wanted to find people who would **underwrite** the project in return for financial benefits from the government once the railway had been built. The second half of the nineteenth century was a period of frantic railway building, especially in the United States. Many railway owners looked to Canada as a way to increase their economic power, since Canada was a natural market for American goods. One prominent **industrialist** was Jay Cooke, who immediately saw the economic potential of the Canadian Northwest.

The only major industrialist in Canada who had enough money to finance a railway was Sir Hugh Allan, who had made his fortune in shipping and manufacturing, and in railway building in eastern Canada.

backers: people who back a project with money

underwrite: to finance

industrialist: someone who owns or controls an industry

Figure 5–12 John A. Macdonald

Figure 5–13 Sir Hugh Allan

power, they lost many seats. During this election, the Conservatives realized they didn't have enough money to woo voters successfully. Macdonald appealed to George-Étienne Cartier, his associate in Quebec, to find out if Hugh Allan would finance the election in return for a guaranteed railway contract. Cartier wrote two **memos**, one promising Allan the CPR contract, the other listing the contributions Allan was to make to the Conservative Party. The text of one of these memos follows:

> The friends of the Government will expect to be assisted with funds in the pending elections, and any amount which you or your Company shall advance for that purpose shall be recouped by you. A memorandum of immediate requirements is below.
>
> | Sir John A. Macdonald | $25 000 |
> | Hon. Mr. Langevin | $15 000 |
> | Sir G.E.C. | $20 000 |

This memo made it seem as though Macdonald was on Allan's payroll. This episode is known as the "Pacific Scandal," and it led to the resignation of Macdonald's government in 1873.

Mackenzie and that "Damned Railway"

Alexander Mackenzie, who led the Liberals to power in 1873, disagreed with Macdonald's vision of a nation linked by rail from sea to sea. As far as Mackenzie was concerned, the railway scheme was a lot of expensive trouble. The Liberals had come to power just as a major economic depression was sweeping North America; the railway was a huge undertaking. As a result, there was no

memos: informal written communications used in business

In the summer of 1871, the Minister of Finance, Francis Hincks, proposed that Allan undertake to build the transcontinental railway. Allan decided that it made good economic sense to build the railway, but only with American backing. By the autumn of 1871, Allan had created the Canadian Pacific Railway, a company which seemed to be Canadian but was really controlled by Jay Cooke's Northern Pacific Railway. Allan and his American backers were not prepared to build a real transcontinental railway because it would be far too difficult. What they intended to build was a branch line to the Northern Pacific.

In 1872, Macdonald called a general election—the first since Confederation. While Macdonald's Conservatives managed to stay in

Political Scandals

Political scandals occur when a politician or a government undertakes an action that is illegal, inappropriate, or both. Sometimes, the mere **perception** on the part of the public that an action is inappropriate is enough to sink someone's career or force a government to resign.

Like the governments of most nations, Canadian governments have dealt with various political scandals over the years. Scandals that involve bribes, such as the Pacific Scandal, are always taken seriously. Sometimes scandals damage a government or a politician's **credibility** for just a few years, especially if the actions in question were not illegal but just tasteless. Journalists have a good sense about when a scandal has passed because they are always monitoring the stories that attract the public's attention.

In the past twenty years, the federal and provincial governments have enacted conflict-of-interest legislation in an effort to reduce the occurrence of scandals. These efforts have reduced the incidence of scandals, but they still occur.

perception: the way things appear

credibility: believability

"WE IN CANADA SEEM TO HAVE LOST ALL IDEA OF JUSTICE, HONOR AND INTEGRITY."—THE MAIL, 26TH SEPTEMBER.

Figure 5–14 Could you put Macdonald's words in any other politician's mouth today?

WHAT DO YOU THINK?

1. This group activity will require you to do some library research about contemporary political scandals.

   a) First, select a scandal you would like to investigate.

   b) Within your group, assign the following investigative roles:

   - **Background researcher** One student will obtain the background information on the scandal—what did the government or politician do that was wrong?

   - **Cartoon-viewpoints researcher** One student will collect political cartoons that reflect diverse viewpoints concerning the scandal.

   - **Editorial-viewpoints researcher** One student will collect editorial writings that provide additional viewpoints concerning the scandal.

   - **Damage-control researcher** One student will research the steps taken to resolve the scandal, and the eventual outcome.

railway construction during his administration. He did, however, allow the Canadian Pacific Survey to continue under the direction of Sandford Fleming. The survey would investigate all possible routes the railway could take. It was a relatively inexpensive project, and Fleming realized that the information collected might one day be useful. Railway aside, it was giving a brand new picture of the geography of the nation.

In British Columbia, reaction to Mackenzie's "do nothing" attitude was extremely negative. Politicians from the province lobbied the federal government, protested to Lord Dufferin, the Governor General, and even talked about **seceding** from Confederation if the promised railway did not get built. There was also a lot of debate in the province about where the railway would run (see Chapter 6 for more information on the battle over the routes).

The National Policy: Formula for Nation Building

As the 1870s progressed, Macdonald and the Conservative Party began to recover from the effects of the Pacific Scandal. Macdonald was convinced that the CPR was essential to the survival of Canada, but he needed a political platform to convince the voters. In 1876, he developed the National Policy, which became the basis of the Conservative election platform during the 1878 election. Macdonald and his party were returned to office with a substantial majority.

The National Policy was more than an election scheme. Macdonald truly believed that it was a formula for nation building, and it remained an essential part of Canadian government policy well into the twentieth century. The policy dealt with three main issues, which are described below.

A System of Protective Tariffs

During the 1870s, the Canadian economy had been damaged by the economic policies of the United States. American companies could produce goods more cheaply than Canadian companies could, and they often **dumped** goods on the Canadian market to increase their profits. Macdonald devised a system of tariffs that would protect Canadian manufacturing, mining, and agriculture from American dumping by making US goods too expensive for the Canadian market.

Western Settlement

Eastern politicians viewed the Canadian West as a vast potential market. Because the prairies were well-suited to agriculture, the Canadian government wanted to encourage the settlement of the West by farmers. These farmers would produce grain crops, primarily for export abroad. This income could then be spent on Canadian manufactured goods, produced in eastern Canada. Macdonald and succeeding governments discouraged the development of manufacturing in the West so that western farmers could become a captive market for the industrial east.

The CPR

The CPR was the cornerstone of the National Policy. The West could not develop as a centre for agricultural export until goods could be transported in and out of the region. Macdonald also thought that the

to secede: to withdraw from a union

to dump: to sell goods at a low price

CPR could be a part of the British Empire's trading network by providing the means to ship goods to and from Asia. The construction of the CPR became the government's top priority. Between 1878 and 1880, the government searched in vain for a group of investors.

The CPR Syndicate

The CPR could not be built, however, until the government found private investors, which it finally did. George Stephen of the Bank of Montreal, Donald Smith of the Hudson's Bay Company, and James J. Hill, an expatriate Canadian investing in United States railways, had bought the floundering St. Paul and Pacific railway in 1877 for just $100 000. Within just four years, they had turned the railway around and had made a profit of $17 million.

In 1880, Macdonald pitched his proposal. Predictably, he offered terms that the trio could not refuse. Upon completion of the railway line, the government would hand over $25 million, along with a land grant of 25 million acres [10.11 million hectares], most of it on the prairies. The CPR Syndicate, as the group came to be known, also received a monopoly on all rail traffic west of Lake Superior for the next 20 years, and an exemption from tax on all lands until they were sold. In return, the syndicate promised to complete the transcontinental railway within ten years. This contract was approved by Parliament on February 1, 1881.

As soon as the contract was approved, the CPR Syndicate changed the route of the railway. The original route was supposed to travel along the fertile belt through Saskatoon. Many speculators had moved into the area, buying up land they hoped would be near the rail line. But the syndicate members, especially James Hill, wanted to have complete control of the project. Hill suggested that the line be moved about 300 miles south, into the

Figure 5–15 The change of route demanded by the CPR Syndicate

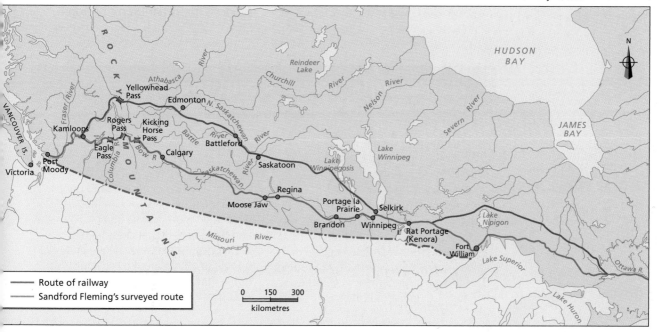

Figure 5–16 William Van Horne

southern prairies—an area that was still not occupied by homesteaders or speculators. This would give the CPR much more control over the location of new towns and railway stations. The southern prairies were far more arid than the the fertile belt, but the syndicate had heard that the region was also suitable for agriculture. Once the main line was completed, the CPR intended to build branch lines north to the fertile belt, because it also had the potential to be profitable.

The change in route meant that most of the information collected by the Canadian Pacific Survey was irrelevant. In addition, it was still unclear how the railway would pass through the Rocky Mountains into British Columbia. The syndicate was looking for a pass through the Rockies, along with possible entry points in two more mountain ranges—the Monashees and the Selkirks. Even as the railway was being built across the southern prairies, the way through British Columbia was still unknown.

The building of the CPR, which began in 1881, did not go well at first. Construction was limited to the line running between Winnipeg and Brandon, but by the time winter had set in, only 230 kilometres of track had been laid. At this rate, the CPR would never be finished within the contracted time period. James Hill spent the early fall of 1881 looking for a new general manager for the railway. He knew he needed someone of exceptional energy and drive, or the whole project would fail.

Van Horne and the CPR

Hill's choice was William Van Horne, a 38-year-old general manager of a smaller railway in the American Midwest. Van Horne was the ideal choice. He was intelligent and dedicated and the word "cannot" did not exist in his vocabulary. He would spend the next four years driving himself and his employees unmercifully until the CPR was completed. Van Horne was also a man of many talents—he could operate any locomotive and understood Morse code as though it were a second language. In the words of modern historian Pierre Berton:

"Hell's Bells" Rogers and the Rogers Pass

The surveyor who found a way through the Selkirk Mountains was Major A. B. Rogers, an expatriate American. Rogers was a foul-mouthed, feisty, and determined man. He was sure that a pass existed through the Selkirks, and he spent two years (between 1881 and 1882) looking for it, travelling through some of the most rugged country in the British Columbia mountains.

Rogers finally found the pass that bears his name in the summer of 1882. Delighted and relieved, the CPR executives paid Rogers a $5000 bonus and named the pass for him. Rogers, who cared more for the immortality—and the name "Rogers Pass"—than the money, framed the cheque and hung it in a prominent place in his home, much to the dismay of the CPR Accounting Department.

He ate prodigiously and was known as a man who fed his workmen generously. He liked his cognac, his whiskey, and his fine French vintages, but he did not tolerate drunkenness in himself or others. Inebriates were fired out of hand. So were slackers … slowpokes, and labour organizers. Van Horne did not suffer laziness, stupidity, inefficiency, or revolt.

The arrival of Van Horne **galvanized** the CPR. He immediately injected a high level of efficiency into the railway company. Five-hundred miles of railway track were laid during the 1882 season, and another 500 miles were laid the following year. With Van Horne in control, the CPR would be able to complete the railway line in the contracted period—as long as the money held out. One problem for the CPR was that the government subsidy was paid out only as each section of work was completed. By the fall of 1883, the company was running out of money. Even the personal resources of George Stephen and Donald Smith, which they pledged to the CPR, could not cover the expenses. Moreover, all the money had been spent on the construction of the Prairie section of the line. Laying the track in the mountainous terrain of eastern British Columbia and the rocky shores of Lake Superior would cost even more money.

As funds dried up, so did the workers' salaries, and they were forced to strike. The Canadian government reluctantly passed a bill that gave the CPR $22.5 million, enough, Macdonald hoped, to finish the railway. During 1884, rail construction proceeded, with Van Horne cutting

to galvanize: to stir into action

Figure 5–17 A temporary railway trestle, later replaced by a permanent bridge

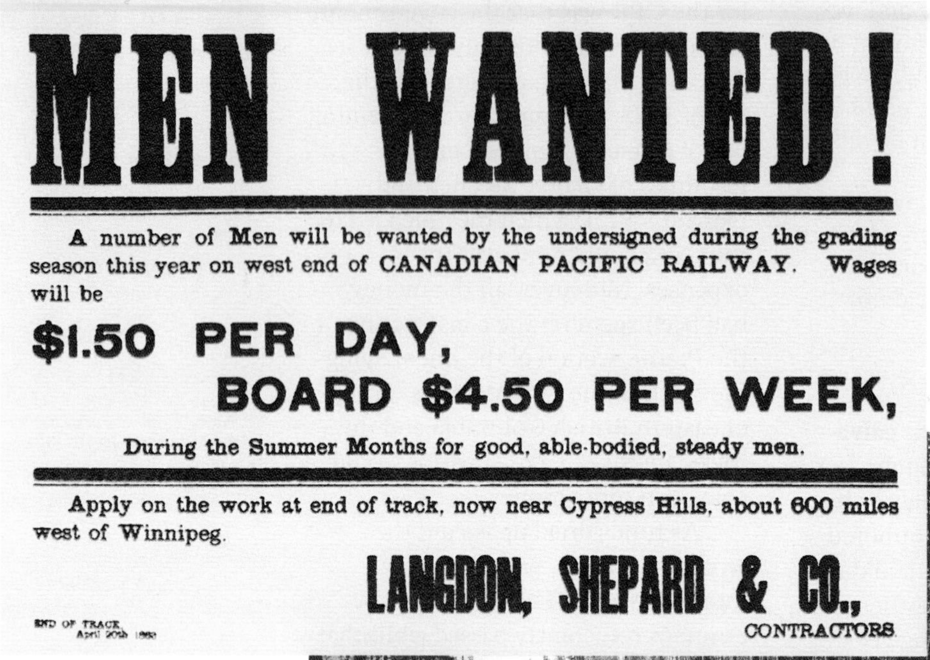

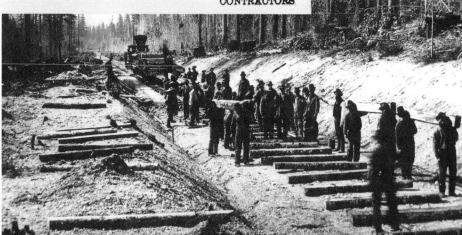

MEN WANTED!

A number of Men will be wanted by the undersigned during the grading season this year on west end of CANADIAN PACIFIC RAILWAY. Wages will be

$1.50 PER DAY,

BOARD $4.50 PER WEEK,

During the Summer Months for good, able-bodied, steady men.

Apply on the work at end of track, now near Cypress Hills, about 600 miles west of Winnipeg.

LANGDON, SHEPARD & CO.,
CONTRACTORS.

END OF TRACK,
April 20th [illegible]

Figure 5–18 An advertisement for workers on the CPR

Figure 5–19 Laying the railway ties was exhausting work.

DID YOU KNOW?

When the "pay car" left Winnipeg each month for the Lake Superior section, it carried $1 100 000, which worked out to an average of $73.33 for each of the 15 000 workers.

corners as best he could. For example, he decided to use temporary wooden trestles to carry the line over difficult terrain. These trestles could be assembled quickly and be replaced by more permanent structures at a later date. But even with these economies, the money advanced by the government was almost used up by the end of 1884, and the CPR was once again strapped for cash.

The CPR was built entirely by hand, and thousands of people were needed to finish the job. When construction reached its height between 1882 and mid-1885, more than 35 000 workers were involved—15 000 working north of Lake Superior, 10 000 working inland from the British Columbia coast, and another 10 000 working on the prairies. Their living and working conditions were terrible—dust from the dynamite blasts, insects, overcrowding and filth in the bunk houses, leaky roofs, and no plumbing. In addition, the diet was boring and often unhealthy. In the Lake Superior

DID YOU KNOW?

Railway workers were called "navvies"—short for "navigators." This term was first used to describe those workers who built canals in the eighteenth and nineteenth centuries.

region, for example, the workers had little access to fresh fruits and vegetables during the winter season. On the job, conditions were often dangerous. There were no medical facilities, and workers' compensation did not exist. Those who were injured on the job were discharged from employment, and would never receive any compensation for their injuries.

The CPR main line eventually crossed the Rockies at Kicking Horse Pass. Here Van Horne had the line built so that it descended the pass at a grade that was twice as steep as safety allowed. The track switched back and forth over the Kicking Horse River, crossing and recrossing it nine times on its way down. In some places, the grade was so steep that it took four miles of track to cover a straight-line distance of one mile.

The CPR "Saves the Nation"

In March 1885, the Northwest Rebellion broke out. The rebellion was a climax of the events you read about at the beginning of this chapter. Because the federal government had to get troops to the Northwest as quickly as possible, it needed to use the CPR. Unfortunately, four gaps broke the rail line north of Lake Superior. Soldiers crossed these gaps on foot, in one instance marching 18 kilometres across the frozen surface of Lake Superior.

However, Van Horne did manage to transport the troops with his typical efficiency, and the first soldiers arrived in Winnipeg in just five days. Thanks to the CPR, it looked as though the federal government could react quickly to a crisis. Indeed, this was the event that saved the CPR from financial ruin. Many Canadians now understood why such a transportation link was necessary. George Stephens, the beleaguered CPR president, could now go back to Macdonald for more money without looking foolish. On July 10, 1885, within hours of running out of credit, the CPR received enough cash from Ottawa to finish the railway. The transcontinental link was actually completed by the fall of 1885—five years ahead of its original schedule.

Figure 5–20 This image is probably Canada's most famous photograph. Here, Donald Smith, one of the railway architects, is shown driving the last spike of the CPR at Craigellechie in the British Columbia mountains on November 7, 1885. How does this photograph reflect the era in which it was taken?

1. Why was Prime Minister Mackenzie so unwilling to spend more money on the CPR?

2. Examine the National Policy. With a partner, determine which aspects of this policy favour certain parts of the country. Explain your answer.

3. The final cost of the railway was about $100 million. Why do you suppose the CPR Syndicate was willing to agree to the deal they made with the federal government?

4. Why was Van Horne necessary for the successful completion of the CPR?

5. Why do you think John A. Macdonald was so unwilling to provide extra funds for the CPR, when its failure would mean the end of his "National Dream"? Explain your answer in a short paragraph.

6. In what ways was the CPR an unfair employer? Why were people willing to work under the circumstances they did?

7. Railway workers normally worked a six-day week. Assuming that three days a week were lost during the winter, calculate the net pay of a worker between December 1 and March 1.

8. Imagine you are a worker on the railway. Write a letter to your family describing your experiences as a railway worker.

9. You are a Canadian living in 1885. In a letter or poem, describe your feelings on learning that the CPR has finally been completed. You might wish to take the role of a western farmer, a Native person now living on a reserve, a Quebecker, or a businessperson living in Ontario.

THE NORTHWEST REBELLION OF 1885

By the early 1880s, the Métis were beginning to lose patience with the Canadian government. As you read earlier, many Métis had moved into the Northwest in the 1870s because the Manitoba government had made it difficult for them to get title to their land. In the Northwest, the Métis continued to press for title to the land they occupied, and they also wanted some financial aid to help them become successful farmers. They did not want to rebel against the authority of the Canadian government.

But the Canadian government had its own agenda for the land occupied by the Métis—an agenda driven by the high cost of the CPR.

The government had surveyed the prairies in the 1870s, and knew that there were some 16 million acres [6.4 million hectares] suitable for cultivation. Much of this land was owned by land speculators who sold it to farmers and gave a portion of the proceeds to the government. Macdonald had calculated that if most of the land was sold, the government would collect about $71 million—more than all the money the government had poured into the CPR. There was no way that the government was going to jeopardize this potential revenue by hearing Métis petitions about "their" land.

The building of the railway also affected the government's treatment of the aboriginal peoples with whom they had just concluded treaties. As railway costs rose between 1882 and 1883, the government slashed the budget of its Indian department. The promised aid to start new lives as farmers never materialized, and the Native peoples had to rely on food handouts from the government just to survive. The government made it clear to the Native peoples that receiving food was conditional on not causing trouble. In other words, the government used the handouts as a form of social control, and "difficult Indians" would receive no food. By 1884, many aboriginal peoples were facing starvation.

In 1884, Gabriel Dumont, the Métis leader, wrote:

> The Government should not be surprised if we side with the Indians. They are our relatives, and when they are starving, they come to us for relief and we have to feed them. The Government is not doing right by them ... I heard the speeches and explanations given of the Treaty [Treaty Number 6], not only they would live as well as they had before, but better ... Is that taking place now? Now they are allowed to go about starving and the burden of feeding them falls on us. We desire the Indians to be fed; because if they are not we ourselves will be kept in poverty.

Louis Riel Returns

In the summer of 1884, the Métis sent a delegation to Montana, where Louis Riel had lived since the mid-1870s working as a school teacher. Riel was moved by the plight of his people, and agreed to fight for justice on their behalf. Riel returned with peaceful intentions, but his very presence in the Northwest signalled to the government and its supporters that another rebellion was a possibility. Conservative businessmen in Prince Albert wrote letters to the government, warning that the Métis were planning an armed revolt. The NWMP investigated and determined that between 500 and 1100 Métis and aboriginal people were ready to take up arms against the government.

In late 1884, a sympathetic European farmer and Riel collaborated on a Métis Bill of Rights. They hoped this document would address the grievances of the Métis and form the basis of a new province in the Northwest, but it was ignored by the Canadian government. The Bill of Rights was far more detailed than the 1869 List of Rights. It reflected both the frustration of the Métis and their desire to be treated as equals with the other peoples in the Northwest. As such, it bore a closer resemblance to the Declaration of Independence which the American colonists had sent the British government in 1776. Here are some of the grievances listed in the Bill of Rights:

- that the Indians are so reduced that the settlers in many localities are compelled to furnish them with food, partly to prevent them from dying at their door, and partly to preserve the peace in the Territory
- that the Métis of the Territory have not received 240 acres of land, each, as did the Manitoba [Métis]
- that the Métis who are in possession of tracts of land have not received patents (title)
- that settlers are charged dues on timber, nails, and firewood required for home use

Figure 5–21 A modern-day photo of Fort Carlton

- that customs duties are levied on the necessaries of life
- that no effective measures have yet been taken to put the people of the Northwest in direct communication with the European Markets, via Hudson Bay
- that settlers are exposed to coercion at elections, owing to the fact that votes are not taken by ballot

Section 17 detailed a number of grievances relating to the government not living up to its arrangements for the North-West Territories, and detailed in the Manitoba Act.

By the end of 1884, tensions were building in the Northwest, and the Macdonald government was facing a crisis. The CPR was almost bankrupt and still not finished. If troops were needed to suppress a rebellion, they would have to travel quickly by rail. Macdonald saw an opportunity to finish the CPR and put down a rebellion in the Northwest. If war broke out, the public would view the money spent on the railway as politically acceptable.

By the spring of 1885, the Canadian government was ready to call out the eastern militia. At the same time, the Manitoba militia started moving into the Northwest, and the Lieutenant-Governor of the North-West Territories banned the sale of ammunition in his jurisdiction. This meant that the Métis would not have any weapons if they decided to rebel. Ottawa's only force near St. Laurent, in the heart of Métis territory, was Superintendent Lief Crozier's small group of NWMP officers at Fort Carlton. But Crozier did not think he had enough officers to fight the Métis.

On March 19, Louis Riel addressed the Métis at St. Laurent. He told them that a peaceful resolution was impossible, and that the Canadian government was determined to make war on the Métis. He concluded his speech with the statement "Justice commands us to take up arms," and he demanded the surrender of Fort Carlton.

The first clash between the NWMP and the Métis began with an attempt at negotiation, but it quickly disintegrated. Angry words were exchanged between the two sides at Duck Lake, near Batoche, and two Métis delegates were shot. Both sides opened fire. Within thirty minutes, twelve NWMP officers lay dead, and another twenty-five lay wounded. Crozier retreated to Fort Carlton—the Northwest Rebellion had begun.

More than 5000 Canadian troops were deployed throughout the Northwest to contain the rebellion. The main force was sent from Regina to deal with the centre of the rebellion—Batoche and St. Laurent. In April, 1600 militia clashed with Gabriel Dumont and fewer than sixty Métis at Fish Creek, just south of Batoche. This small group held off the Canadian troops for a day, and prevented them from moving on to Batoche. Reinforcements arrived, but the militia did not reach Batoche until May 9.

At Batoche, some 725 militia attacked 175 Métis. In spite of the assault, the Métis held their ground for three days. As the battle was drawing to a close, Riel and Dumont met for the last time near Batoche. Riel was distraught over the Métis defeat and the loss of life. He asked Dumont, "What are we going to do?" Dumont replied, "We are defeated. We shall perish. But you must have known this when we took up arms that we would be beaten. So they will destroy us." Riel was captured on May 15; Dumont escaped to the United States, where he spent the next decade in exile.

After the Métis defeat at Batoche, Canadian troops tracked down and arrested the aboriginal leaders who had taken part in the Rebellion. In most cases, these leaders were either pardoned or sentenced to a short prison term. The government's view of the Native peoples was paternalistic—it viewed them as wayward children who had been misled by Riel, rather than as people driven to desperate actions by the Canadian government.

After Riel's arrest, he was taken to Regina and charged with high

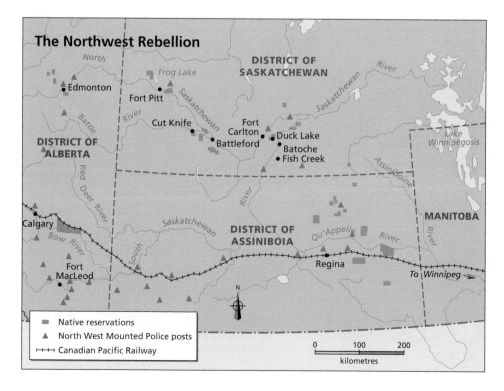

Figure 5–22 Battle sites during the Northwest Rebellion

Chief Crowfoot and the CPR

Throughout the Northwest Rebellion, the Cree, who also wanted a better deal from the federal government, supported the Métis cause. Following the skirmish at Duck Lake, they attacked a settlement on Frog Lake, and the NWMP post at Fort Pitt.

But while the Cree rose in rebellion with the Métis, the Blackfoot nation, led by Chief Crowfoot, did not. The Blackfoot's large reserve lay very close to the CPR line. In 1883, CPR construction encroached on the reserve. Father Lacombe, the **Oblate** missionary who had lived among the Blackfoot since 1870, negotiated with Crowfoot, and the Blackfoot received additional land as compensation. Lacombe's argument to Crowfoot appears at right.

Crowfoot did not like the Europeans or what they had done on the prairies, but he was a **pragmatist**. He understood that change would happen anyway, and he saw no reason to put his people through more difficulty. After the CPR was finished, it rewarded both Lacombe and Crowfoot with lifetime passes on the railway. Crowfoot had his pass glazed, framed, and inscribed with his Blackfoot name, *Sapomaxicow*. Deeply moved, Crowfoot wrote Van Horne, thanking him for his gesture.

Oblate: a Roman Catholic order of missionaries

pragmatist: someone who can see the practical, realistic side of an issue

---

PRIMARY SOURCE

Well, my friends, I have some advice to give you today. Let the white people pass through your lands and let them build their roads. They are not here to rob you of your lands. These white men obey their chiefs, and it is with the chiefs that the matter must be settled. I have already told these chiefs that you were not pleased with the way in which the work was being pushed through your lands. The Governor himself will come to meet you. He will listen to your griefs; he will propose a remedy. And if the compromise does not suit you, that will be the time to order the builders out of your reserve.

Figure 5–23 Chief Crowfoot and his family

treason—taking up arms against the Canadian government. Treason was punishable by death, and the Canadian government probably wanted to make an example of Riel. The trial took place in July 1885. Riel was defended by three lawyers from Quebec, who decided that he should plea not guilty by reason of insanity. They believed that this was the only way his life could be saved. Riel refused. Before Judge Richardson, a staunch Conservative supporter, and a six-man jury of English Protestants, Riel pleaded his case and that of his people.

By this time, Riel was resigned to his fate, but he was also determined to show that the Métis had been mistreated and goaded into rebellion so that they would no longer be a force in the Northwest. In his summation to the jury, Riel not only described the deprivation of his people ("I found the Indians suffering ... I found the [Métis] eating the rotten pork of the Hudson Bay Company ..."), he also placed the responsibility of the rebellion on the shoulders of the Canadian government:

The agitation of the North-West Territories would have been constitutional, and would certainly be constitutional today. If, in my opinion, we had not been attacked. Perhaps the Crown has not been able to find out the particulars, that we were attacked, but as we were on the scene, it was easy to understand. When we sent petitions to the government, they answered us by sending police ..."

... So irresponsible is that government ... that in the course of several years, besides doing nothing to satisfy the people of this great land, it has even hardly been able to answer once or give a single response. That fact would indicate an absolute lack of responsibility, and therefore, insanity complicated with paralysis.

Riel was found guilty of high treason, but the jury and judge recommended clemency. The Canadian government refused to consider mercy, and Riel was hanged on November 16, 1885.

Figure 5–24 The jury that convicted Louis Riel. Why would this jury have posed for this photograph? What emotion do you read on the face of each juror?

Apply Your Knowledge

Comparing Maps and Drawing Conclusions

One year after the Northwest Rebellion, passenger service between Montreal and the Pacific Coast began, and the railway age was underway. These maps show how travel time between Ottawa and the West Coast changed after the building of the railway. Using these two maps as a resource, try to answer the questions that follow. You could work with a partner or in a small group.

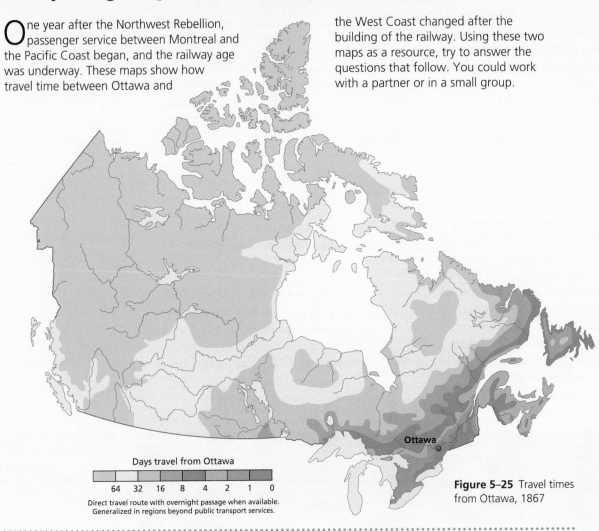

Days travel from Ottawa

64 32 16 8 4 2 1 0

Direct travel route with overnight passage when available.
Generalized in regions beyond public transport services.

Figure 5–25 Travel times from Ottawa, 1867

....

ACTIVITIES

1. Create an organizer to compare the travel times between Ottawa and the following cities in 1867 and 1891.
   - **a)** Toronto
   - **b)** Winnipeg
   - **c)** Edmonton
   - **d)** Vancouver

2. Why did it take longer to reach the British Columbia interior as opposed to the British Columbia Coast from Ottawa in 1867?

3. What areas of Canada still remained inaccessible by rail or by water in 1891?

4. Create a brochure for the CPR in the late nineteenth century that would persuade people to take a long train trip. Your brochure should speak to people living in a specific area, for example, Lethbridge, and include any special instructions about their starting point, along with information about sights en route to their destination.

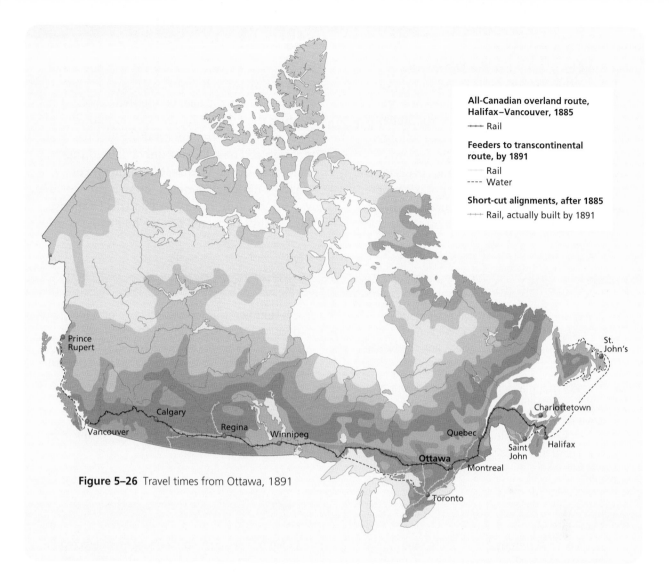

All-Canadian overland route,
Halifax–Vancouver, 1885
⊦⊦⊦⊦ Rail

Feeders to transcontinental
route, by 1891
⎯⎯ Rail
---- Water

Short-cut alignments, after 1885
⊦⊦⊦⊦ Rail, actually built by 1891

Figure 5–26 Travel times from Ottawa, 1891

ACTIVITIES

1. Why do you suppose the government ignored the Métis's pleas for help?

2. How did the government maintain social control over the Native peoples of the Northwest?

3. For what reasons did Sir John A. Macdonald want a Northwest Rebellion?

4. Examine Dumont's statement to Riel (page 195). Why is this statement true? If so, why did the Métis rebel?

5. Your teacher will provide you with more detailed materials regarding the trial of Louis Riel. Examine this evidence, and try to come to a verdict in his case. You could do this as a group assignment, or you could conduct a re-enactment of Riel's trial.

6. With a partner, discuss the options Macdonald had once Riel was found guilty. Be sure to assess the political aspects of any decision—in other words, which option might be the most politically dangerous for Macdonald? Share your findings with the class.

CONCLUSION

It has been said that the Northwest Rebellion of 1885 and the execution of Louis Riel forever ended any sense of Métis national unity. Certainly the Rebellion had a great impact on Canada as a whole. It inflamed English-French and Protestant-Roman Catholic tensions almost everywhere, and it probably raised the level of prejudice against all Native peoples. Canada is still living with the legacy of these events.

The completion of the CPR was the other big event of 1885. In the next chapter, you will read about the special challenges of building the CPR in British Columbia, where the terrain made the undertaking all but impossible. The CPR not only ensured the settlement of the West—it became one of Canada's national symbols, known the world over. At great monetary and political expense, Macdonald's National Dream had come true.

SUMMARY ACTIVITIES

1. In a group or with a partner, evaluate the policies and actions of the Canadian government towards the Métis and the Native peoples in the Northwest.

2. This is a group assignment. You and your group are cabinet members in the Canadian government of 1870. Taking into account the material you have studied in this chapter, try to find solutions to the problems associated with the Northwest. The only restriction on your decision is that you must try to accommodate the needs and concerns of all groups living in the Northwest. Share your findings with the rest of the class.

3. Many historians have said that the CPR is the reason this nation exists today. Assess the correctness of this statement in light of the contents of Chapter 5.

ON YOUR OWN

1. Research the current status of the Métis in the Northwest. What are their current political issues? If possible, invite a representative from the Métis community to speak to your class.

2. Several monuments to Louis Riel have been erected since his death. Find out more information about each of these. You could begin by investigating the monument erected in front of the Manitoba Legislature in the 1970s (now dismantled). What happened to it? Locate a picture of this monument and share it with the class. How does it symbolize Riel's struggle for the Métis? Compare it with the photograph of the Riel monument on page 129.

6 BRITISH COLUMBIA TO 1896

LEARNING OUTCOMES

In this chapter, you will follow the development of British Columbia from its early days as a territory controlled by the Hudson's Bay Company until the time it joined Confederation and became the setting for the "last spike" of the CPR. By the end of this chapter, you will

- compare and contrast British and US attitudes towards the Oregon Territory
- describe the reasons for the creation of the colony of Vancouver Island
- analyze historical records for bias
- describe the evolution of a town and identify its stages of development
- identify three main points of view concerning the entry of British Columbia into Confederation
- provide evidence to show how the CPR led to economic growth in British Columbia

A Mountain of Grief

During the second half of the nineteenth century, living conditions in South China were extremely harsh. The land was overcrowded, and farmers were heavily taxed. It was a struggle for most farmers to survive, let alone make a decent living. In the 1850s and 1860s, several uprisings took place against the Qing Dynasty, and many farms were overrun or abandoned. In the midst of this strife, farmers in South China heard wonderful stories about the riches to be made in North America during the days of the California Gold Rush. So, when railway construction in British Columbia began in the 1880s, thousands of Chinese farmers came to Canada to make their fortune. The reality they confronted was very different from the stories they had heard, as this fictionalized account based on historical records shows.

My name is Woo Xi Feng. I was born in a village near Guangzhou, the capital city of Guangdong province. Our village is small. Right now, there are very few opportunities here for young men to work and to earn a living. I was married in the winter of 1881, and I am not able to provide at all well for my wife. In that winter, a man from Guangzhou came to our village. He spoke to all the young men who were without work, and he told us of a fabulous place across the ocean. He called it "The Golden Mountain."

There, he said, a man could gain his fortune, if he was prepared to work hard. The work he described sounded very difficult, but he promised us wages of one dollar for every day that we worked. He said that the man he represented would pay for our passage to this place, and that we could expect to work for at least three years. My fellow villagers and I calculated that a man who accepted this offer could easily make $1000 in those three years. In our village, such a sum would make us wealthy and allow us to buy a good-sized farm. So we accepted his offer and followed him, first to Guangzhou, and then to Hong Kong, where we boarded the ship that would take us to the Golden Mountain.

January 15, 1882

We have spent over a month on this ship. The ocean is a frightening place for men who have never travelled on it. The ship is very crowded, and the air below decks, where we stay, is very foul. The food is not good, but many of us cannot eat anyway, as we are sea-sick. My friends and I wonder if we have made the right choice.

February 2, 1882

We have arrived at a place the Europeans call "New West-minster." There are many people here, but few Chinese. These people call out angrily at us as we pass through the town on our way to the riverboat, which will take us to where we

will start work. We do not understand their language, and we are frightened. Why are they so angry at us, as they have never seen us before?

February 7, 1882

We have arrived at a place called "Yale," another strange-sounding European name. We have been placed in a building the Europeans call a "bunkhouse." It is a long, wooden structure, with a door, one window, and wooden beds that are stacked vertically along the walls. An iron stove in the centre of the big room gives us some heat, and we also use it to cook the rice and fish we live on. This land is very strange to us. South China is a warm place, but here the air is very cold, and there is a substance called "snow" that covers the ground. Many of us have become ill from the cold. There are thirty of us in this bunkhouse, as well as two cooks. We follow the instructions of a Chinese man, Mr. Chen, who has the title **bookman**. Mr. Chen has explained to us that he is in charge of our wages and supplies. And, since he speaks English, he is also responsible for telling us the orders of the men who have hired us. We will be working to build a railway, which is an iron road on which trains will run. We had never heard of such a thing! Our job will be to carry away rocks from the tunnels which are being built here.

The cargo steamer that took Woo Xi Feng to Canada

The bunkhouse offered few comforts and the land seemed very strange.

The landscape is also very strange. A wild river runs through this place, between enormous walls of rock. The Europeans are using a variety of gunpowder to blast tunnels through the rock so the railway can be built.

May 3, 1882

We have been working on the railway for two months now. The work is difficult and very dangerous. When the blasting takes place, all men must clear out of the tunnel. If they do not, the falling rock can easily kill them. We have heard of accidents that occur when men do not get away quickly enough. We are under the direction of a European man named "Miller," who is our **herder**. We

do not like him, for he is often abusive in his language, especially when we do not work hard enough to satisfy him. Mr. Chen is always polite, but Miller does not return this politeness. We still do not understand why the Europeans dislike us. We have heard that European workers are paid twice as much as we are, yet they do not work as hard as we do. Also, while we keep to ourselves, they often leave the workplace and go to Yale, which is quite far away, where they drink and gamble.

August 8, 1882

Miller has finally caused a great disturbance. Today, when the signal to leave the area before a blast took place, Miller did not

get us far enough away. A big rock flew trough the air, striking one of our workers. The rock took his head off completely. We were so angry, we all—our whole crew—ran after Miller. I am sure that we would have killed him, except he leapt into the river and swam away. Mr. Chen told us later that Miller had been fired for his carelessness, and that a new herder would take his place.

September 11, 1882

One of our men has died. He fell off the side of the rail bed, and lay on a big rock far below. We will not work in the presence of the dead because it is bad fortune. If we did, perhaps another man would die. So we all sat down and refused to work. The big boss—Mr. Haney—came by and was angered by our refusal to work under these conditions. He asked the European workers to remove the body, but they refused, as the corpse was in a place they could not reach. Later that day, a Native man announced he could remove the body. He did so in a very ingenious way. He collected some sticks of dynamite and lowered them on a rope to where the body lay. The explosion totally destroyed the body, and we resumed our work.

November 12, 1882

The Europeans have cheated us. When it came time for us to receive our pay, we discovered we had been underpaid by a whole cent per hour. As we do not get much pay in any case, we refused to work. Mr. Chen went to the boss, Mr. Haney. He soon realized the error, and we were paid the missing cent for our work. Mr. Haney does not understand our ways, but he is an honest man, and for that we respect him. Once, he had to get a work crew quickly to **move up the line** fifty miles. He said that no crew could move that distance, but we told him that we could do so. Within a day, we had moved ourselves and our belongings the required distance, and had begun clearing the way for the rails to be laid. Mr. Haney was most pleased, and thanked us for our efforts.

Later that day, a Native man helped us remove the body.

June 18, 1883

We are now working further up the canyon of the Fraser River than where we were last year. The work is still hard, and men are still injured and die in accidents, but we have become more used to the work, and to the climate. While the last winter was just as cold as the first we encountered, it did not seem so cold. Mr. Chen also obtained some quilted coats for us, and these helped keep out the cold.

August 20, 1883

One of our men has become sick. He can no longer work, and he lies in the tent. There is nothing we can do for him. So we keep working. Yesterday, Mr. Haney asked Mr. Chen about the man.

"Will he die today?" he asked.

Mr. Chen said, "No, tomorrow, at three o'clock."

This was in fact the time for his death—and it came to pass as Mr. Chen had said. Mr.

Haney also asked about our food. We eat rice with fish, and we are used to this food. Sometimes, though, men take sick and die. Mr. Haney says it is our food, but we rather think that it is both the hard work and living in this strange land which causes death from sickness.

October 20, 1884

It seems strange, but we have been working now for over two years on the railway. For most of us, the work has become familiar, and we are now out of the hardest area. Every day we carry rocks, or clear brush, or flatten the ground for the rails to be laid. The work is hard, but we are all looking forward to the day when the railway is finished and we can collect our wages and travel home to our families, whom we have not seen for so long.

November 5, 1885

The work is finally over. The railway will be finished in a week or less, and Mr. Chen has come to tell us that we are discharged. Unfortunately, the railway company lied to us about our wages. We understood that our passage to this place was paid for. They did not tell us

Woo Xi Feng learns how much money was deducted from his wages.

that the cost of passage was deducted from our wages. Nor did they tell us that all the costs of our work were also charged to us. Our rent (in tents and bunkhouses), our food, our tools, our clothing—in fact, all that we used—was subtracted from our pay. And also, in the winter months, when we could not work for the snow and the cold, we were not paid, but our expenses continued! This year alone, I expected to earn at least $250. I actually was paid $43.

Like most of my fellow workers, I am now unable to return to China. I must travel back to the coast at my own expense, and try to find work in Vancouver or New Westminster. I do not believe I will ever see my village or my wife again. I will disgrace my ancestors if I die here. I am, after nearly four years in this country, a stranger in a strange land.

Dynasty: a period of rule in China by the same family

bookman: the boss

herder: the person in charge of the workers

to move up the line: to travel a distance along the designated route

ACTIVITIES

1. How did Woo Xi Feng hear about the opportunities in British Columbia? Why would he and his friends be eager to work on the railway?

2. Why do you suppose people in British Columbia were hostile to the Chinese workers?

3. Find three examples of Chinese customs which would have perplexed the Europeans. Find aspects of life on the Fraser that would have perplexed the Chinese railway workers.

4. What do you suppose the fate of Woo Xi Feng was? Form groups and investigate possibilities.

TIME LINE

1826 — SIMPSON BECOMES GOVERNOR OF HBC

1843 — JAMES DOUGLAS ARRIVES IN FORT VICTORIA

1845 — US GETS BRITISH TERRITORY SOUTH OF 49TH PARALLEL

1856 — FIRST LEGISLATIVE ASSEMBLY ON VANCOUVER ISLAND

1860 — CARIBOO GOLD RUSH BEGINS

1862 — CONSTRUCTION OF CARIBOO ROAD BEGINS

SMALLPOX EPIDEMIC AMONG THE NATIVE PEOPLES

1866 — VANCOUVER ISLAND AND BRITISH COLUMBIA ARE JOINED

1868 — VICTORIA BECOMES CAPITAL OF BRITISH COLUMBIA

1871 — BC JOINS CONFEDERATION

1884 — VANCOUVER BECOMES THE TERMINUS FOR THE CPR

1885 — ROYAL COMMISSION ON CHINESE IMMIGRATION TO BC

The stupendous difficulty of travel here in British Columbia has caused us to admit the utter fallaciousness of certain writers who have sent home glowing reports of the land and its advantages.

–BRITISH TOURIST W. CHAMPNESS, 1862

Champness, who embarked on a journey to British Columbia during the Cariboo Gold Rush, later wrote about his adventures in a British magazine. Why should someone from Britain find travelling in British Columbia a "stupendous difficulty"? Would Walter Cheadle (Window on the Past, Chapter 2) make such a remark? Why or why not?

INTRODUCTION

The Pacific Northwest was the last part of North America to be explored and settled by Europeans. Home to more than twenty-five different aboriginal groups for approximately 10 000 years, the area must have dazzled the new visitors—mountains covered with spruce and fir trees, Western red cedars growing to 60 metres, and an abundance of fur-bearing animals.

A Russian ship was the first to record reaching the Northwest Coast in 1741. It landed in the territory of the Tlingit, and the Russians immediately launched a successful trade in sea otter fur. Ships from Spain, Britain, and the United States soon followed, and the trade in sea otter and seal flourished. By 1826, when the HBC sent George Simpson to govern New Caledonia and Columbia—the future British Columbia—the fur trade was a focus of intense rivalry between Britain and the United States.

In this chapter, you will follow the history of our province from the 1820s, when British Columbia was a territory controlled by the Hudson's Bay Company, to the 1880s, when Vancouver became the last stop on the Canadian Pacific Railway. There were many growing spurts along the way—two fantastic gold rushes, the creation of the first Legislative Assembly, and the entry of British Columbia to Confederation in 1871. In the process, immigrants from many parts of the world, including the United States, Britain, and Asia, came here to work. Some settled permanently, creating the dynamic culture we have inherited today.

Figure 6–1 Fort Vancouver

THE OREGON TERRITORY

When George Simpson became governor of the expanded Hudson's Bay Company in 1826, his greatest challenge was the territory of New Caledonia and Columbia. Many interests had a stake in the region. Russia claimed the coast as far south as northern Vancouver Island. West of the Lake of the Woods, the forty-ninth **parallel** drew a firm boundary between the United States and British North America, but the boundary ended at the eastern slopes of the Rocky Mountains. The Americans claimed the Oregon Territory, on the other side of the mountains. The HBC had other ideas—it saw the region as an extension of Rupert's Land, the vast territory granted by King Charles II in 1670.

Both the Americans and the British wanted to use the Oregon Territory to their advantage. The Hudson's Bay Company had no interest in encouraging settlement. It could disrupt a lucrative fur trade, or, even worse, undermine the Company's trade monopoly in the area. On the other hand, America's population was growing rapidly. Having acquired large amounts of territory west of the Mississippi, the United States seemed fated to control all of North America—an idea promoted by Manifest Destiny. As a result, the Americans pursued an aggressive policy towards the Oregon Territory, one that encouraged settlers to move into the area.

From the American point of view, there were two good locations for settlement: north of the Columbia River, to Puget Sound; and south of the Columbia, along the valley of the Williamette River. As the 1830s progressed, more and more American settlers travelled overland along the Oregon Trail, and most settled in the valley of the Williamette.

parallel: an imaginary line north or south of the equator

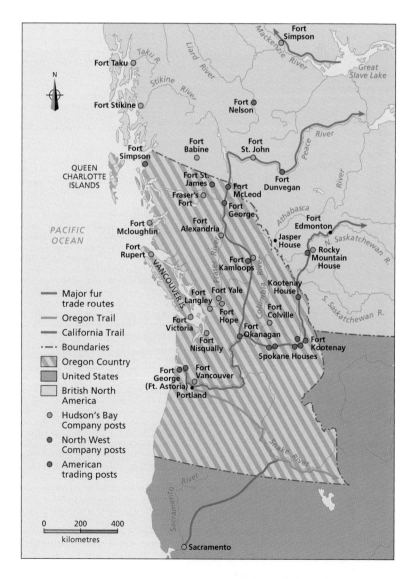

Figure 6–2 The Oregon Territory in 1835

unnerving: unsettling

When Simpson toured the Company's forts in the Oregon Territory, he decided that the HBC was not making the best use of area resources. He created a new post on the north bank of the Columbia River, opposite the Williamette River. Fort Vancouver was immediately placed under the direction of Chief Factor John McLoughlin. Simpson also ordered HBC employees to open up trade in the Fraser Valley and to expand trading networks with the Native peoples in the region. The area seemed to be rich in furs, and dwindling fur stocks had become a real problem.

Figure 6–3 While he was HBC governor, Simpson made a point of touring most of British Columbia. Here, he arrives at Fort St. James in 1828. He is greeted by James Douglas, who would eventually become the first governor of British Columbia. Simpson reportedly enjoyed a "cracking pace" on tour. If you were a member of his expedition, you would be woken at two in the morning and travel at least six hours before breakfast.

In 1827, Simpson established a second HBC post, Fort Langley, on the Fraser River.

McLoughlin was a capable administrator with an **unnerving** physical presence. With his mane of white hair and smoldering eyes, he resembled a character from a Dickens novel. He favoured patched clothes, and often forgot to bathe. Even Simpson found McLoughlin's appearance alarming.

Nevertheless, McLoughlin was known for his fairness, and for rewarding employees with parties and banquets. He was also something of a political realist. He saw that the Americans were going to settle the region south of the Columbia River. In order to reduce American competition with the HBC, he encouraged Americans to go there and to stay out of HBC territory north of the Columbia. He offered money and supplies to Americans arriving overland, although he was supposed to extend help only to HBC employees. Simpson, by contrast, thought the American immigrants should be treated harshly. By the end of the 1830s, McLoughlin's plan had led to a very strong American presence in the Oregon Territory. Neither Britain nor the HBC, however, paid much attention to this development because McLoughlin managed the fur trade in the region effectively.

The HBC also had to contend with the Russians on the Pacific Coast. By now the Russians had established a number of fur-trading posts in Alaska and had extended their influence south along the northern Northwest Coast. In 1839, the HBC and the Russians agreed that the Russians would cease operations south of the 54° 40′ N. In exchange, the HBC would supply

Figure 6–4 The *Beaver* changed a great deal during its fifty-three years on the BC coast. The ship eventually sank off Prospect Point, in Vancouver, in 1888. A commemorative plaque on the Stanley Park seawall tells the ship's story.

Russian posts in Alaska with food. The *Beaver*, an HBC steamship that had arrived on the coast in 1835, supplied the Russian posts. It was also used as a mobile base for trading with the Northwest Coast peoples. It also, of course, added to the British presence in the area.

In 1841, Simpson toured the area again and discovered that the fur trade was not expanding as he had hoped. He decided to consolidate the operations of the maritime fur trade. All coastal posts were to be closed, with the exception of Fort Simpson, and the *Beaver* would be used as a floating fur-trade post to trade with other villages on the coast. McLoughlin was furious; he believed that the chain of forts along the coast made the HBC strong. Simpson had eliminated all the hard work he had done in the last fifteen years.

McLoughlin's anger deepened when his son was killed in a brawl at Fort Stikine in 1842. When Simpson recommended a charge of "justifiable homicide," McLoughlin was furious. Grief-stricken, he developed an active hatred for both Simpson and the HBC. He continued to promote American settlement south of the Columbia, and discouraged newcomers, including those who arrived from Canada, from settling north of the river.

By now, Simpson was alarmed. With the rising population of American settlers in the Oregon Territory, the British could lose control of the area. Fort Vancouver could be lost. Simpson ordered Fort Vancouver's Chief Factor, James Douglas, to establish a new depot on Vancouver Island. In 1843, it would become Fort Victoria, in honour of Queen Victoria.

Danger at the Fort: Amelia Douglas Saves the Day

The murder of John McLoughlin's son was not an isolated incident of violence at the HBC forts in New Caledonia and Columbia. Brawling and lawlessness were a way of life in Canada's "Wild West." Even in the workplace, people behaved in ways that we would find repugnant today. Bosses such as McLoughlin often enforced order and discipline with their fists, and there was no union or human rights code to protect workers.

One of the most intriguing episodes of violence occurred at Fort George and Fort St. James in the 1820s. A chain of events was set in motion when a young clerk, James Yale, was invited to visit another clerk, John Macdonnell, at Fort Fraser. Although Yale was not supposed to leave his post, he decided to make the 200-kilometre journey because Macdonell was feeling gloomy about being stuck alone at his post.

During the visit, Yale heard that two murders had been committed at his fort. He hurried back to find that the men left in charge had been killed with an axe, and that one of the men had been "eaten by dogs, partially so ..." Following the murders, some people claimed that Yale had become too interested in a woman loved by another man, but Yale also learned that there were bad feelings between the murdered men and one of the suspected killers.

Yale wrote to his boss, who promised to exact revenge in the form of a small army of Dene from the Peace River area. The men accused of the murders were from the Carrier nation. In

Figure 6–5 Amelia Douglas is said to have saved her husband's life when she negotiated with Chief Kwah by offering him merchandise at the post.

the meantime, other traders heard that the killers were waiting to ambush Yale at Chinlac, a camp located where the Stuart River flows into the Nechako River. Yale's boss learned that one of the accused had "lately purchased a gun with part of the property he stole, and declares his intention of killing Mr. Yale."

The saga continued through 1823 and 1824. The Carrier became involved after the HBC negotiated with community leaders to execute the men. But one of the accused escaped and survived for several years before taking refuge in the home of Chief Kwah. There, a group of HBC employees, including James Douglas (the future governor of British Columbia), confronted the suspect, dragged him away, and killed him with a shovel. The

high-handed attitude displayed by the group offended the chief, who immediately set out to confront Douglas at his post. As fate would have it, Douglas did not return home immediately, and Chief Kwah found himself dealing with Amelia Douglas, James's wife. The record shows that she remained calm, and negotiated skilfully in order to end the violence.

Of course, the entire story comes to us courtesy of the HBC and its employees. It is recorded in the *Hudson Bay Archives Correspondence Books* and was discovered by a researcher looking for data on trading-post economics. How might this story be different if told from the point of view of the accused, or from the standpoint of someone from the Carrier nation?

Deeply embittered, McLoughlin retired two years later from the HBC. He obtained a decent pension in recognition of his years of service, and settled south of the Columbia River in Oregon City. His place in history confirmed by his kindness to American settlers, McLoughlin would become known as the "Father of Oregon." Few Americans realize that he was born in Rivière-du-Loup, Quebec.

ACTIVITIES

1. In an organizer, compare and contrast American and British attitudes towards the Oregon Territory.

2. Why do you suppose McLoughlin went out of his way to assist American settlers? Give two pieces of evidence.

3. How could the HBC have changed its policies in the 1830s in order to gain control of at least a portion of the Oregon Territory south of the forty-ninth parallel?

THE COLONY OF VANCOUVER ISLAND TO 1858

By the mid-1840s, the United States wanted to expand its territory. In 1844, a Democratic candidate for the presidency, James Polk, ran on the slogan "54° 40' or fight." It meant that the US claimed the Oregon Territory up to 54° 40' N. This slogan proved to be extremely popular with American voters, and Polk won the election.

In 1845, Polk also tried to negotiate with the British government for the Oregon Territory. In spite of his aggressive stance in the 1844 election, Polk had no desire to wage war with the British. When Britain absolutely refused to give up its claim, the old boundary of 1818 was finally extended along the forty-ninth parallel to the Pacific Ocean. Vancouver Island would remain in British hands, but all British territory south of the forty-ninth parallel became US territory, including Fort Vancouver and the farmlands of Puget Sound.

By 1848, the British government decided that its territory on the Pacific coast required a more official presence than the HBC, and it created the Crown colony of Vancouver Island. Britain gave the HBC a trade monopoly in the new colony, but it had to sell land to British settlers who came to live there.

The colony's new governor, James Douglas, was not keen to see any more Americans in the area, so he actively encouraged British settlement of the colony. He thought that free grants of land should be given to prospective colonists. The British government had different ideas. It wanted to recreate the English class system on Vancouver Island. Settlers were required to purchase land at the rate of £1 an acre, with a minimum purchase of 20 acres. Any settler who bought more than 100 acres was required to bring along at least five people to work the

£: a British pound, today, about $2.75 Canadian

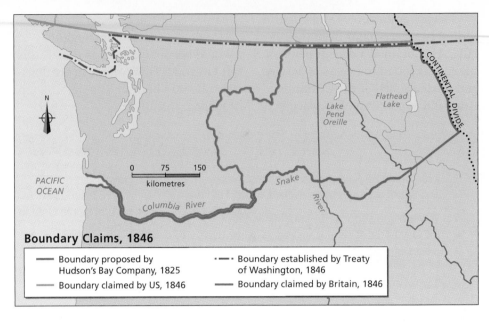

Figure 6–6 This map shows the boundary claims that were made final in 1846.

Boundary Claims, 1846

— Boundary proposed by Hudson's Bay Company, 1825
—·— Boundary established by Treaty of Washington, 1846
— Boundary claimed by US, 1846
— Boundary claimed by Britain, 1846

CONTINENTAL DIVIDE

Flathead Lake

Lake Pend Oreille

PACIFIC OCEAN

Snake River

Columbia River

0 75 150
kilometres

N

land. Once again, the old system of rural England was being transported to Canada. A relatively small number of settlers would be landowners, and they would have many servants to farm the land. In reality, the only settlers in Vancouver Island in 1849 were ex-HBC employees. They had already acquired much of the best farmland in the colony.

Though dominated by the HBC in the 1850s, the colony began to diversify economically. Coal had been discovered near Nanaimo in the 1840s and immigrants arrived in the region with the intention of starting a mining operation. They even had a customer lined up—the Royal Navy. Britain had established Esquimault harbour, next to Fort Victoria, as a naval base, and the warships stationed there needed coal supplies. More mines were established in the mid-1850s at Cumberland further north on Vancouver Island.

The Royal Navy played a huge role in the social life of Fort Victoria. Its officers were considered to be gentlemen because they came from the privileged class in England—they were always invited to parties and other social functions given by the English landowners in the area. While Douglas encouraged these social activities, he was not impressed by the new upper class. Douglas had been a fur trader and was married to Amelia Douglas, a Métis. His dim view of Victorian high society was shared by many of the former HBC employees, who often were shunned by the prejudiced and class-conscious newcomers.

Figure 6–7 Amelia Douglas

In 1856, Governor Douglas created a Legislative Assembly in the colony, partly in response to complaints from ex-HBC employees that Vancouver Island was becoming a private club for the **landed gentry**. The Assembly was small, with just seven elected representatives. Because people couldn't vote unless they owned property, only about forty of the colony's 450 adult citizens had the right to vote. Douglas also insisted on retaining final authority in the colony—the Legislative Assembly could pass resolutions, but it had no authority to enforce them. However, the Assembly did have the authority to grant monies for the government's use.

Douglas was worried about another issue. While a census of the immigrant population of Vancouver Island showed a population of just 774 persons in 1855, there were more than 30 000 aboriginal peoples living on the island. In order for the colony to prosper and attract more settlers, Douglas would have to negotiate with the people who had lived there longer than anyone else. This was especially true of the rich farmlands occupied by the Native peoples living between Fort Victoria and Nanaimo.

Douglas decided to negotiate treaties with the aboriginal peoples: they would surrender their lands to the Europeans, but would retain hunting and fishing rights. The following is an excerpt from one of the treaties he negotiated in 1854. In this instance, "our" refers to the Native peoples.

The condition of, or understanding of, this sale is this, that our village sites and enclosed fields are to be kept for our own use, for the use of our children, and for those who may follow after us; and the land shall be properly surveyed hereafter. It is understood, however, that the land itself, with these small exceptions, becomes the entire property of the white people forever; it is also understood that we are at liberty to hunt over the unoccupied lands, and to carry on our fisheries as formerly.

landed gentry: the British upper class "landed" in another country

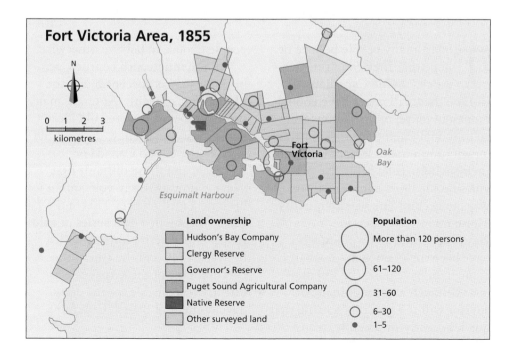

Fort Victoria Area, 1855

N

0 1 2 3
kilometres

Fort Victoria

Oak Bay

Esquimalt Harbour

Land ownership
- Hudson's Bay Company
- Clergy Reserve
- Governor's Reserve
- Puget Sound Agricultural Company
- Native Reserve
- Other surveyed land

Population
- More than 120 persons
- 61–120
- 31–60
- 6–30
- 1–5

Figure 6–8 Landholdings and population concentrations around Victoria in 1855. How successful had the British government's policy of settlement been?

Because Douglas seemed to be leasing the land from the Native peoples—there was an annual compensation of £2 10 **shillings** per family—some people say that he confirmed that the aboriginal peoples had title to these lands. In fact, the governments of Britain, Canada, and British Columbia have all acknowledged this title. The Douglas treaties on Vancouver Island were the only treaties of this nature negotiated in British Columbia in the nineteenth century.

ACTIVITIES

1. Why do you think the British government granted a trade monopoly to the HBC on Vancouver Island?

2. What was unusual about the landholding policy in the colony? Why would immigrants from Canada object to such a policy?

3. How was the Legislative Assembly set up by Governor Douglas not a representative government? How do you think the inhabitants of the colony would react to this state of affairs?

4. Why did Governor Douglas make treaties with many of the Vancouver Island First Nations?

5. Examine the primary source on page 215. With a partner, discuss how this text could be interpreted as meaning First Nations peoples owned their lands. Do you agree with this interpretation? Discuss your findings with the rest of the class.

THE CARIBOO GOLD RUSH

shilling: an old British coinage, about one twentieth of a pound

title: established or recognized right to something

infomercial: an extended commercial that seems like a news show

Today, many people believe or hope that they can "get rich quick." Some Canadians assume they will never have enough money to retire, or buy a house, or go to school—and they are counting on winning a major lottery to top up their savings. Television also provides hundreds of **infomercials** on ways to accumulate wealth quickly. These infomercials feature interviews with men and women who have been lucky enough, or smart enough, to have done the impossible. Although any good financial advisor will tell you that getting rich quick is nearly impossible, many people choose to believe otherwise.

In the nineteenth century, people were just as susceptible to the idea of quick wealth. After all, many immigrants had rejected old ideas about class and money. If you could survive the trip to Canada or America, and those difficult first years, who was to say you couldn't become a millionaire? This optimism was fuelled by a series of gold rushes in western North America between 1849 and the end of the century. One of these rushes was directly responsible for the early development of British Columbia.

Miners Everywhere

In 1848, gold was discovered along the Sacramento River in central California. By 1849, thousands of people had left their jobs and homes to travel to California. They came overland, across the United States, or they travelled by sea, around the tip of South America and then up the Pacific Coast. Many perished along the way. The vast majority of these gold seekers never did get rich, and many never made it back home. As much as it was real, the gold rush was also a fantasy. The fantasy promised that you could scramble along the banks of a gold-bearing creek, pick up nuggets the size of your fist, and become wealthy overnight. In reality, gold seekers had to **stake** a **claim** along a creek, and then sink a mine shaft down to **bedrock.** Gold-bearing clay and sand would be brought to the surface, and the lighter material would be washed away to reveal the gold. Most of the claims had been staked in California by the time people started arriving for the rush of 1849. Most of those driven to California by the fantasy of instant wealth found themselves instead working as miners for the original claim holders. Many were broke and unemployed again by the mid-1850s.

Then, in late 1857, a Hudson's Bay Company trader arrived in Fort Victoria. Along with his cargo of furs for the Company, he carried two vials filled with gold dust and some small nuggets that he had **panned** along the banks of the Thompson River. He presented these to Governor Douglas, who examined them one night at dinner. Douglas believed that news of another gold strike would unleash an influx of greedy miners into the colony. His fear was borne out during the winter of 1857–58. Miners who had moved to Washington and Oregon after the California rush had ended moved north to the banks of the Thompson and Fraser rivers, and began prospecting for gold. Most discovered that the best sources for easily found gold were on the sandbars along both rivers.

Word reached San Francisco in early 1858. Soon, hundreds of unemployed miners were trying to book tickets on any ship that would take them north. The first ship to arrive at Fort Victoria was the side-wheel steamer *Yosemite*. Some 450 miners disembarked on April 25, 1858. Almost immediately, they moved on to the mainland. The miners had to be creative about getting across the Strait of Georgia—some even used makeshift rafts. More ships arrived as the year progressed. By the end of the summer, more than 10 000 miners—mostly Americans—were working on the Fraser River.

Because the majority of miners were Americans, Douglas saw that the mainland had become more vulnerable to US territorial expansion.

to stake claim: the legal right to mine gold, or other minerals, on a specific piece of land

bedrock: solid rock underneath looser materials such as soil

to pan: to search for gold by panning gravel

Figure 6–9 A miner's camp near Yale in 1858

He immediately communicated his concern to the Colonial Office in London. The response from London was swift. First, Douglas was made governor of the new Crown colony of British Columbia, which encompassed the mainland as far north as 54° 40′N. Second, Britain dispatched a contingent of Royal Engineers under Colonel Richard Moody. The Engineers would provide some degree of military presence in the new colony. They would also survey the region and provide technical assistance in building roads and towns, as Douglas required. Moody and the Royal Engineers arrived in 1859.

That year, the gold deposits along the sandbars of the lower Fraser were almost all gone. Prospectors now assumed that the gold found in the river sands and gravels had been eroded from a

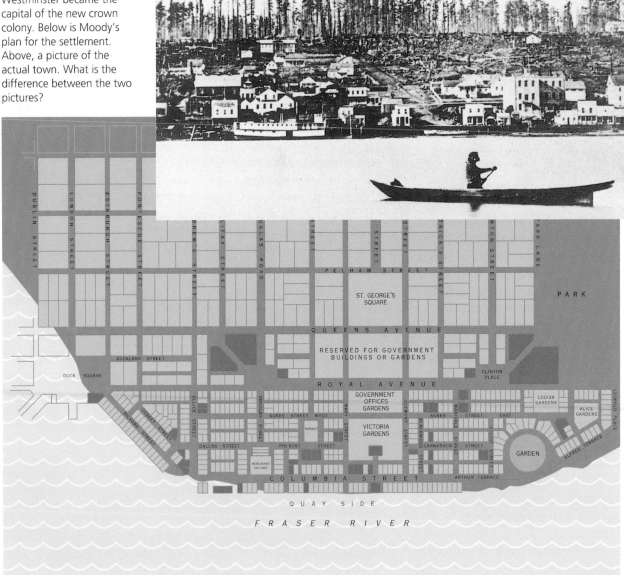

Figure 6–10 New Westminster became the capital of the new crown colony. Below is Moody's plan for the settlement. Above, a picture of the actual town. What is the difference between the two pictures?

larger deposit upstream. That year, the miners moved north along the Fraser, searching for the source of the gold. Between 1860 and 1861, several miners arrived in the Cariboo region of southcentral British Columbia. Here they found sizable gold deposits in the creeks that fed the Fraser.

The Cariboo Road

In the early 1860s, Governor Douglas realized that profitable mining operations in the Cariboo were happening right under his nose—yet the colony wasn't seeing a penny of revenue. Since all the gold removed from British Columbia was taxable, Douglas decided to build a road to the goldfields. In this way, he could ensure that the gold would leave the region via the Fraser, not through US territory. Moreover, a roadway would promote settlement and encourage economic development.

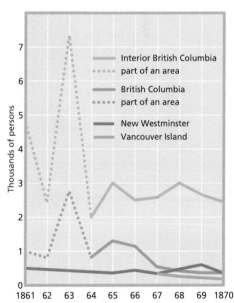

Figure 6–11 Mining in the Cariboo region, at the old Caledonia Mine. What effects to you think such operations would have on the environment?

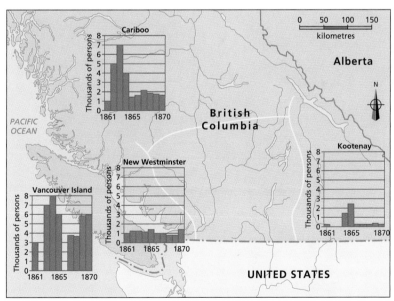

Figure 6–12 Great shifts in population occurred in parts of British Columbia and Vancouver Island during the Cariboo Gold Rush. Examine these population graphs, which show the fluctuating size of four areas: Vancouver Island, the Cariboo region, New Westminster, and the Kootenay region. How do you account for the different patterns seen here?

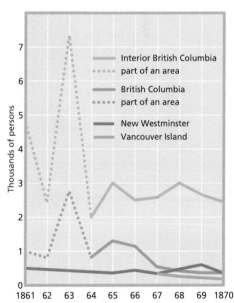

Figure 6–13 What does this graph tell you about the society of the Cariboo region compared to that in the southern part of the colony?

Two possible routes existed. The long route was via Lake Harrison and the Lillooet River. The short route was via the treacherous Fraser Canyon. The Harrison route, which took several steamer routes along the lakes of the interior, probably would have cost more than the second, more difficult, option. So, in 1862, construction of the Cariboo Road began. It covered 650 kilometres, from Yale, along the Fraser Canyon, to the new centre of the Cariboo, Barkerville. The road was a marvellous feat of engineering, and took four years and more than $750 000 to complete. In many places, the roadway had to be blasted from solid rock. Unfortunately, the gold rush was coming to an end by the mid-1860s. The Cariboo Road, built at such expense, was finished only after possible revenues were in steep decline. The colony had a tough time recouping the cost of its construction.

In 1864, James Douglas retired as governor of the two colonies. He was replaced by Frederick Seymour, in British Columbia, and by Arthur Kennedy, on Vancouver Island. Seymour, an active, enthusiastic man, quickly took charge of the colony and seemed to have the best interests of the inhabitants at heart. Kennedy, on the other hand, was autocratic and hard to get along with. He quickly found himself embroiled in all sorts of disputes with the elected Assembly on Vancouver Island.

Figure 6–14 The Cariboo Road

Tragedy for the Native Peoples: When Death Came to Call

Before construction of the Cariboo Road, the oldest trails along the Fraser Canyon had belonged to the Native peoples. Those who knew these trails intimately—and had often escorted miners to the goldfields—also helped to build the Cariboo Road. Although European construction workers always got the first jobs, by 1862, gold prospecting had caused a labour shortage. Contractors working under the Royal Engineers began hiring Chinese immigrants, as well as workers from the aboriginal nations. Eventually, Chinese immigrants would comprise approximately one-third of miners working in the Cariboo region. The Native peoples did not fare so well.

That same year, an outbreak of smallpox started outside of Victoria and spread to other parts of the colony. Smallpox was a dreaded disease in Europe, and one that affected the settlers and miners. For the Native peoples of the Americas, it was almost always fatal—they had never been exposed to it before, and had no immunity to it. It is estimated that after European contact, smallpox was responsible for the deaths of more than 70 percent of all aboriginal peoples.

Following the outbreak in Victoria, the authorities responded swiftly but misguidedly. Homes of the Native peoples were destroyed, and the occupants were ordered to leave Victoria. As they travelled up the coast, they infected other Native peoples. By summertime, smallpox had reached the Native com-

Figure 6–15 The rifle pit dug by some prospectors on their way to the Cariboo. They were attacked by the Chilcotin in 1864.

munities in the northern part of the colony.

The effect was devastating. Whole villages began to die, and survivors scattered into the hinterland. With no one left to perform burial rites, corpses rotted in the abandoned villages, and travellers along the coast reported the scene to the press. Among the Haida of the Queen Charlotte Islands, the effect of smallpox was perhaps the most pronounced. More than 80 percent of the Haida died that summer, and villages that had existed for thousands of years became ghost towns. Along the entire coast, it is estimated that over half of a total population of some 60 000 people died of the disease in 1862.

Unscrupulous—or ignorant— European traders and prospectors compounded the tragedy. They collected blankets and other

possessions from the dead and sold these to other Native communities. The smallpox virus can live for more than six months in contaminated clothing, and so the recipients of these goods quickly contracted the disease. During 1863, even more aboriginal peoples died of the disease inland.

Among the Chilcotin, the smallpox epidemic was a catalyst for rebellion. Their traditional land overrun by road construction and an unwelcome influx of American and European miners— who also disturbed their **salmon weirs**—they staged a brief war in 1864. Smallpox survivors attacked several labourers as they were building a railway right-of-way from the coast to the interior. Eventually, five Chilcotin were tried and executed for their role in the uprising.

salmon weir: a fenced-in stream for easier salmon fishing

Apply Your Knowledge

Barkerville: The Evolution of a Town

The largest town in the Cariboo was Barkerville, situated on the western edge of the Cariboo Mountains. It was named after Billy Barker, a sailor from Cambridgeshire, England, who struck gold in 1862. Barkerville grew up almost overnight, and was a case of "growth via word of mouth." Barkerville grew as fast as word of Barker's strike spread. His claim would eventually yield 1100 kilograms of gold.

Before the construction of the Cariboo Road, people had hauled their own supplies to Barkerville, either on their backs, or in a **pack train**. Because supplies were scarce, even the prices of most everyday items were **inflated**. Inflation in Barkerville did not ease up until the Cariboo Road had been finished, when goods could be transported by huge freight wagons. Soon, movers of freight boasted that they could pack and carry a set of champagne glasses without any breakage—for a price, of course. More women also came to Barkerville after the construction of the Cariboo Road.

At first, the town consisted only of makeshift cabins and tents. By the mid-1860s, however, Barkerville had a population of approximately

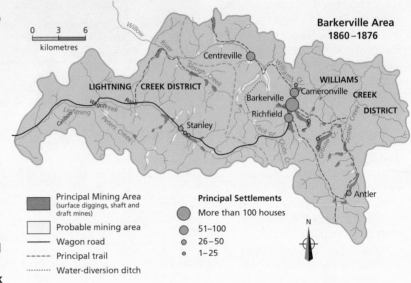

Figure 6–16 The Barkerville area

5000 people—it was the largest town north of San Francisco and west of Chicago. Even though its population was **transient** and largely dependent on mining, Barkerville was becoming less of a service **town** and more of a real community. It had several general stores and boarding houses, a drugstore that also sold newspapers and cigars, a barbershop that also cut

Figure 6–17 Historic Barkerville before the fire. The landscape has been heavily altered by the activities of the gold miners. What possible problems are likely to develop? How would such a town be extremely vulnerable to fire?

women's hair, the "Wake-Up Jake Restaurant and Coffee Saloon," a theatre (the Theatre Royal), and a literary society (the Cariboo Literary Society). Horse racing and prize fighting were common entertainments. Among the so-called "sober set," church services were extremely well attended.

Chinese immigrants were an important part of Barkerville life for almost a hundred years. They established a number of businesses, including the Kwong Lee Company, a general store that sold groceries, clothing, hardware, and mining tools. The Kwong Lee Company also had other stores in other parts of British Columbia, but the Barkerville store was one of the most impressive in town.

The Chinese community also built cabins for Chinese miners, where they saved money by sharing four or five to a cabin, and Tai Ping (the "Peace Room"), the equivalent of a modern nursing home. Chinese immigrants who came to Canada

Figure 6–18 Barkerville as it has been recreated today

during the Cariboo Gold Rush or the building of the Canadian Pacific Railway always wanted to return to their homeland for burial—to do otherwise was an insult to one's ancestors. When a Chinese person was buried in

Barkerville, it was the Chinese community's duty to ensure that the grave was excavated after a suitable time and that the body was sent to China for reburial.

On September 16, 1868, Barkerville was destroyed by a fire that spread quickly through the wooden buildings. Rebuilding began immediately, and at an impressive pace. Within six weeks, ninety buildings had been rebuilt. Even the sidewalks were improved. By 1880, there were enough children in the area to build the Barkerville School. It had just thirteen pupils and one piece of school equipment—a chalkboard. Even so, Barkerville's population was declining by the end of the century, and it eventually became a ghost town. It did, however, have a small

Figure 6–19 The old schoolhouse, which accommodated thirteen students

revival in the 1930s, when the Great Depression caused widespread unemployment, and the price of gold skyrocketed.

In 1958, the government of British Columbia decided that the town should be restored and operated as a tourist attraction. Today, Barkerville appears as it did in its heyday, and visitors can step back in time and marvel at its past. "Barkerville Historic Town" now greets visitors from all over Canada and other parts of the world, including thousands of students. The history of each building has been meticulously researched and documented. No actual residents remain. They were either bought out or moved to New Barkerville during the restoration of the site.

pack train: a line of people or animals carrying heavy packs

to inflate: to increase the price of something dramatically

transient: not lasting very long

service town: a town that provides services to people engaged in one main industry

Figure 6–20 Billy Barker

ACTIVITIES

1. Examine Figure 6–16 and explain Barkerville's location with respect to the main mining areas.

2. Are there any physical characteristics of Barkerville that would discourage settlement? Explain.

3. How many stages of development has Barkerville experienced? Create a time line to illustrate these stages.

4. Why were there no schools in Barkerville before 1880?

5. Using the text and pictures above as a reference, describe the changing cultural landscape of Barkerville. See Chapter 3, pages 115 to 118, for more information about cultural landscapes.

6. What economic and social tensions might have existed in Barkerville during the early 1860s?

7. If you had been a resident of Barkerville during its gold rush, would you have preferred to mine or to operate a business that supported the miners? Explain your answer.

ACTIVITIES

1. How did the fantasy of the gold rush differ from the reality? Which version was more popular? Why?

2. Where was gold first mined in British Columbia? What goal drove miners onward?

3. Douglas was concerned about an anti-British bias among the miners. What was the basis of his concerns? What steps did the British government take to deal with these concerns?

4. Why was the construction of the Cariboo Road so important? With a partner, examine the maps in this section and/or in an atlas. Based on the distance covered, the topography, and the water routes, determine what you feel would have been the best route inland. Share your findings with the rest of the class.

5. Imagine you are a Native person on the BC coast in early 1863. Describe, in a paragraph, poem, or poster, your feelings regarding what has happened to your community and your feelings towards the non-Native people of the colony.

THE COLONY OF BRITISH COLUMBIA—AND CONFEDERATION

During the Cariboo Gold Rush (1858 to 1863) more than 35 000 prospectors arrived in British Columbia from many parts of the world—Britain, the Canadas, and Europe. Most people did not find gold, and very few became rich. By the mid-1860s, the gold was running out. People started to leave the Cariboo region, and eventually, the colony. The rapid loss of population and revenue was a great blow to the governments of Vancouver Island and British Columbia. British Columbia suffered the greatest financial losses, especially considering the amount of money it had spent on the Cariboo Road.

Elected representatives of both colonies began to press their respective governors for a union of the two colonies. They felt that this would make more sense from an economic standpoint. By 1866, the colony of Vancouver Island had debts totalling nearly $300 000. British Columbia's debt, most of it incurred during construction of the Cariboo Road, was just over $1 000 000. In May of that year, both colonies were horrified to learn that their credit with local banks had run out.

The colonial office in Britain agreed with the idea of union. Britain was not interested in providing large **subsidies** to keep colonies operating—especially when the mainland had a huge natural resource base that could eventually generate revenue. On August 6, 1866, the British government formally joined the two colonies together as British Columbia.

Governor Seymour, who was by far the more popular leader, became governor of the new colony. A Legislative Council was established, with twenty-three members. Only nine members were elected, however. There were five representatives from the mainland and four from the Island. British Columbia would not have **responsible government** until later in the century.

Union of the two colonies did not solve their economic woes. The population of British Columbia continued to decline, and the money problems continued. It was obvious that a more permanent solution was needed.

The Confederation Debate

In Chapter 2, you learned that British colonies outside central Canada had concerns about Confederation. British Columbia was no exception, and had three main factions. One faction strongly opposed Confederation, another strongly supported it. The third group, composed mostly of Victoria business people, favoured annexation by the United States. Between 1868 and 1870, the debate about British Columbia's future was ongoing and, at times, bitter.

The elected representatives from the mainland were all in favour of Confederation. In January, 1868, they adopted a series of resolutions, which they forwarded to the government of Canada. In particular, they proposed that Canada become liable for British Columbia's debt, and that the fed-

subsidy: direct financial aid from a higher level of government

responsible government: a government in which the executive council is responsible to the legislative assembly, whose members are representatives of the people

Figure 6–21 Victoria was more established than New Westminster, and the Legislative Council members preferred to live there.

to co-opt: to bring someone into a group by capitalizing on their strengths, even if they disagree with you

eral government build a transcontinental railway to link it to the East. The resolutions had little clout, and were defeated in the Legislative Assembly by a vote of twelve to four. However, the mainland representatives spent the rest of the year promoting Confederation in the press. They believed that only a public clearly in favour of the idea would convince the governor and his supporters to change their minds.

The small group of Victoria business people who supported annexation to the United States had something in common with the confederationists. They believed that British Columbia could not continue to operate without being connected to a larger body. Unlike the confederationists, however, they thought that Canada was too distant from the Pacific Coast to be relevant to British Columbia. They also believed that the United States would be a better market for the colony's forest, mineral, and other resources, and that immigration to British Columbia would flow from the United States rather than from Canada.

The Tide Turns

In late 1868, an election was held for the Legislative Assembly. On the mainland, all the candidates elected were confederationist, but on Vancouver Island, the anti-confederationists triumphed. Then, in June 1869, the situation changed dramatically. While on a tour of northern communities, Governor Seymour died suddenly. The British Colonial Office immediately chose Anthony Musgrave as his successor. Musgrave was a personal friend of John A. Macdonald, who had recommended Musgrave for the post of governor. Musgrave's instructions from the British Colonial Office were simple: Get British Columbia to join Canada as quickly as possible.

In the meantime, the annexationists responded by circulating a petition, which they intended to send to President Grant in Washington. In Victoria—a community of about 3000 people—they managed to collect only 125 signatures. It was obvious that annexation was not a popular concept.

Musgrave now had to persuade the anti-confederationists to join Canada, so he decided to **co-opt** the anti-confederation supporters. They would draft a policy together on the terms of union and then travel to Ottawa as a delegation, where they would present their proposal. His plan was successful. The Canadian government agreed to virtually all the delegation's terms, and promised to start work on a railroad within two years, to be completed in ten years.

In early 1871, the Legislative Assembly met to vote on the Canadian offer. It was accepted after

Figure 6–22 The death of Governor Seymour was one of the catalysts for British Columbia to join Confederation.

Governor Musgrave promised a wholly elected Legislature once Confederation was achieved. With a promise of responsible government finally underway, the terms of Confederation were accepted unanimously. On July 20, 1871, British Columbia officially joined Canada.

ACTIVITIES

1. Identify the main reason for the union between the colonies of Vancouver Island and British Columbia. How would such a union help solve this problem?

2. Why would the British government encourage the union of British Columbia and Vancouver Island? Why would it encourage British Columbia to join Confederation?

3. Who were the annexationists? What were their views on the necessity of Confederation? Were these views popular?

4. Create a poster to advertise the cause of one of:
   - the Confederationists
   - the anti-Confederationists
   - the annexationists
   Try to think of a slogan to use on your poster.

THE RAILWAY SURVEY

The future that seemed so bright on the eve of July 20, 1871 dimmed quickly. Although the federal government had agreed to build a railway to British Columbia, Macdonald had no idea what a railroad would cost. Furthermore, the interior of British Columbia was not at all well known—no one knew where to place a rail line between the Rocky Mountains and the coast. By the early 1870s, there were only two major population centres in the province, southern Vancouver Island and New Westminster, and the Fraser Valley.

The federal government dispatched surveyors to investigate all possible routes. This would buy time for the government to arrange financing for the railway. In British Columbia, two rival factions developed over where the route should be located. Politicians from Vancouver Island thought the railway should travel across the central interior, down the Homathco River to Bute Inlet, and then cross the Strait of Georgia at its narrowest point to the Island. Politicians from the mainland favoured a route that would travel down the Fraser Canyon to Burrard Inlet.

Throughout the 1870s, the "Battle of the Routes" raged as both groups pressured the government. The federal Liberal government of Alexander Mackenzie, now in power, was reluctant to build the railway in any case (see Chapter 5). In fact, the conflict allowed the federal government to delay making a decision. Surveyors also entered the debate passionately, and most developed their own ideal routes. By

Figure 6–23 Politicians from Vancouver Island thought the railway should travel through Bute Inlet, shown here.

1878, a staggering twenty-one routes were being considered. Sandford Fleming, the Chief Surveyor of Canada, was busy promoting a route that would cross the Rockies at Yellowhead Pass and then travel south to Burrard Inlet. His own deputy, however, disagreed with him. Marcus Smith, in charge of the Surveying Department when Fleming went on leave in the mid-1870s, promoted a route through the northern Pine Pass, and west along the Skeena River. Smith favoured this route because the terminus on the Pacific Coast was 900 kilometres closer to Asia than many southern ports.

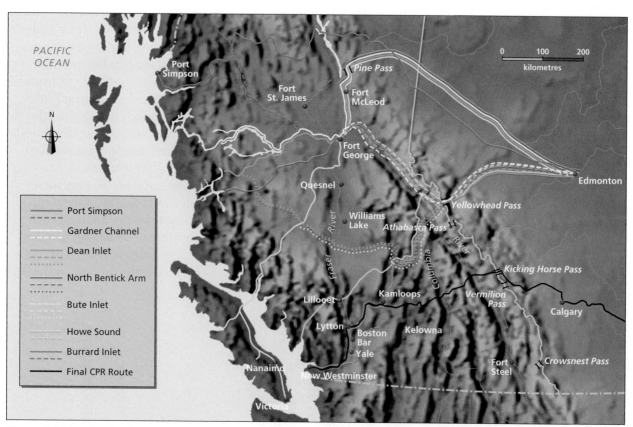

Figure 6–24 The battle of the routes

ACTIVITIES

1. This is a group activity. Each group should take the role of one of the following major players in the Routes debate:
   - Sandford Fleming
   - Marcus Smith
   - Island politicians
   - Mainland politicians
   - Alfred Waddington, who had surveyed a townsite at the head of Bute Inlet
   - Miners and ranchers of the Cariboo
   - Sawmill owners on Burrard Inlet

   Referring to the maps and other information provided by your teacher, develop a case for the route assigned to your group. Present your findings to the class and then have the class vote on the route which it prefers.

THE EMERGENCE OF VANCOUVER

DID YOU KNOW?

In 1886, the new Vancouver city council asked the federal government to set aside the 162 hectares of a military reserve within the city limits as a park. Stanley Park was created in1889.

Vancouver is the youngest major community in British Columbia. Virtually every other major centre got its start during the period of the fur trade or of the Cariboo Gold Rush. Burrard Inlet is not fed by a major river, and the peninsula on which Vancouver developed is covered by thick forest. During the fur-trading period and the Cariboo Gold Rush, these factors discouraged people from settling the area.

When Colonel Moody arrived in New Westminster, it was clear that the Fraser River froze during winter months. He knew this was a problem—defending the colony required access to an ice-free harbour. He ordered three trails to be cut from New Westminster to Burrard Inlet. He also set aside land on the Inlet as military reserves, in case the British Government decided that the harbour needed protection.

In the early 1860s, Vancouver remained as it had been for thousands of years—the home of the Musqueam and Squamish peoples. By 1865, the area was changing. The Hastings Sawmill opened on the

Figure 6–25 The changing face of Vancouver. By the second half of the nineteenth century, Native women had begun to dress in non-traditional clothing, such as the long skirts shown here. This clothing trend disturbed some of the Native men from the West Coast communities. The Hasting Sawmill, which opened in 1865, is pictured at right.

south side of the Inlet, and the company obtained timber rights to much of the southern peninsula. It eventually controlled some 19 000 acres. On the north side of the Inlet, Sewell Moody also opened a mill, in an area that is now North Vancouver. The mill and the surrounding community eventually became known as Moodyville at the time. Moody's Mill began logging Lynn Valley, specializing in "toothpicks," for sailing masts. These were logs that were free of knots and that measured 21 metres long and 4 metres in diameter. Until the 1880s, trees were transported on greased log tracks that were called "skid roads" to tidewater. From here, they were floated to the two mills for processing.

In 1868, colourful "Gassy Jack" Deighton arrived on the Inlet. Because Hastings Mill was officially **dry,** Gassy Jack opened a saloon about a kilometre-and-a-half away from the mill, much to the relief of the mill workers. Soon other saloons and stores appeared around Deighton's saloon, and the little settlement, officially known as "Granville," was known to all as "Gastown," after its founder.

Until the mid 1880s, there was little other activity on Burrard Inlet. In 1881, Port Moody (named after Colonel Moody), was designated as the terminus of the CPR. At once, the focus of activity shifted to the eastern end of the Inlet. Speculators quickly bought up land, and surveyed and sold lots, eager to cash in on the future **metropolis**.

In 1884, William Van Horne arrived in Port Moody to establish the exact location of the CPR terminus. To his dismay, he discovered that the harbour was made up of

Figure 6–26 Vancouver's Gastown as it appears today

tidal flats. It could not possibly accommodate deep-sea vessels, which needed to dock, and load and unload cargo. He travelled further down the Inlet to Gastown, and found what he was looking for—a deep-water anchorage with an expanse of flat land ideal for rail yards. He named the site Vancouver. Of course, the Port Moody **speculators** were outraged, but there was nothing they could do.

In late 1885, the CPR was completed and the future townsite of Vancouver laid out. Now development could begin in earnest. However, on June 13, 1886, a spell of hot, dry weather suddenly made the land-clearing and the slash-burning extremely dangerous. A catastrophic fire levelled the new city in under an hour. Despite this setback, Vancouver was rebuilt quickly, and by the end of 1890, the new city had a population of more than 5000.

dry: forbidding the sale or consumption of liquor

metropolis: a chief city

tidal flat: a low-lying marsh

speculators: people who buy and sell land for profit

The Oppenheimers

The Cariboo Gold Rush attracted many immigrants from around the world, including a large number of Jewish immigrants. Unlike the Chinese, who came to mine the gold, almost all Jewish immigrants to British Columbia made a living selling goods to the prospectors and miners.

In 1848, the five Oppenheimer brothers—David, Charles, Meyer, Isaac, and Godfrey—emigrated from Germany to California, where they opened several stores. In 1858, when news of the gold rush in British Columbia reached San Francisco, Charles Oppenheimer travelled north to investigate. Within a year, his brothers had joined him in the colony.

The Oppenheimers set up a trading firm in Victoria, with branch offices in Yale. By 1862, they also had a store in Barkerville. Their biggest problem was also everyone else's problem. In an era before the Cariboo Road, transportation was terribly slow. The whole area operated as a **black market economy**. In 1862, David Oppenheimer lobbied Governor Douglas to build a road from Yale to the Cariboo. Armed with petitions from Cariboo merchants, Oppenheimer was successful in persuading Douglas to consider the project. As you have already learned, construction of the Cariboo Road began that year.

In 1868, when Barkerville burned, the Oppenheimers' store was destroyed. They lost more than $100 000 worth of goods. Like other merchants in Barkerville, they built a new store immediately. David also bought a fire engine from San Francisco, partly as a **public relations** gesture, and his brother Isaac became the volunteer fire chief.

As the Cariboo Gold Rush declined, David and Isaac Oppenheimer moved south in search of new opportunities. At the time, Burrard Inlet was not heavily populated, but David thought that it would become a major port, especially after the railroad was completed. He was confident that Vancouver would be the winner in the Battle of the Routes and would become the terminus for the CPR. He bought a great deal of land on the south shore of the Inlet in 1877, just west of Gastown, where he opened a store.

In 1884, when William Van Horne arrived in Port Moody, he was greeted by David Oppenheimer. Oppenheimer took the CPR general manager to Gastown, and rowed him around

Figure 6–27 David Oppenheimer is the man in the light coloured top hat.

the inner and outer harbours. Van Horne was impressed by all the land that could be used for the rail terminus. To clinch Vancouver as the favoured location, Oppenheimer offered the CPR half of his landholdings, as well as half of the holdings of other landholders, at no cost. Van Horne readily agreed. It was a shrewd move—Oppenheimer realized that the value of the landholdings would rise dramatically once the railroad arrived.

When the CPR finally arrived, in 1885, David Oppenheimer owned most of the land in the new city of Vancouver. In 1888, he ran for the office of mayor and was elected by **acclamation**. In his four years as mayor, he concentrated on Vancouver's infrastructure. He had pipes laid under Burrard Inlet to carry water from the watersheds on the north shore. Today, much of Vancouver's water supply still comes from this source. He also

bankrolled an electric streetcar system (the third such in North America), and a power company, BC Electric, to run the system. He built a sewage system, donated land for schools and parks and, with the new city council, established Stanley Park as a permanent green space. Oppenheimer also encouraged steamer companies to open up in the area and to trade across the Pacific. Fittingly, he is known as the "Father of Vancouver."

black market economy: an illegal or completely unregulated economy where normal price controls do not apply

public relations: promoting good will

acclamation: elected to office unopposed

bankrolled: funded

Figure 6–28 A parade on Cordova Street, Vancouver, in 1890

ACTIVITIES

1. Why was the Vancouver area developed later than other areas of British Columbia?

2. Name three business ventures that started in Vancouver after 1865. Describe each one of them in a few point-form notes.

3. Imagine you are David Oppenheimer. Write a letter persuading William Van Horne to relocate the CPR terminus from Port Moody to Gastown.

4. It can be said that the Oppenheimers were responsible opportunists. Provide examples to support this hypothesis.

THE CHINESE IN BRITISH COLUMBIA

to rework: to go back and try to extract more gold from an area after it has already been worked

frugal: careful with money

The first Chinese immigrants to North America came during the California Gold Rush of the early 1850s. A few years later, thousands arrived in British Columbia during the Cariboo Gold Rush. As in California, they faced prejudice and discrimination because they differed from European miners in their language, dress, religion, and customs. Realizing that their opportunities in British Columbia were limited by racism, many Chinese miners started **reworking** claims abandoned by White miners intent on quick wealth. Such claims were less expensive to acquire and, if worked patiently, usually produced a reasonable amount of gold. In 1883, a provincial mining inspector noted the following:

The larger number of claims in the province are owned and worked by Chinese, their more **frugal** living habits, their greater industry and more moderate expectations of reward making profitable to them claims that the white miners regard as not having sufficient attraction. Thus, but for the Chinese, the production of gold in this country would not reach nearly the sum shown.

In 1883, of the roughly 2000 gold miners left in British Columbia, 1500 were Chinese. The newcomers helped to build the frontier economy of the province in other ways. They opened general stores and restaurants in the mining towns and operated vegetable farms both in the interior and near the coastal cities. Some Chinese immigrants also worked for wealthy White families in British Columbia, but they always kept close ties with their community.

In 1881, the CPR was faced with an acute shortage of labour for the construction of the BC section of the railway (see Chapter 5), so it hired large numbers of Chinese labourers. Between 1881 and 1885, more than 17 000 Chinese immigrants came to BC to work on the railway. As you read in this chapter's Window on the Past, they were paid one dollar a day (less than half the salary paid to White workers). They lived in separate camps, and generally provided

Figure 6–29 A camp for Chinese workers

their own food and lodging. The work was dangerous and difficult. It is estimated that more than 600 Chinese workers died through accidents or illness during the four years of railway construction.

Life in the Cities

When the railway was completed in 1885, many Chinese labourers could not afford to travel back to China. They had been misled about the cost of food and equipment, which rather than being provided was deducted from their wages. They moved to Vancouver and Victoria in search of work.

This influx of Chinese immigrants into British Columbia's major population centres led to renewed acts of discrimination and prejudice. Racist actions by Whites were both spontaneous and organized. The Knights of Labour, for example, campaigned to have all Chinese removed from Vancouver. The Knights would also often force Chinese residents out of town through intimidation and violence. They also organized a boycott against all businesses that sold goods to Chinese customers.

In the urban areas, Chinese immigrants often did heavy manual labour that other British Columbians avoided. Usually, an English-speaking Chinese **contractor** would bid on a specific job (often land clearing), and would recruit a group of Chinese workers. He would pay and house them out of the monies received for the contract, and would keep anything left over as profit. This system usually ended up cheating Chinese workers. Many Chinese contractors made a fortune from providing work crews. In 1900,

the two largest contractors, Loo Gee Wing and Sam Kee, each had fortunes approaching $1 million.

The account that follows was provided by Sam Lum to a royal commission on Chinese and Japanese immigration in 1902. Sam Lum worked as a labourer in a Vancouver brickyard.

> I get two dollars a day, a dollar fifty in winter. I only have about six months' work in the year; sometimes we get two days in the week, sometimes none at all. My wife and children are in China; I have never been back. I send thirty or forty dollars home every year. I board myself; there is a house in the brickyard. It costs me fifteen or sixteen dollars a month to live, two dollars for rice, eight dollars for meat, nine dollars for beer and whiskey.

Chinese immigrants did displace White workers in some jobs—brick manufacturing was one notable example. The Chinese system of labour contracting also ensured lower wages for Chinese workers because their contractors assisted with living arrangements. Of course, these expenses were deducted from workers' pay, but the situation still angered many White workers, who thought they were being **undercut**.

Discrimination against the Chinese was also purely social. Most non-Native residents of British Columbia in the later nineteenth century were British, and wanted to recreate a homogeneous British culture in the province. The presence of Chinese made this goal impossible. Therefore, the Chinese were depicted as being inferior and dangerous, and incapable of assimilation.

contractor: one who supplies workers

to undercut: to sell work at a lower price than average

The government even legalized racial discrimination. Until the railway was completed, there were no government restrictions on Chinese immigration. In 1885, however, after a series of hearings, the government decided to limit Chinese immigration. Each immigrant was required to pay a fifty-dollar **head tax** upon landing in Canada, and ships were allowed to carry no more than one Chinese person per 50 tonnes. Since most ships weighed about 2000 tonnes, this meant that only about forty Chinese immigrants could enter the country at any one time. While these provisions slowed immigration, they did not entirely stop it. However, they did make it nearly impossible for whole families to come to British Columbia.

ACTIVITIES

1. How did the Chinese turn their experience of discrimination during the Cariboo Gold Rush to their advantage? How do you suppose some local workers would have reacted to this?

2. How did CPR employment practices discriminate against Chinese workers? Why do you suppose Chinese railway workers decided to remain segregated from the other workers?

3. How did the hiring practices of Chinese labour contractors lead to discrimination? How did they exploit Chinese workers?

ECONOMIC DIVERSITY IN BRITISH COLUMBIA

With the completion of the CPR, British Columbia was no longer isolated in the Dominion. Now goods could now flow much more easily through the province, both to the rest of Canada and across the Pacific to Asian markets. Vancouver, in particular, experienced rapid growth in the last decade of the nineteenth century and into the twentieth century.

Other areas of the province also grew in the 1890s. While gold production remained relatively constant, the mining of other minerals grew at an impressive pace. Prospectors discovered silver, copper, and other metals in the Kootenay region in the early 1890s, and mining towns soon dotted the whole region. Giant **smelters** were built in order to extract the metals from the ore of the mines. The new Hall Mines Smelter in Nelson could process 250 tonnes of ore a day. The ore was then transported from the mine, high above the town on Toad Mountain, by a gravity-operated **tramway**. Nelson's population grew from just 400 people in 1890 to 7000 people in 1900. Soon the city could boast of an electric streetcar system, as well as all the other services of a prosperous town.

The Okanagan region also experienced tremendous growth at the end of the century. Here, however, the source of wealth was agriculture, not mining. The area had long been a profitable area for wheat farming, and, in the 1890s, farmers discovered that when they irrigated the dry soil, they had just the right conditions for orchard farming. By the turn of the century, orchards were under rapid development.

While the main purpose of the CPR was to haul freight between the coasts, the managers of the new transcontinental line soon recognized the value of the magnificent and scenic Rocky Mountains. In order to attract tourists, the company started to build large hotels at major stopping points. The original

Figure 6–30 The Silver King Mine tramway. What would be the impact of having such an operation in Nelson?

Figure 6–31 The Okanagan region would eventually become well known for orchard farming.

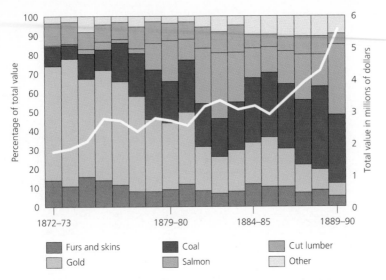

Furs and skins   Coal   Cut lumber
Gold   Salmon   Other

Figure 6–32 Exports from British Columbia between 1860 and 1899

Banff Springs Hotel was completed in 1888 and offered a spectacular view of the Alberta Rockies. Eventually, other chalet-styled hotels were built in Quebec City (1893), Toronto, and Victoria (1908). For tourists to British Columbia, the CPR built several "dining stations" with sleeping accommodations. At the end of the century, tourists came by the thousands to experience the rugged vistas of British Columbia, and to take one of the popular side trips—to Illecillewaet Glacier, for example.

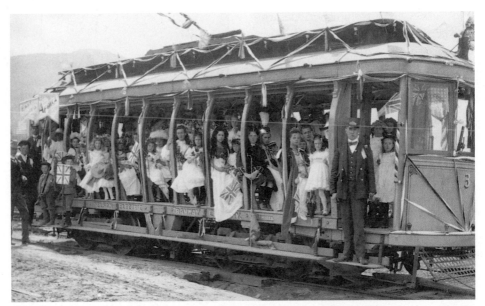

Figure 6–33 Children wave from this streetcar in Nelson on Empire Day, 1902.

ACTIVITIES

1. What led to rapid growth in the Kootenays? Why was this growth short-lived?

2. Why was tourism an early industry in British Columbia?

3. How did the CPR and other railroads serve to boost economic growth in British Columbia?

4. Examine Figure 6–32 and answer the following questions:

a) What export commodity declined after the 1870s?

b) What was the cause of rapid expansion in exports after 1885?

c) Which commodity, of considerable importance in the 1990s, was less important a century ago?

CONCLUSION

The early development of British Columbia was driven by the exploitation of its natural resources, especially furs and gold. During the first half of the nineteenth century, the HBC controlled how the region would be developed. In the late 1850s and early 1860s, the Cariboo Gold Rush attracted large numbers of people to the interior. This event led to the founding of several British Columbia communities. By the mid-1860s, a decline in gold production had led to a rapid decline in population and economic prosperity, and forced a debate on the future of the region. When the colony of British Columbia decided to join Confederation in 1871, it knew it would be linked to the rest of Canada by the CPR. The terrain of British Columbia made the railway a challenge to build, but all obstacles were eventually overcome, and Vancouver became the last stop on the CPR. The last decade of the nineteenth century witnessed the early development of forestry, fishing, and agriculture in British Columbia. These activities helped to form the economic base of our province for the better part of the twentieth century.

SUMMARY ACTIVITIES

1. Create a photo album to show how the physical features of British Columbia influenced its economic development, starting with its history as a territory controlled by the HBC. Supply captions for your photographs, which you could photocopy from other sources or draw.

2. As a class, do a PMI on the Cariboo Gold Rush. Determine how this event affected subsequent events in the history of British Columbia.

ON YOUR OWN

1. Racism is still an issue that is alive in British Columbia today. Write a report on the extent of racism in your community or school, and devise an action plan to combat it. You could contact local anti-racism groups in your community for information, or invite one of their representatives to speak to your class.

2. Investigate your own community's history. How, when, and why was your community founded? Are the current economic activities of your local region indicative of its founding? Why or why not?

3. Organize a visit to your local history museum or invite a local historian to speak to your class about your community. After you complete this activity and the one that precedes it, organize an exhibit of your community's history to raise your school's awareness of the importance of history.

UNIT III
BETWEEN TWO CENTURIES

A s Canada entered the twentieth century, industrialization, technological advances, and immigration made it a modern nation. By 1905, the Dominion stretched from the Atlantic to the Pacific. As Canada moved west, rich natural resources—such as gold, forests, and prairie farmland—drew immigrants, investors, and prospectors from around the world. For homesteading immigrants on the prairies, and for the hundreds of thousands of immigrants and Canadians migrating to Canada's rapidly expanding cities, life was harsh yet full of wondrous change.

A gift economy. This button blanket is an example of the gifts exchanged by Northwest Coast peoples during potlatches. These celebrations confirmed the power of chiefs and redistributed wealth.

Canada adopted policies, such as Laurier's National Policy, to keep the nation united and growing in prosperity. But there were tensions: Native rights in the West; the racial tensions of changing immigration; the drive by workers for unions and by women for political power and representation. As the new century progressed, Canada's economy as a trading nation became more and more intertwined with that of the US. This often threatened

Montreal, in 1929. Montreal was Canada's largest, most industrialized city when Adrien Hebert created this painting, *Place Saint-Henri*. Canada's economy had slowed down, and was about to enter the Great Depression.

New logging. Along British Columbia's coastline, the forest industry has adopted new logging methods. Here a helicopter collects selected logs, leaving the rest of the forest untouched. This has helped to meet environmental concerns and preserve the forests for future generations.

the sense of a Canadian identity and independence. Nonetheless, by the outbreak of World War I, in 1914, a more mature Canada emerged as a distinct presence on the world stage.

As Canada entered the twenty-first century, yet another revolution—the high-tech revolution—was sweeping the globe. While Canada's economy still relied heavily on natural resources, it had diversified. The great majority of Canadians now lived in urban centres. They no longer worked in resource extraction, manufacturing, or agriculture, but in service-related industries. Canadians became innovators in high technology. Prime farmland was absorbed by expanding urban and industrial

development. Environmental and aboriginal concerns started to compete with the interests of forest and mining industries. In British Columbia, as elsewhere in Canada, depleted fish stocks and natural resources, along with industrial and urban pollution, became matters of grave concern.

Because the world had become a global economy, Canada's trade links with other nations became more important. Although Canada was a leading industrialized nation, it had to adjust to the new trade agreements between groups of countries in other regions of the world. In 1989, a trade agreement between Canada and the US came into effect. In 1994, the agreement

was extended to include Mexico. To ensure continued prosperity, Canada also continued to seek closer trade relationships with countries around the globe.

The fall of the Berlin Wall. In 1989, the world watched as the pro-democracy movement overthrew non-democratic governments throughout Europe. Here the Berlin Wall, which had divided East and West Berlin for decades, is demolished by protesters.

7 THE EMERGENCE OF MODERN CANADA 1896–1914

CHAPTER OUTCOMES

In this chapter you will focus on the dramatic changes that occurred in Canada between 1896 and 1914. By the end of the chapter, you will

- make informed judgements about the career of Prime Minister Laurier

- identify the factors influencing nationalist and imperialist sentiment in Canada

- analyze the changing perceptions of Canadian identity

- account for the growth of population in Western Canada and its effects

- evaluate the impact of social change on women, the Native peoples, and immigrants

- describe the impact of technological change

The Lure of the Yukon

This fictional story records the adventures of a young man who sets out to make his fortune in the Klondike Gold Rush of 1898.

News of the Klondike gold strike burst upon the world when ships carrying miners and their gold from the Klondike reached Seattle and San Francisco in the summer of 1897. Men and women from all walks of life swarmed into the Yukon, lured by the ambition to get rich quick.

*More than 100 000 gold seekers started north in the fall and winter of 1897. Few had any knowledge of mining or experience of the harsh land into which they were venturing. By the time many of the adventurers got to Dawson City in late 1897 and 1898, the best **claims** had already been **staked**.*

After 1899, the building of a railway from Skagway to Whitehorse brought in the heavy gold dredges that displaced most of the miners.

Luke staggered the last few metres to the top of the Chilkoot Pass. In the last hour, his backpack had felt unimaginably heavy. He had wanted to stop many times, but once you became part of the long, thin line of struggling gold seekers snaking their way up the pass, you had to keep moving.

For over a week now, the nineteen-year-old from Winnipeg had struggled six hours every day to climb the 1500 steps of frozen snow. Though barely able to carry the 20-kilogram pack, Luke knew that dividing his supplies into lighter packs would mean more trips up the pass—something he wanted to avoid at all cost.

With one final load to go, he slid down the icy slope as fast as he could. He stopped at the "Scales," the flat piece of land at the bottom of the trail where the miners weighed their sup-plies. Luke hoisted his pack and made ready to tackle the "Golden Stairs," as the miners called the trail, for the last time.

He had been told by the out-fitters in Victoria that good tools and tents would be hard to get at any price in Dawson, the new townsite at the goldfields. Flour as high as $6 a sack. Sugar at 50 cents a kilo. Bacon at $1.50 a kilo. Eggs at $4 a dozen. Katherine, one of the women on the trail, had told Luke that she'd heard that anybody willing to cook could sell their bread at 50 cents a loaf and meals for $1.50.

"Wages are $10 a day in Dawson and up to $15 a day out at the mines," she told Luke as they waited their turn at the bottom of the pass. "That's where the money is in Dawson. They say every creek in the Klondike is staked with a claim by now. By the way, if you've got anything unusual in your supplies, keep it safe 'till you get to the goldfields. Dawson's a city where everything's scarce except money. I heard tell of a man who brought in a load of kittens and sold them for $20 each to some lonely miners."

Luke hoped that what Katherine said about the claims wasn't true. Since he'd left school three years ago, he hadn't gotten a steady job. The **depression** just didn't seem to want to end. Sure, there had been some improvement under Laurier and the Liberal govern-ment, but how long could he wait for the Canadian economy to improve? Like many others, he'd been skeptical of the sto-ries of fabulous gold finds in the Klondike. But as more and more prosperous miners arrived in the south, Luke knew he had to take a chance on making his fortune in the goldfields.

243

The long, thin line of struggling gold seekers

After borrowing money from his father, Luke had arrived in the American port of Dyea, on the Alaska Panhandle, at the end of January 1898. From there to Dawson City—and the gold-fields—was 1000 kilometres. He'd set out in winter because he'd been told by a miner he met in Victoria that the frozen trails of the Yukon made travel easier by sled.

"You'll have to pull the sled yourself, though," said the **sourdough** smiling. "Sled dogs go for a premium price up there now. A good'un'll fetch as much as $200 dollars. Now you can always hire some Indian packers, but they know their worth in that wild country and charge $1 a pound to pack or haul your supplies."

Luke started up the Golden Stairs for the last time. Gingerly he found his footing and tried to keep his mind off his aching back and legs. He wondered if the trail from the summit of the Chilkoot Pass to the headwaters of the Yukon River at Lake Bennett would be as difficult. Likely not, he thought—he'd heard it was all down hill. He hoped the clear cold weather would hold. Snow with warming thaws meant the possibility of an avalanche. Last spring sixty men and women on the trail had died under such conditions.

At the top of the Golden Stairs, Luke piled his pack on top of the others and crawled into his tent. Despite exhaustion, he lay awake for some time. He felt more confident

Throughout the spring of 1898, they worked hard to finish the boat.

now that he had overcome the most difficult part of the Klondike trail. Yet, with 1000 kilometres still to go, he knew many difficulties still lay ahead.

The next morning, after a breakfast of cornmeal pancakes, dried fruit, and tea, Luke loaded his sled and adjusted the harness he'd made for himself with ropes. Before he could start, though, he had to get through the Mountie checkpoint. The Chilkoot Pass was the border between Canada and the United States, and the North West Mounted Police wanted to make sure that the newcomers had enough supplies to get to Dawson.

Sighting the Mounties, Luke felt safer than he had since landing at Dyea. Although Dyea wasn't as lawless as Skagway—a place some considered to be the roughest in the world—both Alaska ports were without a police force and were full of crooks eager to separate Klondikers from their money and supplies. Luke felt lucky to have gotten this far without incident.

Luke pulled hard on his sled as he headed downhill from the Mountie checkpoint. Depending on conditions, he hoped to cover the 20 kilometres to Lake Bennett in two to three days.

"You're pulling too hard, son," Luke heard a voice

behind him say. Turning around he saw a small, burly man on the trail behind him. "Don't wear yourself out before you get to Lake Bennett." The man's accent told Luke he was American. Most of the men and women on the trail were Americans, but Luke had also gotten used to meeting Norwegian, Scots, Greeks, Italians, Irish, and even a group of **Maoris.** He'd also heard a rumour of an English lord up ahead on the trail.

Luke stopped and waited for the man and his companion to catch up. "I need to get to the lake as quickly as possible," called Luke, gasping between deep breaths, "and then onto the Yukon River before the spring thaw breaks up the ice."

"Robert Henderson's my name, and this is Seamus Young," the man said as he caught up with Luke. "You'll never haul that sled the 900 kilometres to Dawson before the ice breaks up. You're better to wait at Lake Bennett and build a boat. The ice won't break up on the Yukon River until late May. Why don't you team up with us? The more of us building the boat, the better." Luke readily agreed to the bargain, and the three became friends.

When the trio reached Lake Bennett, they saw many small tents dotting the shores of the lake. There was a constant clamour of sawing and ham-mering. Everybody seemed to be feverishly building boats to carry them and their supplies across the lakes and down the Yukon River.

During the journey to Lake Bennet, Luke realized that Robert and Seamus were old hands at living in the Yukon. They claimed to have been in the Klondike when George Carmack and his Native friends, Charlie and Jim, had struck it rich at **Bonanza** Creek. Robert even claimed that it was he who had first told Carmack of the gold in the creeks running into the Klondike River. Luke had heard lots of **tall tales** since he'd come to the Yukon, and this sounded like another one.

Throughout the spring of 1898, they worked hard to fin-ish their boat. Luke thought its flat, shallow shape made it more like a raft and was con-cerned about its reliability.

"Don't worry," Robert said confidently. "Miles Canyon is the only dangerous place on the river. We just have to be sure to load the craft properly so that the raging waters of the canyon won't tip it. Besides, the Mounties at the checkpoint above the canyon won't let us through if they think we can't make it."

By May the group was ready to go. In late May, the ice began to crack and dozens of the most eager Klondikers risked the ice floes to be the first down the river to the goldfields. Luke and his friends waited another four

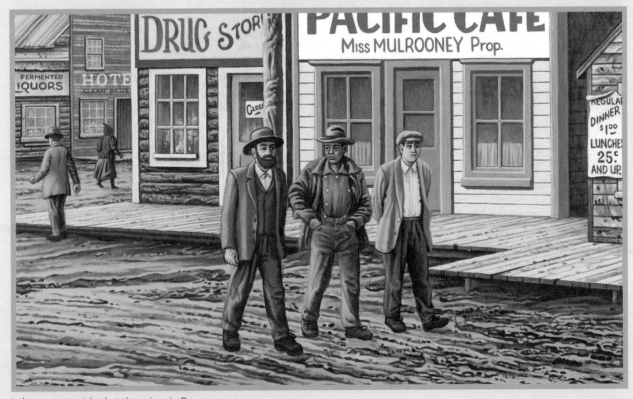

Luke was astonished at the prices in Dawson.

days until the river had cleared. More than a thousand boats of all shapes and sizes headed across the lake and onto the Yukon River for the two week trip to the goldfields.

"I can't believe I'm actually here," Luke said, as he stepped from the boat onto the beach at Dawson. "It's so big—it's a city."

"Nearly 20 000 people here now," laughed Robert as he began unloading supplies from the boat. "What did you expect? Everybody seems to be drawn to Dawson. It's got restaurants, hotels—even telephones. Remember, this is the biggest city north of Seattle and west of Winnipeg."

After unloading their supplies, the three men headed down Front Street, Dawson's main street, then down Broadway and Wall Street. Sure enough, here were several blocks of casinos, saloons, restaurants, and hotels advertising steam baths, running water, electricity, and telephones. Further down the street were banks, hospitals, and a school. There were lots of people coming and going, but most of the buildings were closed.

"What's wrong with the owners?" Luke asked Robert.

"It's 2 o'clock in the afternoon. I thought you said Dawson was a roaring boom town. Don't they want to do business?"

"I bet you it's Sunday," Robert exclaimed. "Sam Steele probably has the place locked up."

Luke was outraged. "That's terrible. Who is he? Some kind of gangster, like 'Soapy' Smith in Skagway?"

"Hardly," observed Seamus, who usually said very little. "He's superintendent of the North West Mounted Police in Dawson, and he's tough as nails. He has 200 Mounties in the area and they maintain strict law and order. There have been only two murders here. Anybody can walk the streets in perfect safety."

"Superintendent Steele enforces the Canadian law against working on Sunday," Robert added. "Saloons, dance halls, and businesses have to close between midnight Saturday and Monday morning. You can't do any work on Sunday—not even cut firewood."

"For what's it's worth, my advice would be to stay here and work in Dawson," said Seamus. "You can make ten times the $2 a day you can get in a job down south. Anyway, the good claims have all been staked. There's 5000 of them prospectors slaving in the diggings with only one in ten finding enough gold to make up for the hardships. Besides, you'll need money for tools, wood, and equipment."

"I'm not ready to give up yet," Luke said firmly, even though he knew he was down to his last few dollars and the prices in the store windows were making him ill. In his heart, he knew he'd have to look for a job the first thing Monday morning.

But later that night, back at the beach where they'd pitched their tents, Luke lay awake. "I'll get to the goldfields," he whispered to himself. "No matter how long I have to wait.

to stake claim: the legal right to mine gold, or other minerals, on a specific piece of land

depression: a period of low economic activity marked by high unemployment

sourdough: someone who had been a prospector for a long time

Maoris: aboriginal people of New Zealand

Bonanza: Spanish word that means "source of wealth"

tall tale: a story that exaggerates the truth

ACTIVITIES

1. What motivated Luke to put up with such hardships in order to reach the Klondike?

2. What hardships do you think Luke will face as he settles in Dawson?

3. Would you have advised Luke to remain in Dawson or to continue on to the goldfields? Why?

4. Robert Service was a young bank clerk who moved to the Yukon during the gold rush. Known as the "Klondike poet," he wrote extensively about the sourdoughs. Find and read one of his poems, such as "Spell of the Yukon," and use it as a model to write your own version of Luke's journey to Dawson.

1896 — WILFRID LAURIER BECOMES PRIME MINISTER

1898 — FIRST AUTOMOBILES ARE IMPORTED INTO CANADA FROM THE US

1899 — BOER WAR BREAKS OUT IN SOUTH AFRICA

1901 — FIRST TRANSATLANTIC WIRELESS MESSAGE IS RECEIVED

1903 — ALASKA BOUNDARY DISPUTE IS SETTLED

1905 — ALBERTA AND SASKATCHEWAN BECOME THE EIGHTH AND NINTH PROVINCES

1906 — BC NATIVE CHIEFS TAKE LAND CLAIM TO THE BRITISH PRIVY COUNCIL

1907 — ASIANS ARE ATTACKED DURING VANCOUVER RIOTS

1909 — FIRST AIRPLANE FLIGHT IN CANADA

1911 — CONSERVATIVES UNDER ROBERT BORDEN WIN THE FEDERAL ELECTION

1912 — THE TITANIC SINKS OFF THE COAST OF NEWFOUNDLAND

1913 — 400 870 IMMIGRANTS COME TO CANADA—HIGHEST LEVEL EVER

1914 — WORLD WAR I BEGINS

CANADA

BUILD YOUR NEST IN WESTERN CANADA.

FOR INFORMATION MAPS AND PAMPHLETS APPLY TO—

Nobody should venture to Canada in the autumn because he will have difficulty in finding work and will have to spend his money, perhaps his last cent, to live through a winter.

—JOSEPH OLESKOW, UKRAINIAN PHYSICIAN

While the Canadian government advertised the glories of the West in Britain and Europe, settlers quickly learned about the realities of living on the Canadian prairies. Over time, Canadian advertising became more realistic, and overseas papers began printing testimonials of immigrants, who told about the bad—as well as the good—side of life in Canada.

INTRODUCTION

In 1905 the new provinces of Alberta and Saskatchewan joined Confederation as the eighth and ninth provinces. Truly, Canada was now a nation that stretched from coast to coast.

The young country faced many obstacles in its quest for survival. It continued to fear a takeover, both economic and political, by its powerful neighbour to the south, the United States. It also struggled for greater independence from Britain, especially when it came to its own foreign affairs. The problem of defining Canada's role as a member of the British Empire had one negative side effect. It caused much fighting between English- and French-Canadians concerning loyalty to Britain. In 1896, Wilfrid Laurier became Canada's first French-Canadian prime minister. His election promised to bring together French- and English-speaking citizens in a united Canada.

Figure 7–1 This painting by Canadian artist William Kurelek shows a group of European settlers arriving on the prairies. Kurelek, who grew up in Saskatchewan, once said that the scenery of the prairies "dwarfs and dominates life, all life … whether it crawls, walks, or flies over its surface, or tries to leave its mark on it, such as dwelling places or modes of travel." How does this observation help you understand this picture?

Laurier's coming to power coincided with the end of a world-wide depression. Global markets opened up for Canada's minerals, lumber, wheat, and manufactured goods. The discovery of gold in the Yukon in 1896 symbolized a shining new age of prosperity and optimism. Hundreds of thousands of immigrants—from Europe, Britain, the United States, and Asia—travelled along newly constructed railways to settle in Canada's West. Wonderful new inventions were on the horizon—telephones, wireless radios, cars, planes, and motion pictures. It seemed as though life was changing forever, and for the better.

The growth in Canada's population provoked some much-needed social reforms. Women and the Native peoples began to assert their equality and human rights. Workers organized into unions. Some immigrants, however, were eventually made to feel unwelcome, and for many, social equality came slowly, or not at all. While the Laurier era marked the beginning of Canada as a multicultural nation, it would be years before the concepts of equality and diversity would truly be part of Canada's emerging identity.

LAURIER IS ELECTED

The Canadian federal election of 1896 ended more than twenty years of Conservative rule. The Liberal party had won a majority of seats in the House of Commons. Wilfrid Laurier, the leader of the Liberals, became Canada's first French-Canadian prime minister. Most Quebec voters were pleased to see a French-Canadian elected. They wanted the federal government to protect their French language and Roman Catholic rights. However, as a Liberal and a French-Canadian, the new prime minister had to be careful when dealing with issues of language and religion. Laurier was aware of the ongoing distrust between French- and English-Canadians—a distrust that had lingered and deepened since the Northwest Rebellion of 1885 and the execution of Louis Riel.

Conflict and Compromise

Laurier wanted to promote national unity at home and to protect Canada's interests abroad. He dreamed that Canada might become a strong nation in which French- and English-speaking citizens would get along with each other. Surprisingly, it was a crisis over French-language rights in the West that had helped Laurier to win the 1896 federal election. In 1890, Manitoba had created an English-only school system, in violation of the Manitoba Act. When the federal government led by Macdonald refused to intervene on behalf of French-Canadians in Manitoba, Quebecers voted in favour of Laurier and the Liberals.

Using a Speech as a Primary Source

When Prime Minister Laurier came to power, he was faced with many issues that were dividing the nation, such as the Manitoba schools question. In this excerpt from a speech he gave 1895, Laurier explains the importance of compromise and **conciliation** in the political arena.

Since speeches are meant to be heard, a good speech usually draws on many **rhetorical** **conventions,** for example, the rousing of emotions through persuasion and repetition, the appeal to common morality, and the use powerful images that evoke pathos or humour.

Have someone in your class read this excerpt. During the reading, concentrate on how this speech makes you feel. If you are persuaded to believe that Laurier must have been an enthusiastic supporter of French rights in Manitoba, you may be interested to learn that this was not the case. The compromise reached by Laurier and Premier Greenway did not support French-language rights: it only entitled Roman Catholic students to some religious instruction within the public school system. On careful reading, Laurier's speech actually promises very little—the mark of a carefully crafted political message.

Well, sir, the governments are very windy. They have blown and raged and threatened and the more they have raged and blown, the more that man Greenway [the premier of Manitoba] had stuck to his coat. If it were in my power, I would try the sunny way. I would approach this man Greenway with the sunny way of patriotism, asking him to be just and to be fair, asking him to be generous to the **minority**, in order that we may have peace among all the creeds and races which it has pleased God to bring upon this corner of our common country. Do you not believe that here is more to be gained by appealing to the heart and soul of men rather than by trying to compel them to do a thing?

Figure 7–2 It has been said that Laurier's greatest gift to Canada was his ability to see both the English and French points of view.

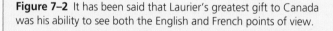

WHAT DO YOU THINK?

1. Create an Organizer with three column headings: R, for repetition; P, for persuasion; and I, for powerful images. Under each heading, copy the portions of Laurier's speech that draw on that rhetorical convention.

2. List the concessions Laurier would make to the French-Canadians in Manitoba.

3. Is being "generous" to minority groups the same as recognizing their rights? Explain.

4. Do you think Laurier's political tactic of compromise and conciliation was an effective one? Could it be used to settle issues of minority rights in present-day Canada?

IMPERIALISM: A FRENCH-ENGLISH SPLIT

conciliation: attempts to resolve differences

rhetorical: speech or writing created in order to persuade and impress

minority: a group having less than the number of votes necessary for control

mother country: an old-fashioned term used to refer to the country from which colonists emigrated

British Empire: the group of countries colonized by Britain, such as Canada, India, South Africa, and so on

imperialist: someone who practises imperialism, the policy of extending control of a region or regions by one nation

Laurier was determined to make English-and French-Canadians get along—not an easy task. There was, for example, the issue of Canada's relationship with its **mother country,** Britain. Most English-Canadians were loyal to Britain and were proud to belong to the worldwide **British Empire.** These supporters of the Empire were known as **imperialists.** French-Canadians felt less pride in Canada's status as a self-governing colony of Britain. As a minority, French-Canadians felt isolated. They certainly did not look to Britain as the seat of their culture.

In the half century following Confederation in 1867, Canada was not concerned with building a large army or navy. For military protection Canada relied on the British navy, which still controlled the seas, and British troops, which were stationed at Halifax, Nova Scotia and at Esquimalt, British Columbia. Many Canadians viewed Canada's military affairs as the responsibility of the British imperial government in London.

As the twentieth century dawned, however, that comfortable view was shattered. Two events—the South African War and the Naval Crisis—reversed Canada's dependency on Britain. Now Britain would turn to Canada for military support in order to strengthen its own world image.

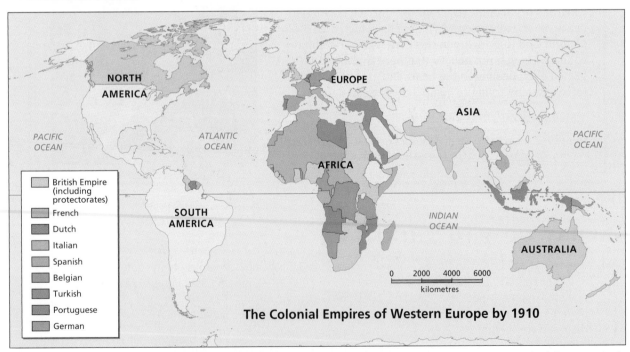

Legend:
- British Empire (including protectorates)
- French
- Dutch
- Italian
- Spanish
- Belgian
- Turkish
- Portuguese
- German

0   2000   4000   6000 kilometres

The Colonial Empires of Western Europe by 1910

Figure 7–3 "The sun never sets on the British Empire." This statement summarized the power and prestige of an empire that circled the globe. Many English-Canadians were proud of their country's status as the senior Dominion of the greatest empire since Rome.

The South African War

For Canada, the most important military event before World War I was the South African War, sometimes called the "Boer War." Canada's involvement in this war split the country along French-English lines once again.

In 1899, the British government controlled many parts of Africa. Now it was trying to extend its control in South Africa north from the Cape Colony. British Settlers met fierce resistance from the Boers, descendants of the early Dutch colonists in the region. Britain insisted that it only wanted to ensure equal rights for British subjects in South Africa. However, the Boers saw the British expansion as seizure of their land. The British seemed keenly interested in South Africa's newly discovered gold and diamond mines, and they were a threat to Boer culture. The Boers declared war on Britain in 1899.

Facing international criticism for its actions, the British government called on the colonies of the British Empire for support. In Canada, there were two views of British actions. Most English-Canadians thought that the prestige of the British Empire was at stake. They supported sending Canadian troops to fight in South Africa, the Boer War, out of duty to Britain. French-Canadians sympathized with the Boers. They did not think Canada should get involved in an unjust imperialist war.

Laurier decided to compromise. Canada, he announced, would equip and transport volunteers to South Africa who would become part of the British forces. As the British military situation in South Africa grew worse, Canada continued to send more volunteers. In all, the government sent 7300 volunteers and spent nearly $3 million on a war that was taking place far away and which did not directly involve Canada.

Laurier's compromise especially irritated French-Canadians. In Quebec, Henri Bourassa, a former Liberal ally, led the opposition to Laurier's decision. He noted that, just because Britain went to war, it did not follow that Canada should also be at war. Bourassa became the most vocal critic of Canada's involvement in Britain's imperial wars.

The Naval Issue

English- and French-Canadians also clashed when it came to the naval issue. Since Confederation, Canada had relied on the British navy to protect Canada's east and west coasts. However, a growing German navy began to challenge British domination of the seas. Britain responded in 1906 with the launching of *HMS Dreadnought,* the first "all-big-gun" battleship. With ten 30-centimetre guns in five turrets and a top speed of 21 **knots,** *Dreadnought* could not be outclassed. The **naval race** between Germany and Britain was on. Britain asked the countries of the British Empire for money to help with this expensive task. Most English-Canadians wanted Canada to contribute ships or money directly to Britain, but French-Canadians wanted Canada to have a navy of its own—one that could be made available to Britain in time of war.

To resolve the conflict, Laurier introduced the Naval Service Act in 1910. According to the terms of the act, Canada would have a navy of its own, which would be turned over to the British in times of emergency. While the eleven warships of the Canadian navy were being con-

knot: a unit of distance used at sea. The British nautical mile is 1853.2 metres

naval race: a competition to have the most powerful navy (the nuclear arms race is a modern day equivalent)

Figure 7–4 The "all-big-gun" *Dreadnought,* made in Britain

DID YOU KNOW?

During the election of 1911, Laurier reeled from his opponents' attacks on his policies of compromise. In a campaign speech he declared: "In Quebec I am branded a Jingo [a nationalist] and in Ontario as a separatist. In Quebec I am attacked as an Imperialist, and in Ontario as an anti-Imperialist. I am neither. I am a Canadian."

free trade: a policy that reduces or eliminates border taxes and regulations between countries

reciprocity: an exchange, or sharing

tariff: a duty or tax a country charges on imports

structed, Britain would lend Canada two cruisers, the *Niobe* for the East Coast and the *Rainbow* for the West Coast.

Both English- and French-Canadians fiercely opposed Laurier's compromise, but for different reasons. Led by the Conservative leader, Robert Borden, imperialists ridiculed the proposed "tin-pot" navy. Quebecers opposed the act because it seemed to tie Canada too closely to British imperial policies. French-Canadian opposition was again led by Henri Bourassa, who founded a newspaper, *Le Devoir*, to publicize his opposition to Laurier's naval policy. By 1914 and the start of World War I, Canada still had no naval policy—and its pathetic navy still consisted of two obsolete British warships.

Reciprocity

During the election of 1911, English-Canadians were preoccupied with the issue of **free trade** with the United States. By 1910, western farmers were tired of being a captive market for Ontario and Quebec manufacturers, who could not make farm machinery as cheaply as the Americans. They had convinced the Liberal government to negotiate a **reciprocity** agreement with the United States, thereby reducing **tariffs** on cheaper US imported goods.

Canadian business leaders and nationalists came together to fight reciprocity. Business people feared that cheaper American goods would hurt their businesses. Railway owners worried about a loss of east-west traffic should the flow of trade became north-south. Canadian nationalists thought that Canadian resources should remain in Canada, and they reminded voters that some Americans actually wanted to take over Canada.

The Liberals under Laurier were defeated in the 1911 election. Laurier would never again serve as Canada's prime minister. He remained leader of Canada's Liberal Opposition until his death in 1919.

The Alaska Boundary Dispute

Canadians did agree on some things. Laurier led a united country when dealing with the Americans in the Alaska boundary dispute. In 1867, when the United States purchased Alaska from Russia, the exact boundary between the remote northwest of British Columbia and Alaska was unclear. No one cared much about the boundary until the discovery of gold led to a surge of miners into the Yukon in 1898. Access to the Klondike goldfields by the easy sea route was only possible by travelling through American territory. This was a serious problem for Canada.

The strip of coastline extending south from Alaska as far as Prince of Wales Island off the coast of British Columbia was called the "Alaska Panhandle." The Pacific Ocean's **inlets** and **fiords,** which led into gold country, were in American territory. Sending Canadian police or militia through the American ports of Dyea and Skagway required permission from the United States.

Laurier was anxious to settle the boundary dispute. In 1903 he agreed to an international **tribunal** that would rule on the boundary. Six judges sat on the tribunal—three from the United States, one from

inlet: a small arm of the ocean that juts into the coast

fiord: an inlet between high cliffs

tribunal: a court or board appointed to judge a particular matter

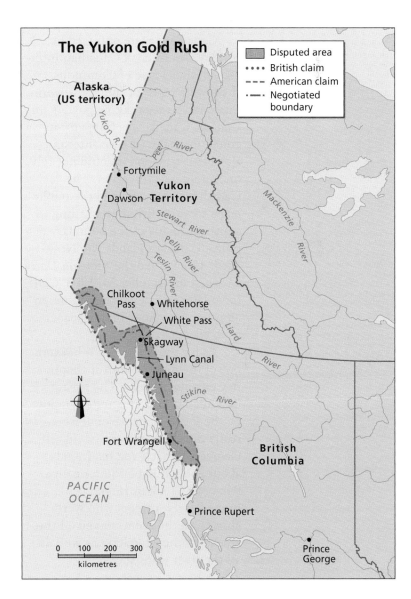

The Yukon Gold Rush

Legend:
- Disputed area
- •••• British claim
- – – – American claim
- –·–·– Negotiated boundary

Alaska (US territory)

Yukon R.

Peel River

Fortymile

Yukon Territory

Dawson

Stewart River

Mackenzie River

Pelly River

Teslin River

Chilkoot Pass • Whitehorse

White Pass

• Skagway

Lynn Canal

• Juneau

Liard River

Stikine River

Fort Wrangell •

British Columbia

PACIFIC OCEAN

• Prince Rupert

• Prince George

N

0 100 200 300
kilometres

Figure 7–5 The Canadian government wanted the boundary measured from the mountains nearest to the ocean. This new boundary would give Canada direct access to the Pacific Ocean by way of a number of inlets. Gold could be taken out of the Yukon Territory and supplies could be carried in without passing through American territory. US President Theodore Roosevelt threatened military action against Canada when he learned of this plan. What difficulties would people and industries in northwestern British Columbia and the Yukon continue to face as a result of the lack of access to the sea?

Britain, and two from Canada. US President Theodore Roosevelt made it clear he wished to see a settlement favourable to the United States.

International politics affected the tribunal's decision. Britain was involved in negotiations with the United States over a border dispute between Venezuela and British Guyana in South America. The British did not want to anger the United States. The British judge, ignoring Canadian protests, voted in favour of the American boundary line. Half the coast of British Columbia would continue to be cut off from access to the Pacific.

Canadians were outraged by Britain's sacrifice of Canadian interests. In the House of Commons, there were calls for full self-government and treaty-making powers for Canada. Canada was trapped—it could not make its own international treaties, and it could not rely on Britain for protection. The Canadian press reflected the public's anger towards Britain for failing to support Canada in the boundary dispute. "Canada's Hands Are Now Tied" proclaimed the *Victoria Daily Colonist* on October 24, 1903. Calls for greater independence in foreign affairs were echoed in newspapers from coast to coast.

As for the gold rush, it became one of the most colourful chapters in Canadian history. The tipster described in this chapter's Window on the Past—Robert Henderson—really did exist, and really did tell George Carmack and his friends about gold on Rabbit (later called Bonanza) Creek in 1896. Immediately, miners who were already on the scene staked all the creeks on the Klondike, as well as all the river watersheds.

It was a year before the world learned of the gold strike through enticing newspaper copy referring to a "ton of gold." The rich and the poor came, by water or by Chilkoot Pass, until 1899, when another strike was announced in Nome. The legacy of these terrible journeys has been recorded in many novels, diaries, plays, and films. Women, including the wives of men who left for the Klondike, often had gripping stories to tell. One woman who ventured north, leaving her children behind, wrote: "I think constantly of my little ones and God knows at times it seems more than I can bear but I must—for Oh deliver me from becoming insane up here."

But there was love to be found, as well, as this account illustrates:

PRIMARY SOURCE

Eighteen-year-old Mabel Long had been married only six months when she and her husband—a man twenty years her senior who had been chosen for her by her parents—set off for the gold fields. What little affection she may have felt for Mr. Long completely vanished when their boat capsized on Lake Bennett and he watched helplessly while she floundered on the water. It was love at first sight, however, between Mabel and the man who did jump in and pull her to shore.

The Klondike Gold Rush helped to ease a great worldwide depression by stimulating investment. And the great surge of people into the area encouraged the Canadian government to establish the Yukon Territory in 1898, with Dawson City as the capital.

1. How successful was Laurier's solution to the school question in Manitoba?

2. Why did English-Canadians and French-Canadians disagree on: a) Canada's involvement in the South African War, and b) the Naval Crisis?

3. Imagine that you are living in the Laurier era. Write a ten-sentence letter to the editor supporting or opposing Laurier's handling of Canada's role in the British Empire.

4. **a)** Examine a modern map of the Northwest Coast. What problems still exist for British Columbia as a result of the Alaska border settlement of 1903?

   b) How would you have settled the Alaska border dispute? If you agree with the idea of an international tribunal, how would you prevent members from voting to protect their countries' interests?

   c) With a partner, investigate the roles of the International Court of Justice and the United Nations in settling international border disputes.

5. Imagine that you are teenager from the prairies who has gone to the Klondike in search of gold. Create a brief character portrait for at least four individuals you encounter at Chilkoot Pass. Include information about their background and reasons for going to the Klondike.

6. What problems confront politicians today in different regions of Canada? As a class, discuss why some issues, such as gun control, are viewed differently in various parts of the country.

THE LAURIER BOOM

Fortunately for Laurier, the worldwide depression that had begun in the 1870s eased during his term of office. The great prosperity of these years resulted from rising world prices and expanding **markets** for Canadian products. Gold from South African mines flowed into London, where it was used by wealthy industrialists to invest in developing British territories such as Canada. Yukon gold also provided a flow of **capital** that could be used to expand factories and buy equipment in North America. The rise in industrial production in turn created a demand for raw materials, which forced up prices. Resource-rich Canada could now charge high prices for its commodities—lumber and minerals. Finally, better shipping technology and lower freight rates helped bulky Canadian resources and agricultural exports to compete in world markets.

New technologies also encouraged the development of Canada's rich storehouse of natural resources. The forests of the Canadian Shield provided raw material for the new pulp and paper mills, which caused the newspaper industry to grow by leaps and bounds. In addition, the Shield was mined for its rich deposits of nickel, copper, and other minerals.

In British Columbia the mining, lumber, and fishing industries grew as the boom extended to the West Coast. When the Canadian Pacific

market: buyers for a specific product, for example, the world market for wheat

capital: money that is used by a company to increase production and which buys a share in that company. Capital stimulates growth and creates more wealth for the investor.

Figure 7–6 British Columbia's forest industry was well developed by the time this photo was taken in 1886. This clearing is at approximately Hastings Street and Westminster Avenue (now Main Street).

homestead lands: public land granted to settlers by the US and Canadian governments in the later nineteenth century. Homesteads were supposed to be developed as farms.

Railway (CPR) expanded into Kootenay along the Crow's Nest Pass (a well-known mining region), it bought its own smelter at Trail. Eventually, the railway company would formalize its involvement in mining with the creation of Cominco Limited. The expansion of the railway lines and prairie development also led to a dramatic growth in lumbering: During the ten years after the turn of the century, investment in the forest industry grew from $2 million to $65 million. It was easy to obtain harvesting rights, and the accessibility of the coast forests led to a cutting frenzy.

Rising world prices helped to increase the pace of agricultural development since higher prices for produce encouraged farmers to expand their production. As the population of the prairies swelled, the region was being transformed from an agricultural hinterland into the "bread basket of the world." This in turn encouraged the expansion of

manufacturing industries. Canada's enormous hydroelectric potential was harnessed to power the new factories and the mines.

The "Last Best West"

"More money" and "more people" became the hallmarks of the Laurier era. The two trends worked together: the flourishing economy attracted immigrants, who in turn stimulated economic growth, which then encouraged more immigration.

By the end of the depression, a growing world demand for wheat, and the end of free **homestead lands** in the United States, made the Canadian West more appealing to Europeans and Americans. From 1896 until 1911, the Liberal government took advantage of these factors and encouraged people to come to Canada. This was a new development. Between 1867 and the early 1890s the number of immigrants to Canada had remained low—nearly all immigration to North America had been to the United States. It was hard to attract settlers to a barren, sparsely populated country like Canada. Many who had made the trip eventually emigrated south to the United States because of the harsh climate or lack of work.

Between 1896 and 1914, the prairie lands swelled with settlers. Clifford Sifton became Laurier's Minister of the Interior, in charge of immigration. A Westerner, he was committed to populating the prairies. Sifton launched a vigorous recruitment program to lure newcomers to prairie homesteads and away from the cities. The promotion campaign targeted prospective immigrants in Europe and the United states who would make good farmers.

Sifton attracted some controversy by welcoming immigrants from the grasslands of eastern and central Europe. These farmers were accustomed to an extreme climate and they understood **dryland farming methods,** but some Canadians were uncomfortable with newcom-

> **dryland farming methods:** farming methods practised in regions with insufficient rainfall, for example, soil cultivation that reduces evaporation

The Power of Advertising

C lifford Sifton's Immigration Department attracted tens of thousands settlers to the Canadian West by offering free homestead land. The department advertised this land through millions of pamphlets, newspaper ads, public lectures, and free trips to promoters who would encourage settlers to come to Canada. Sifton hired agents to distribute posters advertising "The Last Best West," which tried to dispel the commonly held image of the prairies as a frozen wasteland. In all the advertisements, all references to cold and snow were banned. Sifton also offered government officials a bonus for each new person they recruited to Canada.

In 1900, the Superintendent of Immigration updated the House of Commons on the government's strategies to attract immigrants. An excerpt from this report appears below.

> [The] advertising that is done by the department in the United States is pretty extensive. We have advertised in over 7000 American newspapers having a circulation of about 7 000 000 and the states we have advertised in are [a list of twenty states follows]. In the United States, we also have a system of sending [American] delegates to inspect Manitoba and the Northwest and to make their report to the section of the country from which they come. These delegates ... are chosen at a meeting of farmers called together by one of the agents [at the Immigration Department] ... The Canadian Pacific Railroad ... give(s) these delegates free transportation.

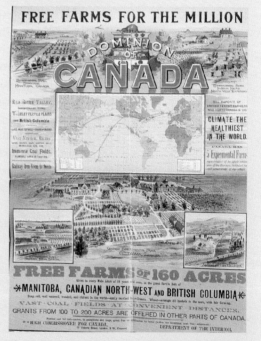

Figure 7–7 Notice the exaggeration in this poster. Newcomers would have to work long and hard before the natural prairie would look anything like the farms shown in the advertisement. Why might readers in Europe be persuaded by such images?

ers whose language and customs differed so much from their own. Sifton defended his **open-door** policy by claiming that "… a stalwart peasant in a sheep-skin coat, born of the soil, whose forefathers have been farmers for ten generations, with a stout [strong] wife and a half-dozen children is good quality." As a result of Sifton's policy, the settlers on the prairies became a much more diverse group, compared to the settlers of eastern Canada. Ukrainians, Russians, Czechs, Hungarians, Poles, Rumanians, Austrians, and many other groups settled in communities throughout the prairies.

Many British settlers also arrived during Sifton's term as Minister of the Interior. In fact, they made up one-third of all immigrants. Because they were usually not from farming backgrounds, they often failed as farmers. British immigrants were mostly working-class people from industrial centres who felt more comfortable living in cities than on the treeless prairies.

American migrants from the plains south of the border were much more successful than their British counterparts. They **assimilated** easily into Canadian society and were welcomed as desirable settlers. Americans had first-hand

knowledge of prairie farming methods, as well as far more money than the average European. The average American immigrant brought $1000 in cash and farming equipment, compared to the average European, who brought $15. American settlers favoured Alberta in particular—to such a degree that, by 1914, the province's population became overwhelmingly American. A million Americans came to Canada between 1896 and 1914.

Thousands of British children were also sent to Canada during these early years. Many had lived in British orphanages, or were the unwanted children of very poor parents. Some were even sent away by the authorities without their parents' knowledge. Many people believed that the farms of Canada would provide an excellent environment where the children would eat well and learn useful skills. This idea appealed to Canadian farming families, who answered the British advertisements placed in Canadian newspapers. Some people took in the "home children," as they were called, because they wanted to adopt them, but many others saw them only as a source of cheap labour. Although the children were supposed to be fed, clothed, and sent to school during the

This table shows the rapid growth of population in western Canada during the Laurier years. Examine the table carefully and make a statement about the rate of growth on the prairies. What reasons can you give for some provinces growing faster than others? Can you explain the decline in population in the Yukon?

Table 7–1	Population Growth by Province, 1891–1921					
Year	Manitoba	Saskatchewan	Alberta	B.C.	Yukon	Canada
1891	152 506	——**	——**	98 173	——**	4.83M
1901	255 211	91 279	73 022	178 657	27 219	5.37M
1911	461 394	492 432	374 295	392 480	8 512	7.21M
1921*	610 118	757 510	588 454	524 582	4 157	8.79M

* Most of the increase occurred by 1914.
** Alberta, Saskatchewan, and Yukon became territories in 1898.

winter, many of them did not enjoy even the basic necessities of life. In some cases, the children were beaten and forced to live in barns or stables.

The Push-Pull Factors in Immigration

Between 1891 and 1921, Canada's population almost doubled. About 60 percent of the immigrants settled in the West: 9 percent settled in British Columbia and 49 percent settled in the prairie provinces. The Maritimes became home to only 3 percent, and the remaining immigrants stayed in central Canada. Canadian immigration policy from 1896 to 1914 succeeded because of "push-pull" factors. Vast migrations of population occur for two reasons: a need to leave one's homeland

(push factor) and/or the lure of opportunity in another country (pull factor). During waves of immigration, push-pull factors often work together.

Americans, Britons, Europeans, and Asians looked to Canada as a place where they could improve their quality of life (pull factor). For poor eastern and central Europeans in particular, free farmland served as a pull factor. By 1891, thousands of Ukrainians had arrived in Edmonton. They had fled repeated crop failures, starvation, and overpopulation in their homeland (push factor).

Push and pull factors also worked together in the case of the Doukhobors, a group of Russians who left their homeland because service in the army was against their

DID YOU KNOW?

"Home children" were sent to Canada until the 1930s.

Figure 7–8 This picture shows some of the thousands of children sent to Canada as "home children." What special problems would children of this age face in coming to a strange environment?

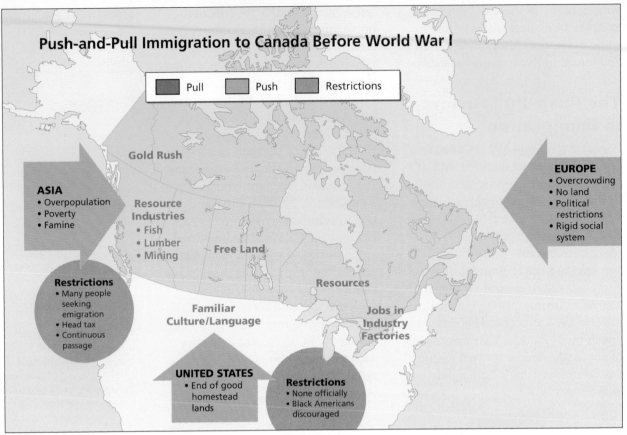

Figure 7–9 Vast migrations of population occur for two reasons: a need to leave one's homeland (push factor), and/or the lure of opportunity in another country (pull factor).

religious beliefs (push factor) and in search of free land (pull factor). Canada exempted them from military service and assisted their passage to the prairies, where they were granted nearly three-quarters of a million acres of land. By 1899, more than 7000 Doukhobors had settled in Saskatchewan. American settlers were motivated to come to Canada by the closing of the homestead frontier of good land in 1892 (push factor). They were drawn to the Canadian prairies because of rising grain prices (pull factor).

Adjusting to Life on the Prairies

Once the new Canadian settlers claimed their land, they had to adjust to a new life. The first task was to raise at least $500 to outfit their homestead with the basics: a plough, a wagon, horses, and a milk cow. To get this start-up money, immigrants often had to work long hours on other people's farms, or in lumber, railway, or mining camps.

For the homesteading family, living conditions were primitive. Comfort was sacrificed to raise the first crop. The first house was often made of mud-covered sod on a wood frame. Affectionately known as a "soddie," it usually featured open

Figure 7–10 This family in Manitoba was well established by 1913. It would have taken years of back-breaking labour to reach this stage of comfort. How could you determine how long the family has occupied the site?

windows covered with sacks and a thatched roof. Walls were created by stacking strips of sod-like bricks. Soddies were full of flies and fleas, and smelled in the summer. They also leaked, as this account shows:

In June we had a spell of very rainy weather and there were few dry spots to be found in the house. Papa spread canvas across poles above the beds to keep them dry. I remember Edie holding an umbrella over Mama while she crouched before the fireplace frying sourdough pancakes for the family.

Other hardships included the long, bitterly cold winters; the monotonous diet and landscape; and natural disasters such as drought, hail, and grasshoppers. Still, most immigrants to the prairies managed to succeed. After a year or two of often very harsh conditions, the settlers would replace

the sod hut with a more substantial home and outbuildings. As more settlers came to an area, roads and bridges were improved, providing better access to towns and markets.

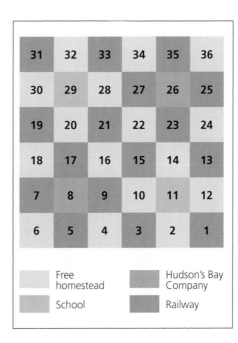

31	32	33	34	35	36
30	29	28	27	26	25
19	20	21	22	23	24
18	17	16	15	14	13
7	8	9	10	11	12
6	5	4	3	2	1

Free homestead
School
Hudson's Bay Company
Railway

Figure 7–11 Most of the farmland of the prairie provinces was surveyed before it was settled. The level topography and the straight Canada-US boundary made a grid system practical. Each province was laid out in square blocks called "townships," measuring six miles (10 kilometres) to a side. Each of the 36 square miles (9 324 hectares), or sections, in a township was further divided into four quarter sections of 160 acres (64.75 hectares). The homesteaders and settlers of the Laurier period were usually granted a quarter section of land.

Newcomers in the Cities

The opening of the West was one of the most dramatic events in Canadian history. Between 1898 and 1914, the population of the prairies increased by nearly one and one-half million. This huge increase had an effect on the entire country.

Although they had been recruited to populate the prairies, almost one-third of the immigrants to Canada during the Laurier era settled in the cities. The development of manufacturing industries also encouraged thousands of Canadians to abandon rural life for work in the cities. Montreal and Toronto doubled in size. Winnipeg, Edmonton, Calgary, and Vancouver grew rapidly as well.

By 1914, Canada's **urban** population was edging towards 50 percent of the total population. Nonetheless, most of the cities in Canada were still relatively small. Only four had a population exceeding 100 000.

Life was often bleak for immigrants in growing Canadian cities. Many of the newcomers were unskilled and spoke little English. They were often exploited in unsafe, low-paying factory jobs. Many lived in **ghettos,** crammed into one- and two-room **tenements** that offered little fresh air, light, or heat. Conditions in the tenements were often unsanitary, which frequently led to disease.

The majority of Canadians and immigrants who moved to cities could find work only as unskilled labourers. They were paid from $10 to $15 a week for working ten to twelve hours a day in noisy, dingy

Figure 7–12 This family lived in a one-room home in Winnipeg in 1912. Primitive and unsanitary conditions were common among poor, working-class families.

surroundings. They worked six days a week, with no job security. While prices for goods were generally low, most household income was spent on housing and food. In many working-class families, women and children took jobs as well to make ends meet. Parents' long working hours led to the neglect of the children, who were unlikely to receive an education.

During this era—before the introduction of social welfare programs such as unemployment insurance or family benefits—the government did not think it was responsible for the needs of the poor. Poor families relied on each other or on charitable organizations for help. Religious and women's groups began to lobby provincial governments for help in addressing the plight of Canada's urban poor.

Between 1911 and 1996, the four largest cities in Canada grew at varying rates. Why might the population of Winnipeg and Vancouver remain relatively small compared to the population of Toronto and Montreal? Think about some of the factors that affect population growth, such as climate, availability of land, and proximity to transportation.

Table 7–2	Largest Cities in Canada, 1911 and 1996	
	1911	**1996** (metropolitan area)
Montreal	491 000	3 328 000
Toronto	382 000	4 338 400
Winnipeg	382 000	676 500
Vancouver	101 000	1 826 800

ACTIVITIES

1. **a)** State three reasons for the rapid growth in immigration to Canada after 1896.

   b) State three problems resulting from the influx of immigrants. Include at least one social problem and one economic problem in your answer.

2. How accurate was it to call western Canada "The Last Best West?" Explain your answer.

3. Design your own brochure or poster promoting immigration to Canada in the Laurier era.

4. Which of the push-and-pull factors listed below would apply to each of these immigrant groups: Americans, Britons, Europeans, and Asians? Create an organizer to display your answers.
   - free land
   - overpopulation
   - scarce land
   - poverty
   - employment
   - political oppression
   - religious oppression
   - economic incentive
   - opportunity for self-improvement

5. Imagine you are an immigrant to the Canadian prairies in the first decade of this century. Draw a sketch map of the prairies showing the location of your homestead along with the nearest cities. Enhance your map with descriptions, illustrations, symbols, and other visual aids to present a colourful picture of the physical/cultural environment of the Canadian West for your relatives in Europe. The geography of the Canadian prairies, described in Chapter 3, and an atlas, will help you complete your map.

6. Imagine you are one of the people shown in Figure 7–10. Write a letter to someone in your homeland describing a significant experience you have had while homesteading in the Canadian prairies.

7. It's 1913. Draw up a petition to take to city council in a major Canadian city. Include in it a list of the problems the city faces and a number of suggestions on how to ease these problems.

RAILWAYS TO EVERYWHERE

subsidy: financial assistance granted by government in support of a business regarded as being in the public interest

Figure 7–13 By 1914, new railways had opened up the northern part of the Canadian West. Settlers could then move away from the CPR-dominated southern route. Many new towns and cities were established as the railways pushed into previously unsettled territory. The railway companies placed stops every 20 kilometres, which allowed towns to grow around the stations.

The economic boom in the West led to the construction of two new transcontinental railways during the Laurier period. As people settled in areas close to the railway, the need for new rail lines became apparent. Prairie farmers were disgruntled with the monopoly of the CPR and the high rates it charged. The CPR had been in business since 1881 and had received millions of acres of land and millions of dollars in cash from the former Macdonald government. Now two rival companies sought federal—and provincial—government aid to build new transcontinental rail lines—and the Laurier government was listening.

The Canadian Northern railway used its government **subsidies** to extend its prairie lines eastward to Quebec and west, along a northern route, to the Pacific. In 1901, the British Columbia government invited its owners, the colourful and shrewd William Mackenzie and Donald Mann, to extend their prairie lines through the Yellowhead Pass and down the North Thompson River to Kamloops, and then on to Vancouver. This extension followed the same route as the CPR. Eventually, Mackenzie and Mann secured over $200 million in government subsidies and land grants, building a financial and business empire that expanded from rail lines to include mining, lumbering, and shipping.

The Grand Trunk Railroad was another Canadian railway that expanded from coast to coast with

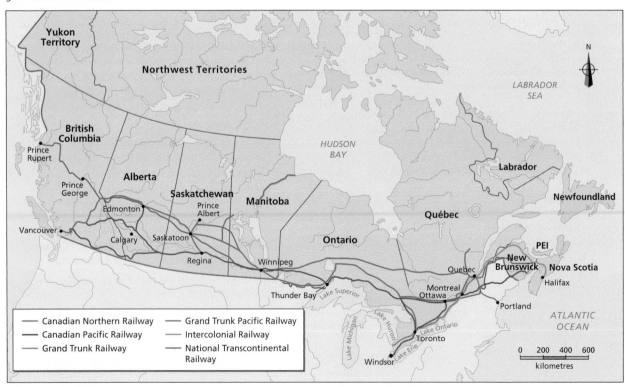

Figure 7–14 Payne Bluff on the Kaslo and Slocan railway lines. This photo shows the rough terrain that challenged railway builders in British Columbia. This particular turning point was so treacherous that passengers had to disembark and follow the train on foot.

hinterland: the remote and less developed area around a community

site: the features of the land on which the settlement is built, such as its elevation and landforms

situation: how a settlement is related to the surrounding area, including its relationship to other settlements and routes

Railway Cities

Many cities in Western Canada owe their existence to the coming of the railway. These cities were often early fur trade centres that were chosen as divisional centres for the expanding railways. As former fur posts, they were usually well situated for development.

Saskatoon, Edmonton, Prince George, and Prince Rupert were communities that were selected as divisional points on the Grand Trunk Pacific Railway (see page 266). At the mouth of the Skeena River, a location that was to become Prince Rupert was chosen as the railway terminus. Kamloops, already on the CPR main line, was chosen by the Canadian Northern as its major divisional point in the interior of the province. These cities, all well-situated, grew in such a way that they could take advantage of their **hinterlands.**

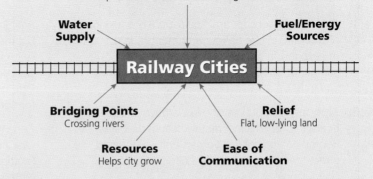

Site and Situation Factors in the Location of Railway Cities

Transportation Nodes
- Route Centres: where several valleys meet
- Confluence Towns: where rivers join
- Gap Towns: offer routes through hills or mountains

Water Supply

Fuel/Energy Sources

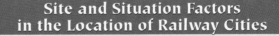
Railway Cities

Bridging Points
Crossing rivers

Relief
Flat, low-lying land

Resources
Helps city grow

Ease of Communication

Figure 7–15 Transportation centres, such as the railway cities of western Canada, grow because of **site** and **situation** factors.

DID YOU KNOW?

Towns along the new rail lines in the prairies and British Columbia were named by starting with A and going through the alphabet to Z as many times as necessary.

topography: the physical features of an area, such as hills, valleys, and bodies of water

government encouragement. The Laurier government even agreed to build the section in eastern Canada in areas not serviced by the CPR or Canadian Northern. The Grand Trunk Pacific built the western section following the same northern route as the Canadian Northern to the Yellowhead Pass. From there it crossed northern BC to a terminus at Prince Rupert.

The outbreak of World War I made the new railways unprofitable because it reduced immigration and ended the flow of British capital to Canada. Fearing the loss of taxpayer support following World War I, the government consolidated all the railways that did not belong to the CPR as the Canadian National Railways, which was "to be owned by the people of Canada."

Figure 7–16 Prince George is located on flat land at the junction of the Fraser and Nechako rivers. It was a major bridging point on the Grand Trunk Railway and a natural nodal point for the northern-central interior of British Columbia. However, only in the 1960s did Prince George experience rapid growth. Around this time, its resource hinterland of forests, minerals, and hydroelectric energy was exploited to the fullest extent. Today, Prince George is the largest city in central British Columbia and the nexus for several railways and roads that serve northern British Columbia.

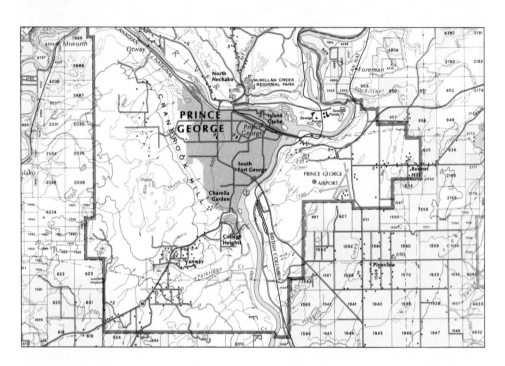

ACTIVITIES

1. Give two reasons for and against the expansion of the CPR. In one of your arguments against the expansion of the CPR, say why other companies should build railways on the prairies and in BC.

2. Draw a simple outline of a locomotive and seven boxcars. Label the locomotive "Laurier's Railway Boom." In each of the boxcars write a different effect that the era's railway-building had on the Canadian West.

3. Canada was a country of only 7 million people in 1910. How many transcontinental railways do you think it should have had? Explain your answer.

4. Examine the map of Prince George in Figure 7–16. List the favourable aspects of the site of Prince George. How has the expansion of Prince George been determined by its **topography?** Refer to Chapter 3 for more information on topography.

5. Copy the map of Prince George's situation into your notebook. Use an atlas to record the location of resources in Prince George's hinterland and add this information to the map. Add any other forms of transportation that could enhance the location of the city.

Figure 7–17 Craigdarroch Castle in Victoria, British Columbia, was built in 1889 for Robert Dunsmuir, the industrialist who founded Dunsmuir Coal. The elaborate home cost $650 000 to build—a large sum at that time—and was still not finished at the time of his death.

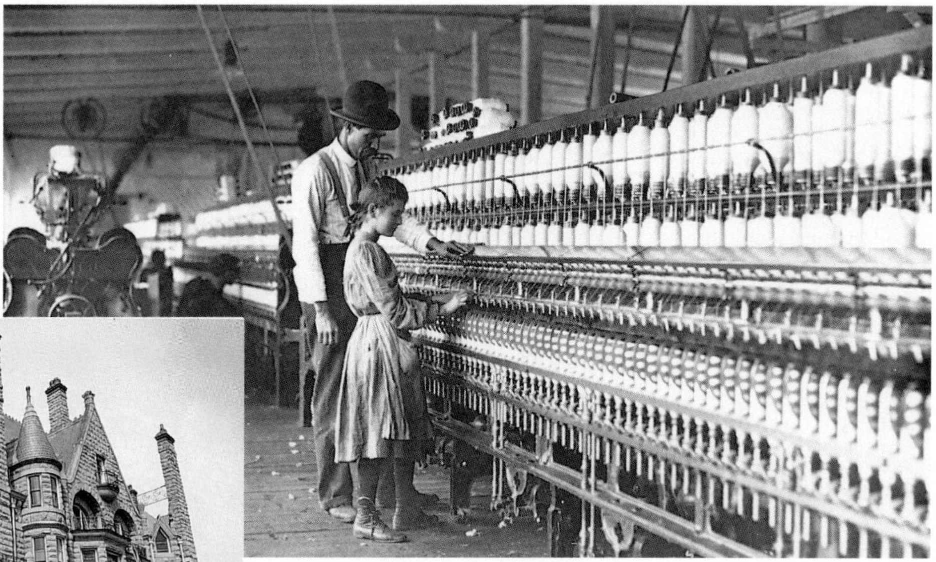

Figure 7–18 The growth of industrialization in Canada created a demand for unskilled labour. Men and women often tended machines for ten to twelve hours a day. Besides the monotony, workers had to endure hazardous and uncomfortable working conditions. Factory owners paid little attention to worker safety or to washroom facilities, and regular rest breaks were unknown. For workers, injury on the job meant time off without pay—or even dismissal.

THE RISE OF UNIONS

The prosperity of the Laurier era did not extend equally to all. Canadian industry and finance were controlled by a few large corporations, such as Imperial Oil, Massey-Harris (which manufactured farm machinery and other equipment), and Dunsmuir Coal. The new concentration of wealth in the hands of relatively few entrepreneurs and investors contrasted sharply with the poverty of those in the working class. Income taxes were insignificant and many entrepreneurs flaunted their wealth. Some built enormous mansions, such as Casa Loma, in Toronto, and the Dunsmuir Craigdarroch Castle, in Victoria. As the gap between rich and poor widened, workers wanted a greater share of the wealth created by their labour.

Between 1880 and 1910, workers began to organize **labour unions** in earnest. Roughly 10 percent of workers in industry joined a union during this time. But the early unions faced an uphill struggle. Unskilled workers could easily be replaced if they went on strike, and the government and the legal system tended to favour employers rather than organized labour. Companies hired private police and called in the militia when workers staged public demonstrations or went on strike. From 1910 to World War I, unrest was widespread and a number of violent confrontations erupted between employers and workers.

labour union: an organization of workers that negotiates matters such as wages and working conditions with employers

Figure 7–19 Strikers at one of the Dunsmuir mines. Thirty-nine of the arrested strikers were given prison sentences ranging from nine months to two years. The Attorney-General of British Columbia said he hoped that these sentences would break the spirit of the other strikers.

Labour Unrest in British Columbia

Some of the most bitter clashes between workers and employers occurred in British Columbia. For years, the Dunsmuir family had controlled the coal industry on Vancouver Island. Working in a Dunsmuir mine meant crawling on one's hands and knees in dark, wet tunnels with only the light of a miner's lamp for guidance. Workers toiled long hours for meagre wages. Hundreds of miners were maimed or killed in frequent explosions. Known for their utter disregard for worker safety, the Dunsmuirs often hired strikebreakers, as well as Asian workers who agreed to work for poor wages, to replace striking miners. Not unexpectedly, mines owned by this powerful family became strongholds of unionism.

In 1910, James Dunsmuir sold his mines to Mackenzie and Mann, the railway entrepreneurs. They immediately tried to increase profits in the Vancouver Island mines while continuing to undercut safety. After two years of wage cuts and unresolved safety issues, miners at the Extension, Cumberland, Nanaimo, and Ladysmith mines began one of the most bitter strikes in the province's history. The conflict dragged on from 1912 until 1914. In 1913, tensions reached an all-time high as the strikers' families were thrown out of their company-owned houses. Strikebreakers were brought in by the company to keep the mines operating. When rioting broke out in Nanaimo and Cumberland, the provincial government called in the militia to stop the violence. In Nanaimo, a mass arrest of strikers followed.

In all, 179 miners were arrested and thirty-nine were sentenced to prison terms. This remained the biggest mass arrest in British Columbia's history until the arrest of environmental activists at Clayoquot Sound eighty years later. The company kept the mines open until the 1930s.

organizing the
FAST FOOD
industry

A sign of the changing times: A press release from the Canadian Auto Workers announces that the newest hero of Canadian labour "can be contacted through her mother."

Figure 7–20 Tessa Lowinger, 16, and Jennifer Wiebe, 17, display their union certification.

This from the aristocrats of industrial unionism, the tough and defiant auto workers?

Please call her mum?

Indeed. In the afterglow of Labour Day, 1998, it is no accident that the bright stars in the CAW firmament are two teenagers who sling fries and burgers when they are not doing Grade 12 homework.

With a little help from their friends, the young Squamish women won CAW certification for staff at the local McDonald's restaurant, making it the chain's only organized outlet in North America.

Given the history of McDonald's and unions, that, as Ryan Mooney, one of their young friends and fellow works said, is monumental.

This summer, after more than two years of working part time at the restaurant, Tessa Lowinger, 16, finally decided that things had become unreasonable.

Fast food is an old-fashioned assembly line. Speed, pressure, and tension. Managers frequently yelled at the young staff, often in front of customers, sometimes reducing them to tears. Workers who fell ill were told they could not take the day off without finding their own replacement.

So, Ms. Lowinger talked to her friend Jennifer Wiebe, 17, and to her father, Hans. Her friend said, yes, they should do

something, and her father said it's up to you, but if you really want to do something, maybe you should talk to a union.

In retrospect, his counsel seems rash. McDonald's beat back every other attempt to organize their workers. Most recently a branch in Saint-Hubert, Que., was closed after its workers voted to join the International Brotherhood of Teamsters.

A few days after their conversation with Mr. Lowinger, the two young women met with Ryan Krell, the Canadian Auto Workers' 24-year-old youth organizer in Vancouver. Like them, he was excited.

"Realistically, I was very scared. I know that if by some miracle it was organized and we were successful and it was going to happen, that they might just close it down."

That was on a Saturday night in July. The next day they phoned back and said they had signatures on union cards for 20 of their 73 fellow workers.

By Sunday night the owner had found out about the drive and by Monday a McDonald's business agent was on the spot, holding meetings. By Tuesday McDonald's was hiring new employees, with a $20 bonus for anyone who brought in a new worker

On Wednesday the CAW calculated that more than half the staff had signed up, and filed for formal certification just before 20 newly hired workers began the afternoon shift.

It's not about money. Fast food workers don't expect to be millionaires. If they're lucky they get a bit above minimum wage, which in BC these days is $7.15 an hour. But they have strong views on working conditions, Mr. Krell said, and that's the problem with the fast food industry.

And that's how the industrial unions have acquired a generation of members with a quite different view of the world.

Young people are strangers in this land. They have no idea of the history of labour or the culture of unionism, no idea of employment standards or working rights. Their parents may be union members, but it never trickled down. Their view of union leaders, as Ryan Krell said, is a bunch of white guys who are over 50 and overweight.

Part of the pitch to young people has been to hire young organizers like Mr. Krell. At 24 he is older than Tessa Lowinger and Jennifer Wiebe, but at least he's not over 50 and overweight.

He believes the CAW is now more sympathetic to young people because a lot of CAW members have sons and daughters who are facing the workplace. They all know General Motors is not opening new factories in BC these days, "and those $30-an-hour jobs just don't exist any more."

A reminder of the brutality of the workplace: The pulp mill where Jennifer Wiebe's father, John, works has been idle all summer, and BC Rail has announced it wants to cut 14 jobs in Squamish, one of which may be Hans Lowinger's.

The surprise of the union drive at McDonald's is that it probably would not have happened if anyone had followed basics of Management 101.

Jennifer Wiebe: "We wanted to be treated the way we treated management—with respect. We didn't yell at them and call them stupid for doing something. I mean, they made mistakes too, right?…

"Nobody liked to go to work. It wasn't fun. Not that work is supposed to be fun, but it was degrading to go to work. You don't want to go and be yelled at just for the heck of it."

WHAT DO YOU THINK?

1. Make a list of reasons that both support and oppose the unionization of the retail and consumer service sector of the economy. With which side do you agree, and why?

2. Use your list to develop three to five questions that you want answered or discussed on the issue of unionizing service-sector workers. Interview both a local employer in the service sector and also a union representative, or invite them to your class. Evaluate their responses. Did the interview/discussions change your opinions?

3. With electronic technology revolutionizing the very nature of work, what roles do you think unions will play in the twenty-first century? How will they change to adapt to the new world of work?

ACTIVITIES

1. Make a list of reasons why workers would wish to form unions during this period.

2. How did the British Columbia mining strike of 1912 to 1914 highlight the differing goals of business, labour, and government?

3. a) As a class, brainstorm a list of ways in which governments today protect the interests of workers. Consider regulations at the local, provincial, and federal level when offering suggestions.

   b) Next brainstorm a list of ways in which governments today protect the interests of business owners. Discuss areas in which these two policies—protecting workers and protecting businesses—conflict with each other and complement one another.

CLOSING THE DOOR TO IMMIGRATION

Many groups of Canadians began to resent Clifford Sifton's "open-door" immigration policy. Some labour organizations saw unskilled immigrant workers as a threat to their members' livelihoods. Some British-Canadians feared that immigrants from eastern, central, and southern Europe would alter the British character of the country. French-Canadians also feared that the influence of their culture would decline as their numbers became proportionately smaller. For the most part, business people supported the growth of immigration during the boom years. These immigrants supplied them with a pool of cheap labour.

Immigration policy was an especially thorny issue in British Columbia. Employers in the mines, forests, and canneries encouraged the arrival of hard-working Asian immigrants, who accepted less pay compared to other workers. But many British Columbians felt their jobs were threatened and pressured the federal government to restrict Asian immigration. In 1905, Frank Oliver replaced Sifton as Minister of the Interior. He agreed with those who wished to reduce the number of immigrants, especially non-White immigrants. Oliver introduced a more selective immigration policy aimed particularly at Asian immigrants, and provincial governments started to restrict Chinese, Japanese, and East Indian immigration.

British Columbia: The "Golden Mountain"

Chinese immigrants comprised the largest single group of Asians in British Columbia at this time. The Cariboo Gold Rush and the construction of the Canadian Pacific Railway had lured many Chinese people to BC. By 1891, 9400 Chinese immigrants were living in the province. Most of them were men who intended to return to China when they had made enough money in British Columbia. Chinese workers lived in isolated "Chinatowns" in Vancouver, Victoria, Nanaimo, and New Westminster. Chinatowns became lively communities with many businesses and cultural organizations.

Most of the Chinese workers were employed in the salmon canneries and in the coal mines of Vancouver Island. Profit-hungry employers were eager to hire

Can you find any pattern in these figures? Name two ways in which the ethnic composition of the BC population differed from that of the prairie provinces in the same years.

Table 7–3	British Columbia Population by Ethnic Origin, 1901–1921		
Year	British	European	Asian
1901	106 403	21 784	19 524
1911	266 295	69 799	30 864
1921	387 513	72 743	39 739

Figure 7–21 The aftermath of a Vancouver riot that destroyed many businesses in the Japanese and Chinese areas of the city.

Chinese immigrants because they worked hard for low pay, but labour councils representing Canadian workers resented the Chinese workers, who seemed to be undercutting the jobs of their members. Labour organizations became leaders in demanding exclusionary legislation that would restrict the number of Chinese entering Canada.

Opponents of Asian immigration formed the Asiatic Exclusion League. Early in 1907, anti-Asian feelings came to a head in British Columbia. When Lieutenant-Governor James Dunsmuir refused to sign a bill to exclude Japanese immigrants from entering Canada, protesters marched to Vancouver's city hall. Some of the speakers inflamed the mob, and roughly a thousand demonstrators left a trail of destruction through Chinatown and the Japanese section of the city. The riot focused international attention on Vancouver, much to the embarrassment of the federal government. Because Japan was an ally

of Great Britain, Prime Minister Laurier apologized to the Japanese government and struck a Royal Commission to report on the riot. Nevertheless, the government set a limit of 400 Japanese immigrants a year into Canada.

By "Continuous Passage" Only

Laurier's Minister of Labour, William Lyon Mackenzie King, led the Royal Commission to investigate the Vancouver riots and to study the damage to property. He was also asked to investigate how workers from Asia had been "enticed" to come to Canada. Since 1904, for example, CPR agents based in Hong Kong had encouraged Sikhs to emigrate to Canada. It was difficult to restrict East-Indian immigration because as British subjects they could not be denied entry to Canada.

To prevent the entry of East Indians into Canada, the government amended the 1906

Figure 7–22 The East Indians aboard the *Komagata Maru* spent two uncomfortable months in Vancouver harbour. In 1994, the eightieth anniversary of the incident, a commemorative plaque was unveiled in Vancouver harbour.

Immigration Act. Immigrants were now required to come to Canada via a non-stop, direct route from their country of origin. A direct, or "continuous passage," from India was impossible. By this means, the Canadian government thought it had resolved the issue of Asian immigration. The continuous-passage amendment was challenged in 1914 when a Sikh businessman, Gurdit Singh, chartered a steamer called the *Komagata Maru* to transport 354 Sikh immigrants to Vancouver. The ship left Hong Kong on April 4, 1914. After stopping in China and Japan, it arrived in Vancouver on May 23. Canadian authorities put the ship in quarantine so that its passengers could not land. Supporters of the Sikhs argued that the continuous-passage rule was invalid, but the government stood firm. Nearly 200 police and immigration officers tried to board the vessel, but they were showered with bottles and sticks. Finally, on July 23, the *Komagata Maru* was escorted out of Vancouver harbour by the cruiser *Rainbow*.

ACTIVITIES

1. What issues were common to the Vancouver Riot and the *Komagata Maru* incident? Which groups benefited from the resolution of each event?

2. Imagine you are an Asian immigrant living in British Columbia in the years before World War I. Compose entries into a journal that you are keeping to describe your experiences in Canada. Mention the jobs you have held, working conditions, interactions with other Canadians, the effect of government restrictions on your personal life, and any other important events that affect you or those close to you.

3. Compare the figures in Table 7–3 on page 273, which shows British Columbia's population by ethnic origin in the years 1901 to 1921, with the most recent figures you can find. Sources such as an atlas or the *Canada Yearbook* may be useful. What principal differences do you find?

THOSE LESS EQUAL: THE STRUGGLE FOR HUMAN RIGHTS

By the time Laurier was elected in 1896, the practice of voting by secret ballot had been the law for more than twenty years. However, only male property owners were entitled to the franchise. Women, Native Canadians, immigrants of Asian ancestry, and many other newcomers to Canada were denied the right to vote. During Laurier's time as prime minister, women, the Native peoples, and other groups began organized efforts to win social and political equality.

Women's Suffrage and Social Reform

Around the turn of the century, most Canadian women had very hard lives. Before the invention of labour-saving devices, such as washing machines, housework and child rearing consumed most of the average woman's day. Families of ten to twelve children were common. For women, the risk of death or disability during childbirth was high, and many babies died at birth. Because women rarely worked outside the home after marriage, educational expectations for women were low. By 1900, women made up only 15 percent of undergraduates at Canadian universities. They were barred from many professions, such as law, and were not eligible for university scholarships.

The campaign for **women's suffrage**—the right to vote—came of age in the Laurier era. **Suffragists** were mainly middle-class women devoted to social reform. They blamed most social ills, including poverty and child neglect, on the evils of alcoholism, which was a growing problem. They demonstrated regularly to persuade the government to extend the franchise to women. Many prominent suffragists were also members of the Women's Christian Temperance Union (WCTU), founded in 1885, to promote prohibition. WCTU members supported women's suffrage because they believed most women supported **prohibition.**

Suffragists of this era were also known as "maternal feminists" because they were convinced that the skills of wives and mothers would bring a fresh, compassionate perspective to male-dominated governments in Canada. They believed that this feminine influence would lead to laws that would improve the lives of women and children.

Canadian suffragists were part of a worldwide movement. To attract

Figure 7–23 The Manitoba-based Political Equality League is pictured here with their petition demanding women's suffrage in the early 1900s.

Nellie McClung

One important suffragist was Nellie McClung (1873–1951). Raised in Manitoba, she became a teacher and well-known author who published many articles and books, including her autobiography. When her family moved to Edmonton, she promoted women's suffrage and prohibition. McClung was an effective speaker and often used wit and humour to "win over" an audience. Devoted to many reform issues affecting women, she worked especially hard to win suffrage for the women of Alberta.

In the excerpt that follows, McClung's words typify the maternal approach to women's rights that characterized the suffragist movement.

Nellie McClung 1873–1951

> **PRIMARY SOURCE** Women must be made to feel their responsibility. All this protective love, this instinctive mother love, must be organized some way, and made effective. There [is] enough of it in the world to do away with all the evils that war upon children, undernourishment, slum conditions, child labour, drunkenness. Women could abolish these if they wanted to."

public attention to their cause, suffragist leaders such as Emmeline Pankhurst in Britain and Susan B. Anthony in the United States organized demonstrations and hunger strikes. In Canada, the generally peaceful suffragist campaign was led by the Canadian Woman's Suffrage Association. This association was supported by Canada's leading women's organization, the National Council of Women of Canada (NCWC), founded by Lady Aberdeen, the wife of Canada's governor general. Lady Aberdeen used her influence to channel what she called "the unused capacity of women in Canada" into efforts to achieve reform.

On the Prairies, the suffragist movement had some of its earliest successes. Perhaps this was because western women had struggled side by side with men against the harsh realities of farm life, and so prairie men were more inclined to regard women as equals. Moreover, western farmers saw women's suffrage as a way to increase the farm vote and farmers' influence in provincial politics. Not surprisingly, the western provinces were the first to grant women's suffrage.

In British Columbia, the fight for suffrage would last more than forty-five years. It began when the province joined Confederation, in 1871. That year, the American suffragist Susan B. Anthony visited Victoria to speak in favour of women's rights. The following year, a bill supporting women's suffrage was roundly defeated in the provincial legislature—only two members of the legislature voted in favour of the bill. By 1873, women who owned property had won the right to vote in **municipal** elections, but in 1899, the suffrage bill was again defeated in the British Columbia legislature. However, this time the vote was close—15 to 17.

In 1912, the provincial Liberals made suffrage part of their election platform and, in 1916, a suffrage referendum passed as part of the

municipal: city or town

Time Line 7–1

The Enfranchisement of Women in Canada

1916	Manitoba, Saskatchewan, Alberta
1917	British Columbia, Ontario
1918	Nova Scotia; federal enfranchisement of women
1919	New Brunswick
1922	Prince Edward Island
1925	Newfoundland (joined Confederation in 1949)
1940	Quebec

VOTE FOR WOMAN'S FREEDOM

THE WOMEN OF BRITISH COLUMBIA WANT THEIR POLITICAL FREEDOM BECAUSE

1. IF WOMAN HAS TO OBEY THE LAWS IT IS ONLY JUST THAT SHE SHOULD HAVE A VOICE IN MAKING THEM.
2. WOMAN'S INFLUENCE WOULD BE INCREASED AND LAWS FOR WOMAN'S PROTECTION WOULD BE MORE EASILY SECURED.
3. AS POLITICAL RIGHTS MAKE MAN NOBLER, SO THEY WOULD MAKE WOMAN NOBLER ALSO.
4. THE BALLOT IS AN EDUCATOR. WOMAN NEEDS THE EDUCATION OF THE BALLOT; THE WORLD NEEDS THE EDUCATION OF THE WOMAN'S BALLOT.
5. WOMAN CAN BETTER PROTECT HER HOME INTERESTS.
6. WOMAN HAS BORNE HER SHARE OF THE TOIL, SUFFERING AND LONELINESS IN THE PIONEER WORK OF THIS PROVINCE AND SHE OUGHT TO HAVE A VOICE IN HOW IT IS GOVERNED.

WOMEN ARE FREED FROM POLITICAL SLAVERY IN NORWAY, SWEDEN, FINLAND, NEW ZEALAND, AUSTRALIA, TASMANIA, ISLE OF MAN, UTAH, WYOMING, COLORADO AND IDAHO, WITH THE RESULT THAT THE LAWS ARE BETTER AND CONDITIONS IMPROVED.

GIVE THE WOMEN THE BALLOT

provincial election. By 1917, British Columbia women finally gained the official right to vote and the right to hold political office.

For the most part, however, change did not come quickly (see Time Line 7–1). During the Laurier years, most Canadians believed that specific areas of life were "natural" to each sex. For example, politics and business were considered "man's work." Such beliefs hindered the struggle for women's equal rights, and many years would pass before women would have their rights recognized in law.

The Rights of the Native Peoples

At the turn of the century, the survival of Native lands and culture was threatened by government policies. The goal of federal government policy was to assimilate Native people into Canadian society and to make treaties with aboriginal groups that would free up land for European settlement. The Native peoples wanted to retain their traditional territory and based their claim to land on the Royal Proclamation of 1763, which recognized them as "Nations or Tribes," extended to them the protection of Britain, and recognized their right to own the land they had used and occupied. An excerpt of the Proclamation follows:

"It is just and reasonable ... that the several Nations or Tribes of Indians with whom We are connected ... should not be molested or disturbed in the Possession of such Parts of Our Dominions and Territories as, not having been ceded to or purchased by Us, are reserved to them, or any of they, as their Hunting Grounds.

"And We do further declare it to be Our Royal Will and Pleasure, for the present ... to reserve under our Sovereignty, Protection, and Dominion, for the use of the said Indians, all lands and Territories not included with limits of Our ... new governments, or within the Limits of the Territory granted to the Hudson's Bay Company, as also all the lands and Territories lying to the Westward of the Sources of the rivers which fall into the Sea from the west and the North West."

The policy of removing Native children from their families and placing them in residential schools further encouraged assimilation. By 1910, more than sixty residential schools existed, most of them run by Christian religious groups. In these schools, Native children received manual, vocational, and religious instruction in the Christian faith. Strict rules forbade the Native students from practising their customs and speaking their languages among themselves. Some Native parents valued the education, training, and skills their children received. However, removing children from their family and familiar surroundings was traumatic for parents and children. The policy had a devastating impact on Native attempts to preserve and pass on their culture to future generations.

The Native peoples of British Columbia were in a unique situation. The remoteness of the province and the delay in large-scale settlement had allowed them to retain their lands longer than the aboriginal peoples of eastern and central Canada. The federal government was responsible for Indian affairs, but control of Native lands lay with the provincial governments. This overlap complicated the question of ownership of Native lands in British Columbia.

As you learned in Chapter 6, the first governor of British Columbia, James Douglas, recognized Native ownership of the land and had negotiated treaties with a number of bands. Then settlers flooded into the West during the Laurier era. The Native peoples felt threatened, and the issues of land and title suddenly became more urgent. From the viewpoint of the federal government, the priority was to establish **reserves** for Native bands through treaties or by special arrangement with individual bands. But by 1900, only fifteen treaties had been concluded with the province's 200 Native bands, and these treaties covered only a small area of British Columbia.

The Native bands of British Columbia united to press for **aboriginal title** to the land. In 1911, Native chiefs from across the province presented the provincial government with claims regarding land title, treaties, and self-government. However, the federal and provincial governments could not agree on how to respond to these claims.

Economic expansion in British Columbia in the early 1900s forced the issue of land onto the back burner. However, the McKenna-McBride **Royal Commission** was established to determine the size and location of Native reserves. In 1916, it recommended adding 136 square miles (35 224 hectares) to the reserves, but also recommended cutting off 74 square miles (19 166 hectares) of more valuable land, to be sold to the public. Since the Indian Act of 1876 had stipulated that **cut-off lands** could be removed from reserves only with the consent of the Native peoples, the **Allied Tribes of British Columbia** rejected the report. The federal government then passed a law that removed the requirement for consent to the sale of cut-off lands. For the government, this decision closed the land-claims issue. For the Native peoples of British Columbia, however, the issue was far from resolved.

reserve: land set aside for the Native peoples

aboriginal title: the concept that Native people have ownership (or control) of the land because they were the first to occupy it

Royal Commission: an investigation by a person, or persons, into a matter on behalf of the federal or provincial government—their decision is not binding on the government

cut-off lands: lands removed from Native reserves, or title to land that was revoked

Allied Tribes of British Columbia: an organization representing most Native peoples living in British Columbia

The Importance of the Potlatch

The federal government had one other problem with the aboriginal people of British Columbia. Here, the cornerstone of Native culture was the **potlatch**, an important ceremony that served many social functions. "Potlatching" involves elaborate feasts to celebrate special occasions, such as the naming of a child, a marriage, or burial. It confirms the powers of chiefs. The potlatch also provides a way to share wealth because hosts give away much of their wealth, including many of their possessions, to the guests. Because it preserved important Native customs, the potlatch was seen by the federal government as an obstacle to assimilation. In an 1884 amendment to the Indian Act, the government banned potlatch ceremonies. However, lax enforcement of the ban until 1914, and the isolation of many villages, allowed the potlatch to continue in many areas of the province.

Figure 7–25 This button blanket was once given away at a potlatch. During the potlatch, gifts are given to all in attendance, so that these people can later be called upon to verify that certain ceremonies took place, for example, a marriage, or to verify the passing on of names or the transfer of rights, for example, hunting or fishing rights.

potlatch: a ritual of giving away property and goods that is observed by many West Coast Native bands

DID YOU KNOW?

Under the terms of the 1998 treaty, 5500 people will qualify as Nisga'a. To be considered Nisga'a, a person must prove that there was a Nisga'a woman among his or her ancestors.

The Nisga'a Land Claim

One historic Native land claim in British Columbia has taken more than ninety years to resolve. On August 4, 1998, representatives of the federal and provincial governments, and the Nisga'a First Nation signed the first treaty in modern British Columbia. This treaty allocates $200 million in treaty-settlement funds (most of it coming from the federal government), along with 1930 square kilometres of land in Lower Nass Valley, as well as ownership of 18 reserves outside the area. The treaty states that the Nisga'a are entitled to all resources on Nisga'a-owned lands, have the right to tim-

ber outside settlement area, and have a guaranteed share of about 20 percent of the allowable catch of Nass River Salmon. The Nisga'a government will also be able to make laws consistent with Canadian law, the Charter of Rights and Freedoms, and the Criminal Code. The struggle for Nisga'a rights began in 1907, when the Nisga'a Land Committee launched a campaign for recognition of title to their ancestral lands. They were the first Native people in British Columbia to pursue their goals within the Canadian political system. These long-time occupants of the Nass Valley in northwestern British Columbia had protested gov-

Figure 7–26 A ceremonial canoe brings Nisga'a chiefs and elders to New Aiyansh for the signing of the treaty.

ernment surveys that were meant to mark off reserves to be occupied by Native peoples in the area. The Nisga'a argued that because they had not signed a treaty with the provincial government, the concept of reserves for the Native peoples was invalid.

In 1913, the Nisga'a Land Committee made their position clear on the issue of reserves and White settlement in their lands:

"We are not opposed to the coming of the white people into our territory, provided this be carried out justly and in accordance with the British principle embodied in the Royal Proclamation (of 1763). What we don't like about the Government is their saying: 'We will give you this much land.' How can they give it when it is our own? We cannot understand it. They have never bought it from us or our forefathers. They have never fought and conquered our people, and taken the land that way, and yet they now say that they will give us so much land—our own land."

The Nisga'a chiefs wanted a treaty to accomplish three things: honour aboriginal title to the land, give the Nisga'a larger reserves on which to live, and compensate the Nisga'a for any land they surrendered.

During a visit to Prince Rupert in 1910, Prime Minister Laurier encouraged the Nisga'a to take their case to the **Judicial Committee of the British Privy Council.** The Nisga'a Land Committee asked the

Judicial Committee of the British Privy Council: at the time, the highest level of legal appeal in Canada

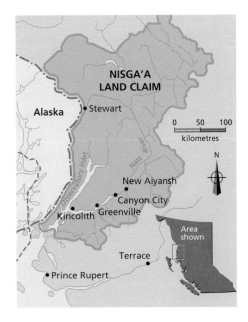

NISGA'A LAND CLAIM

Alaska • Stewart

0   50   100
kilometres

Nass River

Observatory Inlet

New Aiyansh
• Canyon City
Kincolith Greenville

Area shown

• Terrace

• Prince Rupert

Figure 7–27 This map shows the areas designated as Nisga'a land in the 1998 treaty.

Judicial Committee in London, England, to consider their claims. The British government decided that the claims must first be heard in a Canadian court. By then, Laurier was no longer prime minister and neither the Canadian courts nor the Privy Council would have the opportunity to hear the Nisga'a case.

The Nisga'a never abandoned their claim. Despite legal barriers, they were determined to keep the land question alive. Nisga'a chief Frank Calder's election to the British Columbia legislature in 1949, and the granting of suffrage to the Native peoples of Canada in 1960, signalled the winds of change. Soon, favourable court judgements in Native rights cases prompted governments to resolve issues of land claims and Native **self-government.**

The treaty between the Nisga'a and the federal and provincial governments signed on August 4, 1998 was an historic event. It was the first treaty concluded west of the Rockies since British Columbia joined Canada in 1871. In 1999, the treaty was approved by the Nisga'a and the British Columbia legislature. The federal government is expected to pass the treaty in the House of Commons in the fall of 1999.

ACTIVITIES

1. How was "maternal feminism" linked to women's suffrage and social reform during the Laurier era?

2. In small groups, discuss why some members of each of the following groups might have opposed the granting of political and legal rights to women:
   a) politicians, b) employers, c) men, d) women.

3. Design a promotional poster suitable for women's groups in the Laurier era. On the back of the poster indicate why you think the poster would be effective in achieving its goal.

4. "The aims of today's feminists are not significantly different from those of the feminists of the Laurier era." Organize a debate on this statement. You might use a chart like the model below to organize your ideas.

	1890s Feminists	Today's Feminists
Issues on which they agree		
Issues on which they disagree		

5. **a)** Identify the policy of the federal government towards Native Canadians at the turn of the century.

   b) Name two ways in which the government tried to ensure the success of its policy.

6. Summarize the positions of the Native peoples and the federal government on the questions of land title and treaties in BC.

7. Write a legend in the way that a Native elder might tell young people, years from now, about the Nisga'a struggle to claim their land.

8. Write and record the script for a BC government radio commercial which will inform the public about the Nisga'a land claim. If you wish to do a TV commercial, include sketches to accompany the script.

9. Supporters and opponents of the treaty with the Nisga'a have been quick to set out their opinions. Research the positions of each side and compile a two-column list of arguments in favour and in opposition to the 1998 Nisga'a treaty. Use this information to reach your own conclusion on the justice and practicality of this agreement.

10. The BC government has said the Nisga'a treaty will be the model for treaties with the rest of BC's first nations. Find out more about the treaty process in BC and, with the information you gather, decide if the Nisga'a treaty can be used in other situations.

THE NEW CENTURY: WONDERS OF THE LAURIER AGE

Turn-of-the-century Canadians lived in an exciting age filled with new and marvelous technological developments. These "wonders of the age" promised speedy travel by car and by plane, rapid communication with the new wireless radio, and a new view of the world presented in "motion pictures."

The Arrival of the Car

In 1901, automobiles appeared for the first time on the cover of the Eaton's catalogue. As models such as the US-produced Oldsmobile became more affordable, more and more cars appeared on Canadian roads. In 1905, the Oldsmobile inspired a hit song, "Come Away with me Lucille, in my Merry Oldsmobile." Huge profits were possible in automobile manufacturing, and many Canadian companies, such as Massey-Harris and the Canadian Cycle and Motor Company, eagerly went into production. Most automobiles produced in Canada were "hybrids" consisting of American engines and running gear mounted on Canadian bodies. An example of a hybrid car was the McLaughlin Carriage Company's McLaughlin-Buick.

Not everyone greeted the appearance of the automobile with enthusiasm. In 1908, Prince Edward Island banned automobiles in response to complaints that they tore up roads and frightened children and livestock. But reactions elsewhere—in British Columbia, for example—

were positive. Fairly soon, Canadians realized that cars were useful and reliable, and doctors, politicians, business people, and the well-to-do adopted the car as a preferred means of transportation. Adventurous motor excursions, such as from Victoria to Alberni or Courtenay and back, became a favourite pastime on Sundays. Cars were generally restricted to the southern populated parts of British Columbia, where improved roads were available. In the early years of the century, the number of automobiles in British Columbia doubled every year, creating the need to open Canada's first gas station in Vancouver in 1908.

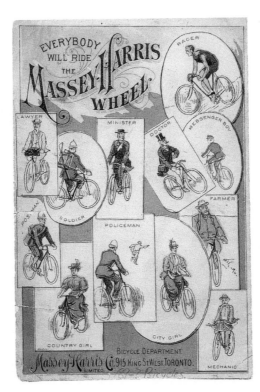

Figure 7–28 In the 1890s, bicycles became the great transportation craze. The high-wheel "penny-farthing" bicycle became obsolete when the modern version, with pneumatic, air-filled tires, made riding comfortable and safe. Both men and women joined bicycle clubs, taking part in tours and in races. An indirect outcome of the bicycle craze was a revolution in women's clothing styles, leading to the abandonment of bustles, corsets, and other constricting garments.

Figure 7–29 Motorists in one of the first cars seen in Vancouver. It was bought for about $200 in 1903.

Soaring Through the Air

It took much longer for airplanes to become as widely accepted as automobiles. Early wooden airplanes were held together by a mass of wire, bamboo, and fabric. Most of the early pilots did their own repairs and maintenance, and crashes were frequent. The first successful flight in Canada took place in 1909 in Baddeck, Nova Scotia, when J. A. D. McCurdy flew a plane called the *Silver Dart* 10 metres above the ground for almost a kilometre at 30 kilometres an hour.

Figure 7–30 The novelty of airplane flight before 1914 is evident in this program for a flying demonstration at Minoru Park in Richmond, British Columbia. What present-day event would match the excitement and glamour of these plane races?

BIRD-MEN

At Minoru Park
3—De Pries and the Manning Bros.—3

Friday, April 14   Saturday, April 15 and Monday, April 17

Grand Easter Holiday Carnival of Flying-Machines
Vancouver Never Saw a Show Like This Before!
3—Flying Machines—3—Flyers—3

Admission, 50c. Grandstand, 50c Extra

A Communications Revolution

Given Canada's size, it is not surprising that Canadians enthusiastically embraced new communications technologies. As the twentieth century dawned, Canadians were the world's greatest users of the telephone. More than 300 000 telephones were counted in Canada's 1901 census—nearly twice as many per person as in the United States and three times as many as in Great Britain. Telephone companies began offering innovative services such as wake-up calls to attract new customers. One company installed a bell in a customer's bedroom. Others, such as the Victoria and Esquimalt Telephone Company, had children run errands for their subscribers, at a rate of 15 cents a half-hour.

Working conditions were much less than desirable for telephone operators, most of whom were women. They wore headphone harnesses that weighed 3 kilograms, and the pay and hours were dismal. An operator who worked in a telephone company in 1900 had these memories:

> ... the local manager ... informed me that my hours would be from eight p.m. to eight a.m., seven days a week. Sunday night I would come in at nine p.m., giving me time to go to church. My salary would be $25 a month, with one week's holidays. After one year's service I would receive $30 a month. In addition to the operating I was to sweep and dust the operating room and look after the furnace during the winter months.

In 1901, Canada also led the way when Guglielmo Marconi received the first wireless telegraph communication from England on Signal Hill in Newfoundland. The message, in **Morse code,** was the first to cross the ocean without the aid of wires. The Marconi Wireless Telegraph Company was set up at Glace Bay, Nova Scotia in 1902. It established permanent radio communication across the Atlantic to Britain. In 1908, the Marconi Company announced it would accept messages from the public for transmission to Britain at a rate of 15 cents a word. The year before, Canadian inventor Frederick Fessenden had transmitted the world's first radio broadcast of music and voice. The new medium was slow to catch on, and people chose to continue listening to sound recordings on cylinders introduced in the 1890s.

Because of the superior reception over water, wireless radio was eventually used in shipping. By 1913, radios were used more widely following the publicity surrounding their role in the *Titanic* rescue. On April 14, 1912, the sinking ocean liner *Titanic* wired a distress message to the rescue ship Carpathia: "We've struck a berg. Sinking Fast. Come to our assistance. Position: latitude 41.46 north, longitude 50.14 west MGY." The transmission of this message saved the lives of more than 700 people who were adrift in lifeboats off the coast of Newfoundland.

Perhaps even more exciting than the telephone or the wireless telegraph was the new moving picture show. The first public screening of a moving picture in Canada was in 1896. Viewers paid 10 cents to crowd into a hall in Ottawa to see several one-minute films showing people doing everyday things.

Morse code: an alphabet composed of long and short signals

Apply Your Knowledge

Using Statistics Like an Historian

The writing of history involves recreating the past by using a variety of historical sources. You are already familiar with documents and photographs as historical sources, and statistics are another. The field of statistics deals with the collection and interpretation of numerical data, such as rates of population growth, immigration, births and deaths, and annual income. Interpreting statistics in order to compose an accurate picture of the past requires great skill, one that historians must develop.

Make a page of point-form notes that summarizes some of the ways in which Canada changed from the years 1891 to 1914. Arrange your points in the order of what you judge to be the most important to the least important developments, then answer the questions that follow.

Table 1 Population of Canada	
1891	4 833 239
1901	5 371 315
1911	7 206 842

Table 2 Urban population: Percentage of Total		
1891	1 440 605	29.8
1901	1 867 260	34.8
1911	3 007 576	41.7

Table 3 Immigrant Arrivals in Canada				
Year	Britain	US	Others	Total
1897	11 383	2 412	7 921	21 716
1901	11 810	17 987	19 352	49 149
1908	120 182	58 312	83 975	262 469
1913	150 542	139 009	112 881	402 432

Table 4 Population of the Prairie Provinces: Alberta, Saskatchewan, Manitoba	
1901	419 512
1906	808 863
1911	1 328 725
1916	1 698 220

Table 5 Acres in Wheat	
1891	18 976 616
1901	65 797 911
1911	102 220 994

Table 6 Total Value of Minerals produced in $	
1891	2 701 213
1901	4 242 542
1911	8 684 154
1916	15 369 709

Table 7 Exports and Imports in $		
1891	88 671	111 533 954
1901	177 431 386	177 930 919
1911	274 316 553	452 724 603

Table 8 Number of Working Days lost to Labour Disputes	
1901	632 311
1905	217 244
1911	2 46 500
1914	430 04

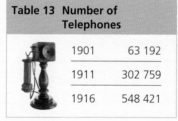

Table 9 Number of Disputes by Industry 1901–14	
Fishing	14
Lumbering	35
Mining	109
Building	390
Metal	260
Printing	31

Table 10 Working Time and Wages	
1901	56.7 hrs/week
Average wage	$829/year
1911	52.2 hrs/week
Average wage	$1097/year

Table 11 Wage on Farms per month		
	Male	**Female**
1910	24.32	N/A
1908	33.69	19.08
1914	35.55	18.81

Table 12 Literacy	
1901	6.00%
1911	11.02%

Table 13 Number of Telephones	
1901	63 192
1911	302 759
1916	548 421

Table 14 Number of Motor Vehicles	
1906	2 810
1911	21 519
1916	123 464

ACTIVITIES

1. Examine Table 3. Based on the data given, which group experienced the greatest jump in immigration between 1897 and 1913? Between what years did the increase occur?

2. Examine Table 8. What might have accounted for the sudden rise in labour disputes in 1911? Reread pages 269 to 270 for background information on this development.

3. Examine Table 10. Make a statement about the relationship between the length of the work week and wages.

4. Examine Tables 1, 13, and 14. Make a statement about the likelihood of owning a telephone versus a car in Canada in 1911. Offer a hypothesis that accounts for this.

5. Compare your original point-form notes with those of another student. Discuss the reasons for differing emphasis or interpretations in your notes.

6. Consider the following:
   - What additional statistics might have given you a fuller picture of the period?
   - How accurate a picture of the period is given by the statistics alone?
   - How accurate would an account of the period be if these statistics were not consulted?
   - How reliable are statistics as sources of historical evidence?

Arts and Leisure

During the Laurier era, a large number of Canadians became world champions in sports. George Dixon, of Halifax, became the first Black man to win a world boxing championship when he captured the bantamweight title in 1890. Tommy Burns became the only Canadian to win the heavyweight title, in 1906, a title he defended ten times and held for nearly three years. Tom Longboat, from the Six Nations Reserve in Ontario, emerged as one of the greatest distance runners of the era. In sculling, another popular sport, oarsman Ned Hanlan, of Toronto, rowed his way in more than 150 races to become world champion. In 1908, Canada sent its first team to the Olympics—and to every Olympics thereafter.

Rapid industrialization and urbanization encouraged the growth of spectator sports and outdoor recreation. Paying spectators watched Babe Ruth's first home run hit at Hanlan's Point, Toronto, as well as the first Grey Cup Game, held at the Point in 1909. On September 2, 1912, 75 000 people watched the hour-long parade through downtown Calgary that kicked off the first Calgary Stampede. Owning an automobile enabled wealthy Canadians to pursue recreation farther from home, such as ski racing, ski jumping, hiking, and camping.

Canadians could also enjoy the work of Canada's poets, writers, and artists. Pauline Johnson's poetry, on Canadian themes, was popular at home and abroad. The daughter of a Mohawk chief and an English-woman, Johnson celebrated her Native heritage in poetry readings across Canada, the United States, and Europe. Other widely admired Canadian writers were Lucy Maude Montgomery, who wrote *Anne of Green Gables*, and Stephen Leacock, who authored *Sunshine Sketches of a Little Town*, a humorous look at small-town Ontario. The frontier adventures of the Yukon Gold Rush were brought to life in the poems of Robert Service. In British Columbia, Emily Carr supported her painting by working as a cartoonist for a weekly Victoria newspaper. She began taking trips to the Queen Charlotte Islands, which provided settings for some of her finest work.

Figure 7–31 Tom Longboat (left) was one of the world's most famous athletes before World War I. His stamina and startling finishing sprints allowed him to dominate most races he entered. He won the Boston Marathon in 1907 and the World Professional Marathon Championship in 1909. His unorthodox training methods led to conflict with managers, but he stuck to his own methods. During World War I he served as a dispatch runner in France.

Canadian taste in foods also began to change. The invention of refrigerated rail cars at the turn of the century made a greater variety of food available across the country. By 1910, processed foods such as Heinz ketchup were common, and the first 5-cent chocolate bars went on sale. The soft-drink craze sweeping the United States also invaded Canada. Marketed at first as a medicine, Coca Cola was now advertised as a soft drink. The craze prompted John McLaughlin, a Toronto pharmacist, to develop Canada Dry Ginger Ale, a brand name now recognized around the world. Canada, it seemed, was truly coming of age.

Figure 7–32 "Bathing" at the beach grew in popularity. Fancy hats and parasols prevented women's skin from burning or tanning. Local governments passed "Public Morals By-Laws" to ensure that proper bathing attire covered the body from the neck to the knees.

ACTIVITIES

1. **a)** What new technological developments excited people at the turn of the century?

   b) How did the new technologies affect Canadian leisure activities?

2. Explain why telephones became so popular in Canada.

3. Examine the photograph shown in Figure 7–29. List as many differences as you can between the car shown in the photo and a modern model. Why do you think the men are dressed as they are?

4. Use the coordinates given in the *Titanic*'s distress call to locate its position at the time of sinking. Write a headline and sub-headline to describe the location of the sinking for readers unfamiliar with the East Coast of Canada.

5. Assume you are a reporter for a newspaper. Your editor has told you to write a brief but exciting article about one of the following:

   a) First screening of a moving picture in 1896

   b) First automobile imported into Canada in 1898

   c) First wireless radio reception in Newfoundland in 1901

   d) First airplane flight in 1909

   In your story, include details about the new invention, your impression of its usefulness, and your opinion of how it might affect the future of Canada.

6. Choose one of the athletes or artists discussed in this section and create a powerful advertisement that would attract people to one of their appearances. Include information on the person, their talents, and achievements. Include some details to show how this person truly reflects the age.

CONCLUSION

From 1896 to 1914, Canadians experienced remarkable social and political changes. As immigrants from Europe, Britain, the United States, and Asia poured into the West, the seeds of a multicultural nation were sown. Farming, fishing, lumbering, and mining prospered. Cities swelled and became increasingly industrialized. Workers began to organize labour unions. Women fought to enter political life, and Native Canadians strove to preserve their cultural identity and to assert aboriginal title to the land.

The Laurier era witnessed some astounding technological changes. Telephones, radios, cars, and airplanes enhanced communications and transportation. However, the full impact of these changes was delayed when, in 1914, the world was thrust into the carnage of a terrible war. The young nation, Canada, was about to step onto the world stage in a new, more mature, role.

SUMMARY ACTIVITIES

1. With a partner, write a dialogue discussing the changes that occurred in Canada during the Laurier era, focusing on one of the following:
   - Native rights
   - Women's rights
   - the labour movement
   - changes in technology
   - changes in arts and leisure

   One partner should take the part of a person who welcomed the changes and the other a person who resisted the changes.

2. Choose five examples each of key people, key events, and key ideas from this chapter. In a notebook, make a chart with the three headings. In each column, list your examples, with a brief explanation for each.

ON YOUR OWN

1. Write an obituary for Prime Minister Laurier that would have appeared in a newspaper. Organize your information in three paragraphs. In the first, deal with his background before he became prime minister. Include such things as date and place of birth, education, occupation before entering politics, and character traits. In the second paragraph outline Laurier's political career, concentrating on his years as leader of the opposition and as prime minister. In the final paragraph discuss his legacy, giving reasons why he might be considered one of Canada's great prime ministers. Finally, you should suggest an appropriate epitaph for his tombstone.

2. Create a collage of images that depicts the changing face of Canada during the Laurier era. Use the images in this chapter as a starting point.

8 THE ECONOMY OF CANADA

CHAPTER OUTCOMES

In this chapter you will focus on key economic concepts, economic regions of Canada, and the economic relationship between Canada and the United States. By the end of this chapter, you will

- analyze statistical information to identify settlement patterns within Canada

- identify technological changes and their impact on Canada and its economic regions

- identify the advantages and disadvantages of new employment trends

- describe Canada's economic sectors and economic regions, along with their activities

- analyze the impact of government regulations on Canadian content in film and television

- evaluate the impact, and the pros and cons, of foreign investment in Canada

- analyze conflicting viewpoints on free trade

The Raven and the Oarsman

High school means different things to different students. In the story that follows, you will meet cousins John, from British Columbia, and Cynthia, from Ontario. They have both completed high school, but there the similarities end. Perhaps the biggest difference between the two is in how they view the future. While the story and characters are fictional, they are based on real questions and real issues that students have discussed—and continue to discuss—among themselves and with school counsellors across British Columbia.

The Spirit of Haida Gwaii

"**I**sn't her flight overdue?" John asked his father impatiently.

"You know as well as I do that it is," his father answered curtly. "It's not as though we're late for the Oscars, you know."

John glanced at his watch again. He couldn't understand why he had to be there when his cousin arrived from Ontario, but his dad had insisted. He had only met Cynthia once—five years before—and he hadn't been impressed by the skinny Grade eight girl. She talked too much, and about nothing that interested him. That had been a terrible vacation. His father and uncle and aunt were forever off somewhere while he spent most of the three weeks avoiding Cynthia.

John shook his head as if to clear it of the unpleasant memories. He looked at this father and muttered, "I'm going to wander around for a bit."

"Keep an eye on the monitors," his father told him, "and make sure you're back when the plane arrives."

John decided to go to the international departures level to see if anything interesting

was happening there. As he wandered around the international wing of the airport he stopped to look at the Bill Reid sculpture, *The Spirit of Haida Gwaii*, that dominates that level. John had been at the airport many times and had noticed the sculpture before, but this was the first time he had paid any attention to it.

"She'd be quicker coming by boat," he muttered to himself as he glanced at each of the people in the canoe. He leaned over and read the plaque:

"*The Spirit of Haida Gwaii* features Raven and Eagle, the two principal Haida figures. The canoe is filled with mythical creatures, animal men and women who symbolize the family of human beings who bite and claw one another as they doggedly paddle along."

John's attention was drawn to the stern of the canoe. There the steersman, Raven, was intent on manoeuvring the boat in a particular direction.

Beneath Raven's wing was the human figure of an oarsman, representing all the common people who obey orders and labour through life performing the tasks allotted to them.

"I wonder what's in store for me," John mused. "Raven or oarsman?" He often wondered what lay ahead for him and had concluded that the future didn't look promising. He'd been out of school for two years now—two of the worst years for fishing on the British Columbia coast. There'd been only two **openings** all summer and, from what he'd heard and read, the situation looked bleak. All through high school he'd assumed he was going to work with his father on their **seiner** and, eventually, buy it and the

licence after his father retired. Now nothing was certain. Money was tight. His father talked about selling the boat and the licence while they were still worth something.

John had been keeping busy doing minimum-wage jobs at fast food outlets and clerking at video stores, just to make ends meet. But in his heart he wanted to go fishing. His earliest recollections were of the summers he'd spent up and down the Strait of Georgia fishing with his father. Sometimes, on their way back from Johnstone Strait, they'd stop at Robson Bight to watch the families of killer whales gliding in and out of the water. Or they'd wander around one of the fishing villages that used to dot the

John and his father on the deck of the seiner

Inside Passage. Nowadays, John thought, you see more tour boats than fishing boats on the Strait in the summer.

"I thought I told you to keep your eye on the arrival times." His father's voice brought John back to present. "We just have enough time to meet her at the arrivals level."

As they hurried away John cast a quick glance back at the raven and the oarsman on *The Spirit of Haida Gwaii.*

At the arrivals terminal they scanned the crowd for Cynthia. It was hard to see as people milled around the luggage carousel.

"Uncle Dan, are you looking for me?"

John and his father turned to face a smiling, self-assured young woman.

"I expect I've changed since you last saw me," Cynthia said confidently. "I see you have too." John wasn't sure how to take the remark.

"Welcome to the West Coast," John's father said as they started for the car. Half an hour later, they were pulling into the driveway of the modest bungalow.

John thought he detected a slight smile as Cynthia waited for him to bring up the luggage. He remembered his uncle's beautiful house in Ontario. An architect, he had designed and built it himself. John's father had dismissed the advice of his parents and had returned to the West Coast after finishing high school in Ontario. They had wanted him to follow his

"Seriously, John, your chances of getting a good job go up dramatically with some kind of post-secondary education."

brother to university but, as he told John later, he'd wanted to be master of his own destiny.

Since his mother had died, John and his dad had spent most of their time on the boat—either fishing or maintaining the vessel. That was, until the last few hard years. His father's desire to keep the boat in its usual tip-top condition seemed to shrink with the size of the yearly catch of salmon.

After Cynthia had put her bags in the spare room she came into the kitchen. She wanted to use their computer to send an e-mail to her parents.

"We don't have a computer," John answered sharply. "We've never had a need for one."

"That's okay—I'll use my laptop and cellphone," Cynthia replied, seemingly unaware of John's frosty tone, "and make the call later."

"Thought we'd have dinner on the pier at Steveston," John's father interjected, smiling.

"They've restored the old canneries and wharves. And besides, the food's better than what John or I could whip up."

"What time do you have to be at the residence at university tomorrow?" John's father asked Cynthia as they settled in at the restaurant.

"Oh, I expect some time after lunch will do." Cynthia responded. "There are a couple of days of orientation for new students before classes start."

The meal was eaten mostly in silence. John found it difficult to talk to Cynthia. He lacked his usual self-confidence when faced with this very self-assured young woman. Maybe it had something to with her going to university.

At school, John hadn't run with the university crowd. He'd always steered away from academic courses, only staying in school because his father had insisted he finish Grade twelve. He liked to work with his hands, but couldn't find many courses that would be useful. The system seemed to be geared to college—and university-bound students. His school counsellor had tried to help him, but had admitted that there were few courses for young men who were not going to university.

The counsellor had also shown him the figures. "The statistics are really clear," Mr. Manji had said, referring to his well-known wall chart. It looked as though John's chances of employment and level of earnings went up dramatically if he continued his education after high school.

John's father nodded towards the pier as they left the restaurant. "Why don't you show Cynthia the boat? I'm sure she'd like to see it. I'll come and pick you two up shortly. I have an errand to run and shouldn't be long." Before John could object, his father was striding toward the car.

As they walked along the pier John struggled to think of something to say. "What will you be taking at UBC?" was the best he could come up with.

"Oh, computer science, information technology, that kind of thing," Cynthia replied. "What about you? Are you thinking of going to university?"

"No," replied John, "I've never given it any thought. I like to work on the boat—be outside, do something useful."

Cynthia stared at him coldly. "Are you implying that computer science is not useful?"

"Not at all," said John, as he helped her step from the pier onto the boat. "It's just that from the little I know about information technology, what comes out today is obsolete tomorrow."

"Talk about obsolescence!" Cynthia exclaimed as she surveyed the seiner. "From the little I know about fishing on either of Canada's coasts, it's a dead-end occupation."

"That's not true," John said. "Sure, the fishing industry in BC has problems, but they can be solved if all the people involved work together."

"Maybe so," Cynthia replied, trying to ensure her clothes didn't come into contact with any of the ropes and nets strewn around the deck, "but I did a paper in geography last year on the world's fisheries and the prospects look grim. The sea is literally dying. The problem is not just here on the West Coast—it's a global problem."

Oh great, she's an environmentalist, thought John.

"Fishermen here are not the problem," he retorted hotly. "It's those big **trawlers**, particularly the foreign ones. They could scoop up all the fish in a week, if they were allowed to."

"It really doesn't matter who's doing it," Cynthia said firmly. "Global overfishing is only the most obvious problem. Look at the millions of gallons

"It's a dead-end occupation," Cynthia proclaimed.

of toxic chemicals that are dumped into the ocean each year, the effects of deforestation on salmon spawning streams, and all those greenhouse gases that seem to be affecting ocean temperatures. Need I go on?"

"Like I already said, everybody has to work together. We can't solve global problems on our own, but we're improving things here in BC," John shot back.

"The pulp mills have really tried to reduce their effluent discharges and the forest industry has strict new regulations that prevent disturbance of salmon-spawning habitats. On top of that, the federal government has reduced the number of fishers through a licence **buyback** scheme. Maybe some of us can survive catching fewer fish though the traditional fishery."

"Well, for you and your father's sake, I hope it works," Cynthia sighed. "But will they be able to clean up all the damage from urbanization, from the mining, the roads, the dam-building, and the bridges, all of which is just going to increase?"

They were sitting in the **wheelhouse** of the seiner now. John looked wistfully out the window at the shimmering water of the south arm of the Fraser River and turned to Cynthia. "It's the way of life that my father and I value. The history of this coast is tied up in the lives of the fishermen."

"That's not the future, though," Cynthia said gently, as if sensing his mood. "Canadians have to stop relying on resource industries to maintain our standard of living. The future is in information technology. That's why I'm going into that field."

"It's okay for you," he sighed. "Girls always did better at the academic subjects in high school. My friends and I never seemed to have the time or incentive for all that studying and homework."

Cynthia gave him a puzzled look. "You don't buy all that stuff about the gender factor in academic achievement, do you? You're young, and there's all kinds of opportunities for upgrading at community colleges. The important thing is to get some training. You can still go fishing, but you have to be prepared for a changing world of work."

"You're starting to sound like my high school counsellor!" John said, chuckling.

Cynthia shrugged. "Well, the advice is free. I don't know everything. But I'm sure the world twenty-five years from now will surprise even those who think they have the future figured out. You might still be fishing, but you should be prepared for any changes that may come along."

"What do you think of the boat?" John's father asked as he stuck his head around the wheelhouse door.

"Oh, it's lovely," said Cynthia. "It's so beautiful out here."

John's father smiled, "I was afraid you two wouldn't find anything to talk about."

Where the future's involved, John thought, there's enough to think about to make your head hurt.

He was surprised at how easy it had been to talk to his cousin in the last few minutes. Maybe having Cynthia around wouldn't be so bad after all.

opening: a period of time in which the Department of Fisheries allows commercial fishing in a designated area

seiner: a fishing boat that uses a net to encircle a school of trapped fish

trawler: a boat that drags a net along the bottom of the sea

wheelhouse: the small, enclosed space on a boat that shelters the steering wheel

buyback: government purchases the licences it has sold

ACTIVITIES

1. How does the title of this Window represent the two points of view held by John and Cynthia? Which way of looking at the world most appeals to you? Why?

2. Should John listen to Cynthia's advice? Why or why not?

3. What additional advice would you give John?

4. What advice might you give Cynthia?

TIME LINE

1867	CONFEDERATION OF CANADA
1930	THE GREAT DEPRESSION BEGINS
1936	CANADIAN BROADCASTING CORPORATION IS FORMED
1947	LEDUC OIL FIELD SOUTHWEST OF EDMONTON OPENS
1965	CANADA-US AUTO PACT
1968	CANADIAN RADIO-TELEVISION COMMISSION (CRTC) IS ESTABLISHED
1980	PRIME MINISTER PIERRE TRUDEAU INTRODUCES NATIONAL ENERGY PROGRAM
1984	PRIME MINISTER BRIAN MULRONEY IS ELECTED; NATIONAL ENERGY POLICY IS DISMANTLED
1989	CANADA-US FREE TRADE AGREEMENT
1994	NORTH AMERICAN FREE TRADE AGREEMENT (NAFTA)

The nineteenth century was the century of the United States. I think we can claim that it is Canada that shall fill the twentieth century.

–WILFRID LAURIER, 1904

Prime Minister Wilfrid Laurier said these words in a speech to the Canadian Club of Ottawa in 1904. What does his statement reveal about his attitude towards the United States? Only seven years later, Laurier advocated free trade with the US and lost the federal election. Why would many people have seen his 1904 speech and his position in the election of 1911 as contradictory?

THE ECONOMY OF CANADA **297**

INTRODUCTION

to downsize: to reduce the workforce through layoffs or early retirement

As a new century begins, Canada's economy continues to change dramatically. You probably have a personal awareness of some of these changes. Maybe a family member has lost a job because of **downsizing**, or maybe someone you know has started a business. You may be asking yourself where you fit into this ever-changing and increasingly global economy. What choices should you make to prosper in the twenty-first century? What must you study to prepare yourself for a job market that seems as fickle as the economy?

As you have learned in previous chapters of *Horizons*, many factors led to the founding of Canada. Some historians have argued that the most important reasons were economic. It was the wealth of natural resources—from land, fur, and fish, to minerals, forests, and gold—that led to colonization in the first place. It was, and is, the promise of a better life that has drawn waves of immigrants to Canada throughout its history.

You learned in Chapter 2 and Chapter 6 that the debates during the drive for Confederation hinged on economic concerns. Those lobbying for Confederation argued successfully that uniting the colonies would bring great economic benefits and prosperity. Once Confederation had been achieved, Canada went on to build an intercontinental railway—a massive financial undertaking that literally transformed the country. Railways linked the country from sea to sea and accelerated

Figure 8–1 Langley, BC, is a thriving, expanding community. How will its growth affect the region's rich farmland?

the pace of industrialization and the growth of cities. Canada and Canadians were on the move.

Today, changing economic forces continue to shape the destiny of Canada. Economic trends are still evolving. Some of these are relatively easy to understand, but others are complex and require critical analysis. In this chapter you will learn the "nuts-and-bolts" of basic economic principles. These will help you better to understand not only the history of Canada, but also the choices we face as a nation. You will also examine the economic regions of Canada—their history, geography, resources, and future prospects.

Canada's relationship with the United States has always played a pivotal role in shaping Canada's development. In this chapter, you will look more closely at that relationship and its history, and how it has affected Canada's economy and politics, indeed, the very way in which Canadians view and define themselves.

◆ ◆

THE CHANGING ECONOMY

Urbanization

Canadians have been leaving the farm and countryside and moving to the city for more than a hundred years. At the time of Confederation, Canada experienced terrific changes. As industrialization continued, cities beckoned with promise of employment and became population magnets. The pull of the city continued throughout the twentieth century. At the end of the nineteenth century, approximately two out of three Canadians lived in rural areas. By 1996, the situation had completely reversed, and three out of four Canadians lived in urban areas.

At the end of the twentieth century, the trend towards urbanization continued. Young people, immigrants, and retirees were attracted to urban areas for a number of reasons. Cities offered more hope for employment and better business prospects. They promised rich opportunities and access to recreational, educational, entertainment, cultural, and healthcare facilities that not even the most prosperous small town could offer. This migration trend was self-perpetuating. As people left for the cities, services had to be cut back in the rural areas and small towns, which in turn encouraged more and more people to leave.

Cities not only acted as population magnets, they expanded physically. The continuing influx of people lead to a phenomenon known as **urban sprawl**. In cities such as Toronto, Montreal, and Vancouver, small towns once on the outskirts were absorbed into the metropolitan area. Surrounding areas, often composed of some of Canada's finest agricultural land, were transformed into housing developments and suburbs. Highways were built, which absorbed even more prime farmland, so that people living in the suburbs could commute to work in the city.

urban sprawl: uncontrolled growth of an urban area

As this table shows, the percentage of Canadians living in urban areas has grown to a large majority. In what twenty-year period did the percentage increase the most? What factors contributed to this? Consider world events, as well as what was happening in Canada.

Table 8–1	Percentage of Canada's Population Living in Urban Areas		
Year	Population of Canada	Urban Population	Percentage of Total
1931	10 377 000	5 469 000	52.7
1951	14 009 000	8 817 000	62.9
1971	21 962 000	16 410 00	76.1
1991	28 031 000	20 907 000	76.6
1996	29 672 000	22 461 000	77.9

DID YOU KNOW?

Rural-to-urban migration is a worldwide phenomenon, and nowhere is it more extreme than in the developing nations. In the People's Republic of China, for example, Special Economic Zones have been established to attract foreign investment. The resulting job opportunities have lured millions of **migrant labourers** *from the interior.*

migrant labourers: workers who must travel to find employment

resource-based: an economy that relies on the extraction or primary processing of raw materials

manufacturing-based: an economy that relies on the manufacturing of goods

regional disparity: different levels of income between regions

primary: an industry that collects natural resources

sector: a clearly defined segment or area

Technological Innovation

Some Canadians left their communities because technology was changing and evolving, and work was only to be found elsewhere. By the 1980s, Canada's economy had shifted from being **resource-based** and **manufacturing-based** to a much more diversified system. As some resource-based towns closed down, cities and towns in other regions grew and thrived, becoming service, transportation, and manufacturing centres. As you learned in Chapter 7, push-pull factors had been at the root of the huge wave of immigration to Canada between 1896 and 1914. Now these factors were becoming a force within the country itself.

In Atlantic Canada, for example, generations of young people ended up "goin' down the road." They went where they could find work, sometimes to urban centres in the Maritimes, but often to cities like Toronto and Montreal. As older traditional industries, such as the cod fishery and coal mining, continued to decline, **regional disparity** became a pressing issue.

Atlantic Canada was not the only area of the country affected. In British Columbia, the forestry industry took a downturn in the 1990s, and forestry towns saw thousands of people migrate. Salmon canneries closed down and threw people out of work. The federal Department of Fisheries and Oceans' conservation programs led to more closures, so that fish stocks could be revived and maintained. Towns along the BC coast that had once prospered and thrived lost their economic basis, a situation described in this chapter's Window on the Past.

As Canada's economy expanded beyond resource-based industries, technological breakthroughs led to increased automation. This meant that the need for human labour decreased, not only in the **primary** industries but also in the manufacturing **sector** of the economy. During the 1980s and 1990s, high-tech innovations increased productivity and efficiency, and reduced costs. As the impact of these changes hit home in the workplace, tens of thousands of Canadian workers lost their lifetime employment. Some manufacturing regions became depressed. Many factories and mills closed down. Others moved into new facilities that relied less on human labour and more on computerized systems. As a result, unemployment itself became a major trend in Canada in the final decades of the twentieth century.

Some **multinational** enterprises decided to locate in Canada, while others abandoned older factories in favour of locations in developing countries. Often they were attracted by lower labour costs and weaker labour and environmental regulations. After Canada signed free-trade agreements in 1989 and 1994, many companies relocated to the United States and Mexico. Part of this movement of companies was because of **globalization**. Again, high-tech innovations in communication, manufacturing, and transportation made it possible for companies to operate differently. Now they could build different components of a finished product anywhere in the world. They could then transport them to another site to be assembled and shipped out to the world market place.

Such changes led to greater competition between the developed and the developing nations, and among businesses. To survive in the new global system, many smaller companies merged with—or were swallowed up by—larger competitors. Some smaller firms disappeared altogether. The term "globalization" was used in the 1980s and 1990s to justify corporate downsizing, **reorganizing**, and **restructuring**. In real life, these terms meant one thing—people lost jobs, whether on the factory floor or in middle-management offices.

As the twentieth century drew to a close, mergers and the drive for higher corporate profits reshaped Canada's economy. The pressure was on Canadian businesses to respond not only as competitors, but as creators, innovators, and leaders. This they did. In the last decade of the twentieth century, Canadians consumed products and services at a record pace, and corporate profits rose. Stock markets enjoyed an extended **bull** run. Canadian companies increased their spending on research and development and began to market new and innovative goods and services around the world. The level of Canadian exports continued to increase, and the economy showed signs of continued growth. Even faced with the challenge of such overwhelming change, Canada's economy continued to diversify and grow.

multinational: a business that operates offices and branches in three or more countries

globalization: a trend towards interdependent national economies

to reorganize: to reduce labour costs by firing managers and redistributing the work among remaining employees

to restructure: to replace full-time employees with part-time or contract employees who receive no benefit packages or guarantees of job security

bull: a trend of rising share prices

Figure 8–2 *Goin' Down the Road*, directed by Don Shebib, marked an international breakthrough for Canadian film in 1969. It tells the story of two Maritimers who travel to find work in Toronto. Their efforts are both comic and sad, and eventually fail. Their struggle, however, captures the human reality of regional disparity, and the sense of dislocation that many Canadians felt as the country became more urban.

Three Types of Unemployment

Three types of unemployment are prevalent today in Canada. Cyclical unemployment refers to work shortages that are seasonal in nature. For example, fishers must abide by regulated openings of fishing banks, and farmers are less active in winter. Fractional unemployment generally means that someone is only temporarily unemployed. They may be between jobs, or just entering the labour force. The third type of unemployment is structural unemployment. This refers to a work shortage that results from the closing of an industry or the major, perhaps permanent, decline of an economic activity. In other words, the jobs are lost forever. Structural unemployment, however, can also mean that an industry needs workers, but that there is a shortage of skilled labour.

Figure 8–3 This crowd in St. John's, Newfoundland is protesting trawler overfishing on the Grand Banks which, with other factors, led to an indefinite moratorium on cod fishing. As fishers, many of these people would have experienced cyclical unemployment in the past. If the damage to the cod stocks is irreversible, however, they will be confronted with structural unemployment.

demographics: study of population statistics, trends, averages, and so on

tertiary: concerned with services

underemployed: a worker employed in a job below his or her level of skill

The New Face of Employment

At the end of the twentieth century, Canada also felt the impact of a major shift in its **demographics**. In the years following World War II, Canada experienced a population and economic boom. The years from 1946 to 1965 came to be known as the "baby boom" era. By the late 1990s, many of the people born in the post-war period, a group popularly labelled the "baby boomers," were retiring or preparing to retire. This trend promised to open up job opportunities for their children and succeeding generations in the future.

More importantly, the new economy, based increasingly on advanced technology and a global perspective, created new job opportunities in the high-tech and information sectors of Canada's economy. However, only the highly skilled and educated need apply. Thousands of older Canadians who suffered structural unemployment faced difficult choices. They had to go back to school to get retrained, or they had to take lower-paying jobs in the **tertiary** sector. This sector of the economy had been growing for decades, but many of the jobs to be found in it required relatively low levels of skill, and they paid accordingly. Many workers had to secure two or three part-time jobs to maintain their standard of living. Other Canadians became chronically **underemployed** and saw their standard of living plummet.

Old perceptions of job-training were changing as well. As always,

These population statistics cover 100 years of Canada's history. Canada's population has been broken down into five different age groups. Study these figures for a few minutes. Can you spot any trends?

Table 8–2	Age Groups in Canada's Population, as a Percentage of Total					
Year	Total population	under 5 years	5–19 years	20–44 years	45–64 years	65 + years
1891	4 833 000	12.64	34.49	35.40	12.91	4.55
1911	7 207 000	12.35	30.15	38.81	14.06	4.66
1931	10 377 000	10.36	31.29	36.07	16.74	5.55
1951	14 009 000	12.29	25.60	36.63	17.74	7.75
1971	21 568 000	8.42	30.97	33.87	18.66	8.09
1991	27 297 000	6.99	20.42	41.33	19.66	11.61
1996	28 847 000	6.65	20.60	39.03	21.49	12.23

A New Model of Mass Production

In the 1980s, General Motors of Canada began an $8-billion re-industrialization program in Oshawa, Ontario. The strategy was to develop a high-tech, synchronized manufacturing complex. This marked a radical change from old manufacturing methods towards the model of the future.

In traditional mass production, automobiles moved along a never-ending assembly line, and each worker completed a specific task until the vehicle was finished. However, with the new system, called "flexible production," automobile frames are placed on automated guidance vehicles and moved to different work areas. Parts for each individual automobile are then assembled at each station. Robotic systems deliver parts to each section so that each car can be built to customer specifications. Robots paint the cars, and then laser and computerized checking systems monitor quality and workmanship.

It's easy to see how the need for human labour is reduced with this type of system. Another cost advantage for GM is that many auto parts do not have to be produced or stored at the Autoplex, since they are manufactured elsewhere by other companies. With modern communication and transportation links, suppliers guarantee delivery of the parts, and only when needed. This shift in technology has resulted in increased productivity and efficiency, better quality cars, and bigger corporate profits. It has also resulted in the creation of new jobs in technology that pay very well. The drawback has been the loss of traditional assembly-line jobs and a lower demand for human labour.

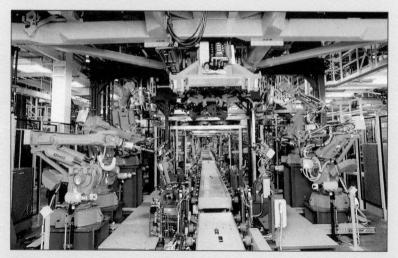

Figure 8–4 GM's high-tech Autoplex in Oshawa

employers wanted hard-working young people with good attitudes towards work. They also needed young people with varied educational backgrounds, people who could be flexible and creative. The new workplace made new demands on workers, and offered different rewards. Lifetime security at one full-time job, a feature of the post-war period, was not one of them. In the new job market, people often were hired on contract, and only for specific projects. New work methods required people to work together in teams, using cooperation to solve problems and collaboration to make decisions.

In a sense, the workplace had changed completely. Employers still required new employees to have traditional literacy and numeracy skills, but they also had to be computer literate. The primary change, perhaps, was that employers needed new workers with highly developed creative-thinking skills. The old training programs that had prepared people for primary and secondary activity jobs needed to change—those jobs were now a declining segment of Canada's economy. In the next sections of this chapter, you will examine our economy in greater detail. A deeper understanding of its history—and its future trends—will help you better to understand your place in it and how best to prepare for working life in the twenty-first century.

ACTIVITIES

1. **a)** Refer to Table 8–1 in this chapter and to Table 2 in Chapter 7, page 265. Plot a line graph showing the urban percentage of Canada's total population in the years 1891, 1911, 1931, 1951, 1971, 1991, and 1996. Based on your graph, make three observations about Canada's rate of urbanization over the last century.

   b) Based on your graph, what predictions would you make about Canada's rate of urbanization in the future?

2. Examine Table 8–2. Offer three pieces of evidence to indicate that one of Canada's challenges in the twenty-first century will be to deal with an aging population.

3. **a)** In groups of four of five students, do one of the following:
   - Ms. Mega Developer acquires some good farmland in order to create a new suburb. List some benefits to society and to the economy resulting from her development.
   - Mr. Magna Developer acquires some good farmland in order to create a new suburb. List some reasons that might be put forward by environmentalists and local farmers who are trying to stop his development.

   b) Design a billboard, based on your points, to win public support for your case. Your group could present your billboard to the class on large construction paper or sketch it on the chalk board. Remember that billboards use text sparingly. Try to distill your message to two short sentences. Select a dramatic image to accompany your text that reinforces your viewpoint.

4. In a paragraph, explain how globalization can be seen as both a threat and a promise for Canada's economy. Refer to pages 294 to 296 and this chapter's Window on the Present.

5. List the advantages and disadvantages of the new style of assembly used at the GM Autoplex from the perspective of
   a) the company
   b) the worker
   c) the consumer.

ECONOMIC ESSENTIALS

When you think of "economics," you probably think of money. True, economics is the social science that studies the production, exchange, and **consumption** of **goods** and **services,** all of which involve the flow of money. But economics is more than that. It is about deciding how to meet the basic needs and desires of individuals, businesses, and nations.

The biggest problem in economic decision-making is the issue of **scarcity**. For example, you may want to buy four new CDs. Perhaps you also need to pay back a friend

consumption: the use or purchase of goods to satisfy wants

scarcity: an insufficient amount

goods: supplies or products that can be sold

services: intangible things that satisfy a want, for example, banking, insurance, and transportation services

The Last Budget Speech of the Twentieth Century

Federal Finance Minister Paul Martin, presented his budget speech to Parliament on February 16, 1999. In the excerpts that follow, he refers to history, economic issues, and to barriers that must be surmounted.

Figure 8–5 Paul Martin claimed the twenty-first century for Canada in his 1999 budget speech. Do you agree with him?

PRIMARY SOURCE

... Government must focus on those areas where it can really make a difference ... We can never lose sight of the need to take a balanced approach. For the social and economic needs of a nation are not separate. They are not in conflict ...

... in the early years of this century, Sir Wilfrid Laurier spoke of our prospects as a people. He said that the twentieth century would belong to Canada. Some since have scoffed at those words ... Well, Mr. Speaker, Laurier was right. Not according to the cold calculations of might, but because of the quality of our life. Not because of any single value we have pursued, but because of the many values we have advanced together. The value of tolerance, of fairness. The value of working together ...

There are barriers we must bring down—of circumstance and of privilege—and new bridges to be built that we can all cross together ... Our goal must be to forge a new alliance—a free market and a fair society supporting one another ...

It is time to imagine a day when we have fully met the challenge of an aging population, met our obligations to the young, and met our responsibility for nature's legacy to us, the environment ... And so, let us come together—all of us—and make a pledge of common purpose: that we will do everything in our power today so that the generations of tomorrow are able to say not only that Canada belongs to the twenty-first century, but that the twenty-first century belongs to Canada.

Figure 8–6 These winter coats are on sale because the demand for them has gone down. How does this demonstrate the law of demand?

The Laws of Supply and Demand

Last year, you learned how early European contact with Canada was based on the need for goods, and not on a need to encourage settlement. In the early 1600s, Champlain viewed his settlement primarily as a trading venture. His purpose was to procure a good supply of beaver pelts, which commanded a high price in France. As a trading nation, Canada's economy and welfare has always been affected by the prices it can set for goods and services in the world **market.** When worldwide prices for Canadian exports are high, the economy booms. The reverse holds true when global prices decrease. When world prices for grain products dropped in the late 1990s, for example, Canadian grain farmers suffered. Many even went bankrupt. They couldn't pay off their debts, because the world price for their goods was lower than their costs of production, or what it cost them to grow their crops. In this and many other possible examples, the laws of **supply** and **demand** directly affect the livelihood of millions of Canadians.

How do the laws of supply and demand work?

The law of demand applies to the consumer side of the market. It works in two ways. When the price for a good or service goes down, demand goes up; conversely, when the price increases, demand falls. This happens for a simple reason— not all people in the market can afford a product or service at its original, high price. When the price of a product or service is lowered, it becomes more affordable to many more consumers. All those sale signs in malls and retail outlets

supply: the relationship between the amount of a good or service available for sale and its price

demand: the relationship between the amount of a good or service that consumers are willing to buy and its price

market: a region or population in which there is demand for a product or service and the good or service can be sold

and set aside some money for your future. The key issue is—you don't have enough money to do it all. You have to make a decision. That is what "scarcity" means in personal terms. In the same way, a society's needs and desires often exceed its resources. It too has to decide how those resources will be used. On a government level, the challenge to balance needs with resources drives economic policy-making, which can lead to angry political debates. Though they may focus on money and resources, these debates also reveal the struggle between different beliefs and values. In fact, a country's economic policies can reveal what it stands for—to itself and to the world.

promising deep discounts are an everyday example of this law at work.

Demand, however, also affects prices. When demand goes up, it pulls the price of the product or service up with it. When demand decreases, so does the price of the product or service. Once again, malls and retail outlets offer clear examples of this law at work. For example, in late January, clothing stores prepare to launch their new lines of spring and summer clothing, even though they haven't sold all their winter stock. Since the demand for winter clothing is fading, the winter clothes are marked down and the new line of clothes is introduced at full price. The prices of fads and fashions are heavily dependent upon demand, which can itself be increased through advertising and **marketing**. Indeed, the extra costs of marketing and advertising become an added cost to the producers—which is passed on to the consumer through higher prices.

The law of supply applies to the producer side of the market, and also affects pricing. When prices are high, producers of goods or services usually increase production. When prices are low, producers tend to cut back on production. By controlling supply, they hope to maximize profits and control prices. For example, if prices for eggs are low, then egg producers cut back on production, creating a shortage. If demand remains the same, prices for eggs will go up. Supply can affect prices in other ways. For instance, a coffee crop failure in Central America would lead to a worldwide shortage in the supply of coffee beans. Assuming that the demand for coffee remains the same, this would

cause an increase in the cost of a cup of coffee. At the same time, if there were a bumper crop of wheat around the world, then wheat prices would fall because of the surplus supply.

As you've already learned, economics is about making decisions. Producers must ask and answer three basic questions whenever they have to make an economic decision. At the core of each is the issue of how best to use available **resources.**

The first question is: What is to be produced? A farmer, for example, must decide whether to grow wheat or canola. A provincial government with a limited budget must choose between increasing funding for health care or education.

The second question is: How is it to be produced? The farmer, for example, would need to consider what technology is required. The provincial government would have to determine if new health-care or education workers had to be trained.

The third question is: For whom is it to be produced? The farmer would need to determine if the crops would be sold within Canada or exported. If the provincial government decided on increasing the education budget, it would have to decide where the funds should go—to public schools, or to private schools?

Defining Resources

When a farmer decides which crop to grow, and a government decides which service to fund, both must assess the available resources. As always, scarcity is an issue. If there is not enough of one type of resource to produce a good or service, steps must be taken, or that choice is eliminated. Resources are generally grouped into three categories.

marketing: promoting goods or services that are for sale

resources: the means available for producing goods and services

Figure 8–7 These Vancouver workers are packing salmon roe for export. They are involved in the fishing industry, a primary activity.

The term "land resources" refers to all natural resources that may be used to produce goods and services. It includes land, air, water, fish, forests, and minerals. The term "human resources" refers to the labour provided by people to produce goods and services, and includes

fishers, factory workers, store owners, educators, research scientists, and so on. "Capital resources" refers to money and human-made goods—which are also known as "capital goods"—which are used to produce other goods and services. Some examples would be transportation infrastructure, technology, research, and education facilities.

Economic Sectors

For most of its existence, Canada has been described as having a resource-based economy. But as you learned in earlier chapters of *Horizons*, our nation's economy has been changing and developing since its earliest days. Today, Canada's economic activities are much more diversified than they were at the time of Confederation.

Economists classify economic activities according to sectors: primary, secondary, tertiary, or quaternary. Primary activities involve collecting, harvesting, or extracting natural resources. Fishing, farming, logging, trapping, and mining are

Figure 8–8 The workers at this site are involved in construction, a key industry in the secondary sector of the economy.

Figure 8–9 The sales team in this women's clothing shop works in the retail industry, a major component of the tertiary sector of the economy.

examples. Secondary activities involve the processing or manufacturing of goods and are broken down into two further levels. For example, milling lumber or smelting iron ore are primary manufacturing activities. Using lumber to construct houses and assembling automobiles or computers are examples of secondary manufacturing activities. Tertiary activities produce services, rather than goods. Machine repair, trucking, sales, banking, and medical services are examples of activities included in the tertiary sector. The creation and transfer of ideas and information makes up the quaternary sector of the economy. Fashion design, medical research, computer software development, journalism, and broadcasting are a few examples of activities in this sector.

Although the quaternary sector is growing slowly, most working Canadians today are employed in the tertiary, or service, sector. In most urban regions, particularly those in southern Ontario and Quebec, manufacturing activities also dominate. However, the primary activities of mining, forestry, fishing, and farming still account for the greatest percentage of the national income. If economic trends continue, the primary sector will continue to decline and the other sectors will grow in relative terms.

Figure 8–10 The medical researcher shown here works in the quaternary sector of the economy.

Using Statistics

When economists study overall economic activity on a national or global level, their work is called "macroeconomics." This is not a remote academic exercise. It's more like detective work—with a touch of fortune telling. Macroeconomic analysis can help us uncover and predict economic patterns. It can also help us assess the economic performance of a person, business, or government. To do this, economists consider a wide range of statistical information. **Unemployment rates**, **consumer price indexes**, and **productivity measurements**, are statistical sources that act like snapshots to reveal the state of the national economy.

The Gross Domestic Product (GDP) and the Gross National Product (GNP) also provide important information. The GDP measures the market value of all goods and services produced in a country during a set period of time—even if the goods and services are produced by a foreign-owned company. The GNP, on the other hand, measures the total market value of all goods and services produced by a particular country's companies—even if they are located in other countries.

Both GDP and GNP can be followed to show how the total value of all final goods and services has grown or has declined. These measurements indicate how robust the economy is. They also tell economists, and the general public, about current economic trends. In turn, these trends can be compared to the **business cycle** and predictions can be made about where the economy is going.

Figure 8–11 This cartoon from the *Vancouver Sun* portrays a sickly economy. What does the cartoonist imply about the ability of economists—or "financial experts"—to make it better, or to predict the future? Explain why you agree or disagree with the cartoonist's viewpoint?

Apply Your Knowledge

Using Economic Statistics to Understand the Past and Predict Future Trends

In Chapter 7, you examined the history of Canada as it became a modern nation. As Canada enters another new century, dramatic economic and technological changes continue to transform the country. Economic statistics can help us to understand the impact these changes had on our history. They can also be helpful in assessing the present and preparing for the future. To get a better understanding of how these economic tools can do all this, look at the graphs and tables below. Then complete the activities.

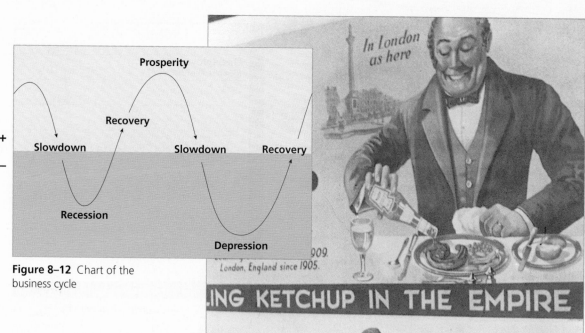

Figure 8–12 Chart of the business cycle

Figure 8–13 This photograph, taken in 1933, puts a human face on the term "economic depression." Many Canadians had no work, and little hope, during the Great Depression of the 1930s. The Depression, in fact, shaped the lives and values of an entire generation of Canadians. It was the last depression of the twentieth century for Canada.

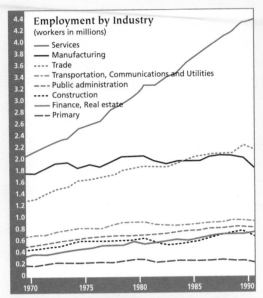

Figure 8–14 Employment in Canada by industry

Employment by Industry
(workers in millions)
— Services
— Manufacturing
---- Trade
--- Transportation, Communications and Utilities
--- Public administration
---- Construction
— Finance, Real estate
-- Primary

Table 8–3 Canada's Real Gross Domestic Product and Annual Change

Year	Constant (1992) Dollars, in Millions	Annual Percentage Change
1970	351 434	3
1974	436 151	4
1978	506 413	4
1982	535 113	-3
1986	628 575	3
1990	705 464	0
1994	744 220	4
1997	798 183	4

Table 8–4 Canada's Real GDP During the Great Depression

Year	Constant (1986) Dollars, in Millions	Annual Percentage Change
1929	52 997	0.9
1930	51 262	–3.3
1931	45 521	–11.2
1932	41 302	–9.3
1933	38 331	–7.2
1934	42 318	10.4
1935	45 357	7.2

Real GDP: gross domestic product adjusted for inflation

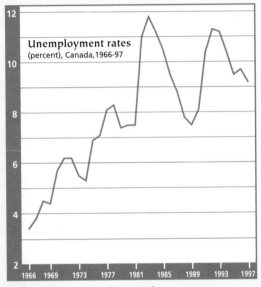

Unemployment rates
(percent), Canada, 1966-97

Figure 8–15 Canada's unemployment rate

....

ACTIVITIES

1. Compare Table 8–3 and Table 8–4 to the chart of the business cycle in Figure 8–12. Based on your observations, would you say that a depression is an inevitable consequence of an economic downturn? Explain.

2. Examine the chart in Figure 8–14. What industry has more than doubled in the number of people it employs? What industry consistently employs the lowest number of workers? Based on this chart, what would you predict about future employment opportunities?

3. Earlier in this chapter you were told that high unemployment may be a trend in the future economy. Look at Figure 8–15 and then give reasons that either support or refute that prediction.

4. Look again at the photograph in Figure 8–13. Imagine that you are a photographer who has been assigned to capture images that show the state of the economy in your region. Describe some of the photographs you might take. Focus on different segments of the economy, both where there is growth and decline.

1. Give an example of one of your recent economic decisions. How did scarcity play a role in your decision? How did you allocate your resources? Why?

2. You have extra tickets to a popular concert that you want to sell. How would the law of demand affect the price of your tickets two hours before the concert? Two hours after? Explain the principle at work.

3. Imagine that you are trying to attract a new business to your community. Prepare a 3-minute pitch that would convince a company to locate there on the basis of your community's land, human, and capital resources. Make your pitch to a partner.

4. Why do you suppose the government of Canada might prefer the GDP statistic while the United States might like the GNP statistic? You may want to keep foreign-owned businesses in mind.

5. Canada's economic sectors are interconnected. Using the chart below as a model, set up your own chart with additional blank rows. In the Primary column, place "copper mining." Next, trace the potential economic activities through the remaining columns. Now place "paper" in another row, but under the "Secondary Manufacturing" column. Place the possible economic activities linked to it in the appropriate columns. You could complete this activity with a partner to come up with many more of the existing—and potential—connections between the economic sectors.

Primary	Secondary		Tertiary	Quaternary
	Primary Manufacturing	Secondary Manufacturing		
wool	yarn	sweater	sales	design
logging	lumber	furniture	transport	testing
fish	cleaning	fish sticks	marketing	research

CANADA'S ECONOMIC REGIONS

Canada is a nation of tremendous diversity. It includes old and new mountain ranges, Arctic deserts, temperate rain forests, vast prairie, rich farmland, and barren shield. Its climates, vegetation, and cultures are equally varied. Canada's economy, naturally, reflects this diversity.

Canada is divided politically by artificial boundaries into provinces and territories. But it can also be divided into **economic regions**, as described in this section. In this case, regions are defined on the basis of the dominant industrial activities in an area. These regions can be very specific, say the business district of a community, or they can be much broader, to include groups of provinces, or even countries. The economic regions in *Horizons* are broad, and loosely follow geographic characteristics. The economic region of BC will be studied in Chapter 9.

economic region: an area defined by common economic activities

The Atlantic Region

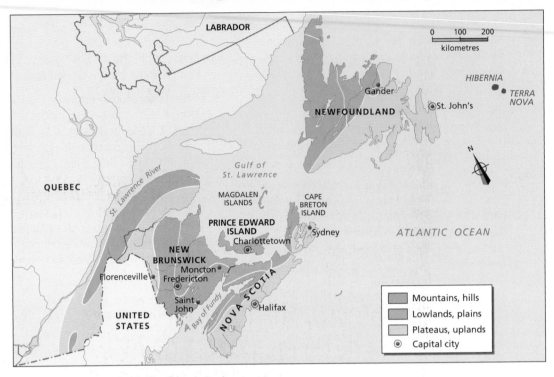

Figure 8–16 The Atlantic Region

The Atlantic Region, Canada's easternmost economic region, is dominated by the Appalachian Mountains and the Atlantic Ocean. It is composed of the present-day provinces of New Brunswick, Prince Edward Island, Nova Scotia, the island of Newfoundland, and the Gaspé region of Quebec. It stretches as far east as St. John's, Newfoundland, and as far west as Rivière-du-Loup, Quebec.

With thousands of kilometres of indented coastlines, the region has many natural harbours. Halifax, for example, is particularly well-situated for trade with Europe and the eastern seaboard of the United States. Major land resources are fish, forests, and farmland. Mineral deposits of lead, zinc, and coal were important to the region's development, although these are becoming depleted. As well, oil reserves off the coast of Newfoundland and **natural gas**

natural gas: a form of petroleum found in a gaseous state

reserves off the coast of Nova Scotia have been discovered and developed.

The region's strategic location resulted in early European contact. John Cabot landed in Newfoundland in 1497, and the teeming banks of fish off the coast of Newfoundland and Nova Scotia later drew fishers from Portugal and France as well. The Native peoples of the region hunted, fished, and farmed before European contact. Fishing has remained a major activity in the region for hundreds of years. Because of the harsh climate in Newfoundland, settlement remained low. In the more southern areas of the region, with areas of fertile land and a less harsh climate, settlement grew more quickly.

Agriculture, which started with Acadian settlers in the seventeenth century, remains a key industry. Today, key agricultural activities include potato farming in the red soils of PEI and New Brunswick, and orchards in Nova Scotia's Annapolis Valley. Forests have also been another major land resource. In the early 1800s, timber became a major export to Britain, where the pines of Nova Scotia and New Brunswick were prized as masts for naval ships.

At the time of Confederation, Halifax and Saint John had internationally important dockyard and shipbuilding facilities. Advances in steam technology and the building of iron ships in the 1890s, however, threatened all that. Forests later came to be harvested for use in pulp and paper mills, which are still vital to the economy in sub-regions of Newfoundland and New Brunswick. Coal mining became a major industry in Cape Breton for generations. At the time of Confederation, the area produced two-thirds of Canada's coal. Steel manufacturing became an important activity near Sydney. The Atlantic region also had a developed financial sector based on trade with Britain and the United States.

After Confederation, central Canada's power increased and eventually came to control the region's mining, financial, and limited manufacturing industries. Changing markets and technology, depleted resources, and a reliance on resource-based activities led to the region's economic decline, relative to the rest of Canada. Regional disparity has been and remains a chronic issue in the Atlantic Region.

Today, the Atlantic economy is changing. The collapse of the cod and **groundfish** stocks has devastated the fishing industry and communities that were built over hundreds of years. This happened for a number of reasons, including trawlers, overfishing by foreign fleets, and overestimates of stocks.

Improved technology—such as sonar locating—led to overfishing as well, and a need for fewer workers. Environmental factors, such as pollution, changes in water temperature—and, possibly, an increase in the seal population—also played a role. It is clear that a way of life is also collapsing. Many people in the fishing industry will have to retrain for work in other sectors, if the industry is to be sustainable.

The agricultural industry has prospered. One striking example is McCain Foods Limited. In 1957, the company began processing french fries in Florenceville, in New Brunswick's Saint John River Valley. It had thirty employees and annual sales of $152 678. By 1997, it employed 16 000 people in a multinational operation that included farming, trucking, and equipment manufacturing. Its 1997 sales were $4.15 billion.

The Hibernia oil field, located 315 kilometres east of St. John's Newfoundland, and the Terra Nova oil field, 35 kilometres south of Hibernia, hold more promise for the region. The estimated size of the Hibernia deposit is 615 million **barrels** of oil. Environmental, economic, and technical studies delayed construction of the drilling and pumping platforms for years. Finally, the first oil was pumped on November 17, 1997. By June 1998, Hibernia was producing 60 000 barrels of crude oil per day. Newfoundland and the Atlantic Region stand to benefit not only from oil royalties and job opportunities, but from optimism at a time when older industries are in decline.

groundfish: fish living on or near the bottom of the sea, such as halibut and cod

barrel: one barrel of oil equals 159 litres of crude oil

Figure 8–17 The Hibernia oil platform

The Great Lakes-St. Lawrence Region

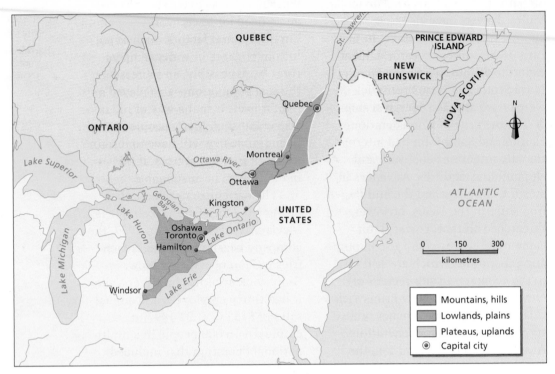

Figure 8–18 The Great Lakes-St. Lawrence Region

The Great Lakes–St. Lawrence Region is Canada's smallest economic region, occupying less than 2 percent of the nation's total land area. It comprises the southern strip of Quebec, along the St. Lawrence River, and the southern tip of Ontario, surrounded by Lake Erie, Lake Ontario, and Lake Huron. Geographically, the region consists of fertile lowlands and has a mild climate. These factors attracted the First Nations to the region, where they became accomplished farmers, fishers, hunters, and trappers.

The St. Lawrence River and the Great Lakes are both valuable resources and superb waterways. European contact brought the fur trade and, later, settlement and the beginnings of manufacturing. Towns were built near rivers so that flour and saw mills could have access to water power. Water transportation routes connected the various communities and allowed raw materials to be transported to more centralized locations for manufacturing activities. As lumbering increased, more land was cleared, and agriculture and settlement expanded.

By the time of Confederation, manufacturing—iron and steel, clothing, saw mills, breweries, even an oil refinery—had become a major component of the economy. Strategically close to the booming US northeast, the region was soon linked by rail to both the Atlantic and the western provinces. The Great Lakes-St. Lawrence Region had extraordinary advantages for industrial development. By the early twentieth century, it was known as Canada's "Industrial Heartland." It had also become the country's financial centre. As you learned in Chapter 2, many of those who opposed Confederation did so because they feared their own regions would be weakened if central Canada gained more power. Indeed, the amount of wealth—and control—concentrated in this region still creates regional tensions across Canada.

In the latter decades of the twentieth century, the automotive sector dominated the region's manufacturing. Today, it employs more than 75 000 Canadians. US automotive giants, Ford, Chrylser, and General Motors, have long operated assembly plants here. For the US corporations, the region provided a pool of skilled labourers and a strong infrastructure. As you will read later in this chapter, their Canadian **branch plants** also gave them a way around Canadian tariffs. Since the 1980s, Japanese automakers Honda and Toyota also have operated highly successful assembly plants in Ontario. Again the labour pool, infrastructure, and a way around tariffs acted as highly attractive incentives to locate here. Canadian auto workers have proven themselves to be among the most productive in North America.

In the last decades of the twentieth century, high-tech industries also expanded and reshaped the economy. For example, Northern Telecom entered its second century in 1995, and is one of the world's leading telecommunications companies. The turning point may have come just after Northern Electric and Bell Canada merged their research and development in 1971. Nortel engineers soon designed the world's first **electronic switching** device, affectionately called the "E thing." This

was followed by breakthroughs in digital technology that helped make Nortel a world leader in global telecommunications. Other high-tech companies have located in Ottawa, which has become something of a high-tech corridor in computer software design.

In the world of high finance, this region is still on top. Most of Canada's banks, trust companies, and insurance companies have head offices in either Toronto or Montreal. Canada's largest stock exchange is located in Toronto, which also has almost fifty foreign chartered banks. When Canadian companies need financing, they must look to this region. The Great Lakes–St. Lawrence Region also has an abundant supply of electrical power. As home to more than half of Canada's population, it is also the largest market in Canada. In other words, the region still has all the advantages required for it to remain the economic engine of Canada.

On the other side of prosperity are environmental concerns. The area between Hamilton and Toronto, known as the "Golden Horseshoe," is heavily industrialized and densely populated. Severe environmental damage has resulted from industrial waste, smog, and urban and industrial developments that have consumed much of the region's richest farmland. The Great Lakes and the St. Lawrence are now heavily polluted as well.

branch plant: a factory or office owned by a company based in another country

electronic switching: a device using electronic components to control the connections in the circuitry of telecommunication systems

Figure 8–19 the "E thing" was a major breakthrough in telecommunications in the 1970s.

The Shield Region

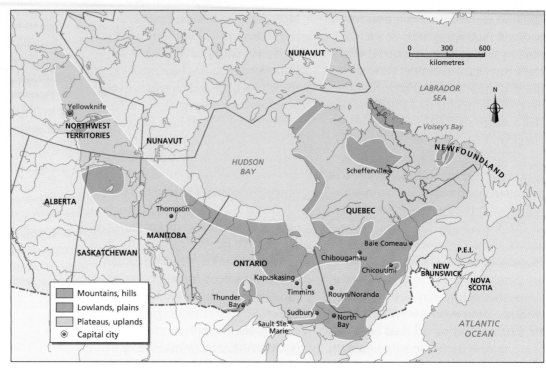

Figure 8–20 The Shield Region

The Shield Region is Canada's largest economic region. It extends east and south from Great Bear Lake in the Northwest Territories, through the three prairie provinces, Ontario, Quebec, and includes all of Labrador and the eastern tips of Baffin Island. The region covers the greater portion of the Canadian Shield, which is composed of some of the Earth's oldest rock.

Igneous and metamorphic rock types are prevalent, and have yielded rich deposits of nickel, copper, gold, silver, lead, and zinc. The region's thin soils, left after the glaciers retreated in the last Ice Age, support boreal forests. Agriculture, however, is very limited. Water is abundant, and the hydroelectric potential of the many river systems has been tapped, starting shortly after Confederation.

The Ojibwa and other Native groups who first settled here hunted and fished for a living. After European contact, the fur trade became the dominant economic activity. Later still, forestry became important, particularly pulp and paper, which remains a major industry. Resource extraction, in the form of mines and smelters, has been critical to the region's economy since the early twentieth century.

Sault Ste. Marie, Ontario, has been dominated by Algoma Steel ever since the company founded its first ironworks there in 1901 and manufactured the first steel rails in 1902. In 1902, the International Nickel Company (Inco) was formed to mine some of the world's richest deposits of nickel, copper, and silver, which had been discovered in the Sudbury Basin. Inco later built smelters in Sudbury, Ontario and Thompson, Manitoba—and sold its products around the world. In the same year, the Aluminum Company of Canada (Alcan) started up in Shawinigan, Quebec. With its second aluminum smelter, in the Saguenay-Lac St. Jean region, Alcan had even more success by building a massive hydroelectric project. In many ways, the mineral riches of the Shield fuelled the industrialization that was transforming Canada. Today, Inco and Alcan have become giant, global corporations.

The region's heavy dependence on resource extraction has also led to major environmental and economic concerns. Mines have produced dangerous stockpiles of **tailings**. Smelter and refining operations have produced high levels of sulphur dioxide and nitrogen oxides, which have polluted lakes and seriously affected forest growth. Massive hydroelectric developments—such as Hydro-Quebec's James Bay project—have flooded once pristine watersheds and threatened the way of life of many aboriginal peoples. Governments have responded to aboriginal and environmental demands—imposing emission-reduction programs, environmental reviews, and aboriginal consultations. But the issues are far from being resolved.

As a region heavily dependent on resources, the Shield's economy is subject to international price pressures. The minerals and metals produced here are **commodities** that fluctuate in value according to global demand and supply. The region's economy can be bumpy as it rides through boom-and-bust cycles. Prices go up and down, but the reserves of metals eventually either run out or become uneconomic. When a mine closes, the town that built up around it also dies, or struggles to survive. This story has been

played out many, many times. Schefferville, Quebec, is just one example. The Iron Ore Company of Canada closed its operation here in 1981, when world prices for iron ore were too low for the company to make a profit. The Quebec government simply provided assistance for residents to move elsewhere.

Other one-resource towns have made efforts to stay alive, often by developing recreation, tourist, and retirement facilities. Many of the larger cities in the area—Sudbury, for example—have taken steps to broaden their economies and develop the tertiary sector. As technological advances in mining and smelting continue to reduce the demand for human labour, the need to shift towards a more diversified, sustainable economic basis is yet another pressing issue in the Shield Region.

tailings: waste left after mining and smelting

commodity: anything that can be bought and sold

slag: refuse left over after ore has been removed

Figure 8–21 A glowing stream of **slag** in Sudbury. By-products of smelting and mining operations are concerns that industry must cope with in the Shield Region.

The North Region

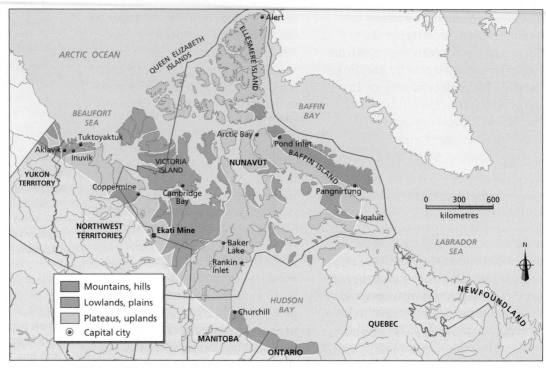

Figure 8–22 The North Region

permafrost: ground that remains permanently frozen

The North Region occupies a vast area of Canada's land mass. Its western limit cuts into a corner of the Yukon on the Beaufort Sea. The boundary then swings east and south through the Northwest Territories and Nunavat, skirts the northern areas of Manitoba and Ontario along Hudson Bay, and swings north again to include the northwestern tip of Quebec and most of Baffin Island.

The region lies north of the line of continuous **permafrost**, and most of it is above the treeline. The landscape is stark and the climate is harsh. Most of the waterways are frozen for most, if not all, of the year. Winters, particularly in the northern areas, are long, cold, and dark. The region consists of mountains, plateaus, lowlands and highlands. The Canadian Shield forms a large portion of the area as well,

extending into Baffin Island and Ellesmere Island.

The aboriginal peoples of the North hunted, trapped, and fished to sustain themselves. Early European contact was based on the fur trade and on whaling and sealing. In the mid-nineteenth century, the search for the Northwest Passage brought more European contact. Gold discoveries in the late 1800s led to increased settlement and resource exploration. During the 1930s, a surge in interest from Canadians in the southern regions led to increased mineral exploration. Geologists found rich deposits of copper, gold, silver, and radium. Eventually, lead and zinc deposits were discovered, as well as reserves of oil and gas.

Environmental damage, however, has always been a primary concern. The construction of an oil pipeline during World War II, which connected Norman Wells with Fairbanks, Alaska, developed leaks along the route. This caused irreparable damage to the environment.

In the 1970s and 1980s, oil companies constructed artificial islands on the Beaufort Sea so that drilling platforms could be built to explore the reserves of oil. They were confronted with environmental challenges typical of the region. The islands had to withstand the pressures of the Arctic ice-pack during the long winters. But because the region had no transportation infrastructure—permafrost makes such an infrastructure almost impossible to build—the Beaufort Sea oil reserves and natural gas fields in the High Arctic were left largely untapped.

Charles Fipke, a geologist from British Columbia, persevered for ten years and discovered **kimberlite** deposits in the Lac de Gras region of the North Region. After five years of environmental impact and economic studies—and two years of engineering challenges during construction, which cost $800 million and employed 800 workers—the Ekati mine began production in October, 1998. It is projected that the mine will produce about 4 million carats of diamonds a year for seventeen years. The mine will have 830 permanent employees, 70 percent of whom will be northerners, including 30 percent aboriginal peoples.

The difficult, fragile environment of the North Region remains a barrier to the development of resource-based industries and to settlement and economic expansion. Environmentalists and aboriginal groups now demand assurances before any pipeline, mining, or transportation **megaproject** is proposed. In many ways, the North Region remains an economic frontier, full of riches and promise, but riddled with challenges.

kimberlite: a rare igneous rock that sometimes contains diamonds

megaproject: an large-scale and expensive engineering or construction project

Figure 8–23 The Inuit maintain many of their thousand-year-old traditions, but now they do it with the help of modern technology.

The Prairie Region

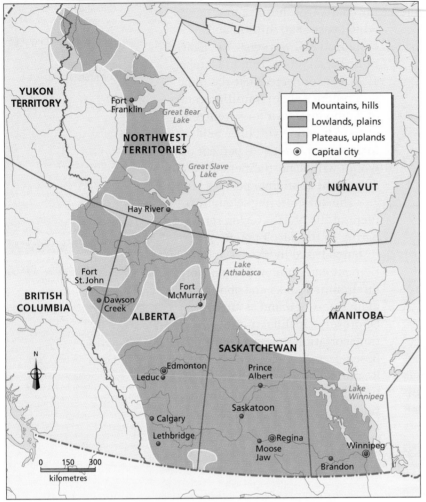

Figure 8–24 The Prairie Region

region hunted the massive herds of migrating bison. Initial European contact centred on the fur trade. After Confederation and the building of the railways, waves of settlers transformed the prairies, altering the aboriginal way of life forever. Forestry became an important activity in the northern regions of the prairies, and today pulp and paper and saw mills remain important industries in these sub-regions.

By 1914, much of the natural grasslands in the southern areas had been ploughed under. New strains of hardy wheat transformed the region into a leading world exporter. Ranching also grew, and remains a major economic activity. Agriculture dominates the prairie economy—more than 80 percent of Canada's farmland is located here. Today, changing world markets dictate what crops are grown, and what animals are raised. Wheat is no longer the undisputed king of crops.

In 1995, the federal government ended the Crow Rate Benefit, a shipping subsidy that had kept crops competitive in the global market. Shipping costs soared. This created alienation towards central Canada, but also forced farmers to avoid dependence on a single cash crop. Today you are as likely to see fields of canola, beans, carrots—even potatoes—as you are wheat. You may also see herds of emu, bison—or ostriches—grazing on the range. To survive, today's farmers and ranchers are attuned to the market place and

The Prairie Region is the northern portion of the Interior Plains. On the east, the region follows the contour of the Canadian Shield. On the west, it reaches to the Western Mountains. It includes the southern portions of Manitoba and Saskatchewan, most of Alberta and the northeastern corner of British Columbia. In the north, the prairie tapers off and turns, occupying a small section of the Yukon.

The Prairie Region consists primarily of rolling plains, which gradually slope downward in three levels from west to east. As you learned in Chapter 3, the Native peoples of the

Table 8–5	Changes in Manitoba Crops, 1992 and 1998 ($ in millions)			
Year	peas and beans	wheat	canola	hogs
1992	$15	$700	n/a	$250
1998	$70	$404	$565	$500

These statistics show how quickly farmers in the Prairie Region adapt to the marketplace. What happened to the importance of wheat as a crop from 1992 to 1998?

the ever-changing prices their commodities can bring.

Another player in the region's economy is the **petroleum** industry. Oil was discovered as early as 1914 in the Turner Valley, southwest of Calgary. The turning point, however, came in 1947 with the opening of the rich Leduc oil field southwest of Edmonton. From this time on, the petroleum industry came to dominate the economy of Alberta. Petroleum was later discovered in Dawson Creek, Fort St. John, and Fort Nelson, in northeastern British Columbia, in Lloydminster, Moose Jaw, and Weyburn, in Saskatchewan, and in Virden, in Manitoba. Much of the petroleum industry is owned and controlled by foreign companies. But in the 1980s and 1990s corporations such as Petro-Canada and Husky Oil emerged as important Canadian-owned companies. Another major petroleum development is the mining of **oil sand** deposits, particularly the Athabasca oil sands, near Fort McMurray.

As in other regions, population has become increasingly urbanized. Technological change has led to fewer and larger farms and a drastic reduction in the number of people employed in farming. Small towns that once provided services to rural communities struggle to survive. In Saskatchewan and Manitoba, many people leave to find work in other regions, even though the economies of the two provinces continue to

diversify. The Prairie Region now has a number of metropolitan areas, such as Edmonton, Calgary, Winnipeg, and Saskatoon. Calgary, in particular, is emerging as a western centre of financial and corporate head offices.

Alberta's petroleum industry has supported growth and diversification in that province's manufacturing sector. As a result, Alberta's economy has a broader spectrum of employment opportunities.

The region's economy is still largely resource-based and subject to global price cycles. But continuing investment in other sectors—especially in secondary manufacturing and quaternary research and development—holds the promise of relative stability.

petroleum: a dark, viscous material found in the upper strata of the Earth

oil sand: sand saturated with heavy crude oil, which usually has seeped to the surface

Figure 8–25 In 1998, these farmers at the US-Saskatchewan border protested government policies that they said were hampering their ability to compete. What does the sign in the foreground tell you about world prices for wheat?

1. Create a table with the name of each of Canada's economic regions as a heading. Under each heading, list points about the region's population. Which, for example, is the most densely populated? Which is the least? Which has the largest number of large cities? Which poses the greatest challenge to settlement?

2. In the past, the federal government has run equalization programs to help poorer provinces. Imagine that you are in charge. Prepare a speech announcing that you are going to either a) eliminate or b) continue the program. Justify your action, taking the consequences on specific regions into account. Also state what you hope to achieve.

3. In a paragraph describe how the economic regions rely on their natural resources.

4. Which economic regions of Canada are the most diversified? the least? Explain, with examples.

5. Which of Canada's economic regions do you think are best prepared for the new century? Explain, with examples.

6. What factors of industrial location led most manufacturing industries to locate in the Great Lakes-St. Lawrence Region, the "Industrial Heartland"?

CANADA AND THE US: AN OVERVIEW

bilateral: between two nations

The United States has an overwhelming influence on Canada. Indeed, Canada's **bilateral** relationship with its neighbour to the south has always been rooted in an awareness of US size and power. Prime Minister Pierre Elliot Trudeau said in 1969:

Living next to you [the United States] is in some ways like sleeping with an elephant. No matter how friendly and even-tempered the beast, if I can call it that, one is affected by every twitch and grunt.

As Trudeau's statement makes clear, the influence of the United States is felt in almost every facet of Canadian life. It is an influence that also courses through Canada's history.

History and Politics

Long before Confederation, the British colonies that would become the United States were a powerful presence for French and British colonists to the north. In 1745, for example, the New England states played a key role in capturing the fortress of Louisbourg from the French. Later, the American Revolution (1775–1783) pitted revolutionary forces against the colonies in the north, which had remained British. Even though American forces failed to take Quebec and other points, these battles, and the War of 1812, had a lasting impact: US military invasion was always a possibility.

In other chapters of *Horizons*, you learned how questions of loyalty inflamed the Rebellions of 1837 in Upper and Lower Canada. Those rebels—including William Lyon Mackenzie—who were seen as being pro-US, were condemned as traitors. Later, the Fenian raids in 1866 galvanized the Confederation debates. These attacks from the US, and the threat of further attacks, undoubtedly pushed some delegates to vote in favour of Confederation. In a perplexing sense, the US was fostering Canada's emergence as a nation by being seen as a threat.

Following Confederation, Canada expanded by purchasing Rupert's Land and securing union with British Columbia. At the same time, the US was also expanding, driven by the idea of Manifest Destiny. In Chapter 5, you learned how John A. Macdonald campaigned in the 1878 election by promising a policy that would bring the territories in the West into the Canadian fold, and out of US control. He won the election, and his National Policy created an east-west infrastructure— and a philosophy of what Canada was and could be as a nation. Macdonald reinforced that vision by erecting tariffs and trade barriers that would defy the north-south pull of trading with the US. It was a policy that guaranteed the survival of Canada for the next 110 years.

Linked Economies

There was one economic development that few had anticipated. As a young, sparsely populated country,

Figure 8–26 Fort Louisbourg, in Cape Breton, today is a popular tourist sight. In 1995, US veterans visited, in uniform, to commemorate its capture by New Englanders in 1745. Might Cape Bretoners view their celebration with mixed emotions?

Canada desperately needed capital in order to develop. In the nineteenth century, British investment had dominated Canada. This usually took the form of debt investment. This meant that British investors lent money to Canadian entrepreneurs who, though indebted, remained owners of their enterprises. As British involvement and investment in Canada diminished, American investment increased, but based on a very different model.

American "equity investment" meant that Americans invested in Canada by buying out Canadian businesses. Under this type of investment, US businesses or individuals also opened enterprises in Canada, but they remained under US control. As a consequence, many new businesses were neither owned nor controlled by Canadians. By the early 1920s, American equity investment had overtaken British investment in Canada.

Initially, Canada's abundant and untapped natural resources attracted US investment. The great pace of

Figure 8–27 Prime Minister Jean Chretien pays a visit to US President Bill Clinton in this editorial cartoon from *The Globe and Mail*. What point is the cartoonist making with the switching of the maps?

protectionist: protecting domestic markets and industries

branch plant: a factory owned by a company based in another country

American industrialization had already started to deplete US resources. In Canada, forestry, particularly pulp and paper, and mining were soon dominated by US interests. Eventually, the energy sector and manufacturing were taken over by the US. American multinational businesses were also drawn to the human capital that Canada could offer—a large pool of well-educated labourers. Once they had set up branches in Canada, American multinationals could also get around the high tariffs that the National Policy had placed on US products as a **protectionist** wall to guard the Canadian market. As companies operating within Canada's borders, they could sell their products and services to the millions of willing consumers in the Canadian marketplace. Soon Canada developed a **branch-plant** economy.

By the late 1920s, the US had replaced Britain as Canada's leading trade partner. American investment continued as US multinationals set up more branch plants, or sub-

sidiaries. As a result of this trend, Canada's economy became well developed. In fact, the National Policy and the branch-plant economy coexisted without much challenge until the late 1960s and early 1970s. Even though American multinationals were beginning to dominate the national economy, most Canadians were pleased with their relatively affluent lifestyles.

Many Canadians, however, worried about the long-term consequences of a branch-plant economy. Often US multinationals sent American managers to run their branch plants, rather than hiring Canadians. They also often spent little—if any—money on research-and-development projects in Canada. The profits from the Canadian branch plants tended to flow southward, back to US headquarters. In a phenomenon known as the "brain drain," many bright young Canadians migrated southward as well, to their branch plant's head office to further their careers and chances of advancement.

During the 1950s and 1960s, as Canada's economy expanded, US investment remained by far the most dominant form of foreign investment. The US wasn't alone—Canada welcomed foreign investment to keep the economy growing.

But the cultural and economic connections between Canada and the United States had a long and complicated history. Canada needed US investment, just as it needed access to the US market to sell its exports.

The Auto Pact

In the early 1960s, Canada's automobile manufacturing industry was struggling. Assembly plants in Oshawa, Oakville, and Windsor were inefficient. They produced limited quantities of four or five different models of cars and trucks, but for the Canadian market only. Production costs were high because of the small market, and Canadian consumers paid the price. They had no choice. Tariffs on US-built automobiles made them far too expensive for most Canadian buyers.

Canada's trade balance suffered. Many of the branch plants in Canada used US parts, and this led to an imbalance of trade. In its automotive trade with the US, Canada bought more than it sold. Something had to change.

In July 1964, negotiations began for a **sectoral** free-trade agreement. The Canada-US Automotive Products Trade Agreement (or the Auto Pact) was signed in January 1965. It guaranteed freer trade between the two countries in auto parts and automobiles. A protective clause stipulated that American-based auto manufacturers must assemble one automobile in Canada for every new automobile that they sold in Canada.

The Auto Pact was not truly a free-trade agreement—it did not abolish all tariffs, or create an

Figure 8–28 Daimler-Chrysler's massive minivan plant in Windsor, Ontario

entirely open market. Instead it was an example of managed trade. If the US-based automobile companies did not meet the one-for-one ratio, then Canada would impose tariffs on imported US-assembled autos. This clause protected the Canadian auto industry, and the Auto Pact benefited the entire economy. In fact, the Auto Pact has been described as Canada's greatest achievement in trade negotiations.

As Canadian consumption of automobiles rose, so did Canadian production. Branch plants began to specialize, building models that were sold to the entire North American market. Streamlining led to greater efficiency and higher profits. With new technology,

improved management styles—and with research and development done in Canada—many Canadian plants outperformed their US counterparts. This led to an expansion of the Canadian auto industry. By the 1980s, it was the leading sector in Canada's international trade, and it usually enjoyed a healthy surplus. In other words, Canada sold more automobiles and auto parts to the US than it bought from the US. Later in the decade, however, dissatisfaction with the Auto Pact was growing. Critics said that Canada's role in the auto industry remained limited to that of an assembler.

sectoral: belonging to a distinct area of economic activity

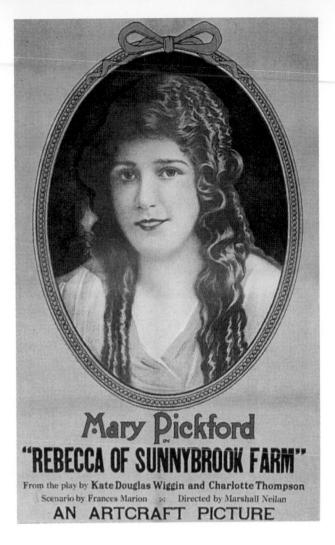

Figure 8–29 In a career that lasted from 1909 to 1933, Mary Pickford was known as "America's Sweetheart." She has been called the "most popular performer in film history." The queen of Hollywood, however, was a Canadian. What other Canadians can you can think of who have had tremendous success in the US? Did their Canadian identity also disappear from their public image?

lished the Canadian Radio Broadcasting Commission. It took over the existing Canadian National Railway's radio broadcasting, which had entertained passengers during long transcontinental journeys. This was one way the government could counter US influence and give Canadians their own voice in broadcasting. The network, however, barely struggled through the Great Depression. In 1936, it was replaced by the Canadian Broadcasting Corporation. The CBC has operated radio programming ever since. Later, television became a new mass medium, and it quickly developed in the US. In 1952, the CBC developed its own television network.

While the CBC maintained its presence as a Canadian **public** broadcaster, economic and market forces continually challenged its purpose and survival. In 1961, for example, CTV became Canada's first **private** television network. More would follow. With the arrival of cable television in the 1960s, Canadians had many more choices in programming—most of it American. In the 1990s, the number of television channels exploded with the appearance of cable specialty channels and the 500-channel Direct Broadcast System.

Many government commissions have studied Canada's cultural industries and made recommendations to preserve and nourish Canadian culture. In 1939, for example, the

Identity Anxiety

As Canada's economy became more and more entwined with the US economy, the influence of American popular culture and mass media swept across the border. This trend went back to the 1920s, when technological innovations led to a flood of American movies, radio broadcasts, and magazines. These attracted millions of Canadian consumers. Soon Canadians drove American cars, listened to American music, and went to American movies. Many Canadians began to worry that they were, in fact, becoming Americans.

Concerned by growing US influence, the federal government estab-

public: owned by the government, to serve the public

private: owned by private individual or business, usually run for profit

Should Government Protect Culture?

In 1968, the federal government established the CRTC, the Canadian Radio-television and Telecommunications Commission. Its purpose was to promote Canadian content in broadcasting. By 1970, the CRTC issued its first Canadian-content regulations. All radio stations in Canada had to broadcast a minimum of 30 percent Canadian content. To qualify as Canadian content, a recording had to meet two of three criteria. It had to be: a) performed by a Canadian; b) written by a Canadian; c) produced in Canada. If a recording did not meet this formula, its air time on Canadian radio stations was restricted.

The regulations were intended to guarantee Canadian artists access to the Canadian airwaves. It was hoped this would spur growth in the Canadian music industry. In this, the policy succeeded. Hundreds of Canadian recording artists did earn air time. And many earned stardom, first in Canada, then internationally. The content regulations, however, were controversial. Many private broadcasters complained that the regulations were forcing them to play music that was unpopular with audiences. It was costing them money by cutting the size of their potential audience.

Nevertheless, many music industry analysts maintained that the regulations had nurtured the industry. In April 1998, the CRTC raised the Canadian-content requirement: now 35 percent of popular music selections played on all radio stations in Canada had to be Canadian.

Figure 8–30 In 1991, BC rock-and-roll star Bryan Adams's "Everything I Do, I Do for You" was an international hit. According to CRTC content regulations, though, it wasn't Canadian: it got only 1.5 points, when it needed 2 points to qualify as Canadian content. Adams was furious, and so were many other Canadians. Do you think the content regulations were justified?

The CRTC also regulates Canadian television, and indirectly influences film production. In 1968, the CRTC ruled that 40 percent of Canadian **prime-time** television had to be Canadian. By 1972, that figure had been raised to 60 percent. As a result, more Canadian productions were developed. Some were successful in Canada and internationally. Most programs and film productions, however, did not have long-term success.

In June 1998, the CRTC released a report on Canadian viewing habits in the new, multichannel world of television. It showed that 74 percent of Canadians subscribed to cable TV and that three-quarters of these had access to more than fifty channels. The report also revealed that the portion of viewers watching English-language Canadian networks had declined from 58.8 percent, in 1992, to 50.7 percent, in 1997. Surprisingly, the number of viewers of US networks had also dropped, from 26.5 percent to 21.3 percent. The specialty channels, both American and

Canadian, had gained new viewers, increasing their share of the audience from 15.7 percent, in 1992, to 28 percent, in 1997.

The CRTC's response to the study was to maintain Canadian-content regulations. If the specialty channels wanted to keep their licences, they would have to follow the content rules.

Canadians in all walks of life have debated the issue of whether Canadian culture should be protected. Some want a completely free market, with unrestricted access to foreign music, films, television programming, and magazines. They want an end to Canadian-content regulations and other government measures that protect cultural industries. Others insist that the government's measures are not only necessary, but that they should be strengthened. These people argue that US cultural industries—film, magazine and book publishing, the recording industry—are so massive and powerful that they would otherwise simply overwhelm Canadian popular culture.

prime-time: the most-watched period of television viewing, usually 7 p.m. to 11 p.m.

Table 8–6	Canadian content for Canadian Specialty Channels (for the year 2001)		
Network	Yearly % Canadian Content	Network	Yearly % Canadian Content
Bravo	60%	Much More Music	60%
CBC Newsworld	90%	Much Music	60%
CMT	40%	Outdoor Life	30%
Comedy Network	58%	Prime TV	50%
CTV News 1	100%	Showcase	60%
CTV Sports Net	60%	Space	30%
Discovery	60%	SuperChannel	25%
Family Channel	25%	Teletoon	60%
Headline Sports	100%	The Movie Network	25%
HGTV	50%	Treehouse	60%
History TV	33.3%	TSN	70%
Life	70%	Vision	50%
Moviemax (west)	20%	WTN	60%
Moviepix (east)	20%	YTV	70%

In the table above, the percentage of Canadian content varies, but it is lowest in the movie channels. Why do you think that is so?

WHAT DO YOU THINK?

1. Make a four-column chart of Canadian writers, actors, musicians, television shows, and sports figures. Analyze your list from the point of view of whether or not their achievements enhance your pride in being a Canadian.

2. Brainstorm a list of Canadian images, institutions, and symbols. Do they help to define a Canadian identity? Why or why not?

3. How have Canadian-content regulations both helped and harmed Canada's music industry? Should these regulations be strengthened, maintained, or removed? Provide at least three reasons for your position.

4. How do CRTC content regulations help the Canadian film and television industry? How do they restrict the business activities of owners of specialty channels? Do you think the regulations are justified? Explain.

National Film Board was created to produce Canadian documentaries and feature films. The National Library of Canada was established in 1953. In 1957, the Canada Council was formed with a mandate to promote the study and enjoyment of Canadian culture through grants to cultural groups ranging from painting, to publishing, to theatre.

Those who believe in government support of culture, believe that culture forms the basis of a nation's sense of itself, and of its citizens sense of identity. But cultural activities and products also form a part of the economy. The Canadian government's role in protecting and promoting Canadian culture has often become a point of angry debate within Canada. It has also become a flashpoint between Canada and the United States as trading patterns change and trade agreements continue to be negotiated and tested.

Freer Trade and Protectionism

Canada welcomed foreign investment during the1950s and 1960s as post-World-War-II development blasted off in a series of megaprojects and branch-plant expansions. In the 1970s, however, the Liberal government of Prime Minister Pierre Elliot Trudeau developed programs to control the growth of foreign investment. Their objective was to protect the Canadian economy from becoming entirely dominated by US and foreign investment.

In 1971, the Trudeau government set up the Canada Development Corporation to promote investment in Canadian-controlled companies. Three years later, it created Petro-Canada as a Canadian-owned pres-

ence in the oil and natural gas industries. At about the same time, the Foreign Investment Review Agency was established to regulate foreign acquisitions of Canadian enterprises and to screen new foreign investment. The Trudeau government clearly had a nationalist economic agenda. In 1980, the Trudeau government introduced the National Energy Program. It was designed to make Canada self-sufficient in its oil supply and to increase Canadian ownership in the energy sector.

All of these programs did significantly reduce US dominance of the Canadian economy. But many

Figure 8–31 Pierre Trudeau's National Energy Program was intended to make Canada self-sufficient in energy, but in Alberta it meant big losses. This protester, who is standing outside the Alberta Legislature in Edmonton in 1980, wears a mask of Trudeau.

trade blocs: groups of nations linked to promote trade

countervail: a special tax to protect domestic products from subsidized foreign imports

anti-dumping duty: a special tariff imposed on imports being sold at an unreasonably low price

Canadian business leaders were critical of the measures and of the government's increasing regulation of the economy. The US government complained about the National Energy Program and the Foreign Investment Review Agency. They also threatened to retaliate against Canadian firms operating in the US.

During the 1980s, new global trends were emerging. New international **trade blocs** were forming. These threatened Canadian-based enterprises, whose exported products and services might be shut out of foreign markets. As developing nations began to compete in the global economy, world prices for commodities started to tumble because of increased supply. At the same time, new technologies were rapidly changing the face of global trade. Many Canadian industries were falling behind.

Particularly disturbing to Canadians was a US Congress that seemed to be filled with protectionist rhetoric. **Countervails** and **anti-dumping duties** were slapped on Canadian products that had been trading relatively freely for years. Trade irritants between Canada and the US became commonplace. Canada's future relationship with its largest trading partner was in doubt.

By 1983, Trudeau's government had become increasingly unpopular, and he resigned. In the 1984 federal election, the Liberals, under John Turner, were defeated. Conservative leader Brian Mulroney became Canada's new prime minister. Almost immediately Canada's economic direction shifted. The Mulroney Conservatives had a continentalist ideology, one which favoured less government interference in the economy and free mar-

kets. The National Energy Program was dismantled. The Foreign Investment Review Agency was replaced by Investment Canada, an agency that was more welcoming to foreign investment. In his first official speech after being elected, Prime Minister Brian Mulroney told US business leaders in New York that Canada was "open for business." But during the Conservative leadership campaign, he had said something to the contrary:

> **PRIMARY SOURCE** "Don't talk to me about free trade. That issue was decided in 1911. Free trade is a danger to Canadian sovereignty. You will hear none of it from me."

It was a fact that global trading patterns were changing quickly. International competition was increasing. Canadian exports faced a very real threat—access to the US market could become dramatically restricted. Consequently, the Mulroney government negotiated the Canada-US Free Trade Agreement, which was signed in 1988.

Mulroney's government was committed to a free-trade philosophy. Negotiations involving Canada, the US, and Mexico quickly followed the Canada-US agreement, and were successfully finalized. Prime Minister Mulroney resigned in 1993. Under Prime Minister Kim Campbell, the Conservatives went down to humiliating defeat in the 1993 federal election. In 1994, the new Liberal government, under Prime Minister Jean Chretien, ratified the North American Free Trade Agreement (NAFTA).

North America was becoming a trading bloc.

Foreign Investment—Does It Always Benefit Canada?

Debates about foreign investment in Canada are often intellectually challenging and emotionally charged. They involve issues of control, both national and personal. At their root is a question: what is the best route for Canada to take with foreign investment in an era of increasing globalization? This question raises even more questions. For example, what role should government play in the Canadian economy? Should it closely regulate foreign investment? Should it court foreign investment?

When making its foreign-investment policies, the Canadian government's decisions directly affect the lives of countless Canadians. In *The Vancouver Sun* reports below, two sides of the debate are revealed.

Figure 8–32 While on a trade mission to China in 1994, Prime Minister Jean Chretien shakes hands with a guard near the Great Wall. In the last years of the twentieth century, the Canadian government actively pursued international trade and foreign investment. Do you think this was the right choice?

PRIMARY SOURCE Governments promise jobs, but foreigners deliver them—nearly 1 million last year alone, says a new ... study for Industry Canada. And that estimate is the minimum, concludes the groundbreaking study, which may put the final nail in the coffin of Canadian economic nationalism ... a draft summary obtained by Southam News claims that every $1 billion in foreign direct investment will generate at least 65,000 jobs within six years. Throw in the potential impact of the ensuing increase in exports and the number could be 114,000 jobs ...

"Basically, what we're finding out," said economist Ross Preston, "is that these pools of capital which are flowing around the world with management expertise, technology, and everything else tied to them are a lot more potent ... than the ... things a domestic economy can do on its own." The job-creation potential of foreign direct investment, he said, is anywhere from double to five times what domestic investment is generally thought to generate ...

"Supercharged" is the term the study uses to explain the multiplier effect of foreign direct investment. Nor does it matter whether the investment is the result of a takeover, a merger, an expansion into Canada, the startup of a new company, or the reinvestment of profits. "Normally, we thought of foreign investment as loss of control or loss of profits," Preston said. "This, in my mind, is something very new and very important for policy makers to sit up and look at." Industry Minister John Manley already has. "We're competing for that investment," Manley said. "We're after the jobs that come with that."

Volvo Canada is shutting down its only North American car-assembly plant, throwing 223 people out of work by Christmas. "We appreciate the efforts of you and your colleagues in your dedicated work at Volvo," vice-president Curt Germundsson told stunned employees … at the Halifax plant. "Unfortunately, your efforts alone do not outweigh the global business factors." Many of the local workers have been with the Swedish automaker for more than twenty years, some since the plant opened in 1963. The decision was made … [that] the S70 and V70 models will now be produced at a giant plant in Europe, which has not been operating at full capacity …

Gord Sonnenberg, president of Volvo Canada Ltd., said there was nothing workers could do to change the situation. "The bottom line is that we have a tremendous amount of excess capacity in our other plants. To make additional investment to repeat what we already have in place in our European plants just doesn't make good business sense."

Larry Wark of the Canadian Autoworkers union said the shutdown is a shock. "This is a fairly new facility; historically, this plant has been at the very top of Volvo corporate productivity charts." Wark blamed Ottawa for steadily dropping tariffs and opening up foreign trade. "That's really the bottom line of what's happening here. The tariffs have been steadily going down for the last eight years to the point where there is no real advantage to having a plant located in Halifax."

WHAT DO YOU THINK?

1. There are two different viewpoints expressed in these newspaper reports. Based on your reading of the reports, complete a PMI chart about foreign investment in Canada.

2. After carefully reviewing your chart, write a letter to the editor of your local newspaper about whether or not you support increased foreign investment.

3. Imagine that you are a worker who has just lost your job at the Volvo plant and that you read the positive report on foreign investment in your morning newspaper. How would you react to this report?

4. Curt Germundsson identified two sides of foreign investment—workers and their "efforts," and "global business factors." List the factors that tipped the balance in one way or the other.

ACTIVITIES

1. What is the "brain drain"? Would you move to the United States for a better job, or would you lose too much by leaving Canada? Explain.

2. In an organizer, list the differences between a sectoral and a comprehensive free-trade agreement.

3. Canadians have been described as having a "branch-plant" mentality. As a class, brainstorm what this description means. Do you believe that it is true?

4. Do you believe that Canada's identity is threatened or supported by its close links with the US? Give examples of why you believe this is so. Keep in mind such things as media, culture, natural resources, technology, and research.

FREER TRADE IN NORTH AMERICA

To understand the concept of freer trade, it is necessary to be familiar with managed trade. Managed trade has developed around the world over hundreds of years. As governments tried to protect their home industries, they developed systems to discourage the free flow of goods across borders. They are called "tariffs" and "non-tariff barriers," such as **quotas,** content regulations, and **embargoes.** Free trade means the complete removal of all these obstacles.

In the last decades of the twentieth century, many trade barriers were challenged and removed. But in the real world, true free trade is hard—if not impossible—to achieve.

What happened instead is "freer trade." Freer trade is a compromise. It means that the trend towards removing barriers continues, but that individual nations retain the right to enact protective measures.

The 1989 Canada-US Free Trade Agreement

The 1965 Auto Pact between Canada and the US set a precedent. Its success led to many other sectoral free-trade agreements between the two countries. In fact, by 1988, nearly 80 percent of all trade between Canada and the United States was bound by bilateral agreements.

quotas: limits on the amounts of various products that can be imported into a county

embargo: suspension of trading or commercial activities

Figure 8–33 Close ties between Prime Minister Mulroney (left) and US President Reagan (centre left) paved the way for the Canada–US Free Trade Agreement. Do you think this agreement was good for Canada? Why or why not?

Table 8–7   **Percentage breakdown of Canada's Total Merchandise Exports**

Year	To US	To Pacific Rim	To Europe
1988	74.5	20	6
1996	81	12	6

In March 1985, during the Shamrock Summit in Quebec City, Prime Minister Brian Mulroney and President Ronald Reagan started to plan a comprehensive free-trade agreement between Canada and the United States. Public reaction during the years of negotiations was passionate and divided in both countries. In Canada, those who opposed the agreement feared that it would allow US business to exploit Canada's economy and overwhelm Canadian culture. Those who supported free trade argued that without it, Canada's economy would decline irretrievably and become uncompetitive.

Nonetheless, an agreement was reached and ratified by both countries. On January 1, 1989, the Canada-US Free Trade Agreement (FTA) came into effect. A comprehensive bilateral agreement, it covered every sector of the two economies, including service industries. Trade restrictions between the two countries were to be phased out by 1998.

The agreement included a number of features and terms. The binational Free Trade Dispute Panel was set up, and its decisions in trade disputes were binding. No export subsidies were permitted. Canada's restrictions on foreign-ownership were reduced. All restrictions on energy exports and imports were removed. The Auto Pact and Canada's agricultural marketing boards were maintained.

Canada's cultural industries—publishing, movies, TV, cable, satellite broadcasting, music, radio—were exempt.

The Free Trade Agreement, obviously, did not create totally free trade. It created freer trade. Trade barriers were reduced, but both nations could, and did, impose retaliatory measures if they felt trading practices were unfair. As the agreement came into effect, many critics on both sides of the border criticized it for not promoting fair trade. Political interference often disrupted trade relations. The binding trade-dispute panel worked, but often slowly. Within five years, however, trade between the two nations increased tremendously. And Canada enjoyed a large trade surplus.

Many Canadian companies restructured their operations and introduced innovative technologies and management systems. They successfully marketed their products and services to American consumers and beyond. Other Canadian companies even relocated or opened offices or branches in the US, drawn by lower labour costs and lower taxes. In the first few years, manufacturing in Canada was hard hit. Many plants closed or moved, with large job losses.

After the first ten years of freer trade between Canada and the United States, it was difficult to evaluate how well the agreement was working, or whether Canada had benefited substantially. The figures were impressive. The value of Canadian exports to the United States more than doubled within the first ten years. In 1997, the value of Canada's exports to the US was $243.36 billion. In 1989, it had been $98.5 billion. The Canadian merchandise trade surplus also grew dramatically. Still, many questions about the impact of the FTA on Canada's economy—and its culture—remained unanswered.

Has Free Trade Been Good for Canada?

Canadians hold strong opinions about the Canada-US Free Trade Agreement. For some, it was a logical step in Canada's historic relationship with the US and an opening towards greater prosperity. For others, it was a blow to Canada's sovereignty, of its absolute power to determine its fate independently. Many Canadians fall somewhere in between these two points of view, as the quotes below reveal.

Figure 8–34 In 1988, anti-free-trade protestors greeted Brian Mulroney in Calgary. Is "fraud" an accurate way to describe the Canada-US Free Trade Agreement? Explain.

> We're doing massive trade with the US, so there's no question in my mind that whatever the weaknesses might be, the general relationship has been an astounding success.
>
> –Simon Reisman, chief Canadian negotiator for the FTA, 1997

Clearly, it [the FTA] was oversold by both sides. We said it was going to be Nirvana; they said it was going to be the apocalypse. It's obviously somewhere in between.

–Sylvia Ostry, a former Canadian trade ambassador, 1997

I always felt Canadians would get a lot more self-confidence when they listened to all those doom and gloom stories and then realized this thing we feared for 100 years [free trade with the US] turned out to be a modest step in the right direction.

–Richard Lipsey, economics professor, 1997

We are progressively moving towards American standards whether you look at the erosion in health care or the erosion in education or unemployment insurance. We were promised this agreement would bring us a better economy, a better standard of living ... more productivity ... it has brought us none of those things.

–Mel Hurtig, publisher, 1997

It's too hard to disentangle this [FTA] from all of the other events that have been happening. We're not even trying to do it.

–Philip Cross, manager of Statistics Canada, Economic Analysis Division, 1997

Some economists believed that the increased trade would have occurred with or without the FTA, since almost 80 percent of Canada-US trade had been covered by sectoral free-trade agreements prior to 1989. Others said that without the FTA, Canada would have lost its access to the US market.

One of the biggest concerns still came down to the sheer size and strength of the US economy compared to Canada's. At times, American interest groups successfully lobbied the US government to impose trade measures that punished Canada. A succession of Canadian products were targeted: softwood lumber, durum wheat, sugar, beer, magazines, pork, raspberries, steel, and so on. In most instances, Canadian trade lawyers successfully appealed the US countervails and had them removed. The Free Trade Dispute Panel, however, could take a very long time to reach its final decision. This could be crip-

pling to small Canadian companies. Many Canadian companies complained that this was an FTA loophole that favoured the Americans in trade disputes. Many American companies complained that Canadian industry was unfairly subsidized by the Canadian government. The cultural issues and the trade disputes are ongoing. They are not easily resolved.

1994 North American Free Trade Agreement

After years of negotiations, the Canada-US Free Trade Agreement expanded and became a continental freer trade system. On January 1, 1994, the North American Free Trade Agreement (NAFTA) came into effect. NAFTA extended the earlier trade arrangement to Mexico and set out a schedule to reduce tariffs between the three countries over a ten-year period. The agreement was hailed by some as creating the

Figure 8–35 This cartoon makes a statement about US power in NAFTA. Do you agree?

world's largest trading bloc. This was not entirely accurate. None of the three countries compromised their sovereignty. They did not adopt a common trade policy—in other words, Mexico, Canada, and the US did not set up common trade barriers against non-member nations. In fact, the three nations have engaged in many trade disputes since the agreement was signed.

Trade disputes aside, NAFTA did establish a "free-trade area." This means that tariffs and non-tariff barriers were eliminated among the member nations. But each partner can independently determine trade policies with other countries. To be a more effective, integrated trade bloc, the NAFTA members would have had to form a customs union, setting up common trade barriers against non-members. This the European Union has done, as you will learn in Chapter 10. Many Canadians, however, opposed NAFTA becoming a trade bloc. They feared it would be dominated by the US, and that Canadian interests would suffer.

From a Canadian perspective, NAFTA's provisions were mostly carry-overs from the 1989 Canada-US Free Trade Agreement. However, there were additions and changes. The Auto Pact, for example, was preserved, but the North American content requirement was raised from 50 percent to 62.5 percent. At first, many Canadian businesses saw this as a setback, but soon the Canadian auto-parts industry adapted and took advantage of the new trade relationship. Canada's marketing boards for eggs, poultry, and dairy products were left untouched, but tariffs on all other food products are to be removed within fifteen years.

Canada also agreed to share available energy sources with the United States when and if the US experienced a shortage. Mexico received an exemption on this clause. This development completely undercut the goals of Trudeau's now-defunct National Energy Program. Canadians with nationalist beliefs viewed the agreement as a threat to the future of Canada's energy supply and to its right to self-determination. Under NAFTA, Canada also agreed to share bulk water supplies with the US, if that country were to experience serious water shortages. Again, this provoked an outcry from those with environmental concerns, and from nationalists. As you learned in Chapter 5, as far back as Macdonald's National Policy, the government of Canada had created a national infrastructure to establish east-west trade within Canada. With NAFTA, the pattern of trade was pulled in a north-south direction.

Some Canadian industries fully supported continental freer trade. Telecommunications, transportation, and environmental-safety companies expected to increase business in Mexico, as did banks, insurance companies, and financial services. Again, those in favour of NAFTA argued that Canada must adapt to the new, highly competitive, global economy. It must look outward and forge stronger international trade links. Other Canadians worried about becoming part of a continental trade system. They were concerned about the state of human rights in Mexico, especially in the poorer provinces. They questioned Mexico's environmental regulations, the low wage structure, and the treatment of female workers in the

DID YOU KNOW?

Maquiladoras are zones in Mexico where component parts can be imported duty-free. Parts are assembled into finished goods, but for export only. Often, low wages and slack environmental laws attract foreign businesses to set up in these zones. In January 1998 alone, forty-two maquiladora assembly plants were constructed in Mexico, generating 7306 new jobs.

maquiladora zones. Also, some worried that low-end assembly jobs would be transferred from Canada to the Mexican maquiladoras, just as American jobs had been. A number of union leaders predicted that Canadian management negotiators might threaten to move operations to Mexico to get labour concessions during contract disputes. Some Canadians believed that a flood of cheaper Mexican goods would jeopardize Canadian companies in the domestic market.

Initial studies of NAFTA's impact on the Canadian economy put some, but not all, of these concerns to rest. In the years following NAFTA's ratification, trade figures between Canada and the United States continued to climb. And in the first year of NAFTA, trade between Canada and Mexico rose a remarkable 21 percent. Also, as predicted, Canadian high-tech and finance companies gained inroads into the Mexican economy.

ACTIVITIES

1. Why are the Canada-US Free Trade Agreement and NAFTA examples of "freer trade" and not "free trade"? Give examples to support your answer.

2. Analyze the primary source quotes on page 337. Classify them according to whether they favour the FTA, oppose the FTA, or fall somewhere in between. Which statements do you most agree with? Explain.

3. What does Mel Hurtig (page 337) mean by "American standards"? Hurtig gives three examples. Can you think of others?

4. After more than a decade, public opinion is still divided over the Canada-US FTA and NAFTA. Why would some Canadians support the idea that these agreements were good for Canada, and others that they were bad? Give details to support your conclusions.

CONCLUSION

In the early twentieth century, Prime Minister Wilfrid Laurier claimed the century for Canada. At the end of the twentieth century, Finance Minister Paul Martin predicted that "the twenty-first century belongs to Canada." The reality for most Canadians, however, was not so simple. As the twentieth century progressed, Canada became urbanized. Its economy went from being resource-and manufacturing-based to one in which most people worked in service industries. In Canada's economic regions, many traditional economic activities declined, while there was growth in other areas. One thing became clear—all regions of Canada had to diversify to remain prosperous.

In the late twentieth century, technological innovations also led to a more globalized economy. Employment patterns and educational needs shifted. Fewer workers were needed in manufacturing, farming, and the resource industries. Canadians adapted, and several Canadian businesses became international leaders in food processing and in high-tech mining, communications, and transportation technology.

In terms of trade, investment, and culture, the influence of the United States grew throughout the century. In 1989, the Canada-US Free Trade Agreement linked Canada more closely to the US. Many saw this as a betrayal of Macdonald's National Policy, and a threat to Canada's identity and sovereignty. Five years later, Canada joined NAFTA. Debates about Canadian independence still erupt, particularly during trade disputes with the US. Economic figures show, however, that trade with the US and Mexico has increased dramatically since the agreements came into effect. As a trading nation, this is good news for Canada.

SUMMARY ACTIVITIES

1. Imagine that it is ten years in the future. After rereading this chapter, prepare a resume with the intention of finding meaningful employment. Include all of the education and training you pursued over the past ten years. Also include a description of your work attitude, particularly your ability to work as a team member in a constantly changing environment.

2. Based on what you have learned in this chapter, make predictions about Canada's economic future. Will Canada survive in the twenty-first century? Why or why not? Will regional disparity remain a major issue?

ON YOUR OWN

1. Using newspapers, the library and/or the Internet, research trade disputes between Canada and the United States. You might consider long-standing disputes such as those over softwood lumber or US magazine split-runs. What has your research uncovered about relations between Canada and the US? Has free trade meant fair trade since the Canada-US FTA was introduced? Why or why not? Give details to support your conclusions. You will find more information about this topic in Chapter 10.

2. Films such as *Goin' Down the Road* (on page 301) can have a social impact. The 1969 film reflected hard times in Atlantic Canada and raised public awareness. Research the film. Find old reviews, for example, and rent the video. Write a report describing how it affected awareness of economic hardship in Canada and whether or not it still has that kind of power.

3. Research an environmental issue that has strained relations between Canada and the United States. For example, the acid rain issue, Great Lakes pollution, water-diversion projects or water for export (you will find information about water for export in Chapter 9.) Prepare a report, based on your research, that assesses whether Canada maintains an independent position or is forced to compromise.

9 THE ECONOMY OF BRITISH COLUMBIA

OUTCOMES

In this chapter you will examine the economic geography of British Columbia. By the end of the chapter, you will

- identify and understand the main economic divisions of British Columbia

- analyze the role of geography in the economy of British Columbia

- identify and understand the principal components of the British Columbia economy

- analyze the changing nature of the British Columbia economy

- account for the disparities between the regions of British Columbia

- demonstrate an understanding of the demographic and locational changes of the British Columbia population

Go North, Young Woman!

This fictional story is set at the University of Northern British Columbia (UNBC), near Prince George. Jennifer Spencer and Kirsty Mills, students at UNBC, are both interested in forest management, but their views have been shaped by very different circumstances. Read on to find out why.

Jennifer could hear someone get up and walk toward the door of the residence apartment. It opened quickly, revealing a tall, athletic girl with a blond pony tail.

"I'm Jennifer Spencer," she said, looking hesitantly at the girl. "I think my room is here?"

"Come on in, you must be in that bedroom to the right—I'm Kirsty Mills, by the way."

Jennifer peeked at the small room. It was half the size of her bedroom at home in Vancouver. Well, she thought, I guess I can handle it for eight months.

"It's all yours. Make yourself at home. Do you need any help unloading stuff?" asked Kirsty.

"Sure," said Jennifer, "My suitcases and boxes are in my car."

"I take it you're not from Prince George," Kirsty asked, as she reached for a box in the trunk.

The University of Northern British Columbia, seen from the air

343

"Well, not anymore," Jennifer explained. "I was born here, but my parents moved to Vancouver before I finished grade school. You know, I didn't recognize much when I drove in. Other than **Mr. P.G.**, that is."

"So why didn't you go to university down south?"

"Oh, I've wanted to go to UNBC ever since it opened in 1994," Jennifer said, grabbing three shopping bags and Doofus, her stuffed bear. "I figured it would be a lot more personal than the big universities down south. Besides, I want to get into tourism and UNBC has some great courses—like resource-based tourism. I've always been interested in the environment and resources,

particularly forestry, so I thought I should get out of the city to do that. And the fact I was born here probably had something to do with it, too."

"Hey, we're on the same track," said Kirsty, smiling. "I'm studying resources management and northern studies. And you're right—we have a great community atmosphere here. The campus is very compact, and everything's in walking distance. They've even connected all the buildings so you don't have to go outside in winter."

"What about you?" asked Jennifer, as they climbed the residence stairs. She noted with awe that Kirsty, weighed down with two boxes, could take them two at a time. "Are you

from around here?"

"Nah, I'm from Fort St. James, northwest of here about 150 kilometres. Just north of Vanderhoof. Hey, you know something? It's amazing this university got built at all. If it weren't here, I'm not sure I could have gone to a university down south. It's a fact that fewer students in northern BC go to university than in southern BC."

"Why would that be?" Jennifer asked, placing her bags on the bed.

"I'm not sure," Kirsty replied. "Probably has to do with the distance and cost, or maybe even a lack of familiarity with higher-ed institutions—you know, having a university nearby and getting the idea of

Jennifer and Kirsty discover that they both want careers in forest management.

The bright and airy courtyard at UNBC immediately appealed to Jennifer.

going there. It probably also has something to do with the availability of jobs in forestry and some of the other resource industries."

"So how did it get built?"

Kirsty flopped down on the bed and picked up Doofus by his ear. "He's so cute. Long-standing attachment?"

Jennifer nodded.

"I guess you could call it 'people power'——the efforts and persistence of some folks in the northern half of British Columbia. I know. My mom was part of the original com-

mittee. Do you know that 16 000 people signed a petition in favour of a northern university and paid $5.00 a piece to show how serious they were?"

Jennifer tried to keep herself from frowning as Kirsty twirled Doofus cheerfully by his ears. "The ball really got rolling in 1989 when the Minister of Advanced Education opened his mouth and changed feet."

"What did he say?"

"Oh, my mother kept the clipping from the *Globe and Mail*. It's practically glued to our fridge door—all that's miss-

ing is a frame. He actually said that in the interior 'people don't think beyond Grade 10. The questions they ask at the end of the day are: How many trees did you cut today? or How were things down in the mine?' As you can see, it's been quoted so often around our house, I've memorized it. Boy, was my mom steaming, and so were all the people up here. I heard the government got 3000 letters over that. My mom used to point at the fridge and say, 'Don't worry Kirsty. When you're ready for university, it'll be there for you in Prince George.' Anyway, enough of that. Do you want a tour?"

"I'm really impressed with the buildings I've seen so far," said Jennifer as she and Kirsty walked through the Student Services Street, one of the connecting buildings. "They're even more beautiful than on the UNBC website. I can't get over how bright and airy they are, and the use of wood really gives it a natural feeling."

"Yeah, they call this whole complex the **agora**," said Kirsty. "That means a 'gathering place' in ancient Greece. The wood's supposed to reflect the forest industry as the economic backbone of this area."

Later in the student food court, Jennifer noticed four long scars on Kirsty's upper arm when she reached for a bottle of ketchup.

"I call those my war wounds," Kirsty laughed, sensing Jennifer's curiosity. "I got them when I was tree planting

345

in the Quesnel area this past summer. Probably a black bear. Looks worse than it is."

"What do you mean 'probably'?" Jennifer asked. "Don't you know?"

"No, I have no idea what hit me. I was sleeping in the tent and I guess the bear was scavenging and must have smelled something in the camp. We'd taken the usual precautions in bear country and secured all the food—most tree planters do. Anyway, I'd rolled over to the side of the tent and I guess it was just determined. It thought my shape looked promising and took a swipe. My screaming must have scared it off, because the next thing I knew, I was on the way to hospital in Quesnel. Nobody saw the bear."

"Why do you think it came to your camp?" Jennifer asked, as she wiped her mouth.

"Oh, I don't know. Bears learn quickly to associate food with people. Also, there are an awful lot of tourists coming into that area now, what with Barkerville and the Bowron Lakes. Some people think it's a big joke to feed bears. And with the dry spring and summer, the berries were probably not very good that year. I'm sure it was really hungry."

"That's so sad," said Jennifer. "I mean, you were attacked, but think of that poor animal. Imagine if it were a mother looking for food for her cub."

"You're absolutely right. I mean, we were invading its habitat. As more areas are logged, bears and other animals

are finding it harder to survive. It's something you just have to accept. Tree planting takes place in bear country."

"So," Jennifer said, draining her juice, and realizing that she was more than slightly impressed by Kirsty's experience, "What did you work at last summer?"

"Tree planting, of course," Kirsty chuckled. "What else? I have my trusty extra-strength pepper spray. Seriously, there aren't too many places a girl can get a good-paying job for the summer. I don't want to finish university with a $20 000 or $30 000 debt. I'm trying to keep the student loans to a minimum."

"I know what you mean. My parents pay most of my costs because I'm so poor. So far, I've gotten only minimum wage jobs, and what I make in a summer doesn't nearly cover the cost of tuition, books, and accommodation. Mind you, there was a little brouhaha when I told them I wanted to go to UNBC. They wanted me to go to their **alma mater**, UBC, and they wanted me to stay home. Anyway, as long as I'm doing well, they'll pay."

"Well, I might be able to get you a job tree planting," Kirsty offered. "That is—ahem—if you aren't scared off by bears. Mind you, your first year won't be any picnic."

"But I don't know a thing about tree planting," Jennifer interjected, though the idea certainly appealed to her.

"Most people don't know

much when they start off. It's backbreaking work and you don't make a lot of money the first year. It's **piecework**. You're paid by the number of trees you plant, or sometimes by the hectare, seldom by the hour. Apart from rain, heat, mosquitoes, black flies, and bears, you have to contend with the conditions in a clear-cut. You have to walk all day on uneven terrain, climb hills, and make your way past all the stumps, rotten trees, and branches. In the meantime, you're rhythmically sticking your trowel into the ground, stuffing a seedling in the hole, flattening it with your foot, and moving on two

metres. Oh, and by the way, you're repeating that for eight to twelve hours."

"Sounds like an awfully hard way to make a living," Jennifer said pensively as they left the Food Court.

"And if the work doesn't get you, the living conditions might. In some camps, hygiene is, well, how do I say this delicately—sometimes not a priority. You can even get sick. And having said all that," Kirsty sighed, "there is no guarantee I'll be planting next year."

"Why is that?" Jennifer asked.

"Since the downturn in the forest industry in the 1990s, lots of workers have been laid off, some permanently. You know, like Gold River, the pulp mill town that closed down in 1999. They obviously get first call on forest-related jobs. Although there are also a lot of jobs in **silviculture**."

"Is that where they work to ensure the seedlings survive," Jennifer offered, "by thinning brush and protecting them from pests and the like?"

"Hmm, that and more," Kirsty nodded as they headed across the campus to the library. "It's probably the most important part of regenerating the forest. Doesn't matter how well the tree planters do their job, if many of the seedlings don't grow to maturity. Hey, I guess that's why we're in resource and environmental courses. At least we're starting to move away from exploitation for immediate gain to long-term economic and environmental sustainability. Oh, honestly, I'm beginning to sound like my professor!" Kirsty burst out laughing.

"I'd like to think that's true," Jennifer nodded, "but sometimes I'm not sure. I remember reading that we're still not reforesting at the rate we're harvesting—something like logging twice as much land as we replant every year. Does that sound right?"

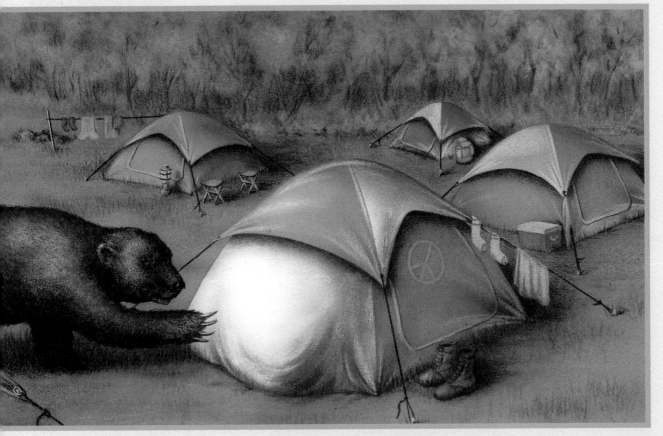

As Kirsty lay sleeping in her tent after a long day of tree planting, the bear took a swipe.

Kirsty paused before answering. "Could be. I've heard all kinds of figures. Most people don't know that 30 percent of logged land can regenerate itself. But one thing I do know for sure is that they are cutting more trees with fewer people. My dad was laid off from the plywood mill he worked in. The company installed a new lathe and cut twice as much wood with half the workforce. It's the same story all over. I know the companies need to introduce technological change to stay competitive, but it has really hurt the workforce in the in the last decade.

"And it's so hard for people to adjust to a new reality. My dad, for instance—he never adjusted. He keeps saying that after thirty-five years in the woods, he doesn't know how to do anything else. In the central interior there wasn't much to do, outside resource industries. He managed to get some work on forest renewal projects—you know, removing old logging roads and thinning 40-hectare blocks of brush, saplings, and weeds."

Jennifer stopped and scanned the beautiful scenery. "I'm sorry to hear that. In the lower mainland you get out of touch with what's happening in the rest of the province."

"It's also why I'm here," Kirsty motioned around the campus. "My mother was determined that I wouldn't be put in the same situation as my dad."

"What really makes me mad about this situation," Jennifer interjected, "is that raw logs are still being exported from BC, amazing as that sounds. We could be **adding value** to our wood, and putting people like your dad to work."

"It's true," Kirsty added, "It's something to do with our international trade agreement. Someone estimated that there is one job lost for every 1000 cubic metres of timber cut. Exporting wood doesn't seem to make a lot of sense."

"You know," Jennifer said, "I don't want to sound noble and all, but it's up to us and coming generations to make sure the forests are managed in a sustainable manner."

Kirsty nodded enthusiastically. "In my two years in resource management I've been looking at the idea of multiple use for our forest resources. Keeping the industry strong, but also doing something to preserve recreational space and habitats—that's a tall order. Forests will be a big part of the provincial economy for years to come, if we do something now."

All of a sudden, Jennifer realized, eight months seemed like no time at all.

Mr. P.G.: a large logger-figure made from logs, standing at the entrance to Prince George

agora: in ancient Greece, a market place

alma mater: the college or university a person attended. Latin for "fostering mother."

piecework: work that is done and paid for by the piece

silviculture: the science of breeding and developing healthy trees

adding value: adding economic value through secondary production

ACTIVITIES

1. Jennifer and Kirsty are very different young women. As a class, itemize all the differences you notice. Can you suggest some reasons for these differences?

2. What do you think of the former minister's comments about the people who live in the province's interior?

3. What happened to Kirsty's father? Why? How did it affect him?

4. Do you think Jennifer will spend the following summer planting trees? Explain.

TIME LINE

1912 • BC PASSES FIRST FORESTRY ACT

1947 • FORESTRY ACT IS REVISED TO ENSURE FORESTS ARE PROTECTED

1973 • BC GOVERNMENT ESTABLISHES LAND COMMISSION TO PROTECT FARMLAND

1987 • UNITED NATIONS REPORT ON THE ENVIRONMENT

1990 • PACIFIC COAST SALMON INDUSTRY HAS BEGUN TO COLLAPSE
BC MINING INDUSTRY STARTS TO DECLINE

1995 • FOREST PRACTICES CODE REGULATES HARVESTING AND REPLANTING

1996 • CANADIAN GOVERNMENT CUTS CANADIAN SALMON FLEET BY HALF

1997 • BC FILM INDUSTRY INJECTS $630 MILLION INTO THE PROVINCIAL ECONOMY

1998 • HIGH-TECH IS THE FASTEST GROWING SECTOR OF THE BC ECONOMY

1999 • DAIMLER-CHRYSLER UNVEILS FIRST DRIVEABLE CAR USING BALLARD POWER TECHNOLOGY

Crossing the Rockies, you are in a new country, as if you had crossed a national frontier. Everyone feels it, even the stranger, feels the change of outlook, tempo, and attitude.

–BRUCE HUTCHISON

British Columbia has always thought of itself as being different from other provinces. The mountains not only separate it from the rest of Canada, but determine the identity of its people. For Emily Carr, for example, the power of British Columbia was in its "power and intensity everywhere." This rugged land has determined the economy, politics, and identity of the nearly 4 million people who call Canada's unique western province home. Do you agree with the views of Bruce Hutchison and Emily Carr?

INTRODUCTION

British Columbia has a vast and varied landscape. Its 952 263 square kilometres include mountains, plateaus, plains, valleys, and coastal islands. Canada's third largest province is nearly three times as big as Japan, four times as big as Great Britain, and bigger than the states of Washington, Oregon, and California combined.

British Columbia's size and physical diversity have affected its economy in many ways. From the earliest times, its people have drawn on its natural resources—fish, furs, metals, and timber. Although the provinces dependency on forestry, fishing, and mining is decreasing, most of its wealth still comes from these primary industries. Today, however, British Columbia's service sector is now a significant part of the economy, a trend seen in many other industrialized nations. Tourism and filmmaking, along with other service industries, are growing at an impressive pace. The province also has a large number of people working in high technology, in both product development and information. These trends indicate that British Columbia's economy is becomingly increasingly global.

As you learned in Chapter 8, many changes occurred in the Canadian economy in the last two decades of the twentieth century. The economy of British Columbia was no exception. Its natural resource base was gradually eroded and its industries expanded and contracted with global economic stresses. Downsizing, fluctuating employment rates, and new trading relationships are examples of how these stresses were—and continue to

to generalize: to draw a conclusion from many pieces of information

Economic data taken over time can be presented in a table to display patterns and trends. In this way, **generalizations** can be made by comparing the data from several years. Make three generalizations that you observe from the data on British Columbia's GDP over the last century.

| Table 9–1 | Percentage Changes in Gross Domestic Product Distribution |

British Columbia, 1880 to 1990

	Primary products	Primary Manufacturing	Secondary Manufacturing	Services
1880	49.7	8.4	8.8	33.1
1890	30.5	7.0	12.1	50.4
1900	41.2	8.6	7.0	43.2
1910	28.9	10.6	8.2	52.3
1920	23.2	9.6	7.5	59.7
1930	18.4	11.0	6.0	63.7
1940	22.0	12.4	8.3	57.3
1950	18.4	14.5	9.6	57.5
1960	10.6	11.3	10.3	67.8
1970	8.9	9.1	8.2	73.8
1980	11.3	10.0	7.6	71.1
1990	10.4	9.2	8.8	72.8
1997	8.8	6.9	10.0	74.4

be—played out. The opening of a mine in Chile or a paper plant in Malaysia—or even a period of slow growth in the European economy—will eventually be noticed in your neighbourhood. In Chapter 10, you will have the opportunity to explore these global links in more detail. In this chapter, you will begin to see how the economic well-being of British Columbia is tied to the well-being, and the interests, of many.

BRITISH COLUMBIA'S RESOURCES: AN OVERVIEW

Natural resources form the backbone of British Columbia's economy. Because of its varied climate and physical geography, our province has many **renewable** and **non-renewable resources**. Abundant forests—coastal and boreal—and Pacific fish stocks have made forestry and fishing the major renewable resource industries in the province. Oil, natural gas, and minerals—coal, copper, gold, silver, lead, and zinc—are the main non-renewable resources; they owe their existence to our land's complex geology (see Chapter 3, pages 99 to 100).

1. **Vancouver Island/Coast**
   Service industries, tourism, forestry, trade, agriculture, manufacturing

2. **Mainland/Southwest**
   Service industries, agriculture, trade, manufacturing

3. **Thompson-Okanagan**
   Forestry, mining, agriculture, tourism

4. **Kootenay**
   Coal mining, mining and smelting, farming, logging, tourism

5. **Cariboo**
   Forestry, mining, agriculture, trade, and manufacturing

6. **North Coast**
   Forestry and commercial fishing, mining and mineral exploration, smelting, pulp milling

7. **Nechako**
   Forestry, some mining, and tourism

8. **North East**
   Coal mining, agriculture, forestry, oil and gas development

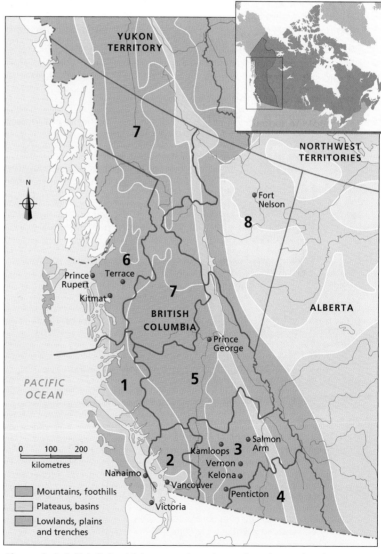

Figure 9–1 British Columbia's economic regions reflect the province's great geographic diversity. These regions are characterized by their principal economic activities, which are determined by many factors, for example, physical features, geology, distance from the coast, and climate.

hydroelectric power: electricity produced by the power of rushing water

The rise and fall in world demand for these non-renewable resources has played a major role in the boom-and-bust nature of British Columbia's economy. **Hydroelectric power** is one of our growing renewable resources. Rivers that roar through the plateaus, basins, and hills of the Cordillera, combined with the right climatic conditions, have encouraged the development of hydroelectricity. British Columbia is home to many large hydroelectric sites, such as Peace River, Kemano, Arrow Lakes, and the West Kootenays.

Sustainability and Stewardship

As British Columbia's population and economy have grown, so too have demands placed on the land and on the resource base. Today, we are beginning to recognize the limits to resource development, and we are concerned about the damage caused by uncontrolled exploitation. Environmentalists and developers alike know that resource industries must adhere to sound environmental practice to ensure that renewable resources are available for future generations. This concept of **sustainability** was first recommended by the United Nations Commission for the Economy and Environment, known as the Brundtland Commission.

The Brundtland Commission called for sustainable development that meets the needs of the present without compromising the ability of future generations to meet their own needs. Sustainability seeks a balance between a sound economy and concern for the environment. In practical terms, this means that the rate of use of a resource should not exceed its rate of replacement. With this model, we are no longer simply consumers of resources, we are also their managers, or stewards, for future generations. **Stewardship** implies a respect for the Earth and its resources and a commitment to protect the environment.

In 1987, the United Nations World Commission on Environment and Development introduced the idea of **sustainable development**. The report opened as follows:

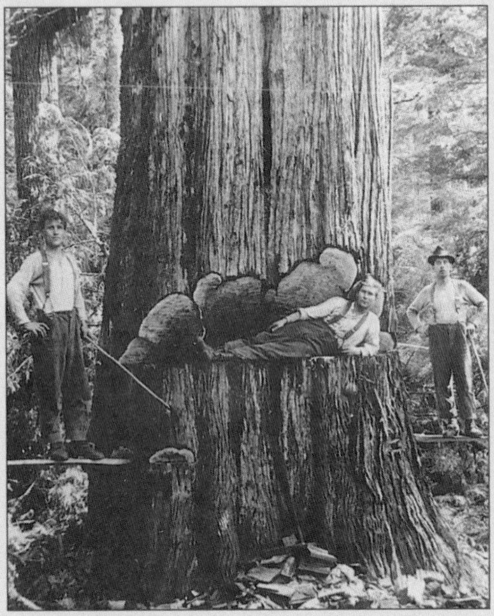

Figure 9–2 Today, leaving a stump this high would be viewed as a wasteful forestry practice. When do you think this picture was taken? Why?

sustainability: the idea that resources should be conserved with an eye on tomorrow

stewardship: the management of resources with regard to the environment and the rights of all

sustainable development: development that preserves an ecological balance so that natural resources are not depleted

PRIMARY SOURCE

> The Earth is one but the world is not. We all depend on one biosphere for sustaining our lives. Yet each community, each country, strives for survival and prosperity with little regard for its impacts on others. Some consume the Earth's resources at a rate that would leave little room for future generations. Others, many more in number, consume far too little and live with the prospects of hunger, squalor, disease, and early deaths.
>
> –*Our Common Future, 1987*

1. **a)** Graphs can simplify the presentation of information and make it easier to compare trends. Draw a multiple-line graph using the GDP data in Table 9–1. When constructing the graph:
   - Plot the vertical axis as percentage of GDP
   - Plot the horizontal axis as decades, from 1880 to 2020
   - Ensure that you can distinguish the four lines from one another
   - Label the axes and each of the lines
   - Give the graph a title

   b) Using dotted lines, extend each of the four lines from 1990 to 2020. Summarize the provincial trends in the first decades of the twenty-first century.

   c) Did you find it easier to compare trends and patterns with the graph or with the table?

   What are the main drawbacks and benefits of these two ways of presenting statistical information?

2. Would it be easier to practise sustainable development in wealthy parts of the world or in poorer areas? Explain your answer.

3. Should wealthy countries bear most of the responsibility for ensuring that the world's resources are available for future generations? Explain your answer.

4. Take an inventory of your personal daily consumption of the Earth's resources. Skim the rest of the chapter for categories of resources, then estimate your consumption by reviewing your daily activities. For example, estimate your water consumption by figuring out how much water you drink, how long you shower, and so forth.

THE FOREST

Nearly 45 percent of all wood logged in Canada is logged in British Columbia. The Western Mountains account for only 14 percent of Canada's forested land, but 40 percent of Canada's **merchantable timber**. The forest industry is the largest segment of British Columbia's economy. Since the late 1800s, British Columbia wood has been shipped around the world. By the mid-1990s, the total value of all forest products exported from British Columbia was $1.5 billion. Logging and the manufacture of forest products provide more employment and contribute more **value-added** than any other industrial sector in British Columbia. Today the industry employs about 30 000 people in jobs ranging from logging to furniture manufacturing.

In recent years, concern has grown about the sustainability of the forest. People have looked for new, innovative ways to add value to harvested wood. In part, this interest has grown because many people realize that the forest has profoundly affected life in British Columbia. It has shaped our trading relationships, determined our standard of living, and even enhanced our artistic and cultural life. The forest industry has always followed the ups and downs of the economic cycle. It lays off workers when times are lean and the demand for housing and forest products goes down. It hires more workers when the economy is booming. Now, however, people are thinking of the industry and the forest itself in the long term, hoping that trees can be a resource for all time.

> **DID YOU KNOW?**
>
> *Most British Columbia lumber is used in saw milling and plywood production, and in the pulp and paper industry.*

merchantable timber: marketable timber

value-added: economic value added through secondary production

The Forests of the Western Mountains

British Columbia's total area is approximately 95 million hectares. Fifty-five percent of this area is forest, most of it coniferous needle-leaf trees. Because it lies at mid-latitude on the Pacific Ocean, British Columbia has a mild climate and a fairly high level of precipitation. These factors have given the province a rich cover of vegetation. On the coast, where the rainfall is greatest, Canada's largest trees grow to a height of nearly 100 metres. As you learned in Chapter 3, topography and climate have a strong influence on the vegetation of British Columbia, producing the dense temperate rain forests of the coastal region and the smaller forests in the interior.

Trees and Us

The expansion of Canada's railway system benefited the lumbering industry in British Columbia. Before the building of the CPR, it was expensive and time-consuming to ship lumber to eastern Canada, which kept lumber exports small. The new rail route to the prairies opened up new markets for British Columbia lumber. In 1900, investment in the forest industry in British Columbia was approximately $2 million. Ten years later, investment had grown to $65 million.

During those years of expansion, the provincial government was anxious to promote the forest industry. It offered a large number of twenty-one-year leases to cut timber in British Columbia's coastal forests. The result was an uncontrolled cutting bonanza and extremely wasteful logging practices. Public pressure forced the government to establish a Royal Commission on Timber and Forestry. The investigation led to the 1912 Forestry Act, which legislated **competitive bidding** for timber leases and established a forestry service to enforce the new regulations.

In 1947, the Forestry Act was revised. For the first time, steps were taken to ensure that forests were not cut down faster than they were growing. Logging companies were limited to an **allowable annual cut,** which would help to preserve the forests. The principle behind the allowable annual cut was **sustained yield,** which means that only as much timber is cut as can be replaced by new growth, assuming a certain amount of loss from fire and disease.

More recently, the science of silviculture has helped to improve the sustained yield. Trees are modified through **genetic alteration** and then carefully nurtured. In addition, more attention is paid to clearing undergrowth, which encourages rapid growth, and to the spacing of trees. In 1995, the British Columbia government introduced the Forest Practices Code, which enforced strict regulations for harvesting and replanting. However, in the face of industry pressure, the regulations have been relaxed. Logging companies say the regulations are excessive and difficult to meet. The government's response angered environmentalists who want more tightly controlled harvesting.

Preserving The Forests: How Much Is Enough?

How much of British Columbia's temperate old-growth forest needs to be preserved in order to protect the forest **ecosystem**? Most people agree that the forest resources of British

competitive bidding: making an offer to buy something that other people also want to buy

allowable annual cut: the volume of trees that can be legally cut down in a year

sustained yield: the number of trees that can be replaced by new growth

genetic alteration: changing trees through grafting

Columbia must be made sustainable so that they will also be available to future generations. Finding a balance between ecological preservation and economic development is difficult, especially since the forestry industry is the biggest employer and revenue generator in the province. In 1992, the provincial government set a goal of preserving 12 percent of the British Columbia forest as park land. Meeting these guidelines, which were inspired by the 1987 United Nations Report on the Environment, has been controversial.

Old-growth Forests

British Columbia's old-growth coastal forest is a temperate rain forest. It has been a lightning rod for disputes between forest companies and environmentalists. The old-growth forests of the coast are a unique resource, but not everyone views them in the same way. Environmentalists say that the number of large, intact **watersheds** left in British Columbia is insufficient to ensure biological diversity and that the old-growth forest must be preserved. (Forests anchor topsoil and absorb excess moisture in a region drained by a river system.) On the other hand, the forest industry faces a declining annual allowable cut of the valuable first-growth forests. Because the forest industry cannot maintain production **quotas** in some areas, it wants to harvest some old-growth areas as well. The aboriginal peoples of the Northwest Coast have a distinctive relationship with the old-growth forest. It plays a central role in their culture, providing building materials for canoes and totem poles, as well as sites for ceremonies. Finally, the growing popularity of **eco-tourism** in wilderness

areas has transformed old-growth forests into recreational areas, which gives them another kind of economic value.

High-profile confrontations between environmentalists and the forest industry—such as those being fought in the Carmanah Valley, Clayoquot Sound, and the Big Bear rain forest—have shown how hard it is to determine just how much of the temperate rain forest needs to be preserved. These cases have, however, raised public awareness about forest preservation and industry practices. In turn, this has changed government and industry attitudes towards forest

ecosystem: a community and its environment functioning as an ecological unit

watershed: an imaginary line between two drainage basins

quota: a set limit

eco-tourism: a sector of the tourist industry that focuses on wilderness areas

Figure 9–3 Old-growth trees can be as high as 100 metres and provide organic matter for a complex ecosystem in the trees and on the forest floor.

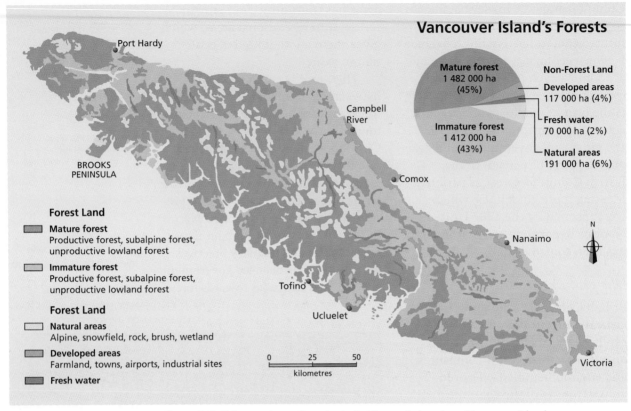

Vancouver Island's Forests

Mature forest
1 482 000 ha
(45%)

Immature forest
1 412 000 ha
(43%)

Non-Forest Land

Developed areas
117 000 ha (4%)

Fresh water
70 000 ha (2%)

Natural areas
191 000 ha (6%)

Port Hardy

Campbell River

BROOKS PENINSULA

Comox

Forest Land

▭ **Mature forest**
Productive forest, subalpine forest, unproductive lowland forest

▭ **Immature forest**
Productive forest, subalpine forest, unproductive lowland forest

Forest Land

▭ **Natural areas**
Alpine, snowfield, rock, brush, wetland

▭ **Developed areas**
Farmland, towns, airports, industrial sites

▭ **Fresh water**

Nanaimo

Tofino

Ucluelet

Victoria

0   25   50
kilometres

N

Figure 9–4 This map shows the extent of old-growth forests on Vancouver Island.

management. In 1995, the government of British Columbia passed a new Forest Practices Act, which ensured a sustained forest resource under strict conservation guidelines. The 1995 legislation not only limited the size of **clear-cuts**, but also protected stream flows and animal habitats, and mandated reforestation along with sound silviculture. Since its introduction, the government has modified some of the legislation's more stringent requirements because of declining overseas markets.

Worldwide campaigns by environmentalists have led to fundamental changes in the practices of British Columbia's big forest companies.

Figure 9–5 Pressure from environmentalists and European customers has led some of British Columbia's largest forest firms to change their harvesting methods.

Environmental groups such as Greenpeace and the Western Canada Wilderness Society want clear-cutting banned as a means of harvesting, and they want old-growth forests to be preserved. In the spring of 1998, one of the largest forest companies, MacMillan Bloedel, announced a phase-out of clear-cut logging and restrictions on harvesting old-growth forests over the next five years in favour of **selective logging**. Western Forest Products also announced that it was applying for certification of its forest practices under the Forest Stewardship Council, the standard endorsed by environmental groups internationally. The companies made these changes in response to demands from US and European customers that British Columbia companies manage the forests in a sustainable fashion.

Clear-cutting versus Selective Logging

Clear-cutting is probably the most controversial of all forest practices. It involves the complete removal of all trees in a given area. In the past, it was not uncommon for huge areas of land to be clear-cut; today, clear-cutting is much less common, primarily because the public disapproves of it. With **selective logging**, only certain trees are logged. Selective logging tries to imitate the natural cycle by leaving dead and live trees standing and leaving the forest floor intact as much as possible. This provides a wildlife habitat and promotes biodiversity. Although selective logging is more expensive than clear-cutting, the higher cost can be offset by improved technology and increased consumer approval. For instance, the cost of helicopter logging on British Columbia's rugged coastal inlets is offset by money saved on building logging roads and on environmental clean-up. Each method has its supporters. With clear-cutting, it costs less to harvest trees, and loggers have more safety on a work site. But clear-cutting also leaves an unsightly area, and causes greater erosion. In addition, it usually harms wildlife habitats. With selective logging, it costs more to harvest trees, and the logging process is more difficult and time-consuming. However, the area looks more attractive than it does after clear-cutting, and there is much less damage to the environment and to wildlife habitats.

clear-cuts: areas in which almost all the trees have been removed in one cut

selective logging: the process whereby mature or diseased trees are removed, leaving the younger trees to grow to maturity

DID YOU KNOW?

In March 1999, the Canadian government gave MacMillan Bloedel 30 000 hectares of Crown forest lands in return for lost cutting rights at Clayoquot Sound.

Figure 9–6 Helicopter logging allows the removal of individual trees (selective logging), thus protecting wildlife habitats.

Protected Areas:
The Twelve-Percent Solution

Opinions on how our resources should be used and valued vary widely. During the 1980s, the conflict between people who wanted to preserve our resources, at all costs, and those whose main concern was to continue harvesting and developing resources, had reached a crisis point. It was time to find a way to balance the province's economic needs with the need to protect its natural resource base.

In 1993, the provincial government launched the Protected Areas Strategy (PAS). Its goal was to increase British Columbia's protected areas from 6 to 12 percent by the year 2000. The PAS also helped the government choose and manage protected areas on land or in fresh water. Four million hectares of park land were added by 1998, bringing the total percentage of protected land close to the government target. The province expanded existing areas with unique or special qualities, such as parks, wildlife refuges, old-growth watersheds, and heritage sites. In some cases, it added new areas. Land and resources in protected areas may not be sold, mined, or logged. Oil, gas, and hydroelectric power development are also prohibited.

Of course, protected areas also have legitimate uses. These include recreation, scientific research, nature preserves, and education. Today, British Columbia's protected areas are providing more nesting and

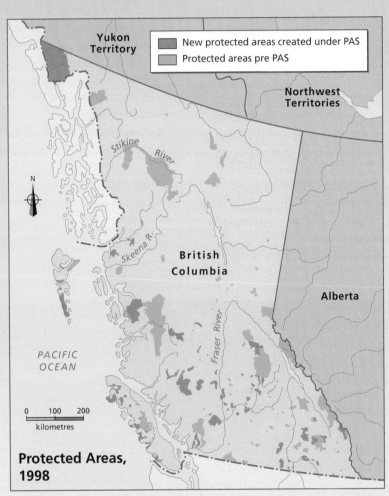

Protected Areas, 1998

Figure 9–7 Part of the Protected Areas Strategy (PAS), the twelve-percent policy has been welcomed as a necessary step towards preserving British Columbia's natural wilderness. Many in the resource industries, however, question the cost of the program.

wintering sites for birds, safeguarding the natural corridors for vulnerable species such as grizzly bears, and ensuring the survival of unique heritage sites.

Preserving the natural and biological diversity of the province has come at a price. In particular,

the forest and mining industries question the wisdom of removing resource-rich lands from the provincial economy. Some companies have launched claims against the provincial government for forest leases and mineral rights that existed before new park lands were designated. The province is committed to compensating forest companies by providing them alternate cutting areas, which will cost approximately $150 million. It will be more difficult to buy out the 300 mineral claims which now lie inside protected areas. The largest settlement so far—for $83.57 million—went to MacMillan Bloedel for the loss of cutting rights on Vancouver Island. Geddes Resources also received a large settlement for lost copper rights when the Tatsheshini-Alsek Park was established along the British Columbia, Yukon, and Alaska borders.

WHAT DO YOU THINK?

1. **a)** Is the loss of resource-rich land offset by the economic benefits of preserving some areas of British Columbia as special sites? Role-play one of the following to arrive at an answer:
   - logger
   - miner
   - environmental activist
   - farmer
   - wilderness outfitter
   - dock worker
   - forestry company executive

   b) As a class, stage an on-the-street survey. One student should assume the role of the surveyor, who asks participants to respond to the question above. The surveyor should ask students to provide information on their background, occupation, and reasons for their position on the issue.

2. Investigate the impact of the PAS on your community. Pool your class findings and list them in order of greatest to least impact.

3. Summarize your attitude to the PAS in a paragraph. Support your opinion with three reasons.

ACTIVITIES

1. Using pages 353 to 359 as background information, create a projected time line for the forest industry to the year 2025. Speculate on at least three major changes that may occur in the British Columbia forest industry in that time.

2. With a partner, script and perform an interview with a retired logger. Discuss changes he or she has witnessed during their logging life in British Columbia.

3. In an organizer, compare and contrast present forest practices in British Columbia with those of the past as described by the logger in the above activity.

4. Should environmental regulations in the forest industry be relaxed during an economic downturn? Use the information in this section and refer to Chapter 8 to arrive at an informed opinion. Summarize your views, with evidence, in a paragraph.

5. **a)** As a class, brainstorm a list of groups who would have an interest in determining the uses of Clayoquot Sound or another old-growth watershed.

   b) In a small group, choose one interest group and use a problem-solving model to determine that group's position on using the watershed's resources. (Your teacher will supply you with information on the problem-solving model.)

   c) Conclude with a negotiating session in which each group presents its findings and all groups try to reach a consensus on the use of the watershed.

FISHERIES: A DWINDLING RESOURCE

In Chapter 8's Window on the Past, you learned how the British Columbia fishing industry reached a state of crisis in the 1990s. Although herring, cod, and other species were part of the yearly catch, the West Coast salmon runs had always been the backbone of the industry. The five varieties of salmon—sockeye, pink, coho, chum, and spring—represent up to 60 percent of the total value of all fish caught on the West Coast.

In the 1990s, the once great salmon runs were no more. Human activity had so reduced the yearly catch that some fishers were allowed on the fishing grounds only two or three times during the season. At one time, there were a hundred major fish-processing plants on the coast—now there are half a dozen. How could this happen? Fishing has been an economic mainstay of British Columbia for thousands of years. The aboriginal peoples of the Northwest Coast depended on salmon, along with other species, and made it a part of their mythology. With the establishment of British Columbia, the Native peoples became an integral part of the emerging commercial fishing industry. Whole families were involved in the industry during the fishing season, working at sea and in the salmon canneries that began to spring up along the coast.

Today, everyone agrees that salmon stocks are dwindling, but few agree on the precise cause. Human interference through overfishing and the degradation of the salmon habitat by industry have certainly played a role. Spawning areas also have been affected by logging, mining, dam-building, road-building and urban sprawl. Water quality has declined because of municipal and industrial pollution (see feature on page 365).

Figure 9–8 One of the early bumper harvests of British Columbia salmon. Less sophisticated technology kept the overall catch down, accomplishing an unplanned sustainability.

Logging has had a huge impact because the cutting of trees on a mountain slope increases soil erosion. In turn, eroded soil, mixed with sediment and rock particles, chokes the spawning habitat. Dams also interfere with salmon migration routes. The survival rate of salmon returning to spawn—as high as 20 percent in the 1970s—has dropped as low as 2 percent in some rivers. It has been estimated that the Snake River Chinook run in the 1800s numbered about 1.5 million. Today, the figure is about 2500.

The solution to dwindling stocks may lie in further studies of ocean ecology. In recent years, researchers have become interested in ocean conditions that affect salmon survival. Changing ocean temperatures resulting from El Nino and La Nina may be responsible for salmon changing their migration routes. The strong El Nino of 1998 may have pushed warmer waters into the North Pacific, driving the salmon further north and into Alaskan fishing nets. These temperature variations could also account for the declining **plankton** population— on which salmon rely for survival— in the western Pacific. Some scientists are now saying that these climatic changes have had as great an impact on salmon as all other factors combined.

Achieving Sustainability

Like the forest industry, the fishing industry is also trying to reach a level of sustainability. However, very few people agree on how British Columbia's fishing industry can be restored to a level of profitability. Many interest groups are involved. The Native peoples, for example, are guaranteed the right to fish in British Columbia. They oppose any

quotas being set on their catches. Canadian and American fishers have disagreed for years not only on how much salmon each country catches, but on where they should be allowed to fish. If salmon bound for British Columbia migrate from the North Pacific through Alaskan waters, who owns the fish—British Columbia or Alaska? Differences of opinion on this very issue led to a collapse of talks between the two countries in 1995. Since that time, both Canada and the United States have continued to overfish. In 1996, the Canadian government cut the commercial salmon fleet by half, taking approximately 1500 fishing boats out of commission. Yet the salmon have not returned as expected. Experts say that even the strictest conservation measures will do little to allow stocks to recover if Alaska will not join Canada, Washington,

plankton: small plant and animal organisms that float in the water

DID YOU KNOW?

Canned salmon was first exported from British Columbia in the 1870s. By the beginning of the twentieth century, British Columbia salmon was exported worldwide. During 1914, the first year of World War I, the entire production of canned salmon in British Columbia was shipped to Britain to help with the war effort.

Figure 9–9 A British Columbia salmon farm

and Oregon in voluntarily reducing the salmon catch.

One strategy to take pressure off the salmon stocks has been to reduce the total number of fishers through **licence buyback** schemes. Under such schemes, fewer fishers survive by catching fewer fish. Of course, this scheme assumes that the rate of returning salmon to British Columbia rivers will improve over time. It also ignores the threat to the industry posed by Asian fleets that use deep-sea drift nets to dredge the seas. The United States and Canada cooperate to track and intercept fishing boats using drift nets in international waters.

Salmon farming, the raising of salmon in a controlled environment, is another possible solution. In 1995, the value of British Columbia's **farmed salmon** outstripped that of wild salmon production. While some claim that farmed salmon is the solution to the fisheries crisis, environmentalists disagree. The David Suzuki Foundation notes that escapee fish from salmon farms could transmit diseases to Pacific salmon if they were to come in contact with each other. Moreover, fish farming could have a negative impact on the biological diversity of the British Columbia salmon population.

Currently, the British Columbia government has a moratorium on further expansion of fish farming because of political and environmental concerns. Fishers of wild salmon and fish farmers have strong lobbies to advocate their point of view, and the government must wade through often-contradictory scientific reports about the safety of salmon farming in British Columbia.

Fishing for sport, once considered secondary to the commercial fishery, has also emerged as an important activity, especially when it comes to claiming a dwindling resource. Recreational anglers take only about 4 percent of the total catch, but the activity is now worth more than commercial fishing—approximately $600 million, versus $400 million for the commercial industry in 1997. Canadian and American sports fishers spend $7 million a year on licences, but the big money comes from the spin-off services provided by guides, outfitters, suppliers, and resort managers. Some people will pay up to $1000 per day to fish in an exclusive fly-in lodge. Advocates of sport fishing say that providing these services creates six times more jobs as are available in the commercial fishing industry.

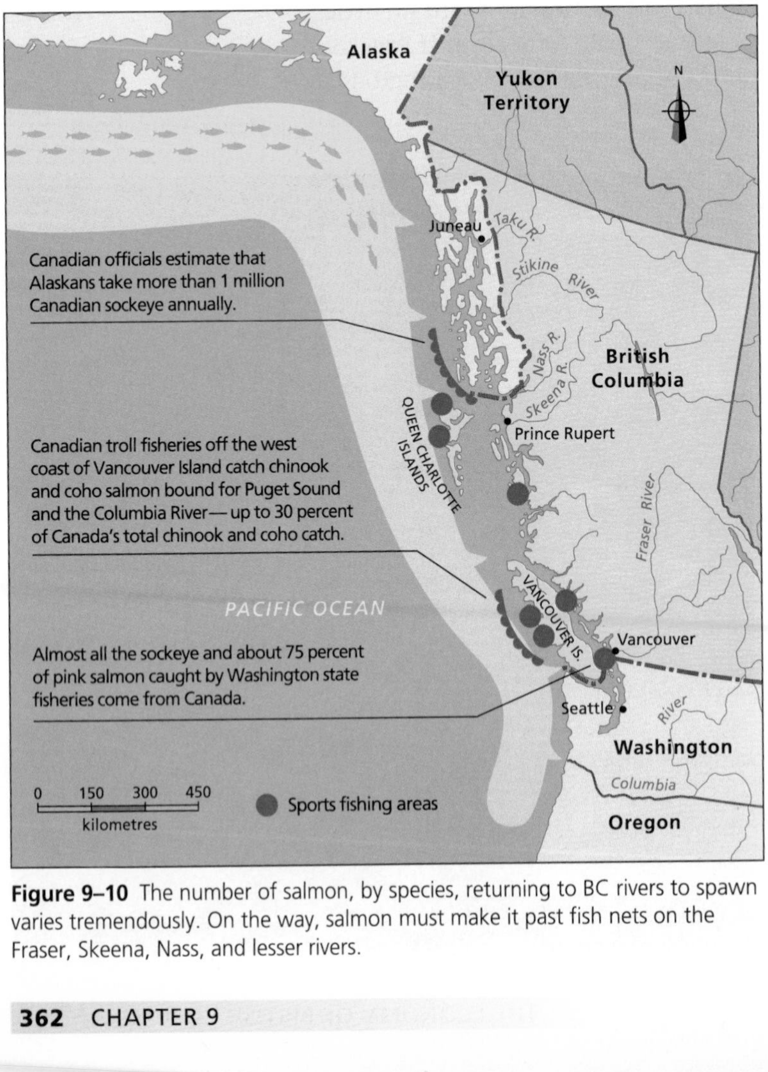

Canadian officials estimate that Alaskans take more than 1 million Canadian sockeye annually.

Canadian troll fisheries off the west coast of Vancouver Island catch chinook and coho salmon bound for Puget Sound and the Columbia River—up to 30 percent of Canada's total chinook and coho catch.

Almost all the sockeye and about 75 percent of pink salmon caught by Washington state fisheries come from Canada.

Sports fishing areas

Figure 9–10 The number of salmon, by species, returning to BC rivers to spawn varies tremendously. On the way, salmon must make it past fish nets on the Fraser, Skeena, Nass, and lesser rivers.

Salmon: Native Mythology and Science

Richard Beamish of Nanaimo, British Columbia, received the Order of Canada in 1999. For years, Beamish has studied the fluctuating temperatures of the North Pacific waters. His studies have tried to connect the effects of global phenomena such as El Nino with changes in marine resources.

Beamish has also tried to relate long-term changes in water temperature with the mythologies of the Northwest Coast peoples—what Beamish calls the "salmon cosmologies" that are encoded in their oral traditions. As examples he cites the Shuswap myth *Epic of Coyote* and the Nuxalk myth *Wanderings of Cormorant*. According to Beamish, "... science is probably about five or ten years away from recognizing that old knowledge, like the aboriginal oral tradition, is close to what scientists are now beginning to talk about."

Figure 9–11 Richard Beamish

Spring Salmon by Roy Henry Vickers

ACTIVITIES

1. List all the possible causes for the decline of the West Coast fishing industry, using pages 360 to 363 as background information along with Chapter 8's Window on the Past.

2. With another student, script a television interview with a commercial fisher. Draw out his or her experiences over these last years of crisis in the industry. You could repeat the exercise for the owner of a sports fishing lodge.

3. What has happened to sports fishing in British Columbia? Explain why.

4. Research the effect of the landslide at Hell's Gate in the early part of the twentieth century on the salmon runs of the Fraser River. Compare its effects and the recovery of the salmon runs with the present crisis in the British Columbia salmon fishery.

5. Contact the Farm Salmon Association of British Columbia and the David Suzuki Foundation for their perspectives on farmed salmon. Write a letter to the British Columbia Department of Fisheries expressing your opinion on lifting or maintaining the moratorium on fish farming in British Columbia.

WATER, THE UNDERRATED RESOURCE

British Columbians take fresh water for granted. High levels of precipitation have created many lakes and rivers that provide fresh water in abundance. We have lots of water, but our consumption of 500 litres a day per person is staggering compared to that of other nations. In India, for example, the average daily consumption is 25 litres. In recent years, population growth and economic development have put more stress on rivers, lakes, and underground water sources, and the need for water management has become a priority.

The rivers of British Columbia play a vital role in the province's economy. They provide water for human consumption and industry, for irrigation, transportation, recreation, and power development. The major salmon rivers of the province, such as the Fraser and the Skeena, are out of bounds for development, but they are still major dumping grounds for municipal and industrial wastes and urban and agricultural runoff.

The rivers and valleys of British Columbia are ideal for the reservoirs required for hydroelectric development. Dams such as the W. A. C. Bennett on the Peace River supply the province with cheap and plentiful hydroelectric power. The Columbia River Treaty of 1964 was a joint Canada-US project to build flood control dams in Canada to regulate the flow of water to the US. In return, Canada got the right to half the power generated in the US. Because Canada did not need

Figure 9–12 Water is a precious commodity, and Canadians are the second largest consumers of water in the world. In India, people survive on 5 percent of our average daily water consumption. Many people believe that water is a public trust that should be available to everyone. If a global water scarcity develops in the twenty-first century, should British Columbia give away some of its water? Should it export some of its water?

The Fraser River

The Fraser River is the fifth longest river in Canada. It starts at Fraser Pass in the Rocky Mountains and flows 1375 kilometres to its mouth at the Strait of Georgia.

In the last thirty kilometres of its journey, the Fraser passes through the 680-square-kilometer estuary it has created. It has Canada's fifth largest drainage basin, which includes thousands of streams and rivers from mountains, forest, and **wetland** that drain 234 000 square kilometres of land—more than one-quarter of the total land mass in British Columbia The basin has a great biological diversity of fish and waterfowl.

As the greatest salmon producing river in the world, the

wetland: an area containing much soil moisture, for example, a swamp

Fraser has never been dammed. The landslide at Hell's Gate in the early years of the nineteenth century destroyed the salmon runs for many years and showed how devastating it could be if the natural flow of the river were disrupted.

Nearly two-thirds of the population of British Columbia live in the Fraser Basin and make daily use of its waters. This population growth has certainly compromised water quality. Fifty percent of the industrial discharges into the Fraser River come from interior pulp mills, and 90 percent of the municipal waste discharged into the river originate in the lower Fraser Basin.

Journalist Mark Hume wrote the following article in response to a government report on the state of the Fraser Basin.

Figure 9–13 The pollution in the Fraser River is evident in this photograph.

By the time it [the Fraser River] finishes its journey to the Pacific, British Columbia's greatest river has become tainted by discharges from a million points of pollution.

Nobody knows where it all comes from. Logging operations upside valleys have kicked in clouds of sediment. Pulp mills ... have used it to carry off small rivers of effluent. Some tributaries have been dammed and diverted, diminishing the flow of the Fraser and elevating water temperatures in the summer, the Fraser has become so warm it kills salmon.

There are farms and golf courses that wash manure and pesticides into ditches that flow into the Fraser. There are landfills that ooze foul-smelling toxic gunk. There are gravel pits that flush sediment as fine as flour into the river.

There are industrial mills, steel plants, paint factories, and rafts of logs treated with preservatives, each making their own ugly contribution.

Even the cars, trucks and busses that clog the highways along the Fraser Valley are helping to pollute the mighty river. Tests in sloughs found elements released in automo-

bile emissions are high enough to kill sensitive aquatic life.

The worst comes at the end, when one million cubic metres of untreated sewage is pumped into the estuary each day.

By the time it hits Georgia Strait, the Fraser has become a watery reflection of the troubled world it runs through. It has become us. The big question, and it is one that is plaguing the world these days, not just the citizens of British Columbia, is how do we live cleaner? How do we continue to flourish as a society without spoiling the natural world we all love?

aquifer: an underground water source usually composed of saturated sand and gravel deposits.

the power at the time the agreement was reached, it opted for a cash payment.

Rapid population growth in the arid southwestern United States regularly raises the issue of bulk water exports. British Columbia's Water Protection Act bans the bulk export of British Columbia water. However, some people in the United States say that water should fall under the jurisdiction of the North American Free Trade Agreement (NAFTA) and should be available for export—a position opposed by Canada's federal government and the government of British Columbia. In December 1998, a California company that wanted to buy Canadian water sued the government of British Columbia because of its ban on bulk-water exports. The California firm said the ban violated the terms of NAFTA, which state that the provinces cannot interfere with international free trade. Canada is having a hard time meeting such legal challenges because the federal government has no official water policy. At the crux of the debate is whether or not water is just like any other resource, or whether its critical importance to the life cycle makes it more than just another commodity.

Figure 9–14 The building of the Brent Lake Dam

ACTIVITIES

1. Use an atlas to add the drainage basin and tributaries of the Fraser River to an outline map provided by your teacher. Annotate the map with the information on the state of the river as outlined on page 365.

2. Use an atlas to locate areas in British Columbia where the quality of fresh water is threatened by industry, agriculture, and contaminants. Write a memo to the provincial Department of the Environment outlining your concerns.

3. Investigate the source and quality of water in your community. Make an inventory of this resource and present your findings in a flyer city officials could send to households.

4. Stage a class debate on the topic: Resolved: British Columbia's Fresh Water is Not for Sale.

THE AGRICULTURAL INDUSTRY

Although less than 10 percent of British Columbia's land is suitable for farming, agriculture has long been practiced here. The Hudson's Bay Company encouraged farming on Vancouver Island as a means of supplying local markets. In addition, the main population centres of Vancouver and Victoria had a climate that favoured agriculture. As the population of the province grew, so too did orchard farming in the Okanagan Valley, cattle ranching in the central interior, and grain farming in the Northeast.

British Columbia farmers tend to specialize, concentrating on one or two products from a variety that includes grain, cattle, dairy products, and orchard fruit. In areas such as the Fraser Valley and Okanagan Valley, farmers practise intensive farming. Here, small growing areas achieve high yields in mainly vegetables, poultry, fruit, and dairy products. The vast expanses of land in the Cariboo and Peace River regions make them suitable for raising cattle and growing grain.

Farming in British Columbia ranks well below the major resource industries in annual production value. It employs less than 3 percent of the province's workforce. The importance of food production, however, cannot be measured solely in terms of income. Farming is a significant source of employment for those people who are drawn to this way of life. Anyone who has grown up on a farm knows that the industry is vulnerable to periods of prosperity and crisis. Not only must today's farmers deal with crop failures due to pests and climatic conditions, they must also manage constantly changing economic factors of the marketplace: price fluctuations; **dumping** of cheap foreign products; rising production costs; and changing industry regulations. Sometimes **marketing boards**, such as those operating in milk, grain, and egg production, set limits to the amount of product a farmer can supply to a particular market.

Farming was traditionally a small-scale family enterprise in British Columbia. By the 1990s, increasing production costs and the introduction of new crops led to consolidation in the industry. Today, agriculture has become much more of a big business. In the Peace River region, family farms are giving way to more profitable large-scale operations that sometimes

dumping: the quick selling of surplus products at a greatly reduced price

marketing board: a government group that regulates the selling of products to protect a region's economic interests

Figure 9–15 New agricultural technology is employed in these fields in the Lillooet Valley to grow a new crop—ginseng—for the Asian market.

tenant farmers: people who farm rented land

employ **tenant farmers**. In the Okanagan Valley, the wine industry has expanded and improved by introducing new grape varieties and implementing better quality control. New crops such as ginseng are also being grown in the dry interior valleys for export to Asia. The hothouse industry has become a major producer of tomatoes and cucumbers for the expanding urban markets of the lower mainland and southern Vancouver Island.

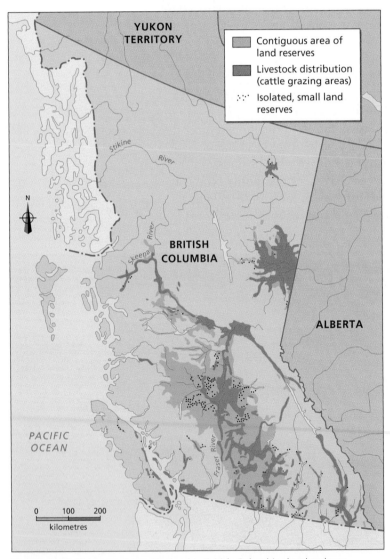

Figure 9–16 This map shows the land in British Columbia that has been designated as part of the Agricultural Land Reserve. It also shows that most of the agricultural output of the province comes from a very small area.

Agricultural Land Reserves

The areas of British Columbia that are ideally suited to agriculture are also ideal for settlement and often become centres of high population concentration and growth. This leads to conflict over how the land should be used. In the second half of the twentieth century, large areas of old rural land were absorbed by industrial and residential development. As more and more people moved to areas surrounding the cities in the 1960s, the province's limited agricultural land base was quickly shrinking. The situation was most serious in the Lower Fraser Valley, the Okanagan Valley, and on southeastern Vancouver Island. The higher economic return from land used for urban development made the continuing loss of farmland seem inevitable.

In 1973, rising public concern over the loss of farmland led the provincial government to take action. It enacted legislation that placed a freeze on developments on agricultural land and established a Land Commission. The commission reserved 4.7 million hectares of land in four categories that measured productivity in an Agricultural Land Reserve (ALR). Only .5 percent of land in the province was considered prime land capable of producing a wide range of crops.

In the 1990s, the Georgia Basin and Okanagan Valley were among the fastest growing regions in Canada. This spreading urbanization placed acute pressure on agricultural land. The Georgia Basin has only 2.7 percent of British Columbia's land area, but nearly 50 percent of its population. In addition, mountain slopes, the US border, and the Strait of

Figure 9–17 Farmland surrounding the lower mainland of British Columbia faces increasing pressure from population growth and industrial development. You can barely see the old farmland in this modern picture of Richmond. Compare this photo to Figure 3–5 on page 97. What has happened?

Georgia restrict the area in which expansion and development can occur. On the east coast of Vancouver Island, population growth to the year 2020 is expected to exceed 50 percent. As a result, urbanization is chipping away at the ALR. By 1993, the ALR had declined by nearly 9 percent in this region—but only .5 percent in the province as a whole. Lands can be removed from the reserve if an application for removal is made to the Land Commission, or the provincial cabinet. Farmlands can be converted to other uses, such as golf courses, and still remain in the reserve if it can be shown that the land can eventually be used again as farmland.

ACTIVITIES

1. How did farming in British Columbia change in the 1990s?

2. What type of farming takes place in your region? If it is an exporter of agricultural products, find out where products are shipped. If your region imports produce, identify some of the foods and their points of origin (the supermarket produce manager can help you with some of these questions).

3. Investigate the status of the Agricultural Land Reserve in your region. Find out if any lands have been removed recently. If so, for what purpose?

4. Imagine that you are a Land Commissioner replying to an application to remove lands from an agricultural reserve. The applicant wants to build a theme park that will create hundreds of jobs. However, in your opinion, the applicant does not understand that the land must eventually return to the reserve. Will you accept or reject this application? Give three reasons in your reply. At least two of your reasons should touch on an environmental or an economic issue.

NON-RENEWABLE RESOURCES: MINING AND FOSSIL FUELS

unprocessed: in their raw form, not processed

Mining has always been an important part of British Columbia's resource-based economy. The Native peoples of British Columbia mined copper before the arrival of the Europeans. Coal mining on the east coast of Vancouver Island was another early operation, starting around 1850. Prospecting along the Fraser and during the Cariboo Gold Rush, which you read about in Chapter 6, expanded mining to the mainland and led to the development of the colony and province of British Columbia. During the Laurier era, mining began in the Cassiar and Omenica gold fields in the northwest corner of the province, and mining of copper, zinc, and lead started in the Kootenay region of the southeast.

British Columbia's mining economy is heavily dependent on export sales. Most minerals are exported **unprocessed** and are therefore vulnerable to shifting world prices and demand. A small change in the price of a mineral can dictate whether or not a mine will make a profit—and whether it remains in operation or closes. Overall, the success of the industry depends on world prices for minerals. But the life of a mine is also limited by the quantity of the mineral it contains. Twenty-five years is the average lifespan for a producing mine. Mine locations in British Columbia change constantly as mines close down, often along

Figure 9–18 An example of open-pit mining

with the communities built around them. Mining ghost towns in British Columbia include Barkerville (see pages 222 to 224), Island Copper on northern Vancouver Island, Britannia mine on Howe Sound, and Babine Lake in the north.

Until the 1950s, most mining in British Columbia was underground. Underground operations give miners access to high-grade mineral **seams** but are very labour-intensive and dangerous. After 1945, large-scale production of lower grade ores was made possible through the development of **open-pit mining**. These vast operations require major initial capital investment and fewer workers, and they are safer than underground operations.

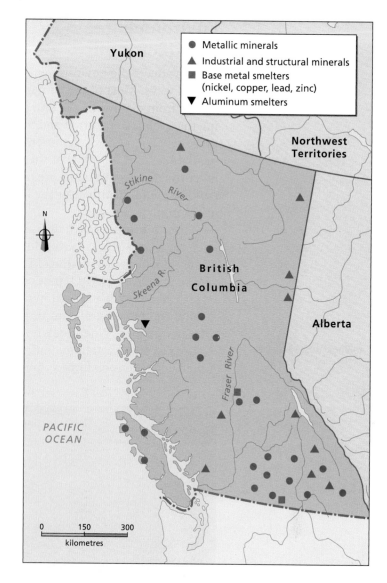

Figure 9–19 The search for new mineral deposits has changed since the days when prospectors went into the wilderness on foot looking for ore samples. Today, geological maps are used to determine the **bedrock** in an area and remote-sensing devices can be used to identify some minerals through aerial survey. Only when there is some certainty of mineral deposits will geologists be sent into the area to obtain rock samples. Before any mine can begin operating, a profitability study is undertaken and then lengthy environmental assessments must be conducted.

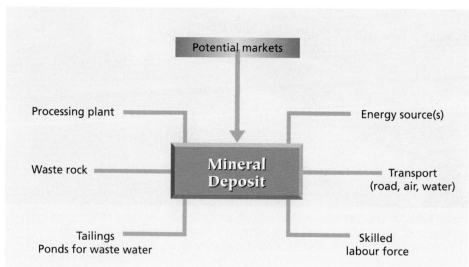

seam: a layer of mineral

open-pit mining: a mining operation that uncovers a mineral deposit by means of excavating a hole

bedrock: solid rock underneath looser materials such as soil

Figure 9–20 Many promising sites with ore deposits are never exploited. This can be attributed to a number of reasons, but usually it comes down to economic or environmental factors.

Environmental Considerations

Mining affects the environment in several ways. Most of the damage results from disturbing the site during the exploration period and from mine development. Government regulations now ensure that the area is returned to its original state of environmental health after the life of the mine is finished.

Open-pit mines leave behind open rock faces and large residues of waste rock known as **tailings**. The acid rock drainage (ARD) that can occur when rock is exposed in this fashion can have significant impact on water quality. When rock is exposed to air or water, sulphuric minerals in the rock form sulphuric acid. Although this process occurs in nature, it can be accelerated by mining activity. Water that comes into contact with the rock becomes acidic. As it re-enters streams, lakes, and rivers, it can damage the aquatic ecosystem. According to the provincial Ministry of the Environment, none of the coal mines and only six of the sixteen operating metal mines in British Columbia generate ARD—and those six mines are taking steps to eliminate it. However, some abandoned mines are known generators of ARD. New mines are now required to post bonds so that if they generate ARD at a later date, or after the mine has closed, the situation can be managed without the cost being absorbed entirely by governments.

tailings: waste left after the mining process

Figure 9–21 The Alcan Smelters aluminum plant at Kitimat was built in the 1950s. It was located at the head of the Douglas Channel in the northwest of the province because it provides a deepwater port. The port is needed for access to world markets and for the supply of major raw materials, which come from Australia and Jamaica. The massive amount of hydroelectric power required by Alcan to process aluminum comes from its own power development at Kemano.

Apply Your Knowledge

Southern Exposure: Where Have All the Mines Gone?

Figure 9–22 In the 1990s, many Canadian mining companies moved all or part of their operations to Chile, in South America. This mine is owned by Teck Corporation.

During the 1990s, the British Columbia mining industry started to decline. Only $50 million was spent on exploring new mines in 1998, down from $227 million in 1990. Today, a shortage of investment capital is only one of a number of problems faced by British Columbia mining companies. It's simply harder to open a mine than it was ten years ago. A new mine cannot open until the company has gone through a lengthy environmental review process and has satisfied any Native land claims associated with the area. In addition, there is always the uncertainty of world market prices.

As a result, many British Columbia mining companies have relocated to other countries. A popular destination has been Chile, in South America. By the close of the 1990s more than 130 British Columbia companies, such as Placer Dome, Teck, and Commence, were operating in Chile. Mining companies say the operating costs are lower and that government regulation of the mines is less stringent than it is in Canada.

The British Columbia Chamber of Mines also claims that the province's Protected Areas Strategy (see page 358) has turned too many of our prime mining sites into park land. Early in 1999, it stopped cooperating with the government. Mining industry representatives say the plan to double the province's park land from 6 percent to 12 percent has resulted in close to 18 percent of the land being regulated as a protected area. They say the process, if continued, will only alienate mining and other resource industries.

Canadian mining companies operating in Chile say they conduct themselves just as they would in Canada. They point to Chile's recently passed Basic Law on the Environment in Chile. However, the Environmental Mining Council of British Columbia disagrees. So do many labour leaders, who are mostly concerned about the loss of Canadian jobs. They cite a World Bank report which states that the shortened environmental review process in Chile could "allow environmentally harmful projects to proceed that previously would have been stopped." Bryan Lee, a member of the United Steel Workers of America union local in Tumbler Ridge, British Columbia, has monitored many projects in South America. He claims that unsafe working conditions and environmental policies are the norm, not the exception.

Jeff Thomson, a Canadian mining executive who has helped to open a number of mines in Chile, thinks a "chain reaction" has developed as a result of Canadian mining interest there.

Canadian mining companies want to develop mines in Chile. This attracts engineering companies and suppliers who establish offices and plants in Chile, often reducing their operation in Canada: the new mines require power which leads to gas pipeline development from Argentina by Alberta companies; all of this activity creates increased travel, which leads to the Vancouver Airport Authority involvement in the Santiago Airport Expansion; and so on.

Table 9–2	British Columbia and Chile: A Snapshot	
	British Columbia	**Chile**
Size in kilometres^2	952 263	756 000
Population (1999)	4 million	4.4 million
Urban population	82 percent	86 percent
GDP (1997)	$86 billion	$26 billion US
GNP per capita	$18 199	$1 940
Exports (1997)	$26.5 billion	$8.6 billion US
Imports (1997)	$23.2 billion	$7.5 billion US
Top 3 origin of exports	United States Japan Korea	United States Japan Germany
Top 3 source of imports	United States Japan China	United States Brazil Japan
Political system	Democracy	Democracy

ACTIVITIES

1. Use the text on pages 373 to 374, especially Table 9–2, and any other information you can gather to complete a organizer that compares and contrasts British Columbia and Chile. In the outside columns place information that is unique to each place. In the centre column, list some points of comparison. Summarize your findings in a short paragraph.

2. Develop a creative way, for example, a flow-chart, to illustrate the "chain reaction" described by Jeff Thomson when a Canadian mining company relocates in a foreign country. Add one or two chain reactions that Thomson might have forgotten to mention.

1. With a partner, generate a list of reasons why British Columbia processes so little of its mineral resources. Share this information with classmates and generate a common list of five to ten reasons.

2. Use the list above to develop three policies that the provincial government might adopt to attract more secondary processing to British Columbia. Be sure to include reasons why these policies might work.

3. Make a two-column list of benefits and environmental concerns resulting from a smelter locating near your community. Poll your class for their opinions on the issue.

THE HIGH-TECH REVOLUTION

A fast-growing sector of the provincial economy is the "high technology," or high-tech, industry. In 1998, this sector comprised more than 2000 companies with total revenues exceeding $3 billion. **Information technology** is the newest area of the industry—its impact on the provincial economy has only been felt in the last fifteen years. While a number of industry leaders are located in British Columbia, most of the information-technology companies are small, in most cases employing fewer than ten people.

Computer services is by far the largest part of the information-technology industry. It encompasses activities such as computer consulting, processing, programming services, systems analysis and design, customized software packages, and multimedia applications. Other industries within this sector specialize in mobile radio communications, television equipment, satellite parts and components, electronic switching equipment, and recording instruments. British Columbia leads all other provinces in the number of companies that are developing products in the field of satellite, mobile, and microwave communications.

This area is the fastest growing segment of the telecommunications equipment industry.

Because high-tech companies tend to cluster in the vicinity of colleges and universities, most are located in the greater Vancouver and Victoria areas. One world leader in the design and development of electronic observation and information systems is MacDonald Dettwiler. Its Richmond-based plant develops some of the most advanced control and communications equipment and software for use on the ground, as well as in space. In fact, most of the non-military Earth observation systems in the world contain hardware and software systems developed at MacDonald Dettwiler.

The company specializes in systems that record and process geographical information, but it is also developing air traffic management systems and defence systems. One company initiative has been the creation of national and international networks for the sharing of spatial data. The Earth Observation Network allows government and private agencies to use public networks such as the Internet for the electronic delivery of satellite images to their archives.

information technology: the use or study of systems that store, send, and collect information (computers and telecommunications, for example)

Ballard Power's Ecological Footprint

The Task Force on Healthy and Sustainable Communities at UBC once put it this way—the "ecological footprint" of human + car is just too big. This group uses land as a way to measure the impact of consumption on the global environment. It works like this: Categories of human consumption are translated into the areas of productive land required to make products and eliminate waste. According to the Task Force the ecological footprint—the amount of land from nature required to support an average Canadian's present consumption—is 6.5 hectares, the equivalent of four city blocks. Of this, 0.9 hectares are required for transport. So if everyone on Earth lived like the average Canadian, we'd need at least four Earths to provide all the materials and energy we currently use.

Transporting people more efficiently and cleanly would reduce this ecological footprint. In all major cities in Canada, lots of approaches have been tried—rapid transit, share-a-ride, and designated lanes for cars carrying more than two passengers—but these have been only moderately successful.

However, Ballard Power Systems Inc., located in Burnaby, has offered a whole new approach. Ballard is one of British Columbia's high-technology success stories. Car manufacturers such as Daimler-Chrysler and Ford have invested in the Ballard Fuel Cell, which will power cars and buses with hydrogen, and will make fuel emissions a worry of the past.

Fuel cells convert chemical energy of a fuel to electricity and heat without combustion. Most fuel cells operate on hydrogen, which combines with oxygen from the air to form water, producing no air emissions. A fuel-cell vehicle powered by hydrogen offers the zero-emission benefits of a battery-powered vehicle but does not have to be recharged. The cars will have few moving parts, and the refuelling process will be quick and efficient.

With grants from the federal and provincial governments, and investments from the world's leading car manufacturers, Ballard Power Systems of Burnaby, British Columbia, is on the cutting edge of a new technology. Its impact will undoubtedly be felt in other areas of power generation.

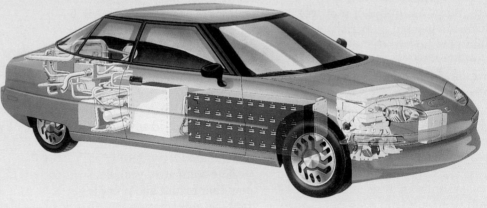

Figure 9–23 On St. Patrick's Day, 1999, Daimler-Chrysler unveiled the first driveable no-emissions car incorporating Ballard Power technology. The company hopes to have the compact car in production by the year 2004.

ACTIVITIES

1. Brainstorm some other ways to improve automobile emissions. Present your findings in the form of a poster encouraging people to reduce automobile pollution.

2. Name three interest groups that could benefit from the sharing of information about the Earth gathered from space. Explain the benefit for each group.

SPLENDOUR UNDIMINISHED

British Columbia's provincial motto, "Splendour Undiminished," is well-deserved. Our province's varied geography and breathtaking scenery, including a desert, have become a resource of expanding economic value. Nowhere is this more apparent than in two of our fastest growing industries—tourism and recreation, and television and film production.

Tourism and Recreation

British Columbia is a worldwide destination for tourism and recreation. From saltwater kayaking to skiing, its many attractions draw sizeable numbers of tourists. And because the number of visitors to British Columbia increases every year, preserving suitable recreational areas for public use has been a primary goal for successive governments.

The completion of the Canadian Pacific Railway in 1885 established tourism in British Columbia as an economic fact of life. To provide accommodation for its passengers, the CPR built hotels in scenic areas such as Banff, Lake Louise, and Victoria (see Chapter 6, page 237). A few decades later, increasing use of the automobile encouraged touring, and tourism. The impact of the automobile continued to grow as the highway system expanded. For example, when the Coquihalla

Highway opened in the 1980s, it made the Okanagan Valley more accessible to the people of the lower mainland—both touring and commercial drivers say this highway provides the fastest route to the interior. The West Coast waters have also attracted sightseers from around the world. In the early twentieth century, tourists were content

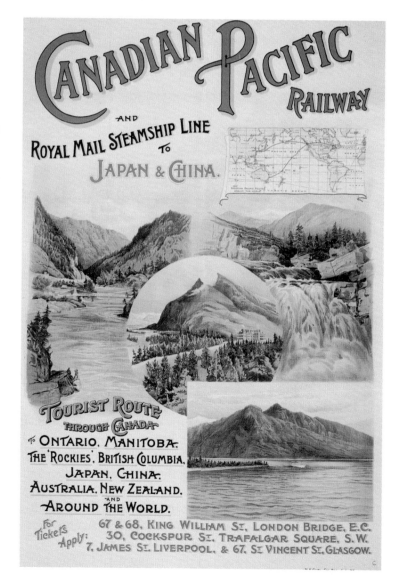

Figure 9–24 Vancouver was a departure point for Canadian Pacific steamships bound for Asia. Sightseers were encouraged to travel across Canada and to Asia through British territory.

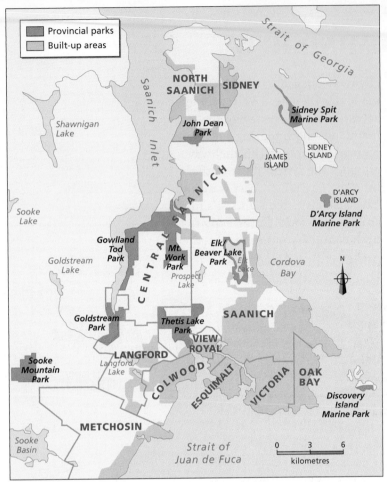

Figure 9–25 British Columbia's national and provincial parks help to preserve some of our province's outstanding natural features, historic sites, and unique habitats. Even in a small area such as Victoria and vicinity, there are many parks to choose from.

built-out: left with no land for homes

condominium hotel: a building with units for sale, but one that also offers hotel services

with day trips from Vancouver to the Gulf Islands. Today, the industry offers luxury cruises to Alaska, whale-watching excursions, and dinner cruises through the many inlets up and down the coast.

The only parks system in Canada larger than British Columbia's is Canada's National Park system. This underlines the fact that Canadian and foreign visitors come to British Columbia to enjoy the variety of outdoor recreation. Hikers can choose from many challenging landscapes, such as the marine West Coast, the

Juan de Fuca trails, or the Rocky Mountains. Kayaking and canoeing are popular on the waters off the West Coast or the fast-flowing rivers of the interior—you can also ride the rapids of the Fraser River in a rubber raft! Abandoned rail lines have been converted into hiking and bicycle paths in areas such as the Kettle Valley, which originally ran from Hope to Midway via Princeton and Penticton. Along the way, some of British Columbia's historic sites and towns have become popular stopping points. Historic sites such as the old gold town of Barkerville (see Chapter 6, pages 222 to 224), the Xá:ytem Longhouse in Mission, and Fort Steele, at the junction of Wildhorse Creek and the Kootenay River, attract more and more visitors each year.

The Ski Industry

One of British Columbia's biggest tourism success stories has been its ski industry. In the past two decades, British Columbia's mountain resorts have enjoyed a 6 percent annual growth rate. Led by the number-one-ranking Whistler-Blackcomb—the fastest-growing ski resort in North America, according to the US Census Bureau—British Columbia has become an international ski destination. An estimated 60 alpine ski areas operate in the province, with huge resorts on Vancouver Island, in the Thompson-Okanagan area, and in the Kootenays. More than five million skiers will visit British Columbia mountain resorts in the year 2000. More than 8000 people are employed at alpine ski resorts, enticing skiers to spend approximately $500 million in the province.

Canada's top ski destination is located 120 kilometres from

Figure 9–26 Blackcomb Mountain in Whistler, British Columbia

Vancouver. A vast, undisturbed landscape in the 1960s, Whistler now boasts more than thirty lifts, thirty-six hotels, nearly a hundred restaurants and nightclubs, and almost 200 retail shops. Whistler expanded by 70 percent between 1990 and 1996, and real estate agents think it will be **"built out"** by 2003. Its numerous **condominium hotels** reflect the trend towards destination vacation resorts, where vacationers can ski and bask in a natural setting, but also enjoy the comforts of city life. Many new condominium hotels are trying to capitalize on the huge influx of people during the ski season. Under Whistler bylaws, buyers of some units can only use them for 65 days out of the year. For the remaining 300 days, they must place them in a rental pool and get back half the rental income (the condominium management receives the other half). This system ensures that more people can buy vacation packages in Whistler, and injects a large amount of cash into the local economy.

The Home of Hollywood North

British Columbia is one of the biggest producers of film and television in all of North America. In 1978, the film production industry in British Columbia did about $12 million worth of business. By 1997, that figure had increased to $630 million. Accounting for the **multiplier effect**, this increase added nearly $2 billion to the provincial economy.

multiplier effect: the total impact on an economy that results when one sector expands

DID YOU KNOW?

The British Columbia Film Commission was established in 1978 to encourage film production in British Columbia. If you think your home or business would make a good location for a film, you can register it with the British Columbia Film Commission.

A mild climate suitable for year-round filming and a wide variety of landscapes are two attractions that bring filmmakers to British Columbia. The Canadian dollar's lower value relative to the US dollar also makes it much cheaper for American companies to film here. In the last few years of the 1990s, the US dollar was worth approximately one-and-a-half times the value of the Canadian dollar.

British Columbia's film industry employs 25 000 full-time and part-time workers in film production and related industries, including construction, special effects, equipment rentals, and food services. Local people form 97 percent of the average crew. Film and television production is an ideal way to add economic growth because it is a **labour-intensive,** non-polluting, value-added industry, and it also increases foreign investment in the province.

In recent years, the Vancouver area of British Columbia has become known as Hollywood North. Here, the British Columbia film industry has produced some of the most popular television series and films, including the top-rated "The X-Files," starring David Duchovny and Gillian Anderson (see feature on page 381).

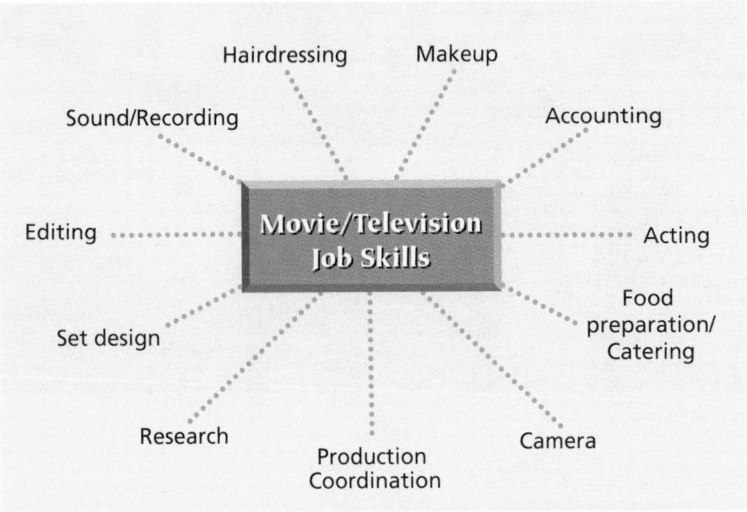

Hairdressing
Makeup
Sound/Recording
Accounting
Editing
Movie/Television Job Skills
Acting
Set design
Food preparation/ Catering
Research
Production Coordination
Camera

Figure 9–27 Careers in the film industry

labour-intensive: requiring a lot of personnel and/or time to do the job

Figure 9–28 Is it Hollywood or Vancouver?

The X-Files in Vancouver: Where Geography and Economics Met

"The X-Files" shot its last show in Vancouver on April 22, 1998. Area residents who got used to seeing huge convoys of trailers parked on their streets—not to mention the bright lights and busy crews—say things are not the same since Mulder and Scully left town. "The X-Files," a television show about two American FBI agents trying to prove that their government has colluded with extraterrestrials, is a top-rated show around the world. It has also been the favourite program of people aged 18 to 48 in Vancouver, the lower mainland, and Victoria.

"The X-Files" creator, Chris Carter, once said that "Vancouver is actually one of the stars of the show." The city's rainy weather and soft, moody light provided a perfect backdrop for five years. The lower mainland was called upon to mimic a variety of locations across North America, including a mountain resort in Virginia, a summer property in Rhode Island, and Lake Okobogec, Iowa. Several local landmarks, such as Grouse Mountain and Lighthouse Park, have now become part of the "The X-Files" film lore.

The economic benefits were obvious. Area businesses received generous location fees and the US Fox network saved a huge amount of money in production costs by using a versatile location where the American dollar would go far. Once the show moved to Los Angeles (at the request of David Duchovny, who wanted to be closer to his wife), the cost per episode shot up by millions of

Figure 9–29 Norm Ghromann confronts David Duchovny in North Vancouver.

dollars. But economics was a factor here as well. Because the show's star was irreplaceable, and because its ratings were so high—occasionally reaching number one in the 18 to 48 age group—Fox could reabsorb these costs by charging even more for its advertising time. Advertisers covet the 18 to 48 demographic group because its members spend more money than any other group.

"The X-Files" has resulted in a number of spin-off industries in Vancouver, such as tours of X-Files sites, complete with hotel accommodation. And when Duchovny said on US television

that Vancouver was too rainy for his liking, the resulting uproar generated even more money for the city's economy. Tourism Vancouver spent $7000 on a publicity stunt intended to reassure American viewers that Vancouver is a great travel destination. Former BCTV weatherman Norm Ghromann arrived in North Vancouver (where the show was filming) dressed up as a tree, and presented Duchovny with a salmon, a provincial flag, and a rain poncho and bonnet. Duchovny was gracious about the stunt and told the *Vancouver Sun*: "I love the rain."

ACTIVITIES

1. In groups of three, research and plan a circle tour of the province and present it in a brochure format. Provide information on distances, means of travel, changing physical features, points of interest, major centres on the route, and any information that you think would interest tourists.

2. The Heritage Branch of the Ministry of Tourism operates thirteen unique historic sites in the province where public programs are presented. With a partner, choose one of the historic sites on their website (www.heritage.gov.bc.ca).Use the information to make a 30-second taped

commercial that highlights the site and a number of its main attractions. Include location information.

3. Use an atlas to find an area of British Columbia which has the potential to be developed as a year-round destination resort. Summarize the reasons for your choice in a letter to the provincial Ministry of Employment and Investment. Support your proposal with maps and illustrations.

4. How many different jobs were affected by the move of "The X-Files" to Los Angeles? Brainstorm a list with your classmates.

POPULATION AND ENVIRONMENT

Demographic changes in British Columbia

Employment opportunities in British Columbia have relocated. Since the 1980s, jobs have migrated from the interior to the lower mainland. Now the Georgia Basin is the centre for new employment in the province. Both the interior and north have experienced job losses as technology has reduced the number of workers needed in the primary industrial sector. These trends are clear in unemployment data. In 1998, Vancouver had an unemployment rate of 6.3 percent, while the Cariboo region had a rate of 15.8 percent. The higher unemployment rate for the Cariboo region reflects the decline of the forest industry.

The Georgia Basin

All of British Columbia is like a colonial system, with the rest of British Columbia supporting Vancouver and Victoria.

The Georgia Basin makes up only 2.7 percent of British Columbia's total area, but it is home to nearly 50 percent of the province's population. This broad, sheltered basin includes the Strait of Georgia, the Lower Fraser Valley, the Sunshine Coast up to Powell River, the Gulf Islands, and the eastern side of Vancouver Island. People are drawn to the region by its mild climate, diverse natural environment of sea, islands, and mountains, relative job abundance, and the many cultural and educational facilities.

Population in the Georgia Basin grew very quickly in the 1990s. In the lower mainland and southern Vancouver Island, some communities grew by more than 20 percent. It is projected that in the next twenty-five years the population in these two areas will grow by about 40 percent—and environmental damage to the air, water, and land is already evident. Pollution from homes, cars, and industries has increased steadily. Greater Vancouver and Victoria already discharge more than 1 billion litres of domestic sewage into the sea every day. Smog from Vancouver can be detected as far north as Texada Island, 120 kilometres away. At one time, pulp mill effluent was also a serious problem. However, this form of pollution has been reduced under strict government regulations and is scheduled to be eliminated by the year 2002.

Many activities are altering the landscape in the Georgia Basin—urbanization and urban development, forestry, agriculture, recreation, and the creation of new transportation corridors. As cities

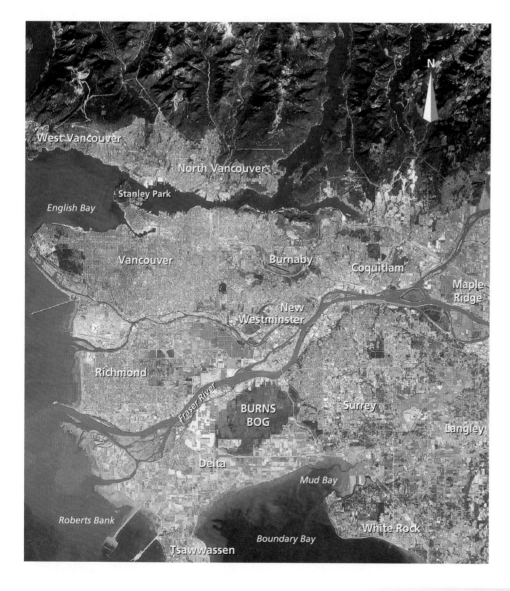

Figure 9–30 This satellite photo shows the extent of development at the mouth of the Fraser River. Encroaching urban sprawl can be seen in Richmond, Delta, and Surrey. Burns Bog, the largest raised peat bog on the Pacific coast of North America—and ten times the size of Stanley Park—is particularly vulnerable. The bog has been called the "lungs of the lower mainland" because of its ability to convert carbon dioxide from the atmosphere into oxygen. It also purifies and stores water, reduces and controls flooding, and provides a habitat for wildlife.

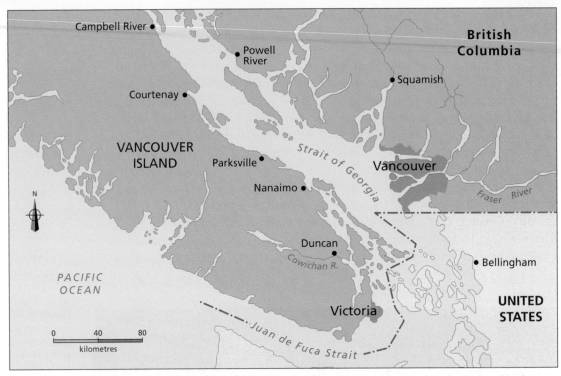

Figure 9–31 Less than 5 percent of the Georgia Basin's population is directly employed in the primary industries of agriculture, forestry, mining, and fishing. However, many jobs in the manufacturing and service sectors depend on these resource industries. As tourism increases in value, the quality of the environment is taking on greater economic importance. If the Georgia Basin is to maintain tourism as one of its major industries, more careful attention will have to be paid to the quality of the environment than has hitherto been the case.

cost of living: what it costs to live in an area, for example, what it costs to rent or buy a home, buy groceries, or pay for local services

expand, they encroach on streams, rivers, and coastal zones such as wetlands. Preserving and sustaining natural systems under these conditions is almost impossible. Some ecological rehabilitation has been attempted, but the cost is high. Too often, the environment takes second place to development.

The technological revolution could also provide some relief for the Basin's growing pains. One of the major sources of pollution is the automobile, a staple of modern life since the end of World War II. In the 1940s and 1950s, industries built their plants in the suburbs, which were planned for cars and trucks. According to many urban planners, however, urban life in the near future may not be so dependent on the car. People may choose to live far away from their source of employment, provided other factors, such as an area's **cost of living**, appeal to them. Fax machines, cell phones, and e-mail make it possible to live almost anywhere and still meet work deadlines. Satellite and cable television bring information and entertainment to the most distant location. Air freight allows manufacturers to locate plants away from urban areas. Already, the decentralizing effect of technology has allowed smaller centres to become competitive. So-called "fringe areas" are emerging on the margins of major North American metropolitan areas. As fewer people find it necessary to make daily trips into the downtown core, air quality will improve.

Witold Rybczynski, a professor of urban studies, and noted author, is an expert on habitats and cities. He says that as the globe becomes more urbanized, the challenge will be to create something more meaningful than sprawl.

> The chief challenge of the coming decades will not be to control sprawl but rather to add to it the ingredients of urbanity: density, walkability, and variety. Large shopping malls have started to combine retail, hotels and entertainment, but they should add apartment buildings; office parks need restaurants. Residential neighborhoods should have a variety of housing, apartments as well as houses, corner stores as well as townhouses. The key to a successful urban environment is to create what real estate developers call a 24-hour place, combining residential, office, retail and entertainment uses in relatively close proximity to create hustle and bustle. This is what makes downtown Vancouver ... so attractive.

The Port of Vancouver

The port of Vancouver began to grow in 1918, following the opening of the Panama Canal to commercial traffic. As grain, lumber, and fish were shipped, Vancouver quickly established itself as Canada's main West Coast port for bulk commodities. Today its most important function is still that of a port. Large terminal grain elevators are found on its docks, and mounds of yellow sulphur and potash sit next to huge containers of imported manufactured goods. The special coal terminal of Robert's Bank, to the south, loads the coal carried by trains from the coalfields of the East Kootenays. Vancouver is also one of the world's busiest cruise ship harbours. More than half a million passengers, in more than twenty cruise ships, sail the Inside Passage to Alaska each year.

Figure 9–32 Vancouver is Canada's gateway to the Pacific Rim.

1. What has happened to employment in the Georgia Basin versus the Cariboo region? What has been the impact on population growth and the environment in the Georgia Basin?

2. With a partner, role play a discussion between someone wishing to preserve Burns Bog and someone who thinks it should be developed.

3. What information can be gathered by examining satellite images? Give examples from Figure 9–30.

4. Examine the satellite photo in Figure 9–30. What indications are there of an international boundary? What other boundaries, natural and other, can you find?

5. Witold Rybczynski is advocating what is known as a "mixed use" approach to buildings in high-density neighbourhoods. Why would this approach be beneficial to a community?

CONCLUSION

During the twentieth century, British Columbia experienced dramatic changes in its economy. The dominance of the primary industries was challenged by the expanding service sector. In forestry, mining, and fishing, technological changes led to increased output with a greatly reduced workforce. A century of harvesting had drained province's resources to a low ebb. Dwindling fish stocks, a reduced supply of timber, and fewer opportunities for mining underscored a change from abundance to scarcity. Conservation and sustainability became the watchwords of the 1990s.

In recent years, BC has set the goal of preserving 12 percent of its provincial land as parkland. There have been many conflicts between environmentalists and developers, and as many high-profile cases. Debates over the best use of the land will continue to be heard as resources are developed, and the interests of the aboriginal peoples, environmentalists, and tourists are heard. Ski holidays, wilderness trips, and eco-tourism are fast replacing resource industries as the mainstay of many interior and coastal communities

In line with global trends, British Columbia's population and production have become centralized in the lower mainland. The settling of many Asian immigrants in and around Vancouver in the last two decades of the century has changed the face of the Greater Vancouver area. The Georgia Basin is now home to more than half the province's population, and the centre for the growing high-tech and knowledge-based industries. However, the growth of population and industry has put a strain on the environment of the Basin. Efforts are now being made to control the deterioration of the Fraser River Estuary and Georgia Strait.

As we begin the twenty-first century, our province will continue to play a role in meeting some global challenges—sustaining an increasing population, a vibrant economy, and a healthy environment, while dealing with the consequences of explosive change. Our health and livelihood will depend on meeting this challenge with foresight and confidence.

SUMMARY ACTIVITIES

1. Create an illustrated timetable for one of BC's primary industries in the twentieth century. Include information on formative changes in the industry, technological developments, and events that have helped or hindered this industry's development.

2. In a group, plan the contents for a website called "Builders of the Economy of BC" or a title of your own choosing. Have each member write up a biographical sketch of a person who had a long-lasting impact on the BC economy, such as H. R. MacMillan, the Dunsmuirs, Jim Pattison, or Jack Monroe. Design an opening page and compile a list of websites that would be good links to your website.

3. In a group, collect several objects related to today's BC economy which could be put into a time capsule. One-hundred-and-fifty years from now, your selections should show what the economy of the province was like, and how people made a living at the close of the twentieth century.

ON YOUR OWN

1. With a partner, do some research on the role of the Japanese and Chinese communities in British Columbia's early fishing industry. Write out a proposal to the National Film Board listing reasons why a documentary film telling their story would be worthwhile.

2. Research examples of the salmon in British Columbia art and illustrations. Make a wall display of your findings.

10 CANADA AND THE GLOBAL COMMUNITY

OUTCOMES

In this chapter, you will focus on Canada's—and British Columbia's—position in the global economy. By the end of the chapter, you will

- use statistics and graphs to understand the Asian economic crisis of 1997–1998

- compare different economies of the Asia-Pacific and identify links with British Columbia

- analyze secondary sources as research materials

- explain the Free Trade Area of the Americas and Canada's role in it

- analyze messages, references, and symbolism in political cartoons

- assess the conflicts between human rights and globalized trade and investment

- explain the origins and structure of the European Union

Hands Across the World

Immigration has turned Vancouver into a multicultural global village. In the following story, two fictional students from immigrant families search out ways to make Vancouver a place where everyone will feel safe and at home.

"Slow down!" Faye gestured to her friend Jackie. "It's supposed to be on this part of Pender Street."

Jackie grinned as she slowed down and manoeuvred the car through traffic. "Well, if you'd written the number down as I suggested ..." The rest of her sentence was cut off by the blaring horns of the cars behind them.

"There it is!" Faye exclaimed as she pointed to a small office on the other side of the street. "Go around the block and grab that parking space in front of it."

Many of their friends found Faye's determination a little irritating at times, but Jackie usually just shrugged good-naturedly and carried on with what she was doing.

As they walked the two blocks back from the car, Jackie turned to Faye. "Tell me again why we're going to this Chinatown Police Centre," she said.

"It's the Chinatown Police *Community Services* Centre," Faye corrected while barrelling towards the crosswalk.

"They're not the police."

"Well then, what are they? Why are we going there?"

Faye looked exasperated. "I told you to do some research. My uncle and aunt—you know the ones who recently arrived from China—they came home and surprised some burglars in their house. Nobody was hurt, but everyone was pretty shaken up. They came over and talked to my dad and mom about it, but weren't going to report it to the police. My parents had a hard time convincing them it was the right thing to do."

"I'm surprised," Jackie said, shaking her head. "Why wouldn't they want to call the police in a situation like that?"

"People like you who have

Jackie and Faye in search of a parking space

lived in Canada all your life know what to do when you need help," said Faye as they waited for the light to change. "But things aren't so simple for new immigrants. That's why I decided to come here. I wanted to find out more about the problems facing people who don't speak English in the Vancouver area."

A young man was stacking some pamphlets on a rack when the girls came through the door. "Hi," he said, "I'm Patrick Kwok, coordinator of the centre. Can I help you?"

"I'm Faye Wong and this is my friend, Jackie Perez," Faye said quickly. "I phoned you about visiting today for information regarding a career-education project."

"Sure, I remember. I'd be glad to answer your questions. Fire away."

"Well," said Faye as she opened her notebook and scanned the questions she'd prepared in class the day before. "Let's start at the beginning. Why was the centre established? What do you hope to achieve?"

"We want to bridge the gap between new immigrants and the police," Patrick said. "Our police force is largely White and English-speaking, but there are many Asian citizens who need its help. We hope to remove some of their uneasiness about the police, which often comes from experiences back home—you know, viewing the police as corrupt and ineffective."

"And how do you do that?"

Faye asked while jotting down some notes.

"Easier said than done," Patrick said smiling. "Apart from advising people who contact the centre and providing pamphlets in Mandarin and Cantonese, I speak to groups of immigrants brought together by Chinese immigrant service groups such as SUCCESS. Sometimes they're confused over simple things—for example, the emergency number in Hong Kong is 999, and over here it's 911. That can be a problem for elderly immigrants."

"How successful do you think you've been?"

Patrick hesitated before answering. "I think you'd have to ask other people about that. But we've been operating since 1992, and the police seem to value our services. We deal with about 2000 people a year, translating legal documents from Chinese into English, providing advice on security, and encouraging people to report crime to the police."

Faye scanned her questions again. "How is the centre financed?"

"Well, sometimes it's touch and go. Principally from the BC Attorney-General's office and the City of Vancouver. We're always short of funds, but we get by."

"Thank you," Faye said as she picked up some brochures to take to her aunt and uncle. "I'm really impressed with the work you're doing. It inspires me to get more involved with the immigrant community."

"Remember," Patrick grinned as he showed them to the door, "There are many immigrant communities in British Columbia, and each one has a unique set of problems. One thing's for sure—there's no shortage of work if you want to get involved."

Jackie was quiet and unusually serious as they left the centre. "You know, Faye, what Patrick told us about Chinese immigrants probably is happening to immigrants from other countries too. And not just with the police. I knew that immigrants have a hard time adapting to a new society, but this visit opened my eyes about the difficulties newcomers face when they're not familiar with Canadian laws and customs."

"That's why I came down here," said Faye as they got into the car. "I see the problems in the Chinese community, and I know it's more widespread. I was looking for a career-ed project that was meaningful and would somehow relate to the volunteer work I've been doing. The experience of my uncle and aunt got me thinking about services that are available to immigrants and the help that's being offered."

"Why don't we work on this together?" Jackie offered. "I really think this is something worth doing."

"Hey—I could use the help, and two heads are better than one. Where should we start?"

Jackie thought for a moment. "Well, we need to find out how many immigrants there are in the Vancouver area and what ethnic groups are represented. The Vancouver Public Library's not far from here. Let's head down there and check out the last census on the Statistics Canada website."

"That's a great idea," Faye replied. "And then we'll check on groups that work with new immigrants."

At the computer, Faye quickly logged on to the Statistics Canada website at www.statcan.ca and began to move through the site. Here she found the information on the last (1996) **census**. It showed that about 380 000, or 20 percent of the 1.89 million people living in the Greater Vancouver **census district**, speak a language at home other than English or French. Almost a third of the population—more than half-a-million people—know a foreign language. More than one third of those living in Richmond speak a foreign language at home, primarily Chinese.

"That's good information," Jackie said from the seat beside Faye. "But we need to know the biggest recent immigrant groups in BC. Go to 'Place of Birth of Immigrants' and we should be able to find out."

The chart Faye brought up on the screen showed that 216 615 immigrants had come to Vancouver between 1991 and 1996, the census year. The largest groups were from Hong Kong (21 percent), People's Republic of China, (13 percent), Taiwan and India (10 percent each), and the Philippines (7 percent).

While Faye printed out the information on immigration, Jackie decided to compile a list of groups that work with immigrants. SUCCESS, the Chinese immigrant service group Patrick Kwok had mentioned, was near the top, right below the Vancouver Immigrant Services Society.

"Let's try these two to begin with," Jackie said. "I've noted the contact person in each case. Why don't we split up and each take one of the agencies? I'll drop you off at SUCCESS and I'll check out the other. We can think of the questions we should ask them as we drive over to their offices."

Later, as they sat in a local coffee bar, they checked their notes.

"Well," Jackie sighed, "that

Faye and Jackie at the Vancouver Public Library

was quite an eye-opener. What did you find out?"

"Interesting information," Faye replied. "Although it just confirmed a lot of experiences that my family has had as immigrants from China. You know, about cultural differences that are often misinterpreted."

"Such as?" Jackie said.

"Oh, for example, in many Asian cultures, people do not make direct eye contact, as a sign of respect. In Canada this can be interpreted as being evasive—you know, not wanting to answer the question. This can become a problem when dealing with government officials, in job interviews, and that kind of thing. What did you find out?"

"Stuff along the same lines," Jackie said as she sipped her latte. "Besides the language barrier, many of the problems that immigrants and refugees face originated in their home countries, and prevent them from integrating into Canadian society. The problems are widespread—poverty, corruption, restricted access to educational opportunities, few rights for women, or even family members being killed in civil wars. It makes some people afraid to report Canadian labour-code infractions and the like to the proper authorities."

"What do you mean?"

"Well, what if the work situation in Canada presents a safety or health hazard, or what if they're getting less than the minimum wage? Or how about

"We'll set up a website," Faye exclaimed.

children being used in criminal activities? Many immigrants, particularly women and refugees, are afraid they'll lose their immigrant status if they become involved in a fight."

"The problem seems to be," Jackie continued, "that some Canadians expect that immigrants from non-European cultures should somehow understand how to behave in every situation. If they were aware of the difficulties, they might be more understanding."

"That's it!" exclaimed Faye. "We need to get the information out to the public and I know how."

Jackie looked puzzled. "How? Writing letters to the newspaper?"

"No!" shouted Faye, gesturing toward the library. "The same way we started our search for information on this topic—on the Net! We'll set up a website with information on immigration and the problems immigrants face in adjusting to life in British Columbia. That would be one way to promote tolerance and understanding for the immigrant experience. What do you think?"

"I think it's a great idea," Jackie replied excitedly. "That's exactly what we've been doing in computer-studies class. We're supposed to submit a project proposal in the next week. We could combine your career-ed project with my project. Teachers are always talking about how we should try to integrate our projects across the curriculum."

"It's almost like teaching," said Faye. "In a way, that's what we're trying to do, teach people to understand the experiences of others. We'll have to have some basic information on immigration on the site. We can start with the information we've gathered today."

"I think it should be interactive." Jackie added. "Let people share their experiences as immigrants, and with immigrants, through chat rooms and bulletin boards."

"Great idea," noted Faye. "It would help to build a sense of community. That's one thing the immigrant agencies stressed. Immigrants don't get to interact with ordinary Canadians other than in official contacts or through work. There's the language barrier: It's hard to have a dialogue when you can't communicate in another language. Which is something that will be a problem on our site."

Jackie shook her head. "Not as much as you might think. There's software that will translate. We'll have to check that out. I've noticed the RIIM website has their immigration research available in seven languages."

"You know," Faye said, looking even more serious than usual, "immigrants might be willing to expose sweatshops and other abuses if they could do it anonymously online in their own language. Which raises the question—how do we get them online?"

"I think most of the immigrant agencies will have computers and access to the Net," Jackie offered. "We'll have to make a list and e-mail them about our site. I have the feeling that's just one of many challenges we'll have before we're successful in getting our site up and running. Right now I think that's enough for one day. Tomorrow we can get down to serious work."

"It's been quite a day," Faye said as they walked out of the library concourse. "This morning I never thought that doing some research on my relatives' break-in would lead to this."

Jackie smiled at her friend. "Someone has to do it. Why not us?"

census: a count of Canada's population done at five-year intervals. Using the census, Statistics Canada provides information on the age, sex, mother tongue, employment, and education of the Canadian population.

census district: census districts of cities incorporate the entire metropolitan area, including suburbs. The census district of Vancouver is 1.89 million people, and includes a wide geographic area.

ACTIVITIES

1. What additional advice would you give Faye and Jackie if they asked you to help them set up their website? Think of technical and content areas they have not considered in the story.

2. Imagine you are a recent immigrant or refugee in the lower mainland of British Columbia. Write out a description of an experience you might have had that could be contributed to the chatline on the website described in this Window.

3. The majority of immigrants locate in Canada's major cities. Make a list of reasons that might explain why. Then make a list of reasons that could be used to convince immigrants to move from the cities into more rural areas of British Columbia.

4. Find out what groups work with new immigrants in your community. Contact one of them and ask their opinion on the biggest problems facing immigrants in your community. Evaluate your findings in light of those outlined in the story.

5. Chinese and East Asian immigrants have a long history in British Columbia. Review the information in Chapters 6, Window on the Past, and 7, Closing the Door to Immigration. How might the problems of Asian immigrants today differ from those in the late-nineteenth and early-twentieth centuries?

1929	RECESSION GRIPS THE WORLD
1939	WORLD WAR II BEGINS
1944	BRETTON WOODS CONFERENCES
1947	GENERAL AGREEMENT ON TARIFFS AND TRADE
1948	UNITED NATIONS ADOPTS UNIVERSAL DECLARATION OF HUMAN RIGHTS
1957	EUROPEAN COMMUNITY IS FORMED
1964	TOKYO HOSTS THE OLYMPIC GAMES
1979	CHINA OPENS SPECIAL ECONOMIC ZONES
1989	BERLIN WALL FALLS
1991	SOVIET UNION IS DISSOLVED
1993	EUROPEAN UNION IS FORMED
1994	NORTH AMERICAN FREE TRADE AGREEMENT
1997	CANADA-CHILE FREE TRADE AGREEMENT

The new electronic interdependence recreates the world in the image of a global village.

–MARSHALL MCLUHAN, 1962

At the end of the twentieth century, technological change transformed Canada's position in the world. It also unleashed forces that would reshape the world into a global community, much as McLuhan had predicted.

INTRODUCTION

The technological revolution that has circled the globe can be summed up in a word: speed. During the last decades of the twentieth century, a high-tech revolution in communications and transportation changed the world in a way that would have been inconceivable during the Industrial Revolution. Canada was part of this great transformation. While the US remained Canada's most important trading partner, Canada forged new links with other nations and regions of the world and moved away from some of its oldest trading partners.

In earlier chapters, you learned how technological advances have cut down the number of workers needed in the primary industries and in manufacturing. Today, multinational businesses operate all over the world, swiftly relocating to areas that allow them to increase profit and expand their markets. You also learned how the Canadian government changed its approach to foreign investment in the 1980s—from tight review and regulation, to openness. In the last years of the twentieth century, Canada's government actively courted international investment and trade because it was seen as an economic necessity. If Canada was to prosper, it needed foreign investment and it needed access to markets to sell its goods.

In this chapter, you will study the evolution of ever-larger international trade blocs, organizations, and agreements. These are changing the way we view—and live in—the world. Examining these developments will help you to understand the powerful economic forces that continue to reshape the world into a global economy.

INTERNATIONAL TRADE AGREEMENTS AND CANADA

When Marshall McLuhan, a famous Canadian thinker on communications, coined the phrase "the global village" in the early 1960s, it was a catchy new concept. The phrase spread around the world in a flash. This was long before the Internet existed as an everyday convenience. McLuhan had looked into the future, and the new world he described was not the world of the past. It was a world in which transportation and communications could shrink distances and eliminate barriers between nations and regions of the world. Almost four decades later, McLuhan's phrase is a part of our language, and the "global village" he predicted is real and present.

Globalization

You have grown up in an age of instantaneous communication and supersonic transportation. At home, at school, or in the public library, the Internet has opened up the world to you. Satellites transmit live images and information immediately—from anywhere in the world to anywhere in the world—with little regard for national boundaries and borders. These are routine facts of life. Technological developments have allowed people to view the world in a completely new way. Indeed, the world has changed. The world's economies operate and interrelate in a new way, with nations negotiating agreements and forming alliances based on changing economic realities.

The global economy that was taking shape in the 1960s has advanced with great speed. Today, cyberspace—the forum in which the global electronics communication system operates—has networked the Earth. Transactions in foreign investment, the stock market, currencies, trade, and commerce are completed with the push of keyboard command. Some **transnational** corporations and multinational businesses have grown to the point where they have more economic power than many developing nations. These businesses can and do move people and ideas around the globe, sometimes very abruptly. The results can be both welcome by a country where a new branch is opened, or devastating for a country in which an old branch is abandoned. In today's global economy, business and trade are competitive. Components for products are often researched and developed in one country, produced in one time zone, assembled in another, distributed in yet another, and sold in still another.

Doing business on a global level has meant that local and national economies have become "international" as well as interdependent.

Figure 10–1 The action at the Toronto Stock Exchange, Canada's largest, in the mid-1990s. Today, Internet trading is revolutionizing stock exchanges around the world. How do you imagine the TSE looks now?

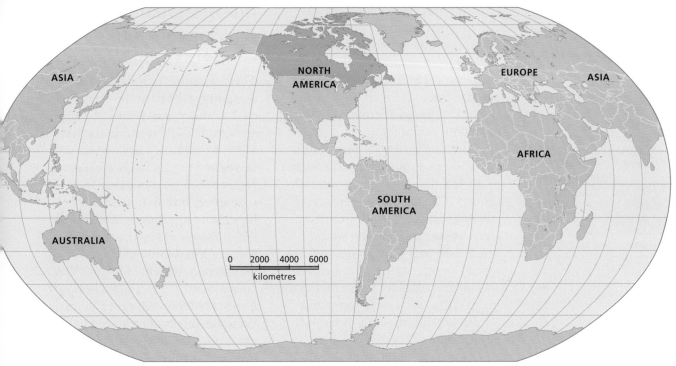

Figure 10–2 Canada is at the centre of this map of the world. How else might Canada's position be represented?

This raises a number of issues. Canada has always needed foreign investment to develop, but being dominated by foreign economies can also threaten its independence. In the twenty-first century, as global businesses continue to merge and expand, this conflict will intensify. Other questions will become more urgent. How can governments enforce regulations and laws—on the environment, labour, and human rights—if multinational businesses can pack up and move at the flick of a switch? If the trend towards **free-market** economics continues, what role will national governments play? Will multinational businesses have more power than democratically elected governments?

The global economy is a new economic order that is still taking shape. It worries many Canadians and excites many others. It offers seemingly unlimited opportunities and potential for growth, but it challenges all regions of Canada to keep up with a dizzying pace of change. It demands that Canada and Canadians do more than simply adapt. To prosper, we must innovate, create, and become world leaders.

Canada's Ideal Location

Canada is ideally located to participate in the global economy. With Pacific and Atlantic coastlines, Canada's transportation connections with Europe, Asia, and Latin America are well-established. Vancouver International Airport in Richmond, BC, for example, is the closest major North American airport to Asia. With connections, passengers can travel through Vancouver to almost anywhere in the Western Hemisphere and the **Asia-Pacific**.

free-market: a market in which prices are controlled by competition

Asia-Pacific: a region of countries, from Asia to Australia, that border on the Pacific Ocean

quotas: set numbers of immigrants allowed to enter a country

Canada's vast geographical expanse also covers many time zones, and this allows business transactions to be completed around the clock. Business people can access European markets from midnight until noon and link with Asian economies from noon until midnight.

Canada's history of immigration has made us a multicultural nation. In the last decades of the twentieth century, Canada's immigration policies were changed—long-standing racist **quotas** and barriers were lifted. Refugees were recognized as a special group. Family reunification was made a basis for immigration. In major cities, such as Toronto and Vancouver, hundreds of thousands of immigrants from Asia, Latin America, and Africa came to call Canada home. This meeting of cultures has prepared us to be citizens not only of a single nation, but citizens of the world—sensitive to, and ready to meet, the challenges of the global economy.

International Trade Agreements and Organizations

The beginnings of today's global economy go back to the early twentieth century. An economic recession gripped the world in the late 1920s as countries isolated themselves and put up trade barriers to protect their own markets and industries. International trade collapsed and international tensions grew. By the 1930s, the recession had deepened into the Great Depression, which devastated countries around the world, including Canada. Along with other factors, these terrible economic and political conditions led to the outbreak of World War II in 1939.

Today's global economy began to take shape before World War II ended, in the summer of 1945. In 1944, in Bretton Woods, New Hampshire, forty-four nations, including Canada, came together.

Figure 10–3 East meets West at Vancouver's International Airport.

They laid plans for a global economic and monetary system that would help the world recover after the catastrophe of World War II. Canada stepped onto the world stage and emerged as an important advocate for freer international trade. This, in fact, has been the cornerstone of Canada's trade policy. The Bretton Woods Conferences led to the creation of the International Monetary Fund (IMF) and the International Bank for Reconstruction and Development, better known as "the World Bank." The Bretton Woods Conferences also helped set the stage for the General Agreement on Tariffs and Trade (GATT) in 1947.

Trade agreements and organizations are often known by their abbreviations, which confuses most people. To add to the confusion, an agreement can become an organization, and sometimes an organization isn't really an organization so much as it is an opportunity for the world's most powerful leaders to come together and discuss international cooperation and trade. Table 10–1 lists some of the most important international trade organizations and agreements. Keep in mind that these are constantly evolving.

exchange rates: the value of one currency compared to another

Table 10–1	International Trade Agreements and Organizations		
Name	**Background**	**Function**	**Issues**
IMF International Monetary Fund	Formed in 1947 to rebuild the global economy after World War II 182 member nations (1999)	Stabilizes **exchange rates** of world currencies Promotes international trade Lends money to nations facing economic problems	Critics say the IMF has too much power and that nations receiving loans often must cut their spending. Supporters say the IMF has stabilized the global economy.
World Bank	Formed in 1947 to help Europe rebuild after World War II	Offers technical assistance and loans to projects in developing nations Provides loans to nations facing economic collapse	Like the IMF, the World Bank sets strict conditions and can tie its loans to economic, social, and environmental reforms. This draws criticism, as well as support.
GATT General Agreement on Tariffs and Trade	Formed in 1947 to reduce trade barriers around the world Canada a charter member	Set policies on international trade practices Member nations expected to make domestic trade legislation comply with GATT	Critics said GATT policies damaged domestic industries and that the US ignored rulings. Supporters said GATT policies increased world trade.
WTO World Trade Organization	Formed in 1995 as the successor to GATT Canada a founding nation 135 member nations (as of 1999)	Referees and promotes the global economy Dispute-settlement body can set rulings that are binding to member nations	Critics say that the WTO is too heavily influenced by the US, and that China must be admitted as a member (see Figures 10–19 and 10–20). Supporters say the WTO is the best organization to create an open global economy.

Table 10–1 (continued)   **International Trade Agreements and Organizations**

Name	Background	Function	Issues
OECD Organization for Economic Cooperation and Development	Formed in 1961 to conduct broad-based economic research 29 member nations Canadian Donald Johnston named Secretary General in 1996	Conducts research for the world's most powerful industrialized democracies Develops policies to improve trade and investment between member nations Coordinates foreign aid policies	Critics say the OECD conducts its affairs with no accountability. (See Cross Currents, page 401, on the Multilateral Agreement on Investment.) Supporters say the OECD improves the flow of international investment and aid.
G7 (8) Group of 7 (8)	Formed as the G6 in 1975 by the world's six major industrialized nations Canada became a member in 1976—now the G7 Russia admitted in 1998—now the G8	Holds an annual summit to discuss inflation and interest rates, job creation, currency, trade and investment, and relations with developing nations	Tagged "the most exclusive club in the world." Summits rarely lead to formal agreements, but they do promote cooperation among member nations.
APEC Asia-Pacific Economic Cooperation	Formed in 1989 to create pan-Pacific trade alliance Canada one of 12 founding members 21 member nations, including Russia (1998)	Meets annually to work towards improved relations and freer trade Objective is to create a Pan-Pacific free-trade agreement by 2020	The Pan-Pacific region is divided politically, which can result in friction. The poor human rights records of some member nations often spark public protests.

sovereignty: the right of a nation to complete self-government

ratified: formally accepted

corporate agenda: the drive by business to make profit regardless of social and environmental consequences

transparent: open to input and understanding; easily seen through

One of the most important developments in global trade was The Multilateral Agreement on Investment (MAI), developed by the Organization for Economic Cooperation and Development in the late 1990s. The MAI sparked protests around the world, for many reasons. First, the OECD had conducted early negotiations about the MAI in secret. Many nations that were pressured to support the MAI were not OECD members and had had little say in original negotiations. Second, many critics saw the proposed agreement as a threat to national **sovereignty**. They feared that the MAI would allow multinational businesses to evade local laws and customs. Third, the MAI could allow multinational businesses and financial institutions to play one country off against another: labour and environmental standards could plummet as countries competed for investment.

In October, 1998, after stiff opposition from worldwide environmental and labour groups, the OECD concluded that the negotiations on the proposed Multilateral Agreement on Investment had ceased.

The MAI and the Net

When Canada announced it would receive feedback on the MAI in 1997, there was no shortage of opinion. Members of the banking industry and some large Canadian multinationals supported the MAI. For them, it represented a step forward in the global economy—the MAI would allow global investment to flow more freely. Canada and Canadians would benefit.

Other groups feared the MAI would give multinational businesses more control over a nation's affairs than its own elected government. For them, social programs, environmental laws, cultural policies—even control of natural resources—could be dismantled if the MAI were **ratified**.

In Canada, the 100 000-member Council of Canadians, a grass-roots organization that opposes the so-called "**corporate agenda**," campaigned against the MAI. Their chairperson was Canadian author Maude Barlow, an outspoken critic of the corporate sector. Barlow travelled across Canada, and to the Paris headquarters of the OECD to oppose the MAI.

The Council of Canadians was hardly alone. Around the world, groups sprang up opposing the MAI—and the Internet provided a forum for MAI advocates and opponents to organize and disperse information.

In these excerpts from their website news releases, you can see how the Council of Canadians, the OECD, and the Government of Canada presented their positions after the MAI was rejected.

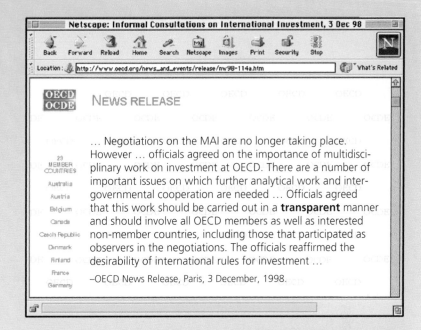

Netscape: Informal Consultations on International Investment, 3 Dec 98

Location: http://www.oecd.org/news_and_events/release/nw98-114a.htm

OECD OCDE   NEWS RELEASE

29 MEMBER COUNTRIES

Australia
Austria
Belgium
Canada
Czech Republic
Denmark
Finland
France
Germany

... Negotiations on the MAI are no longer taking place. However ... officials agreed on the importance of multidisciplinary work on investment at OECD. There are a number of important issues on which further analytical work and intergovernmental cooperation are needed ... Officials agreed that this work should be carried out in a **transparent** manner and should involve all OECD members as well as interested non-member countries, including those that participated as observers in the negotiations. The officials reaffirmed the desirability of international rules for investment ...

–OECD News Release, Paris, 3 December, 1998.

Netscape: Multilateral Agreement on Investment (MAI)

Location: http://www.dfait-maeci.gc.ca/english/trade/backgr~e.htm

Home   E-mail   What's New   Search

The negotiations towards a potential Multilateral Agreement on Investment (MAI) at the Organization for Economic Cooperation and Development (OECD) have now ceased ...

The Government of Canada is committed to an open and constructive dialogue with Canadians on all international trade and investment negotiations. With respect to the MAI, the consultation process allowed the Government to hear from thousands of Canadians ...

Trade and investment are twin engines for job creation, prosperity and economic growth. Canada does better when there are transparent rules governing the international playing field on which our businesses compete. That is why Canada has always been an active participant in the development of a world trading system based on rules rather than on economic might. We believe that the World Trade Organization (WTO) should be the home for any eventual international rules on investment.

–Department of Foreign Affairs and International Trade, 1998.

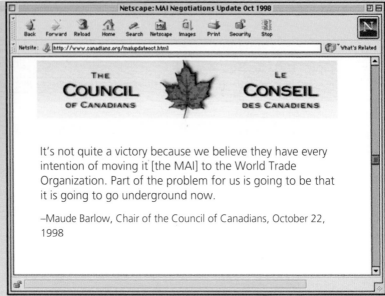

It's not quite a victory because we believe they have every intention of moving it [the MAI] to the World Trade Organization. Part of the problem for us is going to be that it is going to go underground now.

–Maude Barlow, Chair of the Council of Canadians, October 22, 1998

Figure 10–4 Maude Barlow

WHAT DO YOU THINK?

1. In your own words, why do you think so many people opposed the MAI? Why did many multinational businesses and some governments support it?

2. The word "transparent" appears in the news release of the OECD. Why do you think the OECD made this an issue? Refer to the "backgrounder" from the Department of Foreign Affairs and International Trade.

3. Create a two-column organizer listing reasons to support the MAI in one column and reasons to oppose it in another. Based on your organizer, prepare a brief presentation to convince others in the class to either support or oppose the MAI.

4. The quotation from Maude Barlow indicates distrust of the way the OECD and the World Trade Organization conduct their negotiations. Do you think she is justified? Explain, with reasons.

ACTIVITIES

1. Describe why and how the world has become a "global village." Give specific examples.

2. How did immigration to Canada change in the late twentieth century? Did this prepare Canada for the global economy? Explain, with reasons.

3. Refer to Table 10–1.
   a) Which 1947 agreement expected compliance of member nations' domestic trade legislation? What problems could this create?

   b) Which organization has the largest number of member nations? The smallest?

   c) Which organization has been criticized as being too US-dominated?

4. Referring to page 400, list three reasons why the Multilateral Agreement on Investment was rejected. For each reason, list one or two ways in which negotiators could resolve the problem and come up with an acceptable agreement.

TRADE BLOCS

As the global economy has advanced, more and more nations around the world have come together to form regional trade **blocs**. As you learned in Chapter 8, Canada is a member of the North American Free Trade Agreement, which also includes the US and Mexico. While its terms are limited, NAFTA forms what has been called a North American trade bloc. This is the only trade bloc in which Canada is a member.

Types of Trade Blocs

Trade blocs result from agreements that are reached between two or more nations. They involve **preferential** trade arrangements that exclude all other nations. Trade bloc countries have access to more resources and more economic opportunities than they would if they acted separately. Trade blocs also form larger **markets**. In the highly competitive global economy, this can benefit countries by allowing

them to coordinate trade, investment, and development.

There are two levels of trade blocs. Informal trade blocs allow each member nation to maintain independent trade policies outside the bloc. NAFTA is an example. While it created a tariff-free area composed of Canada, the US, and Mexico, each country still maintains separate trade policies with non-NAFTA nations. This is the loosest form of trade bloc.

In formal trade blocs, all members act together in specific trade areas. For example, member nations in a formal trade bloc would impose the same tariff and non-tariff barriers on trade with non-member nations. An economic union is another kind of formal trade bloc. In such a union, member nations have the same labour and environmental laws, a common monetary policy, and even a common currency. The European Union is an example of a full economic union. You will study it more closely later in this chapter.

blocs: combinations of nations formed for a special purpose

preferential: special and advantageous

markets: places where there is a demand for goods and services

Figure 10–5 The euro will replace the national currencies of eleven member nations of the European Union by 2002 (see The Euro, page 433). Do you think it would be a good idea to have a single currency for the entire world?

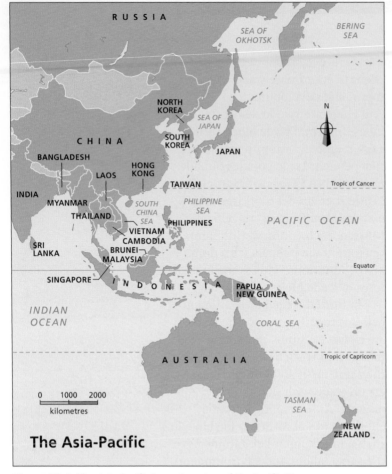

Figure 10–6 The Asia-Pacific is a sub-region of the Pacific Rim.

Canada and the Trade Blocs

While Canada is a member of many multilateral trade organizations and a full member of NAFTA, it is excluded from all other major trade blocs. For a country more dependent on exports than almost any other nation in the world, this is a cause for concern. Before globalization, trade agreements tended to be made nation by nation. Today's trade blocs have changed the way trade is conducted, and they have reduced Canada's access to the world's largest markets. In the case of the European Union, for example, historical trade ties between Canada and European nations have all but vanished. Canada has found it increasingly difficult to trade with the vast market of the European Union. Some trade observers have nicknamed the European Union "Fortress Europe."

In the Pacific region, Canada has been excluded from a closed trade arrangement between Australia and New Zealand and from the 1998 Association of Southeast Asian Nations (ASEAN) Free Trade Agreement. (ASEAN member nations are Indonesia, Malaysia, Thailand, Singapore, Brunei, the Philippines, Vietnam, Myanmar, Laos, and Cambodia.)

Canada has also been excluded from the so-called "Japan" or "**Yen**" bloc, which has existed for decades. In this arrangement, Japanese companies and the government of Japan enjoy partnerships within all the Asian economies. These partnerships have been created through direct foreign investment or foreign aid. China also has alliances with companies and individuals in Hong Kong, Macao, and Taiwan through an informal process known as **guanxi** (gwonchee). Some Canadians of Chinese ancestry have connections with this arrangement, or network, but no formal negotiations have taken place with the Canadian government.

This movement towards trade blocs and alliances reveals how economic globalization leads to the development of regional economic links. It also shows how vulnerable Canada's economy is if it remains excluded from these agreements, alliances, and blocs. This is one important reason why the government of Canada has so actively pursued multilateral trade negotiations and agreements through such bodies as the WTO and APEC.

Globalization in the Auto Industry

In the late 1970s and 1980s, Japan was a pioneer in the technological revolution in automaking. It also helped globalize the auto industry. Responding to fierce competition, Japan's auto giants used their huge profits to tap into emerging foreign markets and labour pools. Toyota set up production in Thailand, Malaysia, Indonesia, and the Philippines. Taking advantage of provisions in the ASEAN Free Trade Agreement, Toyota established a system to manufacture and distribute auto parts. Eventually, it set up assembly operations in these countries. Through these arrangements, these nations gained access to advanced Japanese technology, management systems, and business practices. Toyota gained access to their growing markets and the abundant, cheap, and skilled labour.

Japan also invested in Canada. Toyota now has partnerships with a number of Canadian parts suppliers. It also opened a large assembly plant in Cambridge, Ontario in 1988. Because the plant was so efficient, Toyota expanded its Cambridge plant twice, including a further $600-million investment in 1994. At the time, the rising value of the Japanese yen had raised production costs in Japan, which had gone into a recession in 1992. To be competitive in the US market, Toyota had to produce automobiles in North America. Canada was attractive. The Canadian dollar was lower than the US dollar, and Canada's health care system also cut costs for Toyota.

In 1996, Toyota's Cambridge plant was ranked the second most

Figure 10–7 Toyota's plant in Cambridge, Ontario is one of the most productive auto plants in North America. What industry would you say dominated the area before Toyota built its plant here?

efficient and productive auto assembly plant in North America, using 2.35 workers to produce a compact car. By 1998, the Cambridge plant had increased production to almost 200 000 units a year and employed more than 2600 workers.

This was all good news for Toyota employees in Canada and the ASEAN countries. But back in Japan, auto workers were being laid off as plants closed. The effects of globalization were shattering the traditional Japanese

idea that there was a kind of pact between management and labour. For generations, workers had believed that they had signed on for lifetime employment. As Japanese auto companies continuing to invest outside the country, even more Japanese auto workers were put at risk. Young people graduating from universities and vocational schools faced far different employment prospects than their parents had in the economy of post-war Japan.

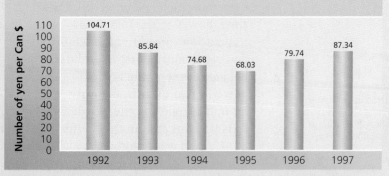

Figure 10–8 Value of Japanese Yen versus the Canadian dollar. In what years did the value of the Yen increase? What impact might this have on Toyota plants outside Japan?

1. **a)** Why is NAFTA considered not to be a formal trade bloc?

   b) What kind of trade bloc is the European Union? The "Japan" bloc? The "guanxi" bloc?

2. Using the "guanxi" bloc as an example, make a list of ways in which you think Canada's immigration patterns might also affect its international trade.

3. In a small group, brainstorm reasons why the government of Canada is concerned about being excluded from trade blocs in the globalized economy. Use specific examples.

Compare your group's findings with those of other groups.

4. Referring to the Cross Currents Globalization in the Auto Industry, create an organizer with four headings: ASEAN autoworkers; Canadian Autoworkers; Japanese autoworkers; and Toyota. Under each heading, list the pros and cons of globalization as seen from this group's perspective. Based on your findings, write a paragraph that describes why you think globalization of the auto industry has been a positive or negative development.

CANADA AND THE PACIFIC RIM

Eurocentric: assuming that Europe, or the North Atlantic, is the centre of the world

elites: groups possessing wealth, knowledge, and power

migration: moving from one country to take up residence in another

As you learned last year, European nations began to dominate the world in the sixteenth century as they colonized enormous areas of Asia, the Americas, and Africa. The North Atlantic came to dominate global economic and political activities for centuries. By the second half of the eighteenth century, Britain had amassed a vast empire. As the first nation in the world to undergo the Industrial Revolution, it became even more rich and powerful. Over time, however, the Industrial Revolution spread to other countries and other continents. As it did, the balance of economic and political power began to shift, not only around Europe and the North Atlantic, but around the world.

Canada was colonized by Europeans, so it is hardly surprising that many Canadians developed a **Eurocentric** view of the world. Europe and the North Atlantic were simply assumed to be the centre of the world, in politics, economics, culture, and daily life. Even in British Columbia, which looks out on the Pacific, leaders and the social and business **elites** maintained their narrow view of the world long after British Columbia entered Confederation. As you learned in Chapter 6, the British had ensured that their class system—and the cultural attitudes that went with it—was the foundation of the colony. In addition, Chinese, Japanese, and East Indian immigrants and labourers faced many barriers in Canada.

In the last third of the twentieth century, it became impossible to ignore Asian countries on the Pacific. Starting in the 1960s, Japan began to re-emerge from the devastation of World War II as a major industrial power. By the 1970s, other Asian economies were also rapidly industrializing. Human **migration,** trade, and commerce between Canada and Asian countries increased dramatically. By the

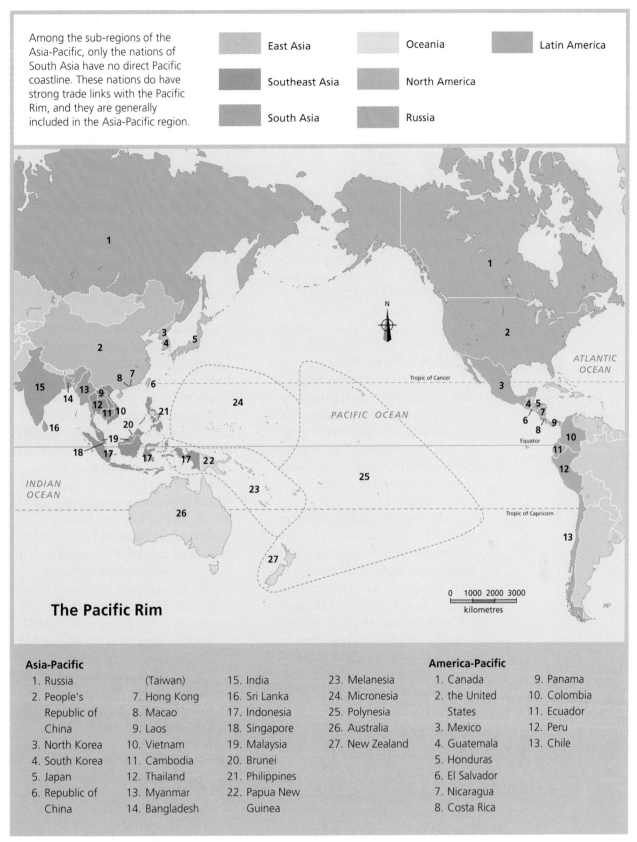

Among the sub-regions of the Asia-Pacific, only the nations of South Asia have no direct Pacific coastline. These nations do have strong trade links with the Pacific Rim, and they are generally included in the Asia-Pacific region.

East Asia   Oceania   Latin America

Southeast Asia   North America

South Asia   Russia

The Pacific Rim

Asia-Pacific

1. Russia
2. People's Republic of China
3. North Korea
4. South Korea
5. Japan
6. Republic of China
7. Hong Kong
8. Macao
9. Laos
10. Vietnam
11. Cambodia
12. Thailand
13. Myanmar
14. Bangladesh
(Taiwan)
15. India
16. Sri Lanka
17. Indonesia
18. Singapore
19. Malaysia
20. Brunei
21. Philippines
22. Papua New Guinea
23. Melanesia
24. Micronesia
25. Polynesia
26. Australia
27. New Zealand

America-Pacific

1. Canada
2. the United States
3. Mexico
4. Guatemala
5. Honduras
6. El Salvador
7. Nicaragua
8. Costa Rica
9. Panama
10. Colombia
11. Ecuador
12. Peru
13. Chile

Figure 10–9 The Pacific Rim and its two major sub-regions

1980s, it was clear that the centres of political and economic power were no longer restricted to the North Atlantic. Asia had became the most economically dynamic region in the world.

The Pacific Rim as a Region

The term "Pacific Rim" usually refers to countries that have a Pacific coastline or that are on the "rim" of the Pacific. This is an extremely broad way to define a region, especially one that includes more than forty independent nations. Yet as diverse as these nations are in history, geography, language, culture, government, and religion, the Pacific Ocean links them all.

The Pacific Rim is usually divided into two sub-regions: the Asia-Pacific and the America-Pacific. The Asia-Pacific includes the nations of Asia and Oceania. The America-Pacific includes nations of North America, Central America, and South America.

The trade blocs and alliances that you examined earlier in this chapter show how vitally important trade is to the Pacific Rim. They also reveal that development in Pacific Rim countries could slow if trade blocs limit the flow of goods between nations. Increased trade in the Pacific Rim has brought with it the need for closer political, economic, and cultural connections.

New Trade Relationships

As you have already learned, Pacific Rim trade and investment has become an important part of Canada's economy. In British Columbia, which is often called "Canada's Gateway to the Pacific," it has completely transformed old trading patterns. June 1989 marked a turning point in British Columbia's economic history. For the first time, trade figures showed that the province had traded more with the Pacific Rim—the Asia-Pacific region—than with the United States and Europe. This shift didn't happen overnight, and trade figures have fluctuated since 1989. A flood of immigration and investment from Hong Kong was another key factor driving the increase. However, trade with the Asia-Pacific countries has consistently dominated British Columbia's economy since that time. British Columbia has developed particularly close ties with Japan, exporting lumber, pulp and paper, coal, copper, sulphur, and food products to the Japanese market. Almost every year, sales of British Columbia products to Japan increase.

During the early 1990s, Canada's economy slipped into a recession. But in British Columbia, from 1989 to 1997, the economy experienced a boom, fuelled by close ties with the Asia-Pacific. Trade and commerce soared, as did Asian investment. Sawmills, pulp and paper mills, shopping malls, ski resorts, hotels, golf courses, and many other enterprises were purchased or initiated by new Asian investors, particularly from Japan and Hong Kong.

In 1992, British Columbia Premier Mike Harcourt described how crucial British Columbia's role would be for Canada in the new century:

British Columbia's role in the medium and long term is to be Canada's front door on the Asia-Pacific, to act as a catalyst and as a meeting place. This is where the action is.

The British Columbia government was also able to diversify its trade and economic development. It was important for the province to develop the quaternary sector of its economy, so high-technology and research and development were targeted. These would create jobs for highly skilled workers and pay high salaries. Without this kind of diversification, British Columbia would become too reliant on the up-and-down cycles of resource-based industries.

In Vancouver and its suburbs, entrepreneurial immigrants, many of them from Hong Kong, invested heavily in real estate and in many different projects. The largest of these was the Concorde Pacific development on the former Expo '86 lands. Hong Kong billionaire Li Ka-Shing and his son Victor, a Canadian citizen, rebuilt the old industrial site into a mini-city of high-rise towers, businesses, and open space located on False Creek. The project revitalized nearby neighbourhoods and brought people back to downtown Vancouver.

The Asian Economies

In 1964, Tokyo hosted the first Olympic Games ever to be held in Asia. At the same time, Japan also unveiled its Shinkansen super-express train system, which linked Tokyo to Osaka—it featured the world's fastest train, nicknamed the "bullet train." The eyes of the world were on Japan and Asia, and Japan's advanced technology and futuristic **infrastructure** made a big impression. Soon Europeans and North Americans began to take notice of the rising industrial and economic power of Japan and the Asian economies. In the next twenty-five years, Japan would become the most economically powerful nation in the Asia-Pacific—in many ways, a world

infrastructure: the basic foundation of a country's economy, including transportation and communication systems

Figure 10–10 The Hong Kong Bank of Canada building is a strong presence in the heart of downtown Vancouver. What does it say about recent investment patterns in British Columbia?

A Turning Point in Hong Kong's History

During the peak of its empire-building days, Britain took control of Hong Kong; in 1898, it became a British **dependency**. Hong Kong also became a global financial and manufacturing centre. In fact, it was often described as the ultimate **capitalist** economy. Britain, however, signed an agreement that the colony of Hong Kong would be returned to the People's Republic of China in 1997.

In the years leading up to 1997, Hong Kong's future was completely uncertain. Its business class invested heavily around the world in case the Chinese government restructured the economy on a **communist** model. It was during this period that Canada—British Columbia, and Vancouver, in particular—experienced a great influx of immigration and investment from Hong Kong. British Columbia was especially attractive because of its Pacific location, natural beauty, political stability, and high standards of education.

On July 1, 1997, at midnight, Hong Kong became a Special Administrative Region of China. The arrangement guaranteed that Hong Kong's government and economic systems would be preserved for fifty years.

dependency: a colony or nation controlled by another nation

capitalist: an economy in which private ownership and enterprise are most important

communist: an economy in which state control and ownership of resources are most important

Figure 10–11 Hong Kong students rehearse in ancient Chinese costumes for a performance to celebrate Hong Kong's return to China on July 1, 1997.

superpower. In the 1980s and early 1990s, the Asian economies—some of them among the poorest in the world—would fuel the expansion of the global economy.

Japan

Many western observers have described Japan's recovery from the devastation of World War II as an "economic miracle." This reveals a certain bias. Because of geography, the Japanese have had a history of surviving and rebuilding after natural disasters. Much of Japan lies in an earthquake zone—the **Pacific Rim of Fire**—and cities such as Tokyo and Yokohama have been levelled by major earthquakes. The Japanese have also had to learn to deal with the random destruction of **tsunamis**, **typhoons**, and even volcanic eruptions. Japan was the first non-western nation to industrialize, in the late nineteenth century. By the outbreak of World War II, in 1939, it was far more industrialized than all but a few Western nations. It was a leader in steel production, shipbuilding, and manufacturing.

By the end of World War II, in 1945, Japan's major industrial centres and cities had been destroyed by bombing. Hiroshima and Nagasaki were destroyed by the first and only atomic bombs ever to be dropped in a war. In Hiroshima, the bomb is estimated to have killed 140 000 people. Tokyo and other factory centres were **firebombed**. As an occupied country after World War II, Japan's redevelopment was guided by the US. The US plan focused on producing quality goods for export and creating good relations between government, labour, and management. Japanese leaders followed this plan, to a degree, and undertook long-term planning, rather than seeking short-term gains.

In 1953, the Japanese government re-established the Ministry of International Trade and Industry. This huge bureaucracy became the driving force for carefully managed economic change, and it developed good relations with corporations throughout the country. The government financed infrastructure projects in communications and transportation, power-generation, and research and development. Labour, banking, and business leaders met regularly with government leaders to work out cooperative strategies. The government also offered grants, subsidies, loans, and protection for new industries. The concept of lifetime employment and company loyalty created good relations between management and labour.

By the 1980s, Japan dominated the Asia-Pacific. Many nations in

superpower: a country with unrivalled power and influence

Pacific Rim of Fire: the earthquake zones and volcanoes that circle the Pacific Rim

tsunamis: long, high tidal waves, usually caused by undersea earthquakes

typhoons: extremely violent storms, usually with high winds, rain, and thunder

to firebomb: to attack with incendiary bombs

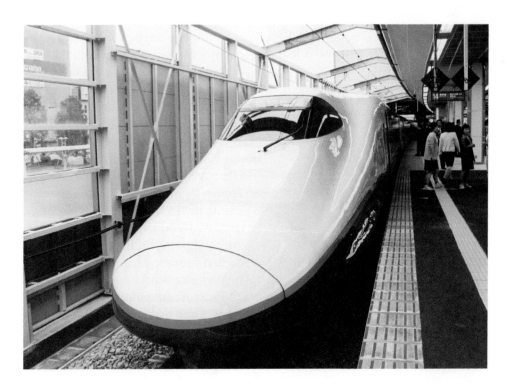

Figure 10–12 Japan's Shinkansen train can cruise at speeds of up to 240 kilometres an hour. Do you know of any trains operating in Canada that can cruise this fast?

Figure 10–13 Mourners float paper lanterns on the Motoyasu River at the Hiroshima Peace Memorial Park on August 6, 1998—fifty-three years after the atomic bomb was dropped. Today, Japan is an economic superpower, but its military power is limited. It has no nuclear arms. Why do you think this is so?

authoritarian government favoured family-owned companies, that operated many different kinds of businesses. Hyundai, for example, runs divisions in iron and steel production, shipbuilding, automobile manufacturing, real estate, and construction. Because of guaranteed government contracts, however, many of these South Korean business groups had a false sense of security and so became less competitive.

Taiwan (or the Republic of China), used a different model of economic development. Family-owned businesses set up small, flexible operations and mass produced consumer products for foreign companies, which were usually based in the US or Europe. Profits were reinvested in the company so that it could diversify and seek out new customers. The businesses also maintained links to other people of Chinese ancestry through the guanxi network. In these ways, Taiwan's economy grew and became less vulnerable to downswings in regional trade patterns.

Hong Kong's economy had very few government regulations on business before being repatriated to China in 1997. In reality, the economy was controlled by a select group of powerful families who owned operations around the world. Investment flowed in and out very quickly. At the first sign of trouble, Hong Kong investors would move their money elsewhere. This proved to be harmful and weakened Hong Kong in times of economic crises.

authoritarian: a government that stresses strict obedience over individual rights and freedoms

the region depended on it for leadership in trade, investment, and commerce. Japan's cash-rich corporations bought or invested in foreign businesses all over the world; and Japanese tourists were travelling the world.

Newly Industrialized Economies

Japan was influential in the rapid industrialization of South Korea, Taiwan, Hong Kong, and Singapore during the 1960s and 1970s. Although these countries also became export-oriented, they differ from Japan. In South Korea, an

The Two Types of Economies

There are two basic types of national economies: mixed economies and centrally planned economies. Most economies in the developed world are social democracies and have mixed economies. This means that the supply of goods and services is determined for the most part by the market place, or private business. Wealth is redistributed through a combination of taxation, state control of key industries, and bargaining by labour. Part of government revenue is used to fund social programs, such as health care and welfare. Canada is an example of a mixed economy.

In centrally planned economies, the state owns all resources and controls production and distribution of goods and services. The state also controls wages and public utilities. Because of this control, the state is expected to redistribute wealth fairly and to provide social, educational, health and welfare services that are accessible to all. Communist economies are centrally planned economies. The People's Republic of China is one example.

joint venture: a business undertaken by two or more countries or companies which otherwise have separate identities

Figure 10–14 In the photo at right, a Chinese worker polishes a Cherokee shell on the modern production line at Beijing Jeep Corporation, a China-US **joint venture**. In the photo below, two women sort tobacco in an old cigarette factory. What advantages might the US be seeking in China? What impact could modern production have on old factories in China?

Starting in the late 1950s, Singapore went from being a city state of slums to an ultra-modern nation of skyscrapers and high-tech factories. Its economy differed from all others in the Asia-Pacific region, and the government was involved in all decision-making. Multinationals had to follow strict government rules and regulations. In exchange, they enjoyed the pluses of this controlled society. Workers were well-educated, technology and infrastructure were up-to-date, and the standard of living was comfortable.

In the People's Republic of China, the world's most populous country, the communist government began a slow change towards a **market-oriented** economy. In 1979, special economic zones were established along the coast of China

market-oriented: allowing competition and the laws of supply and demand to determine the production, distribution, and exchange of goods and services

Figure 10–15 In August 1998, more than 10 000 South Korean riot police were ready to storm a Hyundai auto factory where thousands of workers were staging a strike. What does this say to you about how South Korea's government dealt with labour?

during times of economic turmoil. Old Chinese plants, working under the Chinese communist model, often went out of business, displacing hundreds of thousands of workers. Industrial expansion also led to concerns about pollution and human rights.

Newly Exporting Economies

During the 1980s, the transformation of Asian economies spread to newly exporting economies, such as Thailand, Malaysia, Indonesia, and the Philippines. Thailand set up free-trade zones where foreign companies could assemble products for export to other nations. The Thai people benefited with jobs and increased wages. The capital city of Bangkok suffered the consequences of uncontrolled industrial growth and a huge increase in population, as rural workers migrated to the already overcrowded city.

Malaysia developed high-tech facilities and improved its infrastructure to attract foreign investment. The nation experienced an unprecedented boom in construction and industrial development.

Indonesia went from the agricultural age to the technological age almost overnight by promoting specialized high-tech projects. Unfortunately, government corruption and **favouritism** created divisions in Indonesian society. Friends of the government got richer and richer while the vast majority of the people remained poor. The Philippines, once known as the "sick man of Asia," improved its basic infrastructure—electricity, roads, and communications—and started to attract new businesses. It reached a turning point when it transformed a former US Navy base into a free-trade zone.

favouritism: the unfair favouring of one group, person, or business over another

and foreign multinational businesses were allowed to establish joint ventures with Chinese companies. These operations had access to cheap labour and resources and could sell their products to the emerging markets in China. This provided the Chinese with opportunities to learn modern production techniques. Because the government was directly involved, the businesses were successful, even

In 1991, India, experienced an economic crisis and required help from the International Monetary Fund. India was already industrialized and self-sufficient, but its economy was largely centrally controlled. The government implemented a series of major economic reforms. It created freer trade areas and liberalized regulations for doing business in India, welcoming investment from foreign multinational businesses. The economy grew, and new jobs and products were created. The Indian middle class became the largest of any nation in the world. However, many critics complained that only the rich of India and the foreign investors were making gains.

By the 1990s, many of these nations in the Asia-Pacific were experiencing the fastest growth rates in the world. They were also acting as economic engines for such nations in the developed world as the United States, Germany, and Japan. The future looked extremely promising, although there were problems. Any major downturn in the global economy could lead to a major economic collapse.

Figure 10–16 Indian culture has long had a big influence on popular culture in the West, as shown in this photo of the US pop star Madonna. Do you think Madonna is expanding people's understanding of India? Why or why not?

ACTIVITIES

1. **a)** In 1989, British Columbia's trade statistics showed what significant change? Was this temporary, or the beginning of a trend? Explain, with reasons.

   b) How did British Columbia's government respond to increasing Pacific Rim trade and investment? Was this effective? Explain, with reasons.

2. Create an organizer to compare and contrast China and Japan as economic models. List the differences between each in terms of type of government, population, technology, and so on.

Based on your findings, make predictions about both Japan's and China's future development.

3. The return of Hong Kong to China affected the economy of British Columbia in what ways? Explain, with examples both from before and after the return.

4. Find three newspaper articles on recent economic activities in the Asia-Pacific. Be sure to include Japan and one country from both the newly exporting and newly industrialized economies. Describe the relationship or link between each story and British Columbia.

PACIFIC RIM IMPACT

Time Line 10–1

1992
Japan's real estate and stock markets collapse

January to March, 1997
Thai and South Korean currencies come under pressure

July 1, 1997
Hong Kong returned to China

July 2, 1997
Thai currency sinks 30 percent

July 1997–September 1998
Asian currencies plummet in value

October 20–23, 1997
The Hong Kong stock market suffers greatest decline in its history

October 27, 1997
Stock markets around the world suffer biggest declines in a decade

May 29, 1998
Hong Kong's economy declines 2 percent
Indonesia, Thailand, and South Korea announce negative growth

July 2, 1998
Economic crises in Brazil and Russia

summer 1998
Canadian dollar hits historic low

spring 1999
Asian economies start to recover

All economies are subject to business cycles, and all economies have underlying strengths and weaknesses. The Asian economies of the Pacific Rim experienced stunning growth in the 1980s and 1990s. In the summer of 1997, however, the cycle reversed abruptly. The downturn was triggered by a currency and banking crisis in Thailand that quickly spread throughout Southeast Asia and to most other Asian nations. In the globalized economy, the effects of the Asian economic crisis were soon felt elsewhere. In North America, Latin America, and Europe, levels of exports and sources of foreign investment declined.

The Asian Economic Crisis and Canada

Problems in the Asian economies were clear as early as 1992, when Japan entered a recession. Other Asian nations continued to expand. Factories and stores, real estate projects, stock market ventures—all went ahead, but with borrowed money.

The major roots of the Asian economic crisis can be traced to questionable business practices and weak regulations. In Indonesia, Malaysia, and Thailand, for example, governments barely monitored banks. Many loans were made that would never be repaid. Asian stock

Figure 10–17 This stock trader's face is glum as the Hong Kong stock market suffers its largest decline in history on October 23, 1997.

markets attracted international investors who had one goal in mind: short-term gain. At the first sign of trouble, they would sell their shares and invest somewhere else in the world. This made Asian stock markets far less attractive for stable, long-term investments. While the Asian economies were booming, real estate investors took enormous risks with projects—and financed them with borrowed money. Many businesses also expanded, basing their decisions on the belief that the boom would never slow down.

In countries like South Korea and Indonesia, political corruption had long been a problem. Bribes were common. Some politicians, such as South Korea's former president, Roh Tae Woo, received prison sentences for **graft**. Indonesia's President Suharto favoured family and friends with government appointments, handouts, and deals before he was finally forced to resign in 1998. A former military general, Suharto had been president for thirty years, a period marked by his **dictatorial** powers and widespread human rights abuses. Less than two weeks before he resigned, four student protesters were killed by security forces. Riots and protests swept the country. As the economic crisis deepened, political stability was shaken around the region.

Between July and December 1997, the International Monetary Fund arranged multibillion-dollar emergency loans to the Philippines, Thailand, Indonesia, and South Korea. This helped to stabilize their currencies and to keep the crisis from spreading further. The loans came with conditions, and government spending was restricted. Most of these nations had limited or non-existent social programs, such as employment insurance, health care, or welfare. For those directly affected by the crisis—the middle and working classes—government restraint simply meant more hardship.

With companies, brokerage houses, banks, and factories closing, managers and workers were thrown out of work throughout Asia. Many left the cities and returned to their rural villages; others became homeless. Some survived by creating new opportunities, but they had to live on much lower incomes. Many formerly wealthy people sold off personal possessions in the streets. As governments fell in Thailand, South Korea, and Indonesia, protests and riots broke out.

Canada was also affected by the Asian economic crisis. In British Columbia, the impact was most

dictatorial: like a dictator, with supreme power

graft: underhanded means, such as bribery, used to gain political and business gains

Table 10–2 shows the remarkable social progress achieved in these countries between 1980 and 1995. How secure are these advances in times of economic crisis? Explain, with reasons.

Table 10–2	Living Standards in South Korea, Thailand, and Indonesia					
	South Korea		Thailand		Indonesia	
	1980	**1995**	**1980**	**1995**	**1980**	**1995**
Life Expectancy, years						
male	63	70	58	65	48	60
female	67	78	63	73	48	64
Literacy rate	92%	98%	84%	94%	64%	84%
Income per person US$ (GDP per person)	1200	13 000	444	6900	305	3500

severe. Unemployment increased. As Japanese demand for BC forest products and coal went down, prices sank. Many small forest companies could not maintain production. As a result, 15 500 forestry workers—17 percent of the total forestry work-force—were laid off. Some sawmills closed permanently. In Tumbler Ridge, the town's two coal mines, Bull Moose and Quintette, laid off workers. The future of the town was at risk. Asian investment dried up across the province; some projects were stopped in the middle of construction.

Asian tourism to BC—which had boosted the tourist industry for years—dropped by 20 percent in the first half of 1998. In Vancouver, stores aimed at Asian tourists struggled to survive. British Columbia was the only province in Canada in 1998 to have a declining retail trade. Business immigration to BC from Hong Kong and Taiwan virtually disappeared. In fact, many of the new Canadians from Hong Kong returned home to salvage their businesses. In the Vancouver real estate market, where prices had doubled and tripled since the late 1980s, prices dropped for the first time in a decade. Even Vancouver's school population went down, briefly, but it quickly recovered.

Eventually, the Asian economic crisis of 1997 to 1998 pushed British Columbia into a recession for the first time since the early 1980s. British Columbia had ridden the boom of Asian investment and trade. By the end of 1998, the ride was over. The declining value of the Canadian dollar affected all of Canada, but no other province was threatened with recession. This made it clearer than ever that the rest of Canada depended far more on trade with the United States, whose economy prospered throughout 1997 and 1998. By the spring of 1999, however, Asia's economy was showing strong signs of recovery.

Figure 10–18 The Bull Moose coal mine near Tumbler Ridge, BC, laid off workers during the Asian economic crisis. Why do you think this happened?

Human Rights and Environmental Issues

As trade and investment have increased between different cultures and nations, human rights have become a major global issue. When investments or trade agreements are finalized, however, human rights have usually been placed to the side or entirely ignored. In the Asian nations of the Pacific Rim, a range of political situations made agreements on human rights next to impossible. Cultural values also differ from country to country, and there is not always agreement on what "human rights" means, or if they can apply to all cultures equally.

The Universal Declaration of Human Rights

John Humphrey, a Canadian, wrote the Universal Declaration of Human Rights. Adopted by the United Nations in December, 1948, it categorizes the following themes of rights: (1) all human beings are born free and equal, (2) all are to be treated fairly, without discrimination, (3) all are to have civil and political rights, and (4) all are to enjoy economic, social, and cultural rights. The United Nations Universal Declaration of Human Rights contains thirty **articles**, a selection of which follow.

articles: separate sections or clauses of a document

 Article 1
All human beings are born free and equal in dignity and rights ...

Article 3
Everyone has the right to life, liberty and security of person.

Article 5
No one shall be subjected to torture or to cruel, inhuman or degrading treatment or punishment.

Article 17
(1) Everyone has the right to own property alone as well as in association with others.

Article 21
(3) The will of the people shall be the basis of the authority of government; this will shall be expressed in periodic and genuine elections ...

Article 23
(1) Everyone has the right to work, to free choice of employment, to just and favourable conditions of work and to protection against unemployment.

(2) Everyone, without any discrimination, has the right to equal pay for equal work.

Article 24
Everyone has the right to rest and leisure, including reasonable limitation of working hours and periodic holidays with pay.

Article 25
(1) Everyone has the right to a standard of living adequate for the health and well-being of himself and of his family, including food, clothing, housing and medical care and necessary social services, and the right to security in the event of unemployment, sickness, disability, widowhood, old age or other lack of livelihood in circumstances beyond his control.
...

Article 28
Everyone is entitled to a social and international order in which the rights and freedoms set forth in this Declaration can be fully realized.
...

Figure 10–19 In the spring of 1989, Chinese students held massive pro-democracy demonstrations across China. This photo, taken in Beijing's Tiananmen Square, shows journalists supporting the students. On June 4, 1989, Chinese troops opened fire, killing hundreds of people and quashing the pro-democracy movement.

The dilemma around human rights is not new. In 1948, the United Nations adopted and proclaimed the Universal Declaration of Human Rights. It was a keystone in the UN's mission to promote and maintain world peace after World War II. The Declaration was meant to serve as an objective for the entire international community to strive towards and as the basis for a common understanding of human rights. It still serves these purposes today, but not all nations respond.

Human rights advocates claim that in the global economy the governments of developed nations have a duty to see that human rights are advanced in the developing world. Human rights must not only be respected at home, they say, but in all countries where investments are made and trade agreements are signed. Human rights advocates say that businesses have the same obligation.

Figure 10–20 Chinese Premier Zhu Rhongji stopped in St. John's during a visit to Canada in the spring of 1999. At the time, Canada was supporting China's bid to join the World Trade Organization. Many Canadians remembered Tiananmen Square and were outraged by Canada's trade initiatives with China.

Many of the Asian nations in the Pacific Rim ignored human rights during the period of rapid economic development. The explanation was that economic growth would eventually improve the social and political foundations of their society. But the Asian economic crisis reversed what progress had been made. The same people who had endured human rights abuses during the boom times were the first to suffer when economic growth halted.

Some advocates viewed the crisis as an opportunity to link human rights to international trade, investment, and foreign aid. World leaders such as Prime Minister Jean Chretien, they said, could put the issue in the international spotlight by pressuring repressive Asian governments to act. In countries like Thailand, Indonesia, and South Korea, governments might be forced to adhere to the Universal Declaration of Human Rights, if this were a condition for receiving International Monetary Fund loans.

As the twentieth century drew to a close, Chretien's trade policies drew increasing criticism in the Canadian media, particularly his dealings with Indonesia and China. Trade and investments were being actively pursued—without specific human rights commitments.

Environmental problems also became critical in countries such as Indonesia, India, Malaysia, and Thailand, where the combined effects of economic development and high population growth have been severe. Forests have been devastated—either mismanaged by commercial lumbering or burned and cleared to quickly provide more land for food production. Thailand lost more than 30 percent of its forests in the 1980s alone. In 1997, forest fires in Indonesia affected all of Southeast Asia. International agencies are calling for governments around the world to fund local programs that would reimburse some of the poorest people in the world to manage their local forest lands. This would require a new kind of response from the developed world, one that would assign economic value to the management and preservation of the forests, the world's largest reserves of plants, animals, and clean air.

ACTIVITIES

1. What were the major causes of the Asian economic crisis of 1997 to 1998?

2. Do you think the Asian economic crisis was simply a dip in the "business cycle" or something more permanent? Explain, with reasons.

3. Create a two-column organizer to compare the effects of the Asian economic crisis on Asia and on British Columbia. Based on your findings, where would you say the social impact was felt more deeply? Explain, with reasons.

4. Imagine that you are one of the protesters in Figure 10–19 and that you have witnessed the killings of June 4, 1989. Write a letter to a Western newspaper describing what your protest had hoped to achieve and what the killings mean to your movement. Refer to The Two Types of Economies, on page 413, and The Universal Declaration of Human Rights, on page 419, for background and ideas.

5. Do you support or oppose the linking of human rights and environmental protection to Canada's international trade agreements and initiatives? Provide three reasons that support your opinion.

FREER TRADE WITH THE AMERICAS

As you learned in Chapter 8, Canada, the US, and Mexico are members of the North American Free Trade Agreement (NAFTA). While NAFTA creates a large, tariff-free trading zone for each of the nations involved, some people think the agreement tips the power balance in favour of the United States. The US is a powerful trading nation, and NAFTA allows it to dominate trade relations on the continent.

Since NAFTA was signed, the Canadian federal government has been promoting worldwide trade options that would allow Canada to be less dependent on the US. One part of this global trade strategy has been to encourage better relations with Latin America, a large area that includes Mexico, Central America and the Caribbean, and South

America (see Figure 10–9). According to the Department of Foreign Affairs and International Trade, Canadian exports to Latin America more than doubled in value— from $2.8 billion to $6.4 billion—between 1991 and 1997.

Shortly after NAFTA took effect, there were signs that the agreement might expand to include new members. Canadian trade negotiators hoped that the inclusion of South American nations such as Chile would reduce the trade dominance of the United States. However, the United States Congress stalled the process of allowing Chile into NAFTA, and Canada had to act in its own interests. After lengthy negotiations, the governments of Canada and Chile agreed to enter into their own bilateral free-trade

Figure 10–21 The Canadian company Rio Algom has expanded its massive Cerro Colorado copper mine in Chile since the Canada-Chile Free Trade Agreement took effect in 1997.

agreement, the Canada-Chile Free Trade Agreement (CCFTA). It took effect on July 5, 1997. The agreement eliminated duties on 75 percent of Canadian exports; the remaining tariffs on Canadian exports will be phased out by 2002. One Canadian product that now enters Chile duty-free is durum wheat, used to make pasta.

While environmental and labour concerns were dealt with only in side agreements, the CCFTA benefited Canada in a number of ways. Its terms offered Canadian investment in the Chilean mining sector better protection. Canada's cultural industries, health care and employment insurance programs, marketing boards, and the Auto Pact were left unchallenged, since they were exempted from the agreement. Overall, through the CCFTA, Canadian companies gained better access to Chile than did their major competitors in the US, European Union, Argentina, and Brazil. Two Canadian companies that took advantage of the CCFTA and increased trading with Chile were Rio Algom, which invested $270 million to expand its Cerro Colorado copper mine in northern Chile, and Nortel, which sold $245 million worth of telecommunications equipment to a South American firm to build a cable telephone network for Chile.

Working Towards the FTAA

In 1994, Prime Minister Jean Chretien led a group of Canadian negotiators to the Miami Summit of the Americas. Here, delegates laid out a long-term plan for greater cooperation between the nations of the Western Hemisphere. The key proposal was the Free Trade Area of the Americas (FTAA). The FTAA would create common rules of trade and commerce and would lower or eliminate tariff and non-tariff barriers for all the Western Hemisphere countries. It would make it easier for Canada to conduct business in an emerging market place—with more than 700 million people. The FTAA also promised to clamp down on corruption, which had been a major problem in Latin America.

In 1998, Chretien and leaders from thirty-three other nations of the Western Hemisphere—every nation except Cuba—met in Santiago, Chile, for the Second Summit of the Americas. Here they began the long, slow process of hammering out the details of the FTAA—a process that will not be finished until 2005. Chretien's dream of a large trade bloc

Figure 10–22 Prime Minister Jean Chretien applauds the President of Chile, Eduardo Frei, at the Santiago Summit of the Americas in 1998.

Using a Political Cartoon as a Primary Source

Political cartoons are a barometer for a nation's political weather—they expose all that is unsettling and unflattering about politics and politicians. One reason political cartoons are often so biting is because they bring everyone down to reality. Political **rhetoric** often makes problems sound easy to solve. Political realities, by contrast, are complicated because so many interests are involved.

The cartoons that follow raise some of the issues you have thought about while reading Chapter 10. Before you proceed to the activities, take a few minutes to examine each of the cartoons. Jot down some rough notes about them.

- What is the cartoon about?
- Who appears in the cartoon?
- If you can't identify everyone, can you guess who they might be?
- Did you find the cartoon effective, funny, or both? Think about why.

rhetoric: communication meant to win over or impress

Figure 10–23

Figure 10–24

Figure 10–25

WHAT DO YOU THINK?

1. Why are wall screens being offered for sale in Figure 10–23, and not some other product? How do the screens give the cartoonist the opportunity to express some of the complications of free-trade agreements?

2. Why has the cartoonist put Jean Chretien at a poker table in Figure 10–24? Who seems to be winning the poker game? How do you know? What is the cartoonist saying about the importance of democracy and human rights to Canada? To other nations?

3. What is the setting of the cartoon in Figure 10–25? Why does the cartoonist refer to human sacrifice? What two kinds of human sacrifice are being depicted?

4. What bias is evident in all three political cartoons?

5. After analyzing these cartoons, have your opinions about free trade changed? Explain.

where nations acting together could check the immense power of the United States was inching toward reality. As chair of the negotiations during the first eighteen months, Chretien's greatest challenge was to convince many of the smaller and poorer nations that a free-trade agreement would be in their best interests. Many of those nations depend on tariffs as their main source of revenue. In the long run, however, the greatest obstacle to negotiations surrounding FTAA has been the United States. Its protectionist economic policies have often run counter to the goals of such an agreement.

The Importance of Brazil

Any new trade agreement with the Latin American region will hinge on the stability of Brazil's economy. Brazil has the largest economy in South America and the eighth largest economy in the world. However, Brazil also has a huge

debt, and inflation has been a fact of life since the 1970s. In 1998, Brazil's economy was on the verge of collapse. As often happens in such situations, fear of an economic crisis made the situation worse. Investors lost confidence in the country and moved their investments elsewhere. Development projects were put on hold, further depressing the Brazilian economy. Unemployment became a serious problem.

In November 1998, the IMF organized a $41.5 billion rescue loan to end Brazil's crisis and keep it from spreading to neighbouring countries. The loan came with conditions. Brazil had to reduce government spending and pay down its debt. Brazil also raised interest rates to fight inflation. This, along with the government spending cutbacks, led to even more unemployment. Some analysts feared that these policies would not help Brazil in the long run and that FTAA negotiations would stall as a result.

Figure 10–26 Street vendor in Sao Paulo, Brazil. Sao Paulo has rapidly grown to become one of the largest cities in the world. Rural-to-urban migration has created a city of striking contrasts between rich and poor. How is that played out in this photograph?

Pursuing Pinochet

While political leaders began drafting the CCFTA, a very different drama involving a former Chilean dictator was unfolding halfway around the world.

General Augusto Pinochet had led a military **junta** that seized power in Chile in1973. A right-wing dictator who threatened to "lock up all those people talking about human rights and all those things," Pinochet made good on his promise for seventeen years. Lucky citizens who supported democracy and human rights were expelled from the country. Thousands of others were rounded up, imprisoned, and tortured. Some people simply vanished, never to be seen again. Pinochet's sweep was so wide that, at one time, Catholic Church officials in Chile estimated that one in a hundred Chileans had been arrested at least once following the **coup**.

Pinochet turned Chile into a free-market economy. (Formerly, it had elected a **Marxist** leader.) He eliminated its high tariffs, which encouraged a flood of imported goods, and he stopped subsidizing inefficient domestic industries. These actions plunged Chile into a deep recession in the early 1980s, but the country recovered by the early 1990s. Today, Chile has some prosperous at-home industries, including military arms and computer hardware and software, and its world-famous wines.

Ironically, the CCFTA—an agreement so in tune with Pinochet's economic philosophy—came into effect just a year before the dictator was arrested by the British police on an **extradition** warrant filed by Spain. The warrant was the only way to bring Pinochet to trial for the alleged murders of Chilean citizens while he was in power. Chilean citizens all around the world, including those living in France, Britain, Belgium, and Denmark, fought for the extradition of Pinochet. Their struggle is a reminder that economic gains and protection of human rights are often at odds with each other.

Today, Canadian human rights activists are worried that Latin American democracy is not always supported by multilateral trade agreements. They hope that the Canadian government's trade policies of will stress the importance of democratic

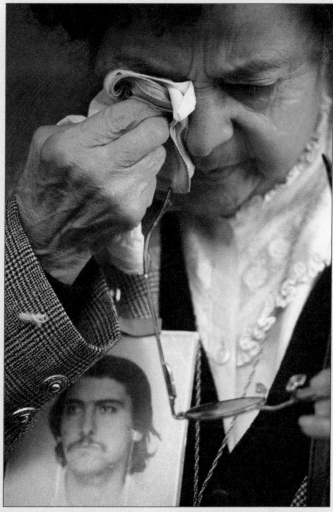

Figure 10–27 News of Pinochet's arrest brought hope and memories to thousands of people who lost loved ones during his reign.

principles, but they fear that such ideals may be overlooked for economic reasons. Whether the issue of human rights stays on the table as officials hammer out the details of the FTAA remains to be seen.

junta: secretive faction or group

coup: brutal taking of power

extradition: the handing over of a person to another country's jurisdiction

Marxist: based on the theories of Karl Marx, which advocate that workers own the means of production

Trade in the Americas: Issues

Environmentalists worry that the migration of companies to Latin America will cause increasing environmental damage. They have not forgotten what happened to the Brazilian rain forest or to the peoples of the rain forest when the Carajás project was launched. In the early 1970s, surveyors discovered possibly the world's largest deposit of iron ore in the Carajás Mountains, in northcentral Brazil. With investment from Europe, the US, and Japan, the government of Brazil constructed an iron mine, smelters, and large hydroelectric dams to provide power. The dams caused the most damage, flooding thousands of square kilometres of rain forest and displacing the aboriginal peoples who had lived there for generations. In addition, the Carajás smelters are fueled by charcoal, which is dirtier but less expensive than coal. In order to make the charcoal, the rain forest is cut down.

As happens with other trade arrangements, many Canadians also fear that their jobs may be lost if Canadian companies move to Latin America. Labour and human rights activists are concerned that Canadian companies will exploit the cheap labour of developing nations, and that children will be victims. They would like to see safeguards included in any trade agreements.

It is estimated that one in five children in Latin America, or about 15 to 18 million children, work. Many of these children live in rural areas and work under conditions that in some cases border on forced labour. In urban areas, local children and those escaping the poverty of the countryside are often employed in manufacturing. In Mexico, some maquiladoras along the US border have become notorious for exploiting impoverished girls who work long hours under strict rules for subsistence wages. In Brazil, working conditions for children working in the footwear industry have been described as "intolerable." As in all developing countries, widespread poverty makes children even more desperate for work and more vulnerable to abuse. International and regional organizations are working towards eliminating child labour, but progress has been slow.

ACTIVITIES

1. Why has Canada pursued freer trade with countries in the Americas?

2. a) What criteria should be used to evaluate whether or not Canada should enter into trade agreements with Latin American countries? For example, one criterion would be environmental impact.

   b) Would countries in Latin America and Canada use the same criteria to judge the success of a trade agreement? Explain your answer.

3. What were the economic gains in Chile during Pinochet's time in power? What were the costs in terms of human rights and freedom? Do you believe Pinochet was justified? Explain your answer.

4. Imagine that you are working for an organization to abolish child labour abuses. Create a cartoon or poster that makes your point quickly and powerfully. Remember to use words sparingly and for impact.

CANADA'S TRADE WITH EUROPE

Then and Now

Canada has had strong trade relations with Europe for hundreds of years. The early settlers who emigrated to Canada usually came from Europe. Canadian fish, furs, lumber, and farm goods were shipped across the Atlantic Ocean to Europe in return for manufactured goods and specialty items. As you learned last year, this kind of trade was to the advantage of countries that imported raw materials and exported manufactured goods. Indeed, many European countries colonized other countries in the world to gain just such advantages.

By the early years of the twentieth century, these European **imperialist** empires needed more and more cheap raw products for their factories. Industrialization had spread around the world, and mass production drew more people into rapidly expanding North American and European cities. As the decades passed, manufactured products became more complex—and the world became more interconnected. Raw products were shipped from many parts of the world, including Canada, to manufacturing centres, usually in Europe. The automobile, for example, first became popular in

imperialist: the domination of another country

Figure 10–28 Map of Europe, 1999

Formation of the European Union

1957 France, West Germany, Italy, Belgium, the Netherlands, and Luxembourg form the European Community (EC)

1962 EC countries adopt a Common Agricultural Policy

1968 EC nations remove all tariffs and adopt a common external trade policy

1973 Denmark, the Irish Republic, and the United Kingdom join the EC

1979 The first elections for the European Parliament are held.

1981 Greece joins the EC

1986 Portugal and Spain join the EC

1990 East and West Germany reunify

1991 EC negotiations begin for economic union

1993 The Treaty of European Union is proclaimed

1995 Austria, Finland, and Sweden join the EU

1996 Bulgaria, Cyprus, the Czech Republic, Estonia, Hungary, Latvia, Lithuania, Poland, Romania, Slovakia and Slovenia start the process to join the EU

1998 11 EU countries join the European Monetary Union (EMU)

1999 The euro becomes an accepted currency

the early years of the century. It required iron and steel, leather, rubber, and oil products, which came from many different countries. Many British capitalists also invested money in Canada, and European investment money helped to build the Canadian Pacific Railway. These investors also took money out of Canada, in profits and dividends. Because the majority of Canadians were of British or European descent, most did not object to these trade arrangements. Many saw Europe as their cultural homeland.

This historic relationship between Canada and Europe remained very important until after World War II. During the two world wars, Canada went to the aid of Britain and its allies to fight Germany and its allies. Canada also provided many essential products—food and war supplies—to Britain.

Canada's merchant sailors also faced grave dangers as enemy submarines tried to sink supply ships in the cold North Atlantic. After World War II, however, Europe became more self-contained and self-sufficient. Preferential trade relations with Canada slipped in importance. As Canada's trade with Europe declined, foreign investment in Canada was far more likely to be from the US than Europe.

By the last decades of the twentieth century, groups of countries in different regions of the world had formed trade alliances and trading blocs. In Chapter 8, you learned about the 1989 Canada-US Free Trade Agreement and its renegotiation to include Mexico in the North American Free Trade Agreement in 1994. In this chapter you have learned of many trade organizations, such as the World Trade

Figure 10–29 Canada's merchant marines took supplies to Europe during World War II.

Organization, which promote global trade and investment.

The technological revolution that was reshaping the global economy was also fuelling massive political change in Europe. Computerized communications systems and satellites linked pro-democracy movements in Eastern Europe to supporters around the world. No borders could stop this flow. Eastern Europe had been dominated by the Soviet Union since the end of World War II, but by the late 1980s that control was crumbling.

The world watched—live, on television—as the Berlin Wall was torn down in 1989 (see the photograph on page 394). Soon other communist governments toppled throughout Europe. The Soviet Union itself collapsed as the pro-democracy movement took power there in 1991. As Marshall McLuhan had predicted, the world was becoming a "global village."

The European Union

After World War II, Europeans looked for ways to enhance national security and improve trade. The countries of Europe had been devastated by the economic and human cost of the war. If they joined together, they could trade more economically with one another. They could also compete in what was becoming a global economy.

The first countries to move in this direction were Belgium, the Netherlands, and Luxembourg. In 1948, they eliminated trade barriers among their three countries. This meant that goods could be made and sold within these countries without any duties or tariffs being added to the price of those goods. In 1952,

France, West Germany, and Italy joined with them to form the European Coal and Steel Community. The move towards today's European Union (EU) had started. The Time Line 10–2 details the entry of countries into the European Community and, later, the European Union.

By 1999, the EU was made up of fifteen countries: Austria, Belgium, Denmark, Finland, France, Germany, Greece, Ireland, Italy, Luxembourg, the Netherlands, Portugal, Spain, Sweden, and the United Kingdom.

The EU has a complex structure, and the negotiations for membership are also complex. The goal was to create a strong economic union where citizens could move freely across the borders of member countries. First, labour and environmental laws had to be harmonized. Next, all countries in the EU had to agree to quality standards for manufactured products that could be imported and exported among the countries. An automobile manufactured in Italy had to have the same fuel-emission standards as one manufactured in France. Common agricultural policies also had to be accepted among all of the countries. These policies sometimes hurt countries that export food to the EU, even those who are members. For example, in 1996 it was discovered that the deadly "mad cow" disease, which had infected British cattle, could be passed on to humans who ate contaminated beef. In response, the European Commission banned British beef and insisted that Britain take drastic measures to get rid of the diseased cattle. Finally, many financial and currency issues had to be resolved (see The Euro on page 433).

Table 10-3   The Structure the European Union

Institutions	The People	Functions and Powers
European Commission	19 commissioners and the president Appointed by the governments of the countries that make up the EU Serve for 5 years	Proposes laws Ensures that policies are put in place and treaties are honoured Represents the EU in international trade negotiations Is independent of the national governments of member countries and must be committed to EU interests
European Parliament	626 members elected by the people of the 15 countries of the EU Sit according to political party rather than according to nationality	Debates issues and offers advice to the Commission Questions the decisions and laws proposed by the European Commission Can dismiss the Commission Approves or rejects the Commission's budget Cannot make laws, but can veto actions of any other branch of the EU
Council of the European Union	The elected ministers of the governments of the 15 member countries	Has the final decision-making power on the Commission's proposals Represent the interests of their countries
European Council	The heads of state of the 15 member countries and the Commission president	Writes conclusions that guide the EU Makes decisions about how the EU's treaties will be put into place
Court of Justice	15 judges and 9 advocates-general Appointed for 6 years by mutual consent of the countries of the EU	The "supreme court" of the EU Interprets the laws of the EU Rules on legal matters

Some nationalists in Europe feared that the European Union would erode their cultural sovereignty. After all, member countries have different cultures, histories, and languages, as well as different currencies and investment procedures. Also, through the centuries, wars had been fought between and among these countries. Other citizens of the European countries, however, believed that they could retain their cultural sovereignty and language even within the European Union.

The European Union and Trade with Canada

After the United States, Europe is Canada's most important trading partner. In 1998, Canada exported almost $18 billion worth of goods to the EU and imported more than $25 billion worth of goods. Investors from EU countries also invest heavily in Canadian businesses, and Canadian investors invest heavily in EU businesses. Anything that creates a barrier for Canadian companies trading in Europe is bad news

The Euro

One of the biggest challenges facing the European Union was (and is) the creation of a common monetary policy and a standard currency. The members of the European Union want a single currency. They believe this will help create a single market, simplify trade and business among the countries of the European Union, and make European products more attractive on the world market because of consistent and stable pricing policies.

On January 1, 1999, eleven of the fifteen countries that are members of the European Union adopted the euro as their common currency. The changeover from their national currencies will take place over a three-year period which will end on January 1, 2002. Between 1999 and 2002, the participating countries will have their own currency and the euro. During this time, for daily buying of goods and services, the countries will use their own national currency. However, the value of their currencies will be permanently based on the euro. On January 1, 2002, euro notes and coins will go into circulation; people will carry them in their pockets and wallets and will use them for all their daily purchases.

Businesses in participating countries will also have to use the euro to buy and sell their products and pay their

Figure 10–30 The euro coin

employees, and they will also have to keep their accounts in euros. This means that by January 1, 2002, these companies will have to change their accounting systems. Canadian companies who do business with European countries will need to do business in euros, and they will need to be able to calculate rates of exchange for contracts.

---

for Canada. So, the Canadian government has developed a strategy to maintain and improve relationships with the EU.

Canada's global trade and business strategy for the twenty-first century has to include Europe because Europe has such a large concentration of wealthy consumers who could buy Canadian goods. Also, with Eastern European countries trying to join the EU, it is quite likely that the European Union will expand.

Because the EU is a united trade bloc, it can exclude Canadian products. At the end of the 1990s, the EU was the world's wealthiest consumer market—so much of Canada's future prosperity depends on maintaining friendly trade relations. This has not always been easily done, as a number of trade and environmental conflicts have shown.

In 1995, for example, the "Turbot War" broke out between Canada and Spain. It was really only a trade war, but shots were fired and threats were made. In March 1995, a Canadian Fisheries patrol ship fired shots across the bow of the *Estai*, a Spanish trawler fishing for turbot, a flatfish very popular in Europe. Brian Tobin, Canada's Minister of Fisheries, had ordered the action. As the Canadian crews tried to board the *Estai*, its crew members cut their nets and tried to escape into the night. Finally, the Canadian ship caught up, seized the ship, and arrested the crew. The incident made front-page news around the world. Government reaction in Spain—and from the EU—was immediate outrage.

> **DID YOU KNOW?**
>
> *A factory freezer trawler (such as the* Estai*) can catch in two 32-minute tows the same amount of fish that were caught in one whole year by the entire French fishing fleet of the 1500s.*

In the following months, Tobin used the explosive situation to publicize overfishing by European fleets off Newfoundland. In press conferences outside the United Nations in New York, he displayed the seized nets, saying the openings were so small that all fish would be picked up in their path. Eventually, with British support, trade retaliation from the EU did not happen and Canada was in a stronger position to enforce fishing quotas and restrictions in the international waters off its coast.

In 1997, the EU stepped up its campaign against the fur-trapping business in Canada by signing the Agreement on International Humane Trapping Standards. If Canadian fur trappers did not follow EU regulations, then Canadian furs would be banned from the EU market. In 1998, there were three disputes between Canada and the EU: an EU initiated complaint about Canadian restrictions on auto parts imports, an EU complaint about Canadian patent protection, and a Canadian concern regarding the European ban on Canadian asbestos products. In each case, the disputes were taken to the World Trade Organization for resolution.

The most important aspect of these disputes was that Canada and the EU were able to reach agreements. Canada's tactic of firm but fair negotiation was working without further jeopardizing Canada's fragile trade relationship with Europe. As a result, Canadian companies continued to find opportunities for investment and sales in the new Europe.

Figure 10–31 Brian Tobin said: "We're down now finally to one last, lonely, unattractive little turbot clinging on by its fingertips to the Grand Banks, saying 'someone reach out and save me in this eleventh hour.'"

ACTIVITIES

1. **a)** Provide three reasons why European countries wanted closer trade relationships with one another.

   b) Why would nationalists resist the movement towards economic union?

2. Examine Table 10–3.

   a) Which of the five EU institutions has the most power? Why?

   b) Which institution is the most democratic? Why?

   c) Can members of the European Commission place the interests of their country above those of the European Union? Why?

3. Design a poster or brochure either a) promoting or b) opposing the euro as the common currency for members of the European Union.

4. Write down one word that describes the trading relationship between Canada and the EU. Volunteer your word, or write it down on the chalkboard. Identify one development in Canada-EU trade to support your word choice.

CONCLUSION

Communication and transportation technology have shaped Canada's history. The canoe gave the Native peoples and the fur-traders the opportunity to explore and map Canada's interior and to establish the fur trade. At the time of Confederation, the railway and steamships led to massive immigration and the building of an industrialized infrastructure. By the dawn of the twenty-first century, revolutionary new technologies had again transformed Canada's economy, and its links with other nations of the globe. In the global economy, trade with Britain and Europe became less important, particularly with the formation of the European Union. International trade agreements and organizations reshaped global trading patterns, and Canada played an active role in their formation.

But the global economy was fiercely competitive. Following the Canada-US Free Trade Agreement and NAFTA, Canada's trade with the US mushroomed. Yet trade with other regions of the world also became more important. In British Columbia, for example, expanded trade with Japan and other Asia-Pacific nations led to a boom while the rest of Canada was in a recession. When the Asian economic crisis hit, BC's economy declined, while the rest of Canada experienced economic growth.

As the global economy continued to grow, conflicts over national sovereignty, the environment, and human rights often galvanized the public. The proposed Multilateral Agreement on Investment, for example, was widely opposed in 1998, and put on hold. Canada's government nonetheless continued to promote international trade and commerce. It pushed to forge closer links with the Asia-Pacific economies, and to create a Free Trade Area of the Americas. Clearly, Canada was seeking broader horizons as it prepared for a more globalized existence in the twenty-first century.

SUMMARY ACTIVITIES

1. Debate the following resolution: "Globalization is a force that cannot be stopped. Free markets and free trade will create a world that is better for all people."

2. With a partner, plan a common currency that Canada would use in a monetary union with other countries. Determine what countries should be members in order to ensure Canada's future prosperity. Will the US be included, or is this union a way to check US power and influence?

ON YOUR OWN

1. Using a variety of media, prepare a presentation on the effects of globalization on popular culture. Consider fashion, popular music, video, magazines, or film, for example.

2. Research the concept of "corporate citizenship." Your teacher will provide you with information to get you started. Based on your findings, draft a document outlining the rights and responsibilities of businesses that operate around the world.

3. With a partner, research Mexican maquiladoras. One of you will look for material that promotes maquiladoras from the viewpoint of economic growth and profit. The other will look for information on labour conditions in maquiladoras and their environmental impact. When you have finished, pool your findings and then write a summary report of what you have discovered.

INDEX

CREDITS

Images

vi and page 1: top left: McCord Museum of Canadian History, Montreal; bottom left: NAC/C-2771, top right: bottom right: Prentice Hall Archives; p.2 National Archives of Canada/C-004453; p.9 The Three Robinson Sisters, George Theodore Berthon, 1845, oil on canvas, 112.1 x 83.8; On loan to the Art Gallery of Ontario by Mr. & Mrs. J.R. Robinson, 1944. Photograph courtesy of The Art Gallery of Ontario; p.11 Al Harvey/The Slide Farm; p.12 Al Harvey/The Slide Farm; p.13 top: Victor Last, bottom: Prentice Hall Archives; p.14 PANB: P37-477-1; p.15 NAC/C-2771; p.17 NAC/C-11811; p.18 Canapress/Peter Dejong; p.19 NAC/C-12649; p.20 NAC/C-17; p.22 James B. Wandesford, Portrait of Colonel Thomas Talbot nd, Watercolour on card, 67.3 x 49.5 cm. Collection of McIntosh Gallery, the University of Western Ontario. Gift of Judge Talbot MacBeth, 1941; p.25 top: NAC/National Library of Canada – Rare Books, Illustrated London News, Vol. XVIII, no. 483, page 387; p.26 Canapress/Jacques Boissinot; p.29 Nova Scotia Archives/N-1220; p.30 Keith Beaty/Toronto Star; p.31 Archives of Ontario/AO 722; p.34 NAC/C-011095; p.35 top: Queen's University Archives, Watercolour (1830) by F.H. Consett, bottom: Canapress/Fred Chartrand; p.38 NAC/Jeffreys/C-73725 p.39 NAC/C-396; p.40 NAC/C-17937; p.41 Metropolitan Toronto Reference Library/MTL 1119; p.43 top: The Granger Collection, New York/4E1104.79, bottom: The Granger Collection, New York/4E275.28; p.44 NAC/C-5456; p.47 NAC/C - 11224]; p.54 Artist Dusan Kadlec; Commissioned by Canadian Heritage (Parks Canada East); p.55 Metropolitan Toronto Reference Library/MTL 1139; p.57 City of Toronto Archives, Health 32-259 p.58 NAC/PA-125840; p.59 Canapress/Moe Doiron; p.60 CORBIS/Bettmann; p.61 Dick Hemingway; p.62 CORBIS-Bettmann; p.63 Courtesy of the Canadian Museum of Health and Medicine at the Toronto Hospital, Canada;

p.64 Mary Evans Picture Library; p.65 top: Canadian Pacific Archives/A6528; bottom: NAC/C-9480; p.67 Canada's Sports Hall of Fame, Toronto; p.68 From High Realism in Canada by Paul Duval. Stoddart Publishing Company Ltd.; p.69 NAC/RD-853 p.70 CORBIS/Bettmann; p.72 SuperStock/Culver Pictures; p.74 McCord Museum of Canadian History, Montreal; p.75 McCord Museum of Canadian History, Montreal; p.78 NAC/C - 14246; p.79 NAC/C-073723; p.83 CORBIS/Michael St. Maur Sheil; p.84 Prentice Hall Archives; p.91 Royal Canadian Mounted Police, Ottawa; p.92 Image Network Inc./The Russ Heinl Group, Sydney, BC; p.93 ; p.95 CORBIS/Caroline Penn, inset: Dick Hemingway; p.97 City of Richmond Archives/Photo 1978-41-30; p.100 top: Al Harvey/The Slide Farm; bottom: Al Harvey/The Slide Farm; p.101 Neil Santin; p.109 Lone Pine Photo/Clarence W. Norris; p.110 Saskatchewan Archives Board/R-A4823; p.111 Image Network, Inc; p.112 Lone Pine Photo/Clarence W. Norris; p.113 Lone Pine Photo/Clarence W. Norris; p.114 Al Harvey/The Slide Farm; p.116 top left: Courtesy of the Geological Survey of Canada/GSC 16753, top right: Al Harvey/The Slide Farm, bottom: Al Harvey/The Slide Farm]; p.119 Al Harvey/The Slide Farm]; p.120 Greg Locke; p.121 Greg Locke; p.124 "Winter Travelling by Dogsled" by Paul Kane. Photography courtesy the Royal Ontario Museum © ROM; p.129 Henry Kalen Limited; p.132 Courtesy Old Fort William, Thunder Bay, Ontario; p.134 Provincial Archives of Manitoba/N-3974; p.135 912.I.8 "Encampment among islands of Lake Huron" by Paul Kane. Photography courtesy of the Royal Ontario Museum © ROM; p.140 Glenbow Archives/NA-249-6; p.141 Provincial Archives of Manitoba/N-13297; p.142 Provincial Archives of Manitoba; p.143 NAC/C-1346; p.145 Hudson's Bay Company Archives, Provincial Archives of Manitoba; p.147 NAC/C-038951; p.148 Hudson's Bay Company Archives, Provincial Archives of

Manitoba; p.150 Courtesy of M. Porritt, Halfway House, South Africa; p.151 Hudson's Bay Company Archives, Provincial Archives of Manitoba; p.152 left: Al Harvey/The Slide Farm, right: Hudson's Bay Company Archives, Provincial Archives of Manitoba; p.154 NAC/1941; p.156 Glenbow Archives/NA-933-1; p.158 Prentice Hall Archives; p.161 Provincial Archives of Manitoba/N-10307; p.162 NAC/C-002775/C-134840; p.164 NAC/C-2424 p.166 Western Canada Pictorial Index/AO173-05404; p.169 NAC/C-95470 p.171 Glenbow Archives, Calgary/NA - 2839-18; p.172 Glenbow Archives, Calgary/NA-1406-27; p.174 Saskatchewan Archives Board/C-1886; p.176 Saskatchewan Archives Board/RA-6277; p.177 Courtesy of Fort Whoop-Up; p.178 Courtesy RCMP, Ottawa; p.179 Winnipeg Art Gallery/G-72-75; p.180 top: Glenbow Archives, Calgary/NA-47-41; bottom: Western Canada Pictorial Index/WCPI 1765; p.183 Prentice Hall Archives; p.184 NAC/C-14246; p.185 NAC/C-78604; p.188 NAC/C-8549; p.189 Prentice Hall Archives; p.190 Canadian Pacific Archives/13561-2; p.191 NAC/C-3693; p.194 Courtesy of Fort Carlton; p.196 Glenbow Archives, Calgary/NA-1104-1; p.197 Saskatchewan Archives Board/RB-278; p.201 Hudson's Bay Company Archives, Provincial Archives of Manitoba/P-389; p.207 Prentice Hall Archives; NAC/C-1619; p.210 Hudson's Bay Company Archives, Provincial Archives of Manitoba; p.211 BC Archives; p.212; p.214 Prentice Hall Archives; p.217 ÒFort Yale and the Gold HuntersÓ Camp, Fraser River,Ó Image #952.61.7. Photograph courtesy of the Royal Ontario Museum, © ROM. p.218 BC Archives/3719; p.219 BC Archives/A-00353; p.220 BC Provincial Archives; p.221 NAC p.222 BC Provincial Archives/A-00355; p.223 top and bottom: Courtesy Barkerville Tourist Bureau; p.224 BC Archives/HP-01144; p.226 City of Victoria Archives; p.227 BC Archives/A-01752; p.228 Al Harvey/The Slide Farm; p.230 top: Vancouver

Public Library; bottom: City of Vancouver Archives; p.231 Al Harvey/The Slide Farm; p.232 City of Vancouver Archives; p.233 BC Archives/B-05081; p.234 Glenbow Archives, Calgary/NA-3740-29; p.237 top: BC Archives/45901, bottom: Greater Vernon Museum and Archives; p.238 BC Archives/8937; p.291 Courtesy of Northern Telecom; p.240 - unit opener/ 242 NAC; p.248 Prentice Hall Archives; p.249 copyright 1985 The Estate of William Kurelek; p.251 NAC 16748; p.254 CORBIS-Bettmann; p.258 Vancouver City Archives; p.259 Prentice Hall Archives; p.261 NAC 417 85; p.263 NAC/C-6605; p.264 NAC/C-30937; p.267 Prentice Hall Archives; top: NAC/C-30927; bottom: Al Harvey/The Slide Farm; p.270 BC Archives; p.271 courtesy The Vancouver Sun; p.274 NAC/C-14118; p.275 Prentice Hall Archives; p.Provincial Archives of Manitoba/N9905; p.277 Canada Post Corporation; p.280 Royal British Columbia Museum; p.281 Archive/Reuters; p.283 Metro Toronto Reference Library; p.284 top: City of Vancouver Archives, bottom: Western Canada Archives; p.288 Sports Hall of Fame; p.289 City of Vancouver Archives; p.291 Courtesy of Northern Telecom; p.292 Ian Smith/Vancouver Sun; p.297 Adrien Hebert (Canadian 1890-1967) Place Saint-Henri, detail 1929, oil on canvas, Art Gallery of Hamilton, Director's Purchase Fund, 1965; p.298 Al Harvey/The Slide Farm; p.301 Used by permission of Don Shebib; p.302 Greg Locke; p.303 Courtesy of General Motors; p.305 Canapress/Fred Chartrand; p.306 Dick Hemingway; p.308 top: Al Harvey/The Slide Farm, bottom: Dick Hemingway; p.309 top: Al Harvey/The Slide Farm, bottom: Al Harvey/The Slide Farm; p.310 Courtesy of Merle Tingley; p.311 NAC/Felix H. Man/PA-145949; p.315 Greg Locke; p.317 Courtesy of Northern Telecom; p.319 Geographical Visual Aids; p.321 Greg Locke; p.323 Canapress/Terry Chevalier; p.325 Courtesy of Louisbourg Archives; p.326 Reprinted with permission from The Globe and Mail; p.327

Copyright 1998 General Motors Corp.Used with permission of GM Media Archives; p.328 Archives Photos; p.329 Canapress/Sandor Fizli; p.331 Canapress/Brennan; p.333 Canapress/Tom Hanson; p.335 Canapress/Gary Hershorn; p.337 Canapress/Calgary Herald/Dean Bicknell; p.338 Roy Peterson, Vancouver Sun; p.342 Al Harvey/the Slide Farm; p.343, 345 The Office of Communications, University of Northern British Columbia; p.349 Al Harvey/The Slide Farm; p.352 New Westminster Public Library/photo #905; p.355 Al Harvey/The Slide Farm; p.356 Al Harvey/The Slide Farm; p.357 Curtis Trent Photography; p.360 City of Vancouver Archives/CVA102.25; p.361 BC Salmon Farmers Association; p.363 top: Courtesy Dr. Richard Beamish; bottom: Roy Henry Vickers; p.364 Jan Becker; p.365 Al Harvey/The Slide Farm; p.366 BC Archives/C-07722 p.367 Al Harvey/The Slide Farm; p.369 Al Harvey/The Slide Farm; p.370 Al Harvey/The Slide Farm; p.372 Courtesy Alcan Aluminium Ltd.; p.373 Courtesy Teck Corporation; p.376 Courtesy Ballad Power Systems Inc.; p.377 Canadian Pacific Archives/A 6528; p.379 top: Al Harvey/The Slide Farm, bottom: Courtesy Lions Gate Studios; p.380 Geographical Visual Aids; p.381 Vancouver Sun; p.385 Al Harvey; p.388 NASA; p.394 Reuters/David Brauchli/Archive Photos; p.396 Dick Hemingway; p.398 Al Harvey; p.402 Canapress/Fred Chartrand; p.403 Courtesy Delegation European Commission; p.405 Courtesy of Toyota Motor Mfg. Canada Inc.; p.409 Al Harvey; p.410 Canapress/Eric Draper ; p.411 Reuters/Scott MacDonald/Archive Photos; p.412 Reuters/Kimimasa Mayama/Archive Photos; p.413 left and right: Reuters/Will Burgess/Archive Photos; p.414 Canapress/Ahn Young-joon; p.415 Canapress/AP Photo/Kevork Djansezian; p.416 Reuters/Larry Chan/Archive Photos; p.418 Image Network, Inc./Bill Tice; p.420 top: Reuters/Carl Ho/Archive Photos, bottom: Greg Locke; p.422 Courtesy Rio Algom Mines; p.423 Canapress/Fred Chartrand; p.424 top and bottom: Roy Peterson, Vancouver Sun; p.425

Cartoon by Alan King, Ottawa Citizen, used by permission of Aspen Graphics and Alan King; p.426 R.Watts/First Light; p.427 Canapress/AP Photo/Carlos Espinoza; p.430 The Marine Museum, Kingston; p.433 Canapress/Bob Edme; p.434 The St. JohnÕs Telegram

Primary Sources
p.3 Excerpts from My Boy Life, Presented in a Succession of True Stories by John Carroll, William Briggs, 1882; p.19 Susanna Moodie, Life in the Clearings; p.21 Excerpts originally published in John Howison, Sketches of Upper Canada (Edinburgh, 1821), reprinted under the auspices of the Social Science Research Council of Canada, 1965; pp.29, 31, 32 Excerpts as appear in Audrey Miller, ed., The Journals of Mary O'Brien, 1828-1838, Toronto, McMillan, 1968; p.34 William Lyon Mackenzie King writing about the Family Compact, as appears in W. Kilbourn, The Firebrand, Clarke, Irwin and Company, 1960; p.36 1, 4 Quotes as appear in C. Lindsey, Life and Times of William Lyon Mackenzie, v. 1, Toronto: P.R. Randal, 1862, 2 Quote as appears in F. Head, A Narrative, London, John Murray, 1839, 3 Quote as appears in G. Smith, Canada and the Canadian Question, Toronto, Hunter Rose and Company, 1891, 5 Quote as appears in Audrey Miller, ed., The Journals of Mary O'Brien, 1828-1838, Toronto, McMillan, 1968; Song as appears in A. Scully et al., Canada Through Time, Toronto, Prentice Hall Canada Inc., 1993, Book 2; p.48 Excerpts as appear in Cheadle's Journal of a Trip Across Canada, 1862-1863, Edmonton, Hurtig, 1971; Excerpt as appears in Richard Proctor, The Gorilla and Other Apes, The Gentlemen's Magazine, July to December 1877, Picadilly, Chatto and Windus, 1877; Editorial as appears in the Owen Sound Comet, December 5, 1862 (reprinted from the Edinburgh Review); Excerpts from both speeches as appear in P. Bennett et al., Emerging Identities, Toronto, Prentice Hall Canada Inc., 1986; pp.85-87 Excerpts from the BNA Act as appear in R. Jackson and D. Jackson, Politics in Canada, Toronto, Prentice Hall Allyn and Bacon Canada, 1998; p.112 Excerpt (left) as

appears in Rudy Wiebe, Temptations of Big Bear, Excerpt (right) from Henri Julien, Diary, 1874, cited in David Cruise and Alison Griffiths, The Great Adventure, Penguin, 1997; Excerpt as appears in Rudy Wiebe, Temptations of Big Bear; p.137 For more original maps, see R. L. Gentilcore et al., The Historical Atlas of Canada, University of Toronto, 1993; pp.141, 150 Excerpts as appear in Manitoba 125. vol 1. Winnipeg, Great Plains Publications, 1993; excerpts as appear in Glyndwr Williams, ed., HudsonÕs Bay Miscellany, 1670-1870; pp.151, 173, 175, 180, 193-194, 197 Excerpts as appear in Don Mclean, Home from the Hill: A history of the Metis in Western Canada. Regina. Gabriel Dumont Institute of Native Studies and Applied Research, 1987; p.165 Excerpts as appear in David and Vincent Arnason, eds. The New Icelanders: a North American Community, Winnipeg, Turnstone Press, 1994; p.189 Excerpt from Pierre Berton, The Last Spike, McLelland and Stewart, Toronto, 1971; Excerpt as appears in Omer Lavalee, Van Horne's Road, Montreal, Railfare Enterprises, 1974; p.215 Excerpts as appear in G. and Helen Vans Akrigg, British Columbia Chronicle 1847-1871, Discovery Press, Victoria, 1977; p.235 Excerpt as appears in Paul Yee, Slatwater City, Vancouver, Douglas & McIntyre, 1988; p.251 Excerpt from a speech given by Wilfrid Laurier in Ontario in 1895; p.256 Excerpt as appears in Frances Backhouse, Women of the Klondike, Whitecap Books, 1995; p.259 House of Commons Journals, 1900, Appendix 1, p.354; Table 7-1 Statistics compiled from various sources, including Historical Statistics of Canada; p.262 Excerpt as appears in A. Rasmussen, A harvest to Reap, Saavage and Wheeler; Table 7-2 Statistics compiled from Canada Year Book, 1914, 1997, and R. L. Gentilcore et al., The Historical Atlas of Canada, University of Toronto, 1993; pp.271-271 Excerpt from John Gray, Is Labour's Mac Attack a Losing Battle?, Reprinted with Permission from The Globe and Mail; Table 7-3 Statistics as appear in Jean Barman, The West Beyond the West: A History of British Columbia, University of Toronto Press, 1991; p.277

Excerpt as appears in Firing the Heather, Fifth House, 1994; p.278 Excerpt as appears in Paul Tennant, Aboriginal Peoples and Politics, University of British Columbia Press, 1990; p.281 Excerpt as appears in Robert Collins, A Voice from Afar, Toronto, McGraw Hill, 1977; pp.286-287 Statistics compiled from various issues of the Canada Yearbook, especially 1911, 1916, 1921; Chapter 8, Table 8-1, Table 8-2, Table 8-3, Table 8-4, Figure 8-15, Table 8-7, data from Statistics Canada, as appear in The 1999 Canadian Global Almanac, Macmillan Canada, 1998; p.323, data from the Manitoba Department of Finance; Table 8-6, CRTC, June 1998; p.333 Eric Beauchesne, Study cites foreign investment as solution to job-creation woes, Vancouver Sun, May 6, 1996, p.A1; p.334, Excerpt Canadian Press, Volvo's Halifax shutdown stuns workers, Vancouver Sun, September 10, 1989; p.337, Excerpts Andrew Duffy, Free trade, 10 years after, Southam newspapers, Vancouver Sun, October 4, 1997; Table 9-1 Statistics from the Government of British Columbia, 1989, 1998; p.365 Mark Hume, A million points of pollution, The Vancouver Sun, May 30, 1995; Table 9-2 Statistics compiled from Canada and the World, Prentice Hall Canada Inc., 1995; p.376 For more information on Ballard Power, see http://www.ballard.com; p.385 Excerpt Witold Rybcznski, Urban all over the world, Essays on the Millennium, Maclean's, September 14, 1998; p.405 Figure 10-8, data from Statistics Canada as appear in The 1999 Canadian Global Almanac, Macmillan Canada, 1998; p.408, Excerpt Window on the Pacific, Maclean's, August 24, 1992; Table 10-2, various sources, World Bank, World Almanac, United Nations Data from Statistics Canada: Readers wishing additional information on data provided through the cooperation of Statistics Canada may obtain copies of related publications by mail from: Publication Sales, Statistics Canada, Ottawa, Ontario, K1A 0T6, by calling 613-951-7277, or toll free 1-800-267-6677. Readers may also facsimile their order at 613-951-1584.